ECONOMICS AND NATIONAL STRATEGY IN THE INFORMATION AGE

Global Networks, Technology Policy, and Cooperative Competition

James R. Golden

Westport, Connecticut
London

Library of Congress Cataloging-in-Publication Data

Golden, James Reed.
    Economics and national strategy in the information age : global
networks, technology policy, and cooperative competition / James R.
Golden.
        p.   cm.
    Includes bibliographical references (p.   ) and index.
    ISBN 0-275-94813-7 (alk. paper)
    1. Information technology—Government policy—United States.
2. National security—United States.   3. International economic
relations.   4. International cooperation.   I. Title.
HC110.I55G65   1994
337.73—dc20   93-48208

British Library Cataloguing in Publication Data is available.

Library of Congress Catalog Card Number: 93-48208
ISBN: 0-275-94813-7

First published in 1994

Praeger Publishers, 88 Post Road West, Westport, CT 06881
An imprint of Greenwood Publishing Group, Inc.

Printed in the United States of America

The paper used in this book complies with the
Permanent Paper Standard issued by the National
Information Standards Organization (Z39.48-1984).

10 9 8 7 6 5 4 3 2 1

For
Elaine

Contents

Figures

Tables

Preface

In their 1960 book, *The Economics of Defense in the Nuclear Age*, Charles J. Hitch and Roland N. McKean argued persuasively that military problems were essentially economic problems involving the allocation of scarce resources to competing objectives. In the bipolar nuclear age, they argued, wars requiring full mobilization were less likely, so the structure of forces in being was more important. They showed how economic analysis could illuminate choices among defense options.

In the nuclear age, the relationship between defense and the broader economic industrial base became more remote. Defense technologies were generally more advanced and specialized than those in the commercial sector. The unique technology requirements for defense production and strict rules for public contracts produced a somewhat isolated military-industrial complex. Hierarchical firms, designed to control information, manage complex production systems, and sell to the Department of Defense monopsony, dominated defense contracting.

Nuclear weapons are still with us, but bipolar confrontation is gone, and the logic of defense production is changing. As dual-use technologies, particularly information technologies, become more important to both commercial competition and defense applications, the separation of defense issues from questions concerning the broader industrial base is no longer an appropriate organizing principle for national strategy.

The developed world is in the midst of a third industrial revolution driven by the logic of new information technologies. The transformation has increased the relative importance of interconnection across teams of workers within corporations, across traditional corporate boundaries, and across technologies. Just as physical networks make it more possible to exchange information instantaneously, organizational networks have emerged to link functions across old organizational boundaries in new ways. Vertical organizations, designed to guard information and promote incremental evolution in standardized, mass-produced products, are giving way. Horizontal organizations, designed to exploit an open exchange of information, develop new products by merging related technologies, and foster continuous interchange among researchers, producers, and consumers, are taking their place.

The key change is the dramatic increase in the information content of products. Organizational adaptation is required to capture the value of information exchanged in transactions and to exploit flexibility in tailoring products to specific applications.

The manifestations of this transformation are everywhere. Corporations are increasingly organized around teams that cut across traditional structural boundaries, and middle levels of management are being thinned to provide for freer information flows. Corporations are cutting back to a core staff and core functions, and are gaining more flexibility by contracting for peripheral support and functions through "ring" employees and firms that are networked to the core operation.

Strategic alliances across corporations provide a basis for long-term cooperation without the constraints imposed by formal mergers. Organizational network behavior is revealed in cooperative agreements on research and development, for example, even among firms that compete at the product level. Networks among suppliers, producers, and consumers now compete with other networks, and competitive advantage increasingly flows from coordination throughout the entire value chain.

The revolution in military affairs is another manifestation of the same phenomena. Even the 20-year-old technologies applied in the war with Iraq demonstrated the impact of integrated sensor, precision strike, and communications systems. The technologies were impressive, but the real revolution was in the organizational adaptations and doctrine that permitted their application in coordinated systems.

The information age has dawned at the same time that the global political system is in transition and economic and technological performance is converging across the three main developed regions of North America, East Asia, and Europe. Indeed, one might argue that the information revolution has accelerated that convergence. If U.S. economic, military, and political leadership is to continue, it will depend less on technological dominance and more on flexible adaptation to the new technical and organizational realities. The heart of that adaptation will be in the evolution of an approach to national technology policy that emphasizes market forces and support for the exploitation of network linkages. The shift will also require a fundamental change in the formulation and application of military technology policy.

In that environment of technological and organizational adaptation, the linkages between economics and national strategy extend beyond the traditional boundaries of national security strategy. The national security apparatus is still essential for dealing with military crises that may unfortunately be even more common in the post-cold war period. But that apparatus should not be the central structure for evaluating broader national strategy, which must now deal more explicitly with the long-term consequences of technological change. It is at that level that the linkages between economics and national strategy have become more important. In the information age, global organizational networks will determine patterns of technological change, and U.S. national strategy must focus on exploiting U.S. advantages within those network structures.

"Cooperative competition" provides a framework for defining that strategy. It recognizes that competition for economic well-being and national influence cannot succeed in national or regional isolation. Cooperation, particularly in constraining and channeling the competition in technology and military capabilities, will be essential. National strategy should focus on exploiting U.S. advantages as a strategic broker in crafting agreements on the rules for technological competition and the principles for military integration. At the same time, the strategy should emphasize the creation of a national environment that promotes technological and organizational innovation in both the commercial and military spheres. In the information age, an alternative strategy of sheltering domestic inefficiencies through commercial or military isolation could have disastrous consequences.

Acknowledgments

The Department of Social Sciences at West Point, where I have taught for over two decades, presents courses on economics, American politics, international relations, and national security studies. The outstanding faculty there provides an extraordinary opportunity for interdisciplinary study in the broad field of political economy. This book has benefited enormously from the counsel of numerous members of that faculty and from the advice of my colleagues in many other departments. I am particularly indebted to those who took the time to work through early drafts of the book and provide critical comments. They include Asa Clark, Thomas Lynch, Casey Wardynski, Michael Meese, Matthew Fung, Damodar Gujarati, and Joseph Collins in the Department of Social Sciences, James Kays in Systems Engineering, John Wattendorf and Donald Horner in Behavioral Sciences, Lanse Leach in Computer Science, Bruce Oldaker in Physics, and Fletcher Lamkin in Civil and Mechanical Engineering.

My deepest debt is to Lee Donne Olvey, who sparked my interest in economic systems when I was a West point cadet, guided me through my graduate work at Harvard, and subsequently, as professor and head of the Department of Social Sciences, created an environment that encouraged an interdisciplinary approach to the analysis of technological, economic, and political change. My earlier book, *Economics of National Security,* written with Donne Olvey and Robert Kelly, helped me think more clearly about the linkages between economics and national strategy. I am also indebted to my thesis adviser and mentor at Harvard, the late Alexander Gerschenkron, who nurtured my interest in patterns of economic development and the dynamics of economic systems.

When my work on this book began in 1992, I envisioned an analysis of the economic factors that might be integrating or separating the three major trading blocs in Europe, North America, and East Asia. My premise was that shifts in those trade relationships would have a major impact on future security regimes. Preliminary research in Europe, generously funded by the Army Research Institute, quickly shifted the focus of my work from trade in general to the impact of technology policies on the location of high-technology activities. The members of the U.S. Mission to the Organization for Economic Cooperation and Development, particularly Daniel Dolan, were very helpful in guiding me toward the large body of work on technology and economic policy under way there. I found the studies of national systems of innovation and the critiques of those studies particularly useful in framing my research.

My subsequent work at the Stiftung Wissenschaft und Politik in Ebenhausen, Germany, where I had spent a year as a Fulbright professor in the early 1980s, helped to outline the interrelationships across technologies, the integration of the European market, and the broader trends and problems in political integration in Europe. The superb documentation staff there provided an outstanding set of preliminary research materials. I owe a special debt to Director Michael Stuermer, Friedemann Mueller, Reinhardt Rummel, Elke Thiel, and Christian Deubner for their support and insights.

I spent the fall of 1992 working through the literature on strategic alliances, productivity growth, patterns of innovation, the factors influencing the location of high-technology activities, trends in information technologies, and relatively recent work, primarily by Japanese and French analysts, on what I subsequently termed "organizational networks." A number of studies played an important role in shaping my subsequent work. Specific contributions are noted at appropriate points in the text, but I must also acknowledge a more general debt to the broader impact that several authors had on the way in which I approached the subject matter. Angus Maddison's work on productivity, Jeffrey Williamson's insights on long swings in productivity growth, Michael Porter's studies of competitive advantage, Chris DeBresson and Fernand Amesse's analysis of innovation networks, Paul David's writing on technological change and patterns of standardization, Shumpei Kumon's insights on network organizations, Frederick Scherer's numerous studies on innovation and growth, the extensive work on systems of innovation by Christopher Freeman, David Mowery, and Nathan Rosenberg, and Paul Krugman's impressive body of work on international trade all helped to shape the structure of the analysis.

Thanks to a second grant from the Army Research Institute, I had the opportunity to test my preliminary findings at a wide variety of public and private organizations. I found the exchanges with the following individuals to be particularly helpful in sharpening the arguments: Andrew Marshall, Thomas Welch, and Andrew Krepenevich in the Office of Net Assessment in the Department of Defense, Dale Vesser and David Ochmanek in the Office of the Secretary of Defense, William Odom at the Hudson Institute, David Abshire, William Taylor, and Don Snider at the Center for Strategic and International Studies, Sherwood Goldberg at Worldwide Associates, Harry Broadman at the Office of the U.S. Trade Representative, John Boright in the Department of State, Steve Drezner at the RAND Critical Technologies Institute, Thomas McNaugher at the Brookings Institute, and Tyrus Cobb and Erik Pages at Business Executives for National Security.

While I owe a debt of thanks to all those I have acknowledged, the responsibility for any errors in the book is mine alone. The ideas expressed here are those of the author and do not purport to represent the official position of the U.S. Military Academy, the Department of the Army, or the Department of Defense. All royalties from the sale of this book will be deposited in a fund for faculty research and development at West Point.

Part I Convergence, Global Networks, and the Productivity Cycle

1 Economics and National Strategy: The New Relationships

The United States needs a national strategy that responds to the central post-cold war political, economic, and military realities: the end of East-West confrontation, economic parity across the developed regions of the West, the information technology revolution, the proliferation of weapons with enormous lethality, and the growing importance of intrastate war. In the emerging environment, the threats to national security are real, but they are more diffuse and less likely to provide a clear focus for standing alliances or to justify the subordination of economic issues to security concerns. Instead, national strategy will have to balance economic and security interests and support approaches that develop international consensus: cooperation will be essential in providing institutions that promote international economic stability and effective crisis management. At the same time the United States must meet the economic challenge of sustaining high and rising levels of national income in the face of intense regional competition. The national strategy, in short, must blend cooperation and competition in ways that respond to the new environment.[1]

The world's new political structure centers on a triangle of competing regions that have achieved economic parity—Europe, North America, and Northeast Asia—loosely tied to developing regions on their peripheries. The three developed regions are integrated by the globalization of production and finance and by the network structures of the information technology revolution, but they are separated by differences in culture and by regional markets and institutions that tie various industries to their respective home bases. The combination of convergence in economic performance and the new structure of global organizational networks has altered the nature of regional competition in ways that have profound strategic implications.

If the first industrial revolution can be characterized by a focus on steam, iron, and railways in national firms, and the second by electricity, chemistry, automobiles, and consumer durables in increasingly multinational firms, the third centers on microelectronics, biological engineering, and new materials in internationally networked firms.[2] The transforming power of the third revolution lies in the impact of information technology in integrating related technologies, reducing transactions and processing costs, increasing the information content of "products," and changing industrial structures.

The information technology revolution is having repercussions for strategy at many levels. One of the most significant has been in the changing structure of industrial organizations and corporate organizational networks. The growing access to and importance of information flows is transforming traditional hierarchical firms into more horizontal organizations that emphasize flexibility, coordination, on-time production, and long-term relationships with suppliers and customers. In the information technology industry in particular, research and development (R&D) relationships extend across firms through horizontal organizational networks that have redefined traditional corporate boundaries. Perhaps ironically, the same firms that cooperate in R&D activities subsequently compete aggressively in product markets. Corporate strategy now requires "cooperative competition," a framework that simultaneously enhances mutual performance and shapes the form of competition. In this sense, cooperation and competition are not alternative approaches to relationships; both elements are always present to some extent. The cooperative component enhances the competition by making both parties more effective, and at the same time the structure of cooperation limits the scope of acceptable competition.

That insight—that competitors must also cooperate in research networks in order to compete effectively in product markets—captures the essential impact of the information revolution for other levels of strategy as well. The new network organizational relationships are redefining regional power balances, altering patterns of economic growth, and shifting the structure of potential alliances that will come into play in dealing with the proliferation of sophisticated threats. In this setting, national strategy must balance cooperation and competition to achieve national objectives. In a strategic sense, the term "cooperative competition" stresses the importance of building cooperative organizational networks that will permit the United States to pursue objectives in concert with other nations while still competing with them for the location of high-value economic activities and for the development of military capabilities consistent with national security strategy. The cooperative element of the strategy recognizes the need to create the public goods, or infrastructure, needed to provide the stability essential for efficient economic interaction and for the integration of military capabilities to meet common security goals.[3] The competitive component recognizes that national objectives still differ, that the distribution of wealth, income, and power will continue to be a national concern, and that, sadly, political and economic competition may occasionally spill over into armed conflict. National strategy must recognize both components by working to create a network of infrastructure relationships to keep the international competition within acceptable limits and by developing the capacity to respond effectively when the competition exceeds those limits.[4]

A NATIONAL STRATEGY

Before examining the new economic environment and the components of a strategy of cooperative competition in more detail, it is important to address the difficulty of sustaining any U.S. national strategy. The term "national strategy" means a vision of the process through which national resources will be used to achieve national objectives. National strategies may be distinguished by the relative roles given to the private and public sectors, the emphasis given to different policy instruments, and the importance assigned to various possible outcomes. National strategies are seldom explicit, and the implementation of strategy rarely flows from objectives to resource allocation. Objectives, concepts, and means normally evolve together.

In modern mixed-market economies, national strategy starts from the premise that a wide range of national objectives will be pursued through decentralized economic markets in which firms and consumers are relatively free to make informed decisions that influence their own welfare. The rationale for government action results from market failures, in the sense that some distortion in information or incentive structures is producing the "wrong" signals for private actions, or from a desire to alter the distribution of income that results from private decisions. Judgments on what constitutes a market failure or an unacceptable distribution of income are obviously intensely political decisions, and those judgments and the extent and form of intervention to correct perceived failures differ substantially from country to country. Japan and France intervene in that process with a structure of indicative planning to coordinate public and private actions in selected industries. The U.S. government has traditionally rejected such explicit industrial planning, although its regulatory framework and its large intervention through defense research, development, and procurement have large sectoral impacts.

In theory, U.S. national strategy would begin with a structure of private activities based on the operation of free markets and then provide a framework for modifying the use of the nation's resources to achieve national objectives derived from enduring national interests. In practice, national objectives conflict, and consensus on how to achieve them is limited. The actual allocation of public resources is settled in an often heated political process that is constitutionally designed to balance competing interests. Policy formulation is rarely driven by overarching strategy: instead, there is an overlapping web of public policies fashioned by a broad array of agencies that compete for resources in the political arena, urged on by many private interest groups with divergent concerns. Effective coordination of those policies in ways that preserve the vitality of the private sector and eliminate the most egregious inconsistencies in public programs is difficult, because the costs of identifying and obtaining the right information and overcoming the frictional problems of defining and implementing policies are enormous. The government's energy and resources are limited, so, at best, the nation might be able to coordinate the use of a subset of national resources in pursuit of its most important national interests.

Security Strategy

As a result of those limitations, the central role of strategy is to elevate a narrow set of policies to prominence for more careful coordination. In the post-World War II period, the analytical device for narrowing national strategy to a manageable scale has been to focus on "security" strategy, based on an assessment of national interests that are at risk in the international arena. Economic policy rarely entered explicitly into this framework, aside from the economic constraints imposed in the budget process. The National Security Act of 1947 institutionalized the security strategy framework in a system centered on the integrating functions of the National Security Council and its staff and a series of Presidential Decision Memoranda. Since 1986 there has been a more concerted effort to articulate an explicit presidential *National Security Strategy of the United States* each year, typically beginning with lists of national interests such as national survival, economic strength, cooperative relations with allies and friendly nations, and a stable world in which democratic institutions can flourish.[5] National security policy attempts to integrate economic, diplomatic, and military policies to deal with threats to those national interests.[6] This post-World War II emphasis on the peacetime coordination of national power to achieve security objectives applied the basic ideas of wartime "grand" strategy to the cold war setting.[7]

The "security" framework for strategy is ultimately based on a system of threat and coercion justified by the importance of preserving vital national interests. Thus, security strategy is distinct from other government policy because of the vital importance of the issues involved and the sensitivity of the policy instruments. In the security framework, elements of national "power" become instruments for achieving security objectives. From this perspective, economic "power," a term used by security analysts but rarely by economists, can be used directly to influence states and other international actors or indirectly as a foundation for generating other elements of power, such as military forces.

The advantages of focusing on national security strategy rather than broader national strategy are manifest. Threats to national security interests provide a clear focus for coordination across relevant agencies, particularly the Departments of State and Defense, in the realm of "high policy," which is presumably less susceptible to partisan bickering than other policy areas. At least to some extent, the security strategy helps to identify capabilities needed to meet threats, informs analysis of tradeoffs across alternative military force structures and weapon systems, and ultimately influences military strategy and budget decisions. The security focus also emphasizes the distinction between long-term planning and what many analysts feel is the *sine qua non* of strategy—the presence of an adversary—and reinforces the concept of "strategic thinking" with its web of moves and countermoves.

Beyond Security Strategy

The disadvantages of the emphasis on *security* strategy as the organizing principle for national strategy are also clear, and they have become more obvious in the post-cold war era. When external threats to vital interests become ambiguous and more remote, the logic and cohesion of the security strategy formulation is less compelling. The threat no longer provides a clear orientation for budget and force structure decisions, and the distinctions between security and other policies break down. Moreover, as economic issues become relatively more important, casting them in a security framework could actually be harmful. In practice, economic policy is not formulated by the actors in the national security system, and it is not driven by national security strategy in any meaningful sense. By focusing on the narrow range of economic policy issues that are influenced by security strategy, the system deemphasizes such key issues as productivity and competitiveness that are handled in other agencies. Moreover, by stressing threats to national interests in the international arena, an emphasis on *economic security* could incorrectly stress coercion against economic competitors rather than domestic policies to enhance competitiveness.

Although economics and security are clearly linked, the idea that economic policy is or should be driven by security interests is inconsistent with the post-cold war environment. More precisely, the *security* framework places economic relationships in a power balance perspective that may seriously distort the economic agenda by emphasizing zero-sum relationships, in which one actor gains at the other's expense, over the normal non-zero-sum relationships of economic exchange, in which both actors gain. The dominance of a security framework as the central focus of national strategy is not appropriate when vital national interests are not directly challenged and the primary policy instruments do not involve threats and coercion. As the relative scope of issues involving military confrontation declines, the security framework provides a less compelling approach for organizing national strategy. Indeed, by making clear threats to national interests or future capabilities to mount such threats the organizing principle for strategy, the security framework may lead decisionmakers to miss the key point that U.S. national interests are increasingly defined in terms of managing competition within the context of cooperative processes.

In the evolving environment, the United States needs a new orientation on economics and security issues. Although the security framework and machinery will remain essential for dealing with direct threats to vital U.S. interests or other cases involving the use of military force, that framework can no longer provide the sole organizing principle for national strategy. Samuel Huntington argues that the United States needs to move beyond the "national security state" of the postwar period to what he calls the "competitive state," whose goal would be "to enhance American economic competitiveness and economic strength in relation to other countries."[8] He notes that economic strength is needed to sustain defense outlays and that interaction in international markets is becoming a relatively more important means of achieving security goals. As he correctly argues, strong growth, productivity, and technological innovation generate international influence through world product, capital, and currency markets. Those markets provide the major forms of interaction among world powers and they have become increasingly important means for influencing international behavior given the declining importance of military power in great power relationships.

Huntington correctly identifies the required shift away from a purely security framework for organizing national strategy, but his emphasis on the "relative" economic performance of the United States casts national strategy in a primarily competitive context. In the highly integrated global economy, however, too narrow an emphasis on competition might lead to policies that reduce efficiency and lower national welfare. An analysis of economic convergence and global organizational networks suggests that cooperation must also be a key element of national strategy. Indeed, competitive steps that serve to isolate the U.S. economy from those networks would actually weaken relative U.S. economic performance.

THE ECONOMIC ENVIRONMENT

The two dominant trends in the international economic environment are convergence in levels of income, growth, and productivity among North America, Europe, and Northeast Asia, and the evolution of global organizational networks with highly integrated, but remarkably stable, regional nodes. Although convergence in economic performance will not mean equality in national economic power because of the differences in scale of national economies, it will mean that U.S. strategy must increasingly involve other major economic powers and that regional political integration could potentially produce alternative power centers equivalent to the

United States. That is not to say that the United States has lost its position among world economic leaders, or that it is destined to fall behind other industrial powers in the coming century. It will still be hegemonic in terms of its overall share of world markets, but it will not and should not be expected to dominate every industrial area.

The evolution of global organizational networks, in which firms in related industries develop long-term R&D as well as trade relationships, means that the three major industrial regions will be tied more and more closely together, enhancing convergence. That does not mean that regional policies will become less effective in the future. On the contrary, regional factors that determine the concentration of niches of particular industries may well become more, not less, important. The combination of convergence and global networks suggests new patterns of specialization that will alter the nature of regional cooperation and competition.

Convergence

Over the past decade, a growth industry has developed around studies of the decline of the U.S. economy. Paul Kennedy's *The Rise and Fall of the Great Powers,* published in 1987—with its thesis that "imperial overstretch" leads to excessive defense spending that crowds out private investment, lowers economic growth, and brings down great powers—came at the crest of a wave of writing on the decline in U.S. productivity growth, the apparent triumph of Japanese corporatism, and the emergence of twin U.S. budget and trade deficits.[9] Improved U.S. economic performance in the mid-1980s muted some of this criticism, but low-growth concerns returned in force with the recession of 1991 and its impact on the 1992 presidential campaign. The facts do not support the thesis of U.S. economic collapse, but they do show that convergence in economic standards and growth rates across Europe, Japan, and the United States is proceeding. That convergence does not imply a sharp reversal in the central position of the U.S. economy, but it does suggest that the extent of U.S. hegemony will decline and that the period of U.S. dominance in most key technologies has clearly ended.

The record of U.S. output per hour worked, or labor productivity, presented in Table 1-1 shows that U.S. workers became the most efficient in the world around the turn of the century. After World War II, the United States briefly held a dominant position, but by the mid-1980s the gap had closed considerably. The precise size of the gap is subject to a number of problems in computing and comparing international productivity figures, but a range of comparisons using different exchange rate benchmarks and labor input concepts suggest that by 1990 France and Germany had moved even with the United States, while Japan and the United Kingdom had reached roughly 70 and 75 percent of the U.S. level, respectively.[10]

Table 1-1

Comparisons of Productivity Levels Across Countries, 1870–1984 (in each year the leader's productivity is set to 100) (Reprinted with permission from the American Economic Association.)

Country	1870	1913	1950	1984
France	49	49	42	98
Germany	53	56	34	90
Japan	17	18	14	56
United Kingdom	100	80	59	81
United States	90	100	100	100

Source: Computed from Angus Maddison, "Growth and Slowdown in Advanced Capitalist Economies: Techniques of Quantitative Assessment," *Journal of Economic Literature* 25 (June 1987): 683.

Note: Maddison estimates gross domestic product per hour worked and converts to dollars using purchasing power parity exchange rates. This table divides the estimates for each year by the figure for the leader, the United Kingdom in 1870 and the United States in other years, and multiplies by 100 to estimate each country's percentage of the leader's productivity.

The surprisingly weak showing of Japanese workers reflects a wide range of productivity across industries, with levels in some industrial sectors equal to the best in the world, but with other sectors trailing far behind.

There has been enormous confusion in interpreting the economic record, primarily because of a lack of precision in differentiating among the concepts of slowing rates of growth, falling behind, deindustrialization, industrial leadership, and convergence.[11] Productivity growth rates in Table 1-2 show that output per worker rose faster in other developed economies than in the United States after 1950, and the pace of productivity improvement fell off sharply in each of the countries listed after 1973. The slower productivity growth in the United States does mean that others are catching up to U.S. levels, but it does not mean that the United States will inevitably fall behind. Growth rates in gross domestic product (GDP) in Table 1-3 show that while each country except the United Kingdom was catching up to the United States in the period from 1950 to 1973, the United States has held its own since then, with France growing at about the same rate and only Japan, the country furthest behind in productivity, growing more rapidly. The decline in productivity growth in all of the countries after 1973 suggests that the root cause is not unique to the U.S. economy. Moreover, the growth rates fall together from earlier levels in the period from 1973 to 1984, and they rise together in the subsequent period, suggesting a convergence in growth patterns.

Table 1-2
Comparisons of Average Annual Growth Rates in Productivity Across Countries in Selected Periods, 1870–1990 (percent per year) (Reprinted with permission from the American Economic Association.)

Country	1870– 1913	1913– 1950	1950– 1973	1973– 1984	1984– 1990
France	1.7	2.0	5.1	3.4	2.4
Germany	1.9	1.0	6.0	3.0	1.9
Japan	1.8	1.7	7.7	3.2	3.4
United Kingdom	1.2	1.6	3.2	2.4	1.4
United States	2.0	2.4	2.5	1.0	1.0

Sources: 1870–1984—Maddison, "Growth and Slowdown," Table 2, p. 650; 1984–1990—
  Computed from Organization for Economic Cooperation and Development, *Economic Outlook Statistics on Microcomputer Diskettes* (Paris, June 1992).

Kennedy's thesis concerns the proposition of moving ahead and falling behind and argues from historical example that great empires lose economic steam from trying to sustain military hegemony too long. Growth rates in the United States and elsewhere, however, have little to do with military outlays. GDP growth rates in Table 1-3 show that the slowdown after 1973 was quite uniform across the major economic powers, and indeed the slowdown in the 1970s occurred at a time of declining, not rising, defense shares of total GDP. Savings and investment are lower in the United States as a share of GDP than in Europe and especially Japan because of the much higher share of GDP that goes to consumption, not to the share that goes to defense.[12]

Another version of the United States in decline emphasizes the loss of U.S. economic leadership, the idea that the nation is losing its position among the leaders in industrial technology. It is certainly true that the United States has lost the dominant technology position it held after World War II, but it still ranks first in most technology areas. In spite of a popular misconception that the decline in overall U.S. productivity growth has resulted from a loss of competitiveness in manufacturing, the growth rate in manufacturing productivity has not declined. Productivity growth in manufacturing per year averaged 3 percent from 1950 to 1973, fell to just over 1 percent for 1974 to 1982, and then soared to 5 percent from 1983 to 1989.[13] The United States still leads the world in output per worker, whether output is measured by GDP, as in Table 1-1, by industrial products in general, or by manufacturing in particular. By one estimate, in 1989 manufacturing productivity in Japan and Germany stood at 80 per-

Table 1-3
Comparisons of Average Annual Growth Rates in Gross Domestic Product Across Countries in Selected Periods, 1870–1990 (percent per year) (Reprinted with permission from the American Economic Association.)

Country	1870– 1913	1913– 1950	1950– 1973	1973– 1984	1984– 1990
France	1.7	1.1	5.1	2.2	3.8
Germany	2.8	1.3	5.9	1.7	3.0
Japan	2.5	2.2	9.4	3.8	4.7
United Kingdom	1.9	1.3	3.0	1.1	3.0
United States	4.2	2.8	3.7	2.3	3.5

Sources: 1870–1984—Maddison, "Growth and Slowdown," Table 1, p. 650; 1984–1990— United Nations, Department of International Economic and Social Affairs, *World Economic Survey, 1991* (New York: United Nations, 1991), 210.

cent of the U.S. level.[14] It is certainly true that Japan now leads the United States in productivity in some key manufacturing categories, including transport equipment, machinery, and electrical equipment, but the overall record would still make the U.S. economy the world's industrial leader by any reasonable standard.

Another related misconception is that the United States is becoming deindustrialized by low manufacturing productivity growth, which is reducing the U.S. share of world manufacturing markets and driving workers to the lower-wage, slow-productivity-growth services sector. However, from 1965 to 1980, service sectors grew more rapidly as a share of total employment overseas than they did in the United States. In fact, the service sector share of real national output in the United States has not been increasing, nor has the industrial sector share been declining. The apparent shift has been caused by the increase in the relative prices of services, and in fact the relative wage of service workers has been rising, not falling. In other words, workers are not being forced out of manufacturing by declining market share; they are being pulled into services by higher wages there. Deindustrialization is not a real phenomenon in terms of output; it is an illusion created by shifting prices and wages.[15] It is certainly true that while the shares of real output remained constant, the portion of the labor force employed in industry and manufacturing declined from 1980 to 1990, but that decline coincided with higher rates of productivity growth in those sectors than in other sectors of the economy. In short, U.S. productivity problems do not originate in the manufacturing and high-technology areas. In fact, the United States maintains its lead in the share of high-technology exports in world markets, and the major shift in the last two decades has been the improved position of Japan relative to Europe.[16]

A more persuasive interpretation of the data is that while the United States is not falling behind or deindustrializing, the economies of Japan and Europe have converged on U.S. productivity levels. Growth rates should converge over time because followers have advantages in being able to borrow the best industrial practices, often embodied in new capital, while the leader must absorb the costs and risks of developing new technologies.[17] Tables 1-1 and 1-2 suggest that other economies have in fact been converging on the levels of U.S. productivity. The puzzle is not why convergence is occurring, but why the United States held out so long as a distant front-runner.

Before racing to implement policies to reverse the decline in U.S. productivity growth, policymakers need to understand the sources of early U.S. productivity leadership. Gavin Wright argues that the U.S. surge to industrial supremacy after 1900 was based on an integrated internal market, the growth of transportation infrastructure, and the simultaneous development of resource extraction and specialization in industrial technologies that complemented those natural resources. Although the U.S. cost advantage in world mineral markets subsequently faded, the accumulated base of an educated workforce and science-based technologies gave the United States a dominant position in a wide range of industries after World War II.[18] From that perspective, the unique advantages that sustained relatively high productivity growth in the immediate postwar period may now have faded. In particular, integration of world markets permitted other countries to gain the advantages of mass production, and large Japanese and European investments in education and R&D created the social conditions required for convergence.[19]

The point is not that the United States is destined to remain the world's productivity leader forever. It would be naive to assume that would be the case, but it is equally naive to expect that the United States will fall behind as other industrialized countries surge past it. Others will encounter problems in sustaining high productivity growth as they lose the advantages of technological followers and are forced to deal with lagging agricultural and services sectors.

Certainly large U.S. budget deficits constrain U.S. public and private investment, and policies to reduce the size of those deficits are clearly in order. U.S. trade imbalances and the loss of competitiveness in some key industries also pose serious challenges for economic policy. But while these are important issues that require attention, they have often been linked with broader arguments about U.S. decline. Convergence in economic performance across regions, however, has far different implications than a systematic process of falling further and further behind. Proponents of reform must, of course, show that U.S. problems are serious in order to stimulate action, and that may lead well-meaning analysts to exaggerate U.S. decline. There is also a danger, however, that excessive alarm could trigger unwarranted and counterproductive intervention in national and international markets. Indeed, the continuing growth of the U.S. economy depends on access to dynamic global networks.

Global Networks

Convergence in economic performance among the major economic powers has been reinforced by the emergence of global industrial networks that, driven by the revolution in information technologies, are transforming international markets, shifting traditional patterns of industrial organization, changing the specialization of labor, altering patterns of R&D and innovation, and accelerating the integration of global capital and product markets. The competition that will determine future U.S. economic performance, living standards at home, and the ability to influence events abroad, will be waged in those global networks. Although the competition begins with the United States still in an economic leadership position, sustaining that lead will require an understanding of how globalization is proceeding and how regions can influence the process.

Global networks spring from regional home bases that provide competitive advantages to industries, or niches within industries, based on economies of scale and scope and the unique characteristics of local markets. Some standardized activities are "footloose," shifting from one region to another in response to fluctuations in the costs of labor and capital or tax incentives. Other high-value, specialized activities concentrate in network nodes, or regions that contain firms linked to several intersecting organizational networks. As a result, regions still matter, but they matter in ways that differ from the classical model of trade based on resource endowments. The key in the new competition is the ability to create the specialized resources that develop nodes in the global network. Economic strategy must therefore come directly to grips with the dynamic nature of "factor creation" and its impact on the location of high-value activities in global organizational networks. Before examining the full implications of convergence and global networks for national strategy, it is important to examine how global networks are evolving and how the location of network nodes might be influenced by public policy.

Networks. Network concepts are transforming the global workplace and creating new forms of interaction across traditional enterprises. The revolution in information technologies has created a new communications network that provides vastly improved physical links among organizations. Organizations connected by the new physical networks have themselves become intertwined in organizational networks designed to pass information quickly and efficiently to enhance coordination in a number of areas, including the following: input-output relationships among suppliers, producers, and consumers; R&D projects among enterprises; financial flows among investors, brokers, and financial markets; and government policy issues. These global input-output, R&D, financial, and policy organizational networks are changing the ways in which the industry structure of competitive advantage and productivity growth are being determined.

The key aspects of the new organizational network structures include shifts from hierarchical to more horizontal relationships and a growing emphasis on long-term cooperation, both driven by the need and possibilities for more complete and timely communication. As Anthony Carnevale, reporting on the work of the Hudson Institute's Workforce 2000 project, argues, the workplace is being transformed by networks that build from individual work teams through links across organizations. Internally the organization is itself a network of interlocking teams, and externally it is part of a network extending across suppliers, consumers, research organizations, financial backers, and government regulators in input-output, R&D, finance, and policy networks.[20]

As a result, jobs are being redefined by the requirements for greater coordination, both within and outside the enterprise. The core corporation is itself a network linking strategic insight at the center to more autonomous points on the periphery, which are in turn connected to other networks.[21] The critical tasks of the network involve the exchange and processing of information, creating a new set of critical skills and increasing the services component of total output. As a result, products are composites produced by networks in which brokers draw on routine components and services in some locations and specialized problem-solving and problem-identifying skills in others.[22]

The new networks extend beyond the traditional exchange of goods and services across enterprises to include expanding cooperation in R&D.[23] The number of interlocking research agreements among corporations in the information technology industry has been exploding over the last decade. Separate clusters of arrangements across information technology firms are dominated by regional groups of Japanese, European, and U.S. companies, although the linkages also extend across regions.[24] This same transfer of technology across horizontally linked Japanese firms goes beyond the traditional keiretsu, or business group, structure. Ken-ichi Imai calls the new configurations "network industrial organizations" to emphasize the central role given to creating and exchanging information in such enterprises.[25]

Although the use of the term "network" is widespread, its precise meaning varies in applications across fields from electronics to sociology. In a sense, everything is networked to everything else: more precision is needed to make the concept useful. Shumpei Kumon has provided the most precise formulation to date by classifying social systems according to the dominant form of interaction among actors in the system, which he divides into three categories: threat coercion, exchange exploitation, and consensus inducement. In this framework, the nation-state is an organization dominated by a threat coercion orientation based on international law; the modern industrial organization based on property rights would be in the exchange exploitation category; and organizations featuring consensus inducement relationships based on information rights would be "modern network organizations" designed to share information about goals and actions to achieve them.[26]

Kumon has identified the critical importance of communications flows in what Chapter 3 defines as "organizational networks." Of course, multinational firms have existed for a long time, but the essential difference is that the new network organizational arrangements are not based on the ownership of subsidiaries in a hierarchical structure, nor on the armslength impersonal interaction of the market, but on shifting patterns of personal interaction across firms based on information exchange. As a result, the key players in the new system are the strategic brokers who are constantly creating and modifying global organizational networks. Vertically structured, hierarchical firms, with clear divisions of responsibility across different corporate levels and a top-down centralized information flow, are being overwhelmed by new organizations structured around a more horizontal flow of information within and across traditional corporate boundaries. These "network industrial organizations" are winning the information technology competition.

Individual firms cannot afford the enormous costs nor bear the high risks of remaining at the cutting edge of all the technologies that are integrated in new products, but they also cannot miss a breakthrough that could create whole new product lines. Sharing proprietary information has enormous risks, but the risks of isolation from new technologies may be even greater. Organizational network structures permit the development of trust needed for balancing exchanges over an extended period without the inflexibility that creeps into hierarchical organizations.

The emergence of global networks provides a clear challenge to traditional ways of thinking about national strategy. If firms are no longer national champions whose profits are closely tied to national markets, but are brokers linked in global networks, the pursuit of national economic interests through the support of national firms becomes problematic. If the exchange of value occurs by electronic transmission rather than the transfer of products, traditional commercial policies may be less important than policies that influence the location of network nodes. The new organizational network structures are changing the organizing principles for the analysis of power. Power depends more on the ability to influence access and interconnection than on the capacity to enforce borders.[27]

From this network perspective, national strategy will depend less on confrontation with opponents and more on the art of cooperation with competitors. National neomercantilist policies that attempt to shield national firms from international competition might simply isolate domestic workers from the high-value jobs available through global networks.

Network Nodes. Global networks are transforming politics and economics by altering the national identity of products, technologies, corporations, and industries.[28] As a result, international competition will increasingly depend on the relative competence of the one resource that does not flow freely across borders in international markets—people. In Robert Reich's terminology, "high-value" businesses, based on specialized problem-solving skills provided by "symbolic analysts," are needed to ensure competitive advantage against "high-volume" foreign firms, because it is not products but skills that are traded in global "webs."[29] One dimension of national strategy must address the education of a labor force with the skills needed in the global economy. From an organizational network perspective, labor with the appropriate skills will create network nodes of high-income activities.

Other factors are also important in capturing high-value network activities, and a substantial literature emphasizes the multiple sources of stability of regional network nodes.[30] For example, Michael Porter shows that data on 10 nations and over 100 industries indicate that leading industrial firms have stable ties to specialized regions. Porter argues persuasively that successful firms become masters of their "value systems," which include the firm's suppliers, distributors, and customers. Operating from a "home base," where the firm defines its strategy, develops its core products and process technologies, and maintains its most sophisticated production, the global firm reaches out through a "global network" of activities. The location of the home base is determined by a "national diamond" composed of factor conditions, demand conditions, related and supporting industries, and firm strategy, structure, and rivalry.[31] Porter's analysis correctly focuses on the new reality that competitive advantage lies not in the nation's endowment of resources, but in the pressure the environment places on the firm to invest and innovate. Sustainable competitive advantage in high-value products and technologies comes from the creation of "advanced" factors—such as communications infrastructure, graduate engineers, and research institutes—and "specialized" factors that are tailored for use in particular industries. The private sector creates those factors in response to constantly shifting international standards.[32]

Network nodes, then, depend on labor skills that evolve in a broader context of factor creation driven by education and training systems, public and private R&D, adaptation of innovations into commercially successful processes and products, and an environment of supporting services. National characteristics such as social and political stability, the definition of property rights, the structure of factor, product, and financial markets, labor-management relationships, the science and technical infrastructure, the education system, and attitudes toward innovation all constrain a nation's approaches to factor creation and thus limit the industries in which the nation can successfully compete. Within that national environment, the complex processes of innovation and factor creation help to determine the structure of industry competitive advantage and hence the rate of productivity growth.

The synergies among the determinants of competitive advantage produce advantages to industrial concentration that cause the structure of competitive advantage, and hence the location of network nodes, to persist over time. The processes of concentration are "path-dependent" in the sense that early. events change costs of future production, so network nodes tend to endure. Transitory advantages become locked into particular regions through the development of a pool of specialized labor, supporting trade and services, and the sharing of technological ideas.[33] The most spectacular current examples of concentration are in the industries that trade services, such as Hartford's insurance, Chicago's futures trading, entertainment in Los Angeles, and even Silicon Valley in California and Route 128 around Boston, which are more centers for technological services than of production.[34] Improved communications and the reduction in transportation costs and trade barriers that have facilitated global markets have arguably increased the importance of these regional concentrations, because firms can lever their local competitive advantages into wider and wider markets.[35]

The persistence of network nodes, or home bases, suggests a potential for strategy to influence the location of economic activity despite the prevalence of globalization. Regional distinctions persist in part because global firms must operate from and sustain large positions in their home markets. As a result, trade and technology policy differences sustain separable regions centered on the United States, Europe, and Japan, in which the rate of intraregional trade is growing faster than interregional trade.[36]

Competing technological policies across regions provide a potential realm for strategic efforts to capture network nodes, particularly in industries with broad impacts on other industrial sectors. If innovation and the creation of advanced and specialized factors are the keys to competitive advantage, many analysts argue that government assistance to promote innovation and factor creation might be in order. The central problem with such assistance is that market competition provides the driving force for innovation and creativity geared to commercial applications, and without that market test it is difficult to assess the future returns to government programs. Government intervention might, however, be useful if it is geared to correcting market failures, such as the private sector's reluctance to pursue projects whose benefits spill over to other firms. For example, if the project benefits all companies in an industry equally, no single company may have sufficient incentive to pursue the investment. In addition, the scale of some forms of R&D and the risks of failure to produce profitable innovations may be so high that the private sector cannot pursue projects for which public benefits may outweigh public costs. Although there are clear theoretical justifications for some government support of innovation and factor creation, the precise level and form of that intervention remain controversial, and differing policies across various nations remain a source of friction.

Some argue that there are strategic industries with large, long-term impacts on other sectors; that capturing them requires domestic production of components as well as products (semiconductors as well as computers); that technological development is path-dependent, so you cannot just jump in at the next technological level; and that while the short-run gains from intervention to capture high-technology markets may be small, the long-term impact of capturing strategic technologies may be very large.[37] Those arguments provide a controversial but widely cited foundation for the use of government policy to attract and defend regional network nodes containing high-value activities with the potential for influencing long-term technological patterns. From that perspective, differences in competing technology policies provide a major potential source of conflict among North America, Europe, and Japan.[38]

In sum, convergence in economic performance among the major economic powers does not mean that the United States is destined to fall behind new industrial leaders, but it does mean that future competition will occur on a more equal footing. That competition will center on efforts to capture the nodes of global networks that have resulted in part from the revolution in information technology. Earlier U.S. advantages from an abundance of natural resources, a large integrated national economy that permitted mass production, and then a large lead in science-based R&D, have faded. In the new competition for network nodes, the United States will have to rely on other sources of competitive advantage by promoting the creation of the advanced and specialized factors valued in emerging global networks. The tactics to be used in the competition remain controversial, but the evidence is that the competition is already well under way and that it will focus on attempts to capture nodes of high-value activities in the context of global networks. As a result, national strategy must reconcile cooperation in building global organizational networks with the competition for high-value activities in network nodes.

COOPERATIVE COMPETITION

Theodore Moran argues that the United States is in decline, but that the process is reversible and that there are two competing grand strategies for achieving this: "sophisticated neomercantilism" and "transnational integration." Sophisticated neomercantilism would include managed trade to ensure market share for "national" firms in critical industries and swift reprisals against unilaterally defined unfair practices in U.S. markets, such as dumping goods below the cost of production or foreign subsidies for exports. Foreign investment in the United States would be carefully reviewed, public investment funds would be targeted on "national" champions, and transborder corporate alliances would be scrutinized to ensure U.S. firms could sustain favorable market positions.

The cluster of policies aimed at transnational integration, on the other hand, would feature trade liberalization along multilateral lines, generally open investment policies with performance requirements to enmesh foreign firms in the U.S. industrial base, the use of R&D credits for both domestic and foreign firms to promote the development of critical technologies, and a general presumption in favor of global alliances. In Moran's view, the ultimate choice of a grand strategy depends not only on technical assessments of the effectiveness of the different policy components, but also on an evaluation of the international repercussions of the regional confrontation implicit in the sophisticated neomercantilist approach and of the burdens of international leadership implicit in the transnational integration approach.[39]

Although Moran overstates the extent of U.S. decline, his presentation of the two alternatives for grand strategy is compelling. The cluster of policies he calls "transnational integration" comes very close to the idea of cooperative competition. Cooperative competition is superior to sophisticated neomercantilism on many counts. In the context of global networks that are increasingly the source of dynamic technological change, the economic risks of isolation implicit in sophisticated neomercantilism are enormous. Moreover, the sophisticated neomercantilist approach is inconsistent with the nature of the broader political and military challenges national strategy must also address, including arms proliferation, internal wars, the AIDS epidemic, environmental decay, drug traffic, and humanitarian relief efforts. The complexity of those challenges and the limitations of national resources and approaches for dealing with them mean that cooperation in political and security networks will be essential. The idea of organizational networks is relevant here because of the increasing importance of the coordination of information flows in dealing with those sophisticated problems and because the precise set of countries willing to cooperate on a given issue will vary over time. As a result, international organizations will require greater flexibility in organizing themselves for specific tasks. Global political and security networks will perform the same kinds of functions as economic organizational networks, providing an infrastructure that will enhance cooperation and constrain the nature of competition. From that perspective, neomercantilism, sophisticated or otherwise, would constitute a set of economic policies that are inconsistent with the broader requirements of grand strategy.

Convergence in the economic performance of the three leading economic regions and the emergence of global organizational networks underscore the importance of cooperative competition. Cooperation across those regions will be essential to avoid confrontations over the location of network nodes, which could undermine the advantages of global networks. A narrow focus on relative U.S. economic performance might well miss the point that the level of economic well-being increasingly depends on the ability to operate in integrated world networks. Although it may well be possible to influence the location of network nodes, the form of the competition must be consistent with the need to cooperate in constructing and sustaining global political, security, and economic organizational networks. In contrast to the zero-sum nature of cold war military confrontation with clear winners and losers, the creation of cooperative global networks is a non-zero-sum exercise in which all competitors can gain, albeit to differing degrees. In short, in the new environment, the "competitive state" must promote cooperative competition.

The essence of the cold war strategy was economic and political isolation of the Soviet Union, bilateral nuclear deterrence, forward deployment of U.S. forces in standing alliances based on containment, economic and technological leadership by U.S.-dominated multinational firms, and catch-up growth in Europe and Japan. The new strategy of cooperative competition will be defined more in terms of global organizational networks that provide for enhanced cooperation on technological developments and potential responses to international crises in a framework of shifting ad hoc coalitions and intense economic competition.

More broadly, the strategy of cooperative competition recognizes the key role of technological innovation and economic growth in meeting broad national goals, including internal well-being as well as external security. The economic dimension of the strategy stresses the reality that while the United States and its allies are building an international infrastructure that will improve the well-being of all the participants, they will still be competing with each other for markets. Although the United States needs to cooperate in providing the essential public goods that make international markets operate effectively and permit the mobilization of resources in response to common interests, it also needs to ensure that domestic firms are not disadvantaged in those markets.

The key arguments for a strategy of cooperative competition centered on technology policy may be summarized succinctly. First, the level and industry structure of productivity growth are the best measures of long-term economic performance and international influence. Second, the most persuasive interpretation of productivity growth data is that performance in the major economies of North America, Europe, and Japan are converging, while the less developed regions are dropping further behind. Third, productivity growth in the advanced economies depends on a productivity cycle based on the interaction—within and across national borders—of factor creation, innovation, and the industry structure of competitive advantage. Fourth, the revolution in information technologies has created new physical communication networks that have generated global input-output, R&D, finance, and policy organizational networks, which create powerful forces for integrating standardized processes. Fifth, despite the growing pressures for standardization in global networks, regional network nodes—produced by divergent national attributes, subtle distinctions in economic systems, unique technologies and skills, and synergies from external economies of scale and scope—still persist. Sixth, commercial policies and traditional industrial policies for picking the winners of the future are far less effective than technology policies in influencing productivity growth, because they do not provide the dynamic incentives for innovation, factor creation, and competitive advantage in high-value industries needed to sustain high growth levels. Seventh, technology policies can influence the competition for nodes of high-value activities if they focus on tacit forms of information, technological infrastructures, and local organizational network relationships that are not easily transmitted through global organizational networks, particularly if those policies address sources of market failure in strategic industries. Eighth, implementing such policies will require an emphasis on dual-use industries with both commercial and military applications and this will demand a new orientation for national technology policy in general and military technology policy in particular.

The book develops these arguments in two sections. Part I assembles the evidence on changes in the economic, technological, and organizational environment. Chapter 2 introduces the ideas behind the productivity cycle and interprets the productivity record. Chapter 3 explores the ways in which the information technology revolution has created new physical communications networks and the associated global organizational networks that give international dimensions to the components of the productivity cycle. Chapter 4 presents a refined approach to distinguishing among modern economic systems based on communications flows, and shows how national and regional differences in factor creation, innovation, and the industry structure of competitive advantage persist despite global networks.

Part II shifts to a U.S. policy perspective. Chapter 5 reviews the performance of commercial, industrial, and technology policies in the new environment of economic convergence, global networks, and competition for high-value activities in regional network nodes. Chapter 6 examines the evolving structure of U.S. national technology policy, and Chapter 7 focuses on military technology policy as a component of the broader national strategy. Finally, Chapter 8 pulls together the implications of the policy analysis for the formulation of an integrated national strategy of cooperative competition.

NOTES

1. An earlier version of portions of Chapter 1 appeared in "Economics and National Strategy: Convergence, Global Networks, and Cooperative Competition," *Washington Quarterly* (Summer 1993): 91–114, copyright MIT Press, 1993. The edited material is reproduced here by permission of the *Washington Quarterly* and MIT Press.

2. In the 1930s, Joseph Schumpeter argued that clusters of innovative breakthroughs tended to produce spurts in economic activity that generated 50 to 60-year-long economic cycles known as "Kondratiev cycles." He identified the spurt in the 1780s associated with the first industrial revolution, the railroad surge in the 1840s, and the simultaneous breakthroughs in electricity, telephones, and automobiles in the 1890s as the beginning of three major long cycles. The classification of the first industrial revolution used in this chapter focuses on the role of the external condenser steam engine and includes Schumpeter's first two waves. See Frederick M. Scherer, "Technological Maturity and Waning Economic Growth," in *Innovation and Growth: Schumpeterian Perspectives*, ed. Scherer (Cambridge, Mass.: MIT Press, 1984), 263–264, for a quick summary of Schumpeter's argument and an application to recent technologies. The use of the term "third industrial revolution" and its association with the three technologies listed in the text is becoming more common. See, for example, David J. Teece, "The Dynamics of Industrial Capitalism: Perspectives on Alfred Chandler's *Scale and Scope*," *Journal of Economic Literature* 31 (March 1993): 216.

3. See William W. Kaufman and John D. Steinbruner, *Decisions for Defense: Prospects for a New Order* (Washington, D.C.: The Brookings Institution, 1991). Kaufman and Steinbruner argue for "cooperative" security based on collective arrangements and arms control agreements as a replacement for the strategy of deterrence and containment.

4. See Samuel P. Huntington, "Advice for a Democratic President: The Economic Renewal of America," *National Interest*, No. 26 (Spring 1992): 17. Huntington calls for an integration of Franklin Roosevelt's welfare state with Truman's national security state in the form of a new competitive state.

5. U.S. National Security Council Staff, *National Security Strategy of the United States* (Washington, D.C.: U.S. Government Printing Office, August 1991), 3.

6. Daniel J. Kaufman, David S. Clark, and Kevin P. Sheehan, eds., *U.S. National Security Strategy for the 1990s* (Baltimore, Md.: The Johns Hopkins University Press, 1991), 5.

7. The term "grand strategy" is often associated with the level of wartime mobilization during World War II. Edward Mead Earle, "Introduction," in *Makers of Modern Strategy*, ed. Earle (Princeton, N.J.: Princeton University Press, 1971), p. viii, defines "grand strategy" as "the art of controlling and utilizing the re-

sources of a nation—or a coalition of nations—including its armed forces, to the end that its vital interests shall be effectively promoted and secured against enemies, actual, potential, or merely presumed."

8. Huntington, "Advice for a Democratic President," 17.

9. Paul Kennedy, *The Rise and Fall of the Great Powers* (New York: Random House, 1987).

10. McKinsey Global Institute et al., *Service Sector Productivity* (Washington, D.C., October 1992), chap. 1, exhibit 1–4, between pp. 2 and 3.

11. Jeffrey G. Williamson, "Productivity and American Leadership: A Review Article," *Journal of Economic Literature* 29 (March 1991): 51–68.

12. Samuel P. Huntington, "The U.S.—Decline or Renewal?" *Foreign Affairs* 67 (Winter 1988/89): 88.

13. Charles Steindel, "Manufacturing Productivity and High Tech Investment," *Federal Reserve Bank of New York Quarterly Review* (Summer 1992): 38–40.

14. McKinsey Global Institute, *Service Sector Productivity,* chap. 1, exhibit 1–3, between pp. 2 and 3.

15. Williamson, "Productivity and American Leadership," 59–60.

16. Richard R. Nelson and Gavin Wright, "The Rise and Fall of American Technological Leadership; the Post-War Era in Historical Perspective," *Journal of Economic Literature* 30 (December 1992): 1955.

17. Alexander Gerschenkron, *Economic Backwardness in Historical Perspective* (Cambridge, Mass.: Harvard University Press, 1962).

18. Gavin Wright, "The Origins of America's Industrial Success, 1879–1940," *American Economic Review* 80 (September 1990): 665.

19. Nelson and Wright, "The Rise and Fall of American Technological Leadership," 1955.

20. Anthony Patrick Carnevale, *America and the New Economy: How Competitive Standards Are Radically Changing American Workplaces* (San Francisco, Calif.: Jossey-Bass Publishers, 1991), 86.

21. Robert B. Reich, *The Work of Nations: Preparing Ourselves for 21st Century Capitalism* (New York: Alfred A. Knopf, 1991), 95–96.

22. Ibid., 113.

23. Albert Bressand, "European Integration: From the System Paradigm to Network Analysis," *International Spectator* 24 (January-March 1989): 24.

24. John Hagedoorn and Jos Schakenraad, "Leading Companies and Networks of Strategic Alliances in Information Technologies," *Research Policy* 21 (April 1992): 163–190.

25. Ken-ichi Imai, "Japan's Corporate Networks," in *The Political Economy of Japan, Volume 3: Cultural and Social Dynamics,* ed. Shumpei Kumon and Henry Rosovsky (Stanford, Calif.: Stanford University Press, 1992), 220.

26. Shumpei Kumon, "Japan as a Network Society," in *The Political Economy of Japan,* ed. Kumon and Rosovsky, 128.

27. Bressand, "European Integration," 26.

28. Reich, *The Work of Nations,* 3.

29. Ibid., 83, 113.

30. For more details on particular network nodes, see the following: AnnaLee Saxenian, "The Origins and Dynamics of Production Networks in Silicon Valley," *Research Policy* 20 (October 1991): 423–437; A. J. Scott, "The Aerospace-Elec-

tronics Industrial Complex of Southern California: The Formative Years, 1940–1960," *Research Policy* 20 (October 1991): 439–456; N. Dorfman, "Route 128: The Development of a Regional High Technology Economy," *Research Policy* 12 (August 1983): 299–316; and Patrizio Bianchi and Nicola Bellini, "Public Policies for Local Networks of Innovators," *Research Policy* 20 (October 1991): 487–497.

31. Michael E. Porter, *The Competitive Advantage of Nations* (New York: Free Press, 1990), 42, 54–55, 71–72.

32. Ibid., 77–80.

33. Paul Krugman, *Geography and Trade* (Cambridge, Mass.: MIT Press, 1991), 36–38.

34. Ibid., 66.

35. Michael J. Enright, "The Geographic Scope of Competitive Advantage," *Netherlands Geographic Studies,* forthcoming.

36. John Zysman with Laura Tyson, Giovanni Dosi, and Stephen Cohen, "Trade, Technology, and National Competition," in *Technology and Investment: Crucial Issues for the 1990s,* ed. Enrico Deiaco, Erik Hornell, and Graham Vickery (London: Pinter Publishers, 1990), 198–199.

37. Zysman, "Trade, Technology, and National Competition," 185–211. For a similar line of argument, see Organization for Economic Cooperation and Development, *Technology in a Changing World,* The Technology/Economy Programme (Paris, 1991), 86–93.

38. Zysman, "Trade, Technology, and National Competition," 185.

39. Theodore H. Moran, *American Economic Policy and National Security* (New York: Council on Foreign Relations Press, 1993), 74–81.

2 Collapse or Convergence?

The central strategic question for the U.S. economy concerns the prospects for long-term rates of economic growth. Growth in output will determine the size of the national pie that can be divided among personal consumption, investment to stimulate further growth, and government spending on defense, infrastructure, and public services. A strong, growing economy provides the foundation for individual well-being and national influence.

Long-term growth depends on an expansion in capital and labor resources and efficiency in using them to provide valued products. Researchers have long known that economic growth is greater than the sum of its parts: output grows faster than increases in the quantity of available capital and labor because of improvements in their quality, changes in technologies for combining inputs into outputs, organizational adaptation, and economies of scale. In short, growth comes from the provision of new and better factors of production and from increased efficiency in using them. Efficiency in factor use is defined as productivity, the ratio of outputs to inputs. This chapter examines the sources of productivity growth, reviews possible explanations for the decline in productivity growth in the developed regions since roughly 1973, and evaluates the evidence that productivity performance is converging across Europe, Japan, and the United States. Subsequent chapters examine the impact of the information technology revolution on changing sources of productivity growth in a global economy linked by international organizational networks.

THE PRODUCTIVITY CYCLE

Figure 2-1 illustrates how national characteristics and public policies influence innovation networks, factor creation, and the industry structure of competitive advantage, which interact in a "productivity cycle" that determines productivity growth. Labor productivity, or output per hour worked, depends on the capital stock of plants and equipment available for workers, the quality of worker skills, the technology for combining inputs to produce outputs, and organizational efficiency in making the entire process work.[1] These factors are "endogenous," or jointly determined, because current industrial structure determines how innovation occurs through training and investment patterns, which, in turn, slowly modify

Figure 2-1
The Productivity Cycle

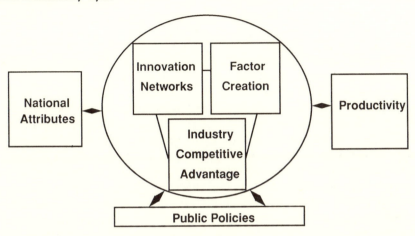

industrial structure.[2] These factors interact in productivity cycles that are "path-dependent," with incremental adjustments to patterns of innovation, factor creation, and industrial structure periodically driven toward new paradigms, or patterns of interrelationship, by external shocks such as technological breakthroughs.

The box labeled "factor creation" in Figure 2-1 emphasizes the importance of generating capital and labor skills tailored to the requirements of each industry. The central idea is that productivity growth depends on the provision of capital and labor appropriate for high-value industries.[3] The "innovation networks" box contains those processes and institutions that contribute most directly to the creation, adaptation, commercialization, and dissemination of new products and production techniques. Innovation networks—including research universities and institutes, government laboratories, and private corporations—facilitate and constrain patterns of research, development, and the infusion and adaptation of new innovations. The international dimensions of the innovation networks are particularly important in evaluating new sources of productivity growth, and subsequent chapters will explore those global networks in detail.

Patterns of innovation and factor creation play a large role in determining the set of industries or niches within industries in which a nation will develop international competitive advantage. The industrial structure, in turn, influences the form of innovation networks and patterns of factor creation by generating a concentration of supporting industries, facilities, and labor skills that guide and benefit from innovation. Innovation networks, factor creation, and the structure of industry competitive advantage are interconnected in patterns that persist for extended periods through long swings that make up the productivity cycle and determine the pace of productivity advance. The process follows a cyclical pattern because it is driven by technological advances that tend to come in waves of related innovations that work their way through the system and produce new patterns of factor creation, innovation, and competitive advantage.

Although the global economy is becoming more and more integrated, differences in national attributes and public policies continue to influence the productivity cycle. National attributes define the environment within which innovation, factor creation, and industrial competition proceed. Those national attributes include social and political stability; property rights; the structure of capital, labor, and product markets; labor-management relationships; the education system; science and technical infrastructures; and attitudes toward innovation.

Differences in public policies also affect the nature of the productivity cycle in each country. The broad macroeconomic setting influences rates of savings and investment that have a direct impact on capital creation. Commercial policies determine patterns of tariffs, quotas, and subsidies that affect industrial structure and openness to international competition. Industrial policies, which include policies whose purpose is to influence the pattern of employment or production across industries or regions, have clear impacts on each part of the productivity cycle. Research or technology policies have their most direct impact on the structure of innovation networks, but they can also affect the other components. These policies are not easily separable into distinct groups in terms of either the processes through which they are implemented or the range of their economic impacts. Indeed, failure to assess the combined impact of these policies on the productivity cycle, and the inability to coordinate across them in the context of a coherent strategy, is a central strategic problem.

The concept of a cycle suggests a pattern of delayed interactions that feed on each other. Innovations must be adapted to new capital, training, and procedures and tailored to commercially profitable products. The full impact of an innovation frequently depends on related innovations in other fields, and the pace of diffusion can be erratic as independent pockets of innovation become more integrated into new production systems. The investment, training, and adaptation required to create new factors of production take time, and the lags between technical innovation and observed productivity improvement often stretch into decades because of slow rates of diffusion and problems in measuring the full impacts of new products and processes.[4]

Three aspects of the productivity cycle warrant special emphasis. First, there is considerable evidence that industrial concentration and competitive advantage are path-dependent. For example, the location of a textile mill in any one of a number of river valleys providing cheap sources of power might be the product of a chance decision, but once the mill is established, the network of suppliers and customers that grows up around the mill may provide the incentive to locate other mills in the same region. In short, history matters, and patterns of international specialization are surprisingly persistent, even in an age of integrated global markets. Second, differences in national attributes do persist over time. They are not fixed, to be sure, and experience with innovation, factor creation, the composition of competitive advantage, and productivity performance can slowly change national attitudes and institutions, but differences in national attributes remain important. Those two elements, path dependence and persistence in national attributes, create strong arguments for national approaches to productivity development. The third key factor, the emergence of integrated global organizational networks that coordinate processes of innovation across regions, limits the effectiveness of strictly national approaches.

Subsequent chapters examine the components and determinants of the productivity cycle in more detail, with emphasis on the transforming impact of global organizational networks. National strategy must build from an assessment of how these sources of productivity are changing in an integrated global economy. This chapter begins at the right side of Figure 2–1, with an assessment of the productivity record as the central criterion for evaluating long-term economic performance and influence.

The record, presented in more detail below, yields the following three central conclusions. First, persistent U.S. budget deficits have lowered national savings and made increases in domestic investment hostage to international capital flows and continuing trade deficits. Second, the downturn in U.S. productivity growth after 1973 does not constitute a dramatic departure from long-term productivity growth trends. This fact does not reduce the importance of the slowdown, but it does shift attention for the causes of the downturn from recent policies to longer-term cycles. Third, the downturn in U.S. productivity growth does not mean that the United States is being "deindustrialized" or that it is destined to fall behind more dynamic competitors. Instead, the major developed economies are converging on the productivity performance of the leader, a process that has clearly been at work since the end of World War II.

NATIONAL SAVINGS AND DOMESTIC INVESTMENT

Persistent U.S. budget deficits have lowered national savings and made increases in domestic investment hostage to international capital flows and continuing trade deficits. The rate of increase in capital, or the level of investment, determines the pace of change in the size and quality of the plants and equipment available to workers. Annual gross investment must not only provide for the replacement of depreciated capital whose usefulness has declined, but also add net investment of new machinery and

Table 2-1
U.S. National Savings, Net Domestic Investment, and Net Foreign Investment,
1960–1990 (billion nominal dollars)

	1960	1965	1970	1975	1980	1985	1990
Personal Savings	21	35	58	100	154	190	207
Net Business Savings	15	32	19	41	34	92	50
Government Surplus Sums to:	4	1	-12	-65	-35	-125	-140
National Savings	39	68	66	76	153	156	117
Minus:							
Domestic Net Investment	32	61	62	61	156	260	208
Equals:							
U.S. Foreign Investment	6	7	4	16	-3	-104	-91

Source: U.S. Council of Economic Advisers, *Economic Report of the President* (Washington,
   D.C.: U.S. Government Printing Office, February 1992), Table B-1, p. 298; Table B-
   14, p. 314; and Table B-26, p. 328.

Notes: Details may not add to totals because of rounding. The government surplus is for
   federal and local governments based on national income and product accounts. Net
   foreign investment includes the statistical discrepancy in Table B-26 net of small capital grants received by the United States in 1970 to 1972 and 1979 to 1981.

factories needed for expanded output. The funds for purchasing capital
goods flow from national savings and purchases of domestic assets by foreign citizens.

National savings include the share of corporate profits plowed back into
new capital, personal savings by individuals, funds that government invests
in new capital, and any excess of government revenues over other spending. Those savings provide a pool of funds that can be channeled through
financial intermediaries, such as commercial banks, to firms that will use
the funds for net investment in new domestic capital. The funds might also
be used for U.S. foreign investment to buy assets owned by foreign citizens. As a result, total U.S. national savings must equal the sum of U.S.
net domestic investment and U.S. foreign investment. Table 2-1 shows this
relationship for the period from 1960 to 1990.

National savings is a driving force behind capital creation and long-term economic growth. As Table 2-2 shows, national savings averaged over 8 percent of U.S. GDP in the 1960s and between 5 and 6 percent in the 1970s, enough to fund domestic investment and to purchase foreign assets. After 1980, however, national savings fell to between 2 and 3 percent of GDP, while domestic investment fell only slightly. The decline in the national savings rate came from a drop in the private savings rate and from a huge increase in government budget deficits as a share of gross national product (GNP). National savings did not provide sufficient funds to meet the demand for domestic investment, so U.S. assets were sold to foreign citizens to meet the high demand for spending. Net U.S. foreign investment disappeared. Instead, funds flowed into the U.S. as foreign citizens purchased U.S. assets.

The use of foreign funds to finance domestic investment meant that the U.S. was buying more that it could produce, so it had to import more than it exported. The trade deficits of the 1980s and 1990s are the mirror image of the flow of investment funds into the United States. In short, large government deficits produced the decline in national savings, the decline in national savings led to the flow of foreign investment into the United

Table 2-2

U.S. National Savings, Net Domestic Investment, and Net Foreign Investment, 1960–1990 (percent of GDP)

	1960	1965	1970	1975	1980	1985	1990
Personal Savings	4.0	4.9	5.7	6.3	5.7	4.7	3.7
Net Business Savings	2.8	4.5	1.9	2.6	1.2	2.3	0.9
Government Surplus	0.7	0.2	-1.1	-4.1	-1.3	-3.1	-2.5
National Savings	7.6	9.6	6.5	4.8	5.6	3.9	2.1
Domestic Net Investment	6.3	8.6	6.1	3.8	5.7	6.4	3.8
U.S. Foreign Investment	1.2	1.0	0.4	1.0	-0.1	-2.6	-1.6

Source: U.S. Council of Economic Advisers, *Economic Report of the President* (Washington, D.C.: U.S. Government Printing Office, February 1992), Table B-1, p. 298; Table B-14, p. 314; and Table B-26, p. 328.

Note: Details may not add to totals because of rounding.

States, and the influx of foreign investment produced the trade deficit. As a result, the government budget deficits and the trade deficit are twins: they arrived together and they look very much alike.

The moral of the story is that domestic investment can only be sustained at levels higher than national savings if there is a net flow of foreign investment into the country, and that means continuing trade deficits. As with any investment, the use of foreign funds to purchase capital goods may well make sense if it increases growth and creates enough income to more than pay back the principal and interest on the loan. Indeed, foreign funds financed a large share of U.S. growth in the nineteenth century. In the 1980s, however, the foreign investment only sustained levels of domestic investment somewhat below the traditional share of GDP in the face of increasing national consumption, particularly by government. Indirectly then, the foreign investment funded high consumption, not capital growth. While it might be possible to sustain inflows of foreign investment in the long run if they actually add to the nation's productive capacity, it is not possible to sustain an influx of funds that only finances consumption. Sooner or later the debts must be paid, and that means lower future income levels.

National savings remain the key to long-term growth, and reductions in U.S. budget deficits are essential to increasing national savings.[5] Persistent budget deficits lower national savings and make the increases in domestic investment hostage to international capital flows and continuing trade deficits. Moreover, international borrowing may not be sufficient to sustain traditional investment levels. According to a study by M. A. Akhtar and Ethan Harris, the lower level of national savings in the 1980s led to a reduction in the ratio of net U.S. private investment to GDP from 7.1 percent in the period from 1971 to 1980 to 5.2 percent from 1981 to 1990, and by their estimates that decline of roughly 2 percent lowered U.S. potential GDP in 1990 by 2.5 to 3.5 percent.[6]

The growth problems that result from budget deficits are clear, and the deficits can be reversed with appropriate fiscal policies. The reversal will be painful, because belt-tightening will lower after-tax income in the short run, and reductions in the growth of government programs are unpopular, but lower deficits are an essential first step toward sustained growth. Solving the deficit problem, however, will not eliminate other concerns about long-term growth patterns, because growth depends on more than investment.

PRODUCTIVITY PATTERNS

The decline in national savings does not fully explain the downturn in U.S. productivity growth after 1973. The explanation requires a longer-term perspective, because the downturn does not constitute a dramatic departure from historic productivity growth trends that have moved in long cycles.

Sustained growth requires increases in productivity that depend on the quality of labor and changes in technology as well as capital formation. As shown in Table 1–1, the United States has held the world lead in the ratio of output to labor input, or labor productivity, for some time, but the rate of growth in U.S. productivity has been declining both in terms of earlier U.S. experience and in terms of growth rates in other countries. Measures of productivity that account for the input of both capital and labor, or total factor productivity, have also been declining. In other words, higher growth in labor and capital are now required to sustain traditional levels of growth in output. The full reasons for the productivity decline are not clearly understood, and, as a result, conflicting explanations and policy prescriptions to reverse the decline abound. National economic strategy must begin with changes in macroeconomic policies to bring down stifling budget deficits, but the next, more controversial steps depend on an assessment of the other reasons behind the decline in productivity.

Productivity and Growth

In the long run, the rate of increase in output per worker determines the pace of improvement in living standards and changes in relative economic power. The decline in U.S. productivity growth rates should produce similar declines in long-term growth rates in output and consumption. U.S. individual welfare and international influence thus depend on an understanding of the sources of the decline in productivity growth and the steps that might correct it.

Of course, it is possible to increase living standards in the short run without improvements in productivity, but those alternatives cannot be sustained over time. Living standards can be raised by lowering savings or by borrowing from abroad to increase consumption, but neither of those approaches works in the longer run, because they will either depress investment in the capital needed for growth or they will drive up the trade deficit. Similarly, the nation can always use its resources more intensively than it normally does, but that could lead to inflationary pressures that are hard to suppress after they have been released.

The government, for example, could easily expand the money supply to stimulate the economy, leading firms to use their capital more intensively or to bid against other firms to obtain more labor services. For a while, output and consumption would rise. Unfortunately, prices will also rise, because the costs of production increase as less efficient capital is brought on line and workers demand higher wages for the extra hours of work. The resulting inflation can have serious impacts on those who did not anticipate it, particularly those on fixed incomes and those who loaned money at fixed interest rates. Moreover, as the record of the 1970s clearly indicates, inflation creates inflationary expectations that lead to further wage demands in a continuing spiral, and the ultimate steps to eliminate the inflation can be painful. The reduction in the growth of the money supply at the end of the 1970s and the early 1980s did succeed in lowering inflation, but it also produced the deep recession of 1982.

Sustained long-term growth in living standards cannot be obtained by drawing down savings, relying on foreign investment, or demand management by government. In the long run, productivity growth determines growth in per capita output.

The Productivity Record

Should productivity growth in economically advanced countries decline over time? In the first half of the twentieth century, this question intrigued economists who speculated that innovation came in bursts that brought surges in growth.[7] As Great Britain surrendered productivity leadership at the turn of the century to Germany and the United States, economists speculated that the great "climacteric," as Britain's slowdown was called, might ultimately apply to the new leaders as well. New technologies would be championed by nations with the flexibility to exploit them. In Joseph Schumpeter's view, entrepreneurs would break out of traditional molds, create new industries, and promote a wave of related innovations.[8] Ultimately, however, the growth spurt would be depleted as demand was saturated and cost savings slowly dried up. In this process of "creative destruction," young rivals would surge ahead with rapid productivity growth, only to be brought down by newer rivals as technological gains declined, cost reductions became more difficult, the market ceased to expand, and sales stopped growing. Of course, the new industries might emerge in the same country, so the technological trajectory did not necessarily mean a shift in national leadership, but many argued that as growth proceeded the leading country might develop a social sclerosis that would limit flexibility in adapting to new economic breakthroughs. Schumpeter felt that capitalism itself would ultimately fall from political reactions to the entrepreneurs and the institutions that supported them: increased regulation would ultimately lead to socialism.[9]

The surge of demand in World War II and the postwar period silenced the discussion about technological trajectories, because the increase in aggregate demand swamped any tendency for declining growth in particular industries. The slower growth of the 1970s, however, brought a renewed interest in the impacts of aging industries. Mancur Olson, for example, proposed the argument that the distributional coalitions of interest groups required to resolve equity concerns make it more and more difficult for advanced economies to compete.[10]

The concept of an aging country, as distinct from an aging industry, however, is fraught with problems such as defining the base period from which aging is to be measured. Moreover, as R. D. Norton has argued so effectively, the concept of national aging is particularly hard to define in a country as regionally diverse as the United States. As industrial trajectories produce social or political coalitions that might restrict growth in one region, for example, new industries can locate in other regions.[11] Moreover, countries can respond to sclerosis once that problem is perceived. Concerns of the early 1980s on the aging of Europe, the failure to create new jobs there, and stifling European social institutions has now given way to euphoria over the dynamic possibilities of the single European market. The potential for such rebirth makes the aging metaphor tenuous.

The national aging argument is frequently applied to the United States as it enters a period of more intense competition with a revitalized Europe and a Japan that has been generating rapid productivity gains in highly visible manufacturing export sectors. According to this argument, key U.S. institutions—the educational system, political processes, corporate structures, and science and engineering infrastructure—have not kept pace with changes in the global economy. Hence, the United States is destined to fall behind unless it can somehow transform those institutions.

The key piece of evidence in this argument is the declining rate of productivity in the United States, both in terms of its own history and in terms of its competitors. That record, however, is difficult to interpret because of long swings in productivity performance. The recent slowdown may suggest a long-term adjustment to a new lower-growth trend, a pattern that would support the idea of a United States falling behind in the regional competition. On the other hand, the pattern may simply reflect an adjustment that is a natural part of convergence in the performance of advanced economies. Neither interpretation provides cause for complacency, because the lower productivity growth that has persisted since 1973 has already had important consequences. On balance, an assessment of the long view and the convergence evidence suggests that although the United States has not fallen behind, it will have to reorient itself for intensified competition with economic equals.

Table 2-3 provides the best available information on annual growth in output per worker hour in five advanced economies stretching back into the nineteenth century. The most striking aspect of the table is that entries average over 2 percent per year, reflecting a century of dramatic economic progress. One can estimate the number of years it takes for output per hour to double by dividing the annual growth rate into the number 72. On average, output per worker doubled every 36 years through the century, so children enjoyed roughly twice the economic standards of their grandparents.

The postwar surge from 1950 to 1973 saw an unprecedented rate of economic growth. Japan's extraordinary productivity growth of over 9 percent per year from 1960 to 1973 means that output per hour was doubling every eight years. The U.S. productivity growth of 2.5 percent per year from 1950 to 1973 was not that impressive by the Japanese standard, but it still meant output per worker was doubling every 30 years. Each generation could expect a dramatic improvement in living standards. From that perspective, the slowdown after 1973 in all these countries meant an enormous loss in potential income. Productivity growth continued, to be sure, but at the U.S. rate of 1 percent per year, output per worker was doubling only every 72 years, a dramatic change from the postwar performance.[12]

The dismal U.S. productivity performance since 1973 has already had enormous consequences. The key strategic questions are whether or not that performance is apt to persist and what can be done about it. The answers require an exploration of the long-run pattern of productivity growth and its sources, an accounting for the explanations of the slowdown after 1973, and an examination of the impacts of the slowdown on different sectors of the economy.

The Long View

In an impressive study, *Productivity and American Leadership: The Long View,* William J. Baumol, Sue Anne Batey Blackman, and Edward N. Wolff reach guardedly optimistic conclusions about U.S. productivity performance from the long-run perspective.[13] First, they emphasize that the decadal data similar to the estimates in Table 2-3 show a trend increase in productivity growth of just over 2 percent per year from 1870 to 1984, with clear cyclical variations. There was a sharp drop below the trend during the depression in the 1930s, a sharp rise above the trend through the wartime expansion of the 1940s, continued growth above the trend line through 1970, and a drop below the trend through 1984. The wartime surge and postwar bulge offset the drop during the depression, bringing the U.S. economy back near its long-term trend. Compared with the postwar surge, the decline after 1973 looks like a sharp collapse, but from a longer-term perspective it appears to be a cyclical downturn around a stable trend. Second, they note that manufacturing productivity, despite drops in 1950 to 1956, 1963 to 1968, and 1971 to 1980, has not shown any long-term downward trend, and indeed it has been rising sharply since 1980. Third, the sectors in which productivity growth has been declining,

Table 2-3
Growth Rates of Labor Productivity for Five Industrial Countries, 1870–1990
(**percent per year**) (Reprinted with permission from the American Economic
Association.)

| From | 1870 | 1890 | 1913 | 1929 | 1938 | 1950 | 1960 | 1973 | 1984 |
To	1890	1913	1929	1938	1950	1960	1973	1984	1990
France	1.5	1.9	2.4	2.9	0.8	4.4	5.7	3.5	2.4
Germany	1.9	1.9	1.4	2.4	-0.4	6.9	5.3	3.0	1.9
Japan	1.8	1.9	3.6	2.5	-1.2	5.9	9.1	3.2	3.4
UK	1.4	1.1	1.5	0.9	2.2	2.3	3.9	2.4	1.4
US	2.2	1.8	2.4	0.7	3.8	2.5	2.5	1.0	1.0

Sources: 1870–1984—Growth in GDP per work hour computed from Maddison, "Growth
and Slowdown in Advanced Capitalist Economies: Techniques of Quantitative Assessment," *Journal of Economic Literature* 25 (June 1987): Table A-5, p. 683;
1981–1990—Growth rate in GDP per worker computed from OECD, *Economic
Outlook Statistics on Microcomputer Diskettes* (Paris, June 1992).

such as finance, insurance, real estate, and other services, are those that
have never had good productivity growth. All three of these considerations
suggest that there is no clear evidence of a downturn in productivity
growth at the aggregate or sectoral levels.[14]

Unfortunately, productivity growth has not rebounded since 1984, the
last year in Angus Maddison's data used by Baumol, Blackman, and
Wolff. As shown in Table 2-3, U.S. productivity growth for the entire
period from 1973 to 1990 has remained at roughly 1 percent per year,
compared with the long-term trend of over 2 percent. The slide into the
recession of 1991 and the modest recovery in 1992 add a cyclical downturn to the weak 1973 to 1990 performance. As a result, the case that
productivity growth has merely dipped below a higher long-term trend to
which it will ultimately return becomes more tenuous. Nonetheless, the
length and size of the productivity decline is not inconsistent with earlier
cyclical patterns.

There is therefore some question as to whether U.S. long-term productivity growth rates have actually declined; but if they have, what would
explain the drop? U.S. economic growth around the turn of the century
received an enormous boost from the interaction of a large national free-
trade area and large investments in transportation. Western railroads in
particular pressed investment ahead of existing demand and forged an integrated national transportation system.[15] As Gavin Wright correctly emphasizes, that transportation network, the discovery of new minerals, and

the innovation of new processing techniques released enormous creativity that spurred growth, developed sophisticated technologies, and prompted improvements in organizational structures.[16] Mineral abundance in this sense was not so much a natural endowment as an integral part of technological progress: it was both cause and effect. American production techniques evolved to exploit the availability of minerals, emphasizing capital- and mineral-intense processes and large-scale production.

With industrial prosperity came investments in an educated work force, funding for scientific research, and increasing exploitation of science-based technologies. After World War II, resource abundance no longer provided the foundation for continued growth, but the United States maintained its productivity lead through the application of skilled labor to science-based technologies that played to U.S. advantages. Those technological advantages have now atrophied. After a period of large investments in research, development, and education overseas in which other economies adapted to U.S. standards, U.S. firms must now adjust to global technologies.[17] The period of declining productivity growth in the United States has also been a period of adaptation to foreign commercialization of new technologies and changes in the organizational structure of global firms. The recovery of the U.S. economy to the long-term trend will have to take place in a transformed international environment.

The Short View

The long-view argument boils down to the case that productivity has always cycled around its long-term trend, and the performance since 1973 does not constitute a permanent departure from that pattern. This argument could be defeated by evidence showing a clear, persisting explanation for the downturn, but unfortunately the available evidence does not provide a persuasive explanation.

The "growth accounting" approach developed by Robert Solow and refined by Edward Denison provides a useful way of organizing the available evidence.[18] In their framework, the rate of growth in output is "explained" by the rate of growth in the inputs of labor and capital weighted by their relative importance. The weights come from the assumption that the share of national income that goes to labor or capital reflects each factor's relative contribution to output. For example, labor receives roughly 70 percent of national income, so labor would receive a weight of 0.7 in explaining output increases.[19] If the number of worker hours grew by 1 percent from one year to the next, growth accountants would say that labor explained a growth in output of 0.7 percent during that year. If capital contributes 30 percent of output and capital grew by 2 percent from one year to the next, capital would explain a growth in output of 0.6 percent. In this case, capital and labor together would explain output growth of 1.3 percent

(0.7 plus 0.6). The growth accountant can then compare actual growth with the "explained" growth to see if there is a residual that needs further explanation.

Using this approach with data for the United States for the periods from 1950 to 1973 and from 1973 to 1984, Maddison obtains the results shown in Table 2-4. The task is to explain why the rate of growth fell from 3.72 percent per year in the early period to 2.32 percent per year in the later period, a decline of 1.4 percent per year. The three sources of growth include increases in capital, labor, and total factor productivity. The reduction in the rate of new capital formation from 1973 to 1984 explains a slowdown of 0.17 percent compared to a total decline in growth of 1.4 percent, or roughly 12 percent of the drop. That decline was largely offset by a matching increase in the quantity of labor, so the total growth of inputs dropped only slightly between the two periods. The decline in annual growth rates is not explained by changes in the quantity of capital and labor input.

One way of restating the puzzle is to observe that the lower growth came from a decline in productivity, although that still leaves the explanation for the lower productivity unresolved. In the period from 1950 to 1973, capital and labor together explained 1.87 percent of total growth of 3.72 percent, or roughly half of the growth in output, and the residual, total factor productivity, also explained half of the growth, findings that are consistent with similar studies for earlier periods.[20] Table 2-4 shows that in the subsequent period from 1973 to 1984, capital and labor explained 1.8 percent of total growth of 2.83 percent, or over 75 percent of total growth, and productivity explained less than one-quarter.[21] The key conclusion here is that the decline in total factor productivity growth is the central explanation for the decline in growth rates between the two periods.

Apparently, something happened that made labor and capital less productive than they had been in the earlier period, but it is not yet clear what it was. Growth before 1973 seemed to get a boost from some factors other than the quantity of capital and labor. If the source of the boost could be identified, policymakers would have a better idea of what approaches might be most helpful. From this perspective, the challenge is to identify factors other than the quantity of capital and labor that might explain the decline in growth.

Unfortunately, none of the other potential explanations is persuasive. A decline in the quality or quantity of education might explain a reduced rate of productivity growth, but education quality is hard to measure. The available estimates of education quantity show that the rate of increase in years of schooling went up between the periods from 1950 to 1973 and from 1973 to 1984 as the rate of growth was going down.[22] As a result, there is little evidence that changes in education caused the slowdown in

Table 2-4
Accounting for U.S. Growth, 1913–1984 (average annual percentage rates)
(Reprinted with permission from the American Economic Association.)

Component	Growth Rate 1950–1973	1973–1984
Growth in Output and Input Quantities:		
Gross Domestic Product (GDP)	3.72	2.32
Labor Quantity	1.22	1.35
Capital Quantity	3.40	2.83
Estimated Contributions to GDP Growth by:		
Labor Quantity	.85	.95
Capital Quantity	1.02	.85
Labor and Capital Quantity	1.87	1.80
Unexplained Residual	1.85	.52
Additional Explanations of GDP Growth from:		
Labor Quality	.29	.36
Capital Quality	.51	.43
Structural Effect	.12	-.07
Energy Effect	.00	-.12
New Unexplained Residual	.93	-.08

Source: Maddison, "Growth and Slowdown in Advanced Capitalist Economies," Table 20, p. 679, using weights of 0.7 for labor and 0.3 for capital. Maddison actually divides capital into residential and nonresidential capital and applies weights of 0.07 and 0.23, respectively.

productivity growth. There is some evidence that the rate of increase in the quality of capital may have declined between the two periods, but the difference is not large enough to explain much of the slowdown.[23] As a result, adjustments in the data for changes in labor or capital quality do not increase understanding of the decline in total factor productivity.

Growth is also affected by shifts in the structure of output among agriculture, industry, and services, caused by changes in demand as income increases and by different rates of technological progress in each sector. Those shifts have followed a consistent pattern across developed countries with the share of agricultural employment falling over time, services rising,

Table 2-5
Compound Rates of Growth in Output per Hour in Selected U.S. Sectors and in
Manufacturing in Selected Countries, 1960–1973 (percent per year)

	1960–1973	1973–1984	1984–1990	1973–1990
United States				
Business	2.9	0.9	0.8	0.8
Nonfarm Business	2.5	0.7	0.6	0.7
Manufacturing	3.3	1.5	2.9	2.0
Manufacturing in				
France	6.4	3.9	3.4	3.7
Germany	5.6	3.0	2.5	2.8
Japan	10.2	4.4	4.5	4.4
United Kingdom	4.2	2.8	4.1	3.3

Source: Computed from U.S. Bureau of Labor Statistics, *Monthly Labor Review* 115 (September 1992): Table 45, p. 92, and Table 49, p. 97.

and industrial employment being squeezed between them, first rising and then falling.[24] The U.S. pattern is typical, with agricultural employment falling from 50 percent of total employment in 1870 to just over 3 percent by 1984, and services employment rising steadily from roughly one-quarter of total employment in 1870 to almost 70 percent by 1984. Changes in industrial employment have been less dramatic, rising from 24 percent in 1870 to a peak of 34 percent in 1960 and then falling back to 28 percent in 1984.[25] The level of productivity and, as Table 2-5 shows, the rate of productivity growth have varied sharply across these sectors, so shifts in the composition of output should help to explain changes in overall productivity growth rates.

Because the level and rate of growth of industrial productivity have been much higher than services, the rise in the industrial share of employment from 1950 to 1973 and the decline from 1973 to 1984 is consistent with the slowdown in overall productivity growth. That shift turns out to be significant. Maddison computes what the rate of increase in output would have been if the sectoral composition had not changed, compares that with the actual increase in output, and uses the difference as the estimate of the impact of the structural effect on growth. As shown in Table 2-4, the structural shifts explain roughly 0.19 percent of the 1.4 percent decline in GDP growth, or roughly 13 percent of the slowdown.[26]

The shift in the sectoral composition of output had an important impact on productivity growth. There is also some evidence that the energy crisis that began in 1973, and was therefore coincident with the productivity slowdown, was also significant. Efforts to conserve on energy in the face of higher energy prices might lower output per worker, and Maddison estimates that those adjustments explain roughly 9 percent of the total decline in GDP growth between 1950 and 1973 and between 1973 and 1984.[27] The conclusion that the increases in energy prices mattered, but that they do not explain the lion's share of the productivity decline, is consistent with the observation that the drop in energy prices in the 1980s did not reverse the low rate of productivity growth of the 1970s.

Table 2-4 assembles the evidence for each explanation. The additional corrections for labor and capital quality, structural change, and energy consumption account for just under 30 percent of the decline between the two periods. That still leaves, however, over 70 percent of the growth slowdown unexplained. Most of the decline in growth must still be attributed to factors that have not yet been measured. The two most important sources of the slowdown that can be identified as continuing areas of concern, however, are the shift in the sectoral composition of output toward the low productivity growth services sector and the decline in the rate of new capital formation, each of which explained slightly over 10 percent of the productivity decline between 1950 and 1973 and between 1973 and 1984. The decline in capital formation may have played an even larger role if new capital embodies new technologies. Those conclusions do not, however, provide a clear foundation for public policies that might reverse the productivity decline, except for steps to enhance capital formation. Indeed, because most of the decline remains unexplained, it is not even clear that the decline will persist.

Manufacturing Productivity: The Sectoral View

If the long-run record leaves some question about the permanence of the slowdown, and the absence of clear explanations draws the persistence of the decline into question, what does the record of productivity growth in different industries suggest about productivity patterns? Dale Jorgenson argues that weighted sums of detailed sectoral studies show an even more precipitous decline in productivity than that observed at the aggregate level.[28] The major problems have been in construction, mining, and services, sectors that have historically exhibited slow productivity growth. Manufacturing productivity, the traditional pacesetter, has remained relatively strong, although it has fallen below its pre-1973 growth rate.

Table 2-5 presents the record of U.S. productivity growth for selected business sectors, including services, agriculture, and industry. Manufacturing productivity grew faster than the rest of the business sectors in each period, following the general slowdown from 1973 to 1984 but rebounding strongly from 1984 to 1990. Manufacturing productivity growth declined somewhat between the periods from 1960 to 1973 and from 1973 to 1990, but not nearly as much as the rest of the business sectors. In fact, the long-term manufacturing record since 1948 is very consistent with the hypothesis that there has been a steady rate of total factor productivity increase over the entire period despite short-term cycles.[29] Nonetheless, U.S. manufacturing productivity growth lagged behind the other major economies in each period, with the exception of 1984 to 1990 when U.S. growth exceeded the German performance.

In sum, the longer-run data suggest that there has been only a modest decline in manufacturing productivity growth and that the sectors pushing overall U.S. productivity below its long-term growth pattern are construction, finance, insurance, real estate, and other services.[30] A slowing of growth in manufacturing productivity would draw the long-term overall productivity pattern into question, because that sector has typically led other sectors. Instead, resiliency in manufacturing productivity growth provides cause for optimism. The persisting low rates of growth in services productivity are a concern because of the steadily increasing employment share in that sector, but they do not constitute a departure from long-term trends. In short, the strong performance in manufacturing supports the hypothesis that although U.S. productivity growth has declined in comparison with the extraordinary postwar spurt, productivity growth may in fact still be on the longer-term trajectory it has followed since the late nineteenth century.

CONVERGENCE OR FALLING BEHIND?

The United States does not face economic collapse. Instead, the major developed economies are converging on the productivity performance of the leader, a process that has clearly been at work since the end of World War II. The downturn in U.S. productivity growth does not mean that the United States is being "deindustrialized" or that it is destined to fall behind more dynamic competitors.

Table 2-3 shows that since 1890 the United States has rarely been the leader in productivity growth. The period from 1938 to 1950, including World War II and the immediate postwar period, provides the one exception. A larger sample of 16 industrial countries reveals that the United States has never led in productivity growth since 1880, and in peacetime periods there have usually been at least five countries ahead of it.[31] The surprise then, is not that the United States continues to lag behind the others in productivity growth, but that it has sustained its lead in absolute productivity for so long.[32] Convergence theory offers a compelling hypothesis to explain why this might be the case.

Convergence

Based on his analysis of nineteenth century European growth, Alexander Gerschenkron argued that follower countries had an advantage over leaders because the followers could borrow new technologies if and when their growth spurt finally occurred. As a result, the more relatively backward the country was at the time of its spurt, the larger the impact of the new technologies and the faster the rate of growth would be, so followers would then tend to converge on the leader. Not all countries would necessarily be able to overcome their relative backwardness, because the adaptation might be too difficult and the required level of investment might be too great. Gerschenkron argued that the spurt required dramatic social changes, and the more backward the nation was, the more it would have to rely on a strong ideology or government intervention to initiate the spurt.[33]

After extensive testing with various long-term time series, Baumol, Blackman, and Wolff concluded that convergence has been a powerful force since roughly 1880. Their technique was to plot initial relative GDP per hour worked versus subsequent productivity growth. Convergence theory would suggest that the initial leaders should have slower productivity growth, and that is exactly what they found: the higher the initial level of productivity the slower the subsequent growth.[34] On the basis of their analysis, the United States showed a slightly higher rate of growth than convergence alone would suggest.[35]

They also used "coefficients of variation" as statistical estimates of the dispersion of productivity growth across countries: the larger the coefficient, the larger the variation in observed productivity growth. Convergence theory suggests that the coefficients should decline over time, indicating less variation across countries. Again, that is exactly what they found using Maddison's data on 16 industrial countries for the period from 1870 to 1984.[36] They repeated their analysis using a larger sample of 72 countries for the period from 1950 to 1980 and discovered that, except for a group of 23 less-developed countries, those furthest behind in productivity growth grew faster.[37] More recent studies have confirmed both the postwar convergence in output per worker in Organization for Economic Cooperation and Development (OECD) countries and the lack of convergence of less-developed countries toward the OECD levels.[38] Convergence in the major OECD economies was driven by the higher rate of physical capital accumulation and technical changes in Japan and Europe than in the United States.[39]

The pace of convergence should decelerate over time as the gap between productivity leaders and followers becomes smaller. Greater mobility of capital, information, and entrepreneurs and the emergence of international organizational networks that link them together and facilitate interaction should prevent nations in the "convergence club" from diverging after they have moved together. The rapid diffusion of technology through imitation lowers the relative gains from the discovery of new products and processes, making it possible for followers to converge on the leaders more quickly. Maddison argues that the growth "catch-up bonus" comes from the savings on R&D that are possible by simply borrowing the best available practices from the leader. The larger the gap, the higher the growth impact of technology transfer should be.[40] Maddison's somewhat arbitrary estimates of the size of the catch-up bonus suggest that the Japanese economy, for example, gained roughly 1 percent per year in real GDP growth from the follower advantages from 1950 to 1973 and just under half a percent per year from 1973 to 1984.[41] The declining follower bonus reflects the reduced advantages from technology transfer as convergence proceeds.

In a separate study, John Kendrick estimated that technological catch-up accounted for almost half of the decline in the productivity gap between the United States and other countries between 1960 and 1973.[42] He concluded that the major factor in the slowing rate of productivity growth from 1973 through 1982 was a decline in the rate of technological progress, which dropped off in each major country, but fell roughly 1 percent per year more quickly in the United States.[43]

The manufacturing productivity growth rates in Table 2-5 are also consistent with the hypothesis of convergence. Japan, the country with the lowest manufacturing productivity of the five countries in 1950, grew most rapidly since then, but the differential declined dramatically after 1970. The French, German, and Japanese lead over the United States in manufacturing growth rates declined after 1973, with only the United Kingdom showing a constant differential. As Table 2-6 indicates, in 1989 the United States still had a significant lead over its competitors in most manufacturing sectors. The United States led Germany in each category and trailed Japan only in the highly publicized machinery, electrical engineering, and transport equipment sectors. Concerns that the United States is falling behind in manufacturing productivity center on a small set of industries that may, however, have large dynamic impacts if they are seen as enabling productivity advances in other sectors. In this sense, it might be more important to track relative performance in different processes than in products. At any rate, appropriate concerns for performance in sectors that might be seen as critical in some dynamic sense should not distort the more general picture of continuing American productivity leadership in most manufacturing areas.

In summary, the convergence hypothesis suggests that the variation in productivity growth performance across countries should decline over time, and that the rate of convergence should decline as the absolute gap in productivity levels is reduced. The data on overall productivity and on

Table 2-6
Factory Productivity for Major Manufacturing Industries in 1989 (U.S.
productivity level equals 100) (Reprinted with permission from the McKinsey
Global Institute.)

	Japan	Germany
Machinery, Electrical Engineering, and Transport Equipment	117	80
Basic Metals and Metal Products	98	85
Chemicals, Petroleum, Rubber and Plastic Products	92	70
Wood, Paper Products, and Others	70	80
Textiles, Apparel, and Leather	63	92
Food Products, Beverages, and Tobacco:	25	69
Total Manufacturing	80	80

Source: McKinsey Global Institute, Service Sector Productivity (Washington, D.C.: McKinsey
     & Company, Inc., October 1992), Exhibit 1–14.

manufacturing productivity are clearly consistent with those hypotheses.
The long-term record of U.S. productivity growth in terms of its own history and in terms of its relative international performance does not suggest
a precipitous decline caused by some dramatic policy change.

Competitiveness and Deindustrialization

The ideas of productivity, competitiveness, and deindustrialization are
related, but often confused. International competitiveness depends on productivity, prices, and exchange rates. Prices in turn depend on unit labor
costs, or average compensation per hour divided by labor productivity.
Competitiveness, then, can be achieved in a variety of ways, including
shifts in exchange rates or average compensation as well as productivity.[44]
Although Britain fell from its productivity leadership in 1870, it was able
to compete in world markets despite faster productivity growth elsewhere
by accepting relative wage cuts.[45] Slow relative growth in industrial productivity, then, does not necessarily mean a loss of competitiveness or deindustrialization, but it would impose declines in the wages received by
industrial workers compared with other countries. Conversely, a short-run
swing in competitiveness does not necessarily imply a long-run shift in
relative productivity.

The rising share of U.S. national employment in the services sector and the decline of the share in the industrial sector is often cited in making the case for the deindustrialization of the American economy; but that argument does not hold up in terms of real national output. In fact, the share of services in GDP evaluated in constant prices has remained remarkably stable at roughly half of real GDP since 1970.[46] Industrial shares of real output have not been falling and service shares have not been rising. Prices in the services sector have, however, been rising more rapidly than in other sectors, because productivity in services has been increasing more slowly. Rising prices of services have driven up their share of nominal output from 45 percent of GDP in 1980 to 52 percent in 1990. The rising prices might be expected to reduce the relative demand for services, but that has not been the case, perhaps because the demand for services rises sharply as income increases or because the industrial sector now draws more heavily on the services sector by contracting for services inputs.[47] As a result, the employment share of services has been increasing to maintain the relative real provision of services despite slower productivity growth. Workers are not being pushed into services by lagging productivity in manufacturing and loss of international competitiveness in the industrial sector; they are being pulled into services by steady demand in the face of rising prices. In other countries where the growth in productivity in manufacturing has been higher than in the United States, the expansion in services employment has been even more pronounced.[48] In short, deindustrialization is not a real phenomenon in terms of output, but an illusion caused by changing prices. Employment is shifting to services because of persistent demand and because services are an increasingly important input to other sectors, not because of a loss of international competitiveness in manufacturing.

Convergence remains a much better description of the current U.S. situation than an alternative formulation that shows the U.S. economy becoming noncompetitive in international markets, losing market share, being forced out of industry in general and manufacturing in particular, and falling further and further behind the competition. There is no absolute guarantee that the U.S. economy will remain in the group of converging economies forever, but there is little evidence that it is about to fall behind the leaders.

THE IMPACT OF INFORMATION TECHNOLOGIES

The next chapter explores the information technology revolution in more detail, but this section considers why the revolution transforming the workplace and interaction across organizations has had such a small impact on measured productivity increases. The advent of the computer and enhanced communications would be expected to drive up productivity in general and particularly in manufacturing and selected service sectors. The answer to this puzzle is particularly important for an assessment of longer-term productivity performance.

Paul David's assessment of the lags between innovation, productivity impacts, and productivity measurement supports the premise that the information technology revolution will have important lagged impacts on long-term productivity growth.[49] He argues that "techno-economic regimes" form around "general-purpose engines," such as the separate condenser steam engine, the electric dynamo, and the computer, whose key components are embodied in standardized modules or designs that can be used throughout the economy. The emergence of a new general-purpose engine produces a difficult "regime transition" as a wide variety of processes and products adapt to the new technology. The electric dynamo created a light show that captured imaginations at the 1900 Paris World's Fair, but the diffusion of the innovation proceeded slowly and the impact on productivity data did not emerge until the 1920s. The key problem in diffusion was the pace of factory electrification, which was delayed until old factories and equipment deteriorated, users adjusted from a cumbersome "group drive" system in which common shafts drove sets of machines to a more efficient "unit drive" system, public utility commissions emerged to coordinate electric monopolies, and corporate holding company organizations developed to facilitate acquisition, integration, and central control.[50] In short, diffusion required extensive technical adaptation and socioeconomic reform.

During the transition, redundant systems coexisted, some based on electricity and some on steam, creating excessive estimates of capital in use that depressed productivity estimates. Moreover, broader improvements in the brightness of lighting, faster streetcar rides, population dispersal to more remote neighborhoods, and factory safety and working conditions did not show up in traditional productivity measures. Ultimately, productivity measures did pick up measurable gains from capital savings in the transition to shift work and input savings from electric motors, which contributed to a surge in manufacturing productivity in the 1920s.[51]

The analogy between the electric dynamo and the computer is not perfect, but it is instructive because both systems operate in integrated networks that require standardization to exploit economies of scale. As David notes, the diffusion of computer technology may be even more difficult than the diffusion of the electric dynamo because of the rapid pace of hardware and software changes, repetitive training requirements, extensive redundancy as paper-based systems are phased out, and lags in redesigning organizations to exploit new patterns of information processing.[52] The wave of new products associated with the computer makes it difficult to assess quality changes and introduces a downward bias into productivity estimates. These lags and measurement problems could explain the limited evidence to date of a productivity surge from the new technologies.[53] Low productivity growth may result from a regime transition as organizations adjust to the new general-purpose engine, which will drive up future productivity. This transition to network organizations is the central theme of the next chapter.

IMPLICATIONS OF CONVERGENCE

Productivity growth serves as the best indicator of long-term economic performance. It is the foundation for individual well-being and national influence. If the U.S. rate of productivity growth does not rebound from the post-1973 levels to its longer-term historic trend, the cumulative long-run consequences will be staggering, both in terms of individual standards of living and in terms of national economic power. If the rate of U.S. productivity increase had been just half a percentage point higher over the last two decades, GDP would have been over $600 billion higher each year in the early 1990s.[54] On the basis of the long view of productivity performance, the lack of clear explanations for the slowdown after 1973, and the recent performance of manufacturing productivity, there is some cause for optimism about the potential for productivity to rebound. The recession of 1991 will cloud the picture for some time until a clear long-term pattern emerges, but in the meantime the continuing slow productivity growth will put the optimistic longer-term assessment into question. On balance, then, U.S. productivity performance is a cause for concern but not for alarm.

Convergence in economic performance will pose important questions for U.S. strategic goals and national policies. Convergence does not mean national economic collapse or that America is now destined to fall behind. It does mean the image of America as the world economic leader will be replaced by one of America as an economic leader. Will that change erode economic, political, or military power? The issue here is clearly one of relative, rather than absolute, economic performance. Should the United States care if per capita income is higher elsewhere as long as American per capita income is high and rising? With comparable productivity levels, the scale of the U.S. economy would guarantee that the United States will retain a much larger share of world GDP than its competitors. The leadership question is not, however, solely one of relative economic power. Status as the world's most efficient economy may translate into political influence through general esteem for a country's processes and institutions. Moreover, loss of leadership in critical sectors that have broad economic impact or military significance might increase national vulnerability. Convergence raises emotional issues touching on national self-esteem and America's vision of its role in the world.

Convergence will require important changes in economic behavior. As a technological leader in virtually every field after World War II, the United States could afford to look inward for sources of technological change. The international technology networks that have accelerated convergence have made national borders less relevant.[55] Keeping up with the technology leaders now requires access to international networks and adaptation to innovation wherever it might occur.

Whether policymakers seek to return the U.S. economy to its long-term productivity growth trajectory or to retain leadership in certain economic sectors, the first step toward a solution will be to correct the macroeconomic environment by reducing government budget deficits, increasing national savings, and lowering dependence on foreign investments to finance domestic capital formation. But while that is the essential first step, it will not be enough. The apparent erosion in the productivity boost from technological change means that a clearer understanding of the productivity cycle and the processes of innovation in global industrial networks is needed. Chapter 3 explores those issues.

NOTES

1. This organizational efficiency is often called "x-efficiency." See Harvey Leibenstein, "Allocative Efficiency vs. X-Efficiency," *American Economic Review* 56 (June 1966): 392–415.

2. One version of "endogenous growth theory" suggests, for example, that new innovations are typically embodied in new capital, so a low rate of national savings and capital formation has long-term impacts by slowing not only the expansion of current forms of capital but the rate of technical change itself.

3. The key ideas about the creation of specialized and advanced factors of production and the linkage with competitive advantage come from Michael E. Porter, *The Competitive Advantage of Nations* (New York: Free Press, 1990), particularly 77–81.

4. For an analysis of these lags, see Paul A. David, "General Purpose Engines, Investment and Productivity Growth: From the Dynamo Revolution to the Computer Revolution," in *Technology and Investment: Crucial Issues for the 1990s,* ed. Enrico Deiaco, Erik Hornell, and Graham Vickery (London: Pinter Publishers, 1990), 141–154.

5. The correlation between national savings, investment, and growth has been well established, but it is not completely clear whether the demand for investment draws forth the required savings or the supply of savings drives investment. The distinction has important policy implications. See Jeffrey G. Williamson, "Productivity and American Leadership: A Review Article," *Journal of Economic Literature* 29 (March 1991): 61–63; and William J. Baumol, Sue Anne Batey Blackman, and Edward N. Wolff, *Productivity and American Leadership* (Cambridge, Mass.: MIT Press, 1989), 184–187.

6. M. A. Akhtar and Ethan S. Harris, "The Supply-Side Consequences of U.S. Fiscal Policy in the 1980s," *Federal Reserve Bank of New York Quarterly Review* 17 (Spring 1992): 5.

7. The following discussion of industrial aging draws on insights provided in R. D. Norton, "Industrial Policy and American Renewal," *Journal of Economic Literature* 24 (March 1986): 1–40.

8. Joseph A. Schumpeter, *The Theory of Economic Development* (Cambridge, Mass.: Harvard University Press, 1934).

9. Joseph A. Schumpeter, *Capitalism, Socialism and Democracy* (New York: Harper & Row, 1942).

10. Mancur Olson, *The Rise and Decline of Nations: Economic Growth, Stagflation, and Social Rigidities* (New Haven, Conn.: Yale University Press, 1982).

11. Norton, "Industrial Policy and American Renewal," 25–27.

12. Productivity data are notoriously difficult to interpret for a number of reasons, including cyclical fluctuations, problems in measuring public sector productivity, and the challenge of measuring labor input. For example, the percentage of the population in the workforce, or the participation rate, and the number of hours worked per week by those in the workforce clearly vary over time. In the United States, participation rates have been increasing with a sharp rise in the number of two-income families, and average hours worked per week have been declining. In 1980, the average number of hours worked per week in private non-agricultural industries was 35.3, and by 1990 that had declined to 34.5. See U.S. Council of Economic Advisers, *Economic Report of the President* (Washington, D.C.: U.S. Government Printing Office, February 1992), Table B-34, p. 337, and Table B-42, p. 346.

13. Baumol, Blackman, and Wolff, *Productivity and American Leadership.*

14. Ibid., 65–83.

15. James R. Golden, *Investment Behavior by United States Railroads, 1870–1914* (New York: Arno Press, 1975).

16. Gavin Wright, "The Origins of America's Industrial Success, 1879–1940," *American Economic Review* 80 (September 1990): 664.

17. Ibid., 666.

18. Robert Solow, "Technical Change and the Aggregate Production Function," *The Review of Economics and Statistics* 39 (August 1957): 312–320, and Edward Denison, *The Sources of Economic Growth* (Washington, D.C.: Committee for Economic Development, 1962).

19. Angus Maddison, "Growth and Slowdown in Advanced Capitalist Economies: Techniques of Quantitative Assessment," *Journal of Economic Literature* 25 (June 1987): 658–660.

20. Solow, "Technological Change and the Aggregate Production Function," and Moses Abramowitz, "Resource and Output Trends in the United States since 1870," *American Economic Review* 46, *Papers and Proceedings* (May 1956): 5–23.

21. See Dale W. Jorgenson, "Productivity and Postwar U.S. Economic Growth," *Journal of Economic Perspectives* 2 (Fall 1988): 24–25. Jorgenson found that capital and labor contributed roughly three-quarters of total growth over the period from 1948 to 1979.

22. See Maddison, "Growth and Slowdown in Advanced Capitalist Economies," Table A-12, p. 688.

23. Ibid., Table 20, p. 679.

24. Ibid., 666.

25. Ibid., Table A-13, p. 689.

26. Ibid., Table 20, p. 679.

27. Maddison, "Growth and Slowdown in Advanced Capitalist Economies," 672. See also Thurow, "Can America Compete in the World Economy?" in *The Quest for Competitiveness: Lessons from American's Productivity and Quality Leaders,* ed. Y.K. Shetty and Vernon M. Buchler (New York: Quorum Books, 1991) 84.

28. Jorgenson, "Productivity and Postwar U.S. Economic Growth," 31.

29. Paul W. Bauer, "Unbalanced Growth and U.S. Productivity Slowdown," *Economic Commentary,* Federal Reserve Bank of Cleveland, January 1, 1992, Figure 2, p. 2.

30. Edward Denison, *Estimates of Productivity Change by Industry,* 40.

31. Baumol, Blackman, and Wolff, *Productivity and American Leadership,* 87.

32. See Table 1-1.

33. Alexander Gerschenkron, *Economic Backwardness in Historical Perspective* (Cambridge, Mass.: Harvard University Press, 1962).

34. See Moses Abramowitz, "Catching Up, Forging Ahead, and Falling Behind," *Journal of Economic History* 46 (June 1986): 385–406.

35. Baumol, Blackman, and Wolff, *Productivity and American Leadership,* 102–103.

36. Ibid., 92–93.

37. Ibid., 96–99. Also, see Williamson, "Productivity and American Leadership," 64.

38. For example, see J. Bradford De Long and Lawrence H. Summers, "Macroeconomic Policy and Long-Run Growth," in *Policies for Long-Run Economic Growth* (Kansas City, Kans.: Federal Reserve Bank of Kansas City, 1992), 99–102. Also, see Steve Dowrick and Duc-Tho Nguyen, "OECD Comparative Economic Growth 1950–1985: Catch-Up and Convergence," *The American Economic Review* 79 (December 1989): 1010–1030. They report a systematic process of catching up in the convergence of total factor productivity. See also Luc Soete and Bart Verspagen, "Convergence and Divergence in Growth and Technical Change: An Empirical Investigation," paper prepared for the American Economic Association Conference, Anaheim, Calif., January 6, 1993, p. 4. They argue that OECD per capita GDP converged during the period from 1950 to 1980 and that the rate of convergence slowed in the early 1980s. Their discussion of a worldwide sample on pp. 5–6, however, shows that the countries furthest behind did not converge on the performance of the leaders in the 1960-to-1985 period.

39. M. Ishaq Nadiri and Ingmar R. Prucha, "Sources of Growth in Output and Convergence of Productivity in Major OECD Countries," paper presented at the annual meeting of the American Economic Association, Anaheim, Calif., January 1993, p. 25.

40. Maddison, "Growth and Slowdown in Advanced Capitalist Economies," 669.

41. Ibid., Table 20, p. 679.

42. John W. Kendrick, "Policy Implications of the Slowdown in U.S. Productivity Growth," in *Productivity Growth and Competitiveness of the American Economy,* ed. Stanley W. Black (Boston, Mass.: Kluwer Academic Publishers, 1989), 80–81.

43. Ibid., 83.

44. Ibid., 84.

45. Williamson, "Productivity and American Leadership," 52.

46. U.S. Council of Economic Advisers, *Economic Report of the President* (Washington, D.C.: U.S. Government Printing Office, 1993), Table B-6, p. 356.

47. Bauer, "Unbalanced Growth and U.S. Productivity Slowdown," 1–4.

48. Williamson, "Productivity and American Leadership," 59.

49. Paul A. David, "General Purpose Engines, Investment and Productivity Growth," 141–154.

50. Ibid., 145–146.

51. Ibid., 149.

52. Ibid., 150–1.

53. There is some evidence that investment in computers has had a larger impact on productivity than other forms of capital. See Charles Steindel, "Manufacturing Productivity and High Tech Investment," *Federal Reserve Bank of New York Quarterly Review* (Summer 1992): 39.

54. Bauer, "Unbalanced Growth and U.S. Productivity Slowdown," 1.

55. Richard R. Nelson and Gavin Wright, "The Rise and Fall of American Technological Leadership; the Post-War Era in Historical Perspective," *Journal of Economic Literature* 30 (December 1992): 1933.

3   Global Networks

The information technology revolution has contributed to the creation of integrated global organizational networks that are changing the structure of international corporations, shifting patterns of R&D, and altering the nature of national economic competition. The elements of the productivity cycle—innovation, factor creation, and the industry composition of competitive advantage—all have important international dimensions, because R&D, input-output, and finance networks link organizations across borders. Similarly, policy networks span overlapping levels of jurisdiction within a nation and across national boundaries, and connect government agencies, policy analysts, and corporations in a web of activities that influence macroeconomic, commercial, industrial, and research policies. Productivity growth now depends on access to and competition within global networks, which have become engines of technological change, adaptation, and diffusion.

This chapter explores four propositions concerning the nature and impact of the new global networks spawned by the revolution in information technology. First, international economic interaction in the postwar period has evolved from a structure of multinational firms based on the coordination of production within enterprises to new global network arrangements that emphasize collaboration across enterprises. Second, the revolution in information technologies has created new physical networks with strong externalities that make network standards very sensitive to early design decisions and create new organizational pressures for external integration. Third, organizations are responding to the rapid pace of technological change and to the lowered cost and improved capabilities for interconnection through the creation of organizational networks. Input-output, R&D, finance, and policy organizational networks are particularly important in understanding the transformation of international economic activity. Fourth, the changes in external network relationships parallel similar shifts in internal organizational structures. A closing section examines the interaction of organizational networks in the productivity cycle, introducing the productivity relationships that are examined in more detail in Chapter 4.

COLLABORATION ACROSS ENTERPRISES

International economic activities may be seen as extensions of the basic principle of arbitrage—buying in markets where prices are low and selling where they are high. Differences in prices endure where transaction costs in the form of information, government restrictions, transportation, and so forth exceed the price differential, or where risks lower the expected return. Typically, price differentials and uneven rates of return on investment in different industries across nations lead first to trade in products, then to portfolio investment in financial instruments, and then to direct investment to establish production facilities in the foreign market. Foreign production typically involves savings in transportation and labor costs, and it also permits better adaptation to local product preferences and administrative procedures, so international investment and trade complement each other.

As firms pursue multinational operations, they can expand horizontally with similar operations in other countries to exploit advantages in finance, management, R&D, and brand recognition, or they can develop vertically to integrate supply, production, distribution, and service activities. Economies of scale in producing standardized products or economies of scope in controlling similar functions must be weighed against other constraints. For example, expansion increases coordination costs, reduces concentration on core competitive advantages, limits organizational flexibility, and adds the complexity of operating in multiple jurisdictions. The global organizational networks that have emerged in response to many of those problems are adding a new dimension to international economic activities and are transforming organizational structures.

Economic interdependence among the major economies has been expanding for decades, but global organizational networks represent a significant shift from earlier patterns.[1] The postwar period can be divided into three phases, with emphasis on internationalization through trade and portfolio investment in the first phase ending in the early 1960s, trade supplemented by direct investment by multinational firms in the second phase through the early 1980s, and internationalization through trade, direct investment, and global organizational networks in the subsequent phase. In the first phase, trade liberalization, proceeding through rounds of General Agreement on Trade and Tariffs (GATT) negotiations, brought down tariff levels and produced sharp increases in the volume of world trade and shares of exports as a part of world GDP. This constituted arms-length internationalization, with production based in national firms and interindustry trade following differences in resource costs. In the second phase, multinational firms increased direct investment in foreign plants, and trade reflected the growing role of transactions within firms and industries. This trend toward intrafirm and intraindustry trade continues, and by some measures over half of U.S. exports and imports are now simply transfers of goods and services within multinational corporations.[2]

In the 1980s the level of interaction had shifted beyond foreign production by a limited number of large multinational firms. Cooperation extended to complex international coordination of production and technology transfer through external strategic alliance agreements and other, less formal relationships that supplemented multinational operations within competing firms. The trend was most apparent across industries with rapid rates of technological change, rising R&D costs, and converging technologies—particularly microelectronics, new materials, and biotechnologies—and in industries that used advanced process technologies, such as automobiles, oil refining, and telecommunication, but it was also apparent in lower-technology food sectors and in a variety of service areas, such as banking and transportation.[3]

One of the essential differences in this recent phase has been the growing importance of continuous process and product modification based on extensive coordination among international suppliers, firms, and customers. Those input-output organizational networks, explored in more detail below, often offset the advantages of centralized operations of large multinationals based on economies of scale or scope. Another major change has been a shift toward collaboration in R&D networks in order to lower costs, reduce risks, and integrate related technologies. These global organizational networks are concentrated in arrangements among firms in North America, Europe, and Japan, and the pace of new agreements is striking.

By some estimates, the rate of new U.S. international joint ventures—forms of strategic alliances that produce a new operating entity—created each year went up by 600 percent over the period from 1976 to 1982, and U.S. firms established over 2,000 strategic agreements with European firms alone in the 1980s.[4] The key point is that these relationships developed externally rather than internally within multinational firms.[5] Although the legal forms of the alliances vary, their objectives have become more and more strategic in scope.[6] In other words, organizational networks are based on horizontal relationships across firms rather than hierarchical relationships within enterprises, and they are designed to enhance the competitive advantage of groups of corporations. In the most recent phase of development in international economic activity, patterns of long-term interaction among firms based on formal agreement or improved communication have grown in importance compared with internal hierarchical relationships with branches and subsidiaries.[7]

Network organizational relationships include negotiated alliances in the form of international consortia, joint ventures, subcontracting, licensing and interfirm agreements, and less formal extended relationships between suppliers, producers, and purchasers. The motivation for formal strategic alliances short of merger among firms is most often a desire to exploit complementarity among the firms' technologies or to transfer technology directly. OECD studies have shown that the form of agreements varies across industries depending on the role of government, the international supply structure, the novelty and sophistication of the technology, the size of firms, the scale and risk of investment, and the extent to which the final product is part of an integrated system.[8]

Agreements in the space satellite, long-range civil aircraft, jet engine, telecommunications, and military systems industries—which have heavy government involvement, high supply concentration, sophisticated technologies, large-scale investments, and strong systemic attributes—typically create international consortia or joint ventures directed at worldwide marketing. For example, the Boeing Company, the world's leading aircraft producer, and the four European partners in the rival Airbus Industrie consortium, the world's second leading producer, agreed in January 1993 to a transatlantic joint venture to study the feasibility of moving toward joint production of an 800-seat superjumbo airliner. Presumably the firms concluded that the high costs of development and limited demand would permit production of only one version of the new plane.[9]

At the other end of the spectrum, in biotechnology, specialized electronics and software, pharmaceuticals, and some new materials industries—in which the government role is weak, international supply structures are less concentrated, radical shifts in technology are frequent, investment scales are small but risks are high, and small knowledge-intensive firms dominate—agreements tend to take the form of R&D contracts between large and small firms.[10] In the semiconductor industry, which lies between those two extremes, R&D agreements are typically bilateral arrangements among rivals for two-way exchanges of technology that reduce R&D outlays and put added pressure on nonparticipants, creating an extensive web of overlapping bilateral agreements and complex R&D networks.[11]

Joel Bleeke and David Ernst examined a sample of 150 top companies by market value, including 50 firms each from the United States, Japan, and Europe, and found that 49 had entered cross-border "strategic alliances." Although two-thirds of the strategic alliances encountered managerial or financial problems in the first two years, more than half ultimately succeeded for both partners, including 60 percent of those spanning different geographic regions and 67 percent of those between financially strong firms. Flexibility in modifying the form of collaboration as cooperative ventures proceeded was particularly important in successful alliances. In contrast to the relative success in forming cross-regional strategic alliances to exploit different core competencies, few companies even attempted to diversify outside their core business through overseas acquisition. Bleeke and Ernst concluded that strategic alliances are preferable to acquisition for moving into new or related businesses.[12]

The structure of formal strategic alliance agreements has been tracked

Table 3-1
Information Technology Agreements by Form of Contract, 1980–1986 (percent)

Type of Agreement	Percent of Agreements
Equity:	29
Joint Venture or Consortia	22
Minority or Parity Shareholdings	7
Joint Development Agreements	25
Licenses	21
Other Non-equity Agreements	26

Source: ARPA database, Polytechnic of Milan, as cited in Gian Carlo Cainarca, Massimo G. Colombo, and Sergio Mariotti "Agreements Between Firms and the Technological Life Cycle Model: Evidence From Information Technologies," *Research Policy* 21 (February 1992): 53.

Note: The database includes 2,014 agreements involving 1,574 sets of partners that belong to 1,177 autonomous organizations.

most thoroughly in information technology industries, including semiconductors, data processing, and telecommunications, where the number of agreements rose by some 500 percent from 1980 to 1986. Table 3-1 shows that those formal arrangements were evenly distributed over equity, joint development, license, and other non-equity agreements, including subcontracting and technology transfer agreements. Almost 60 percent of all those agreements were interregional, with over 40 percent linking U.S. firms with Japanese or European enterprises.[13]

Figure 3-1 illustrates one of the more active industrial technology networks from the perspective of the German Siemens Corporation to show how one firm might perceive its environment within the network.[14] The overlapping bilateral agreements between Siemens and other firms, and their agreements with still other firms, illustrate the network concept. Figure 3-1 shows Siemens at the center, other European firms at the lower right, U.S. firms at the top, and Japanese firms at the lower left.

Using the number of agreements reached as a simplified measure of the intensity of relationships, Siemens has the strongest ties with the Dutch firm Philips, and relatively strong links to International Business Machines (IBM), Digital Equipment Corporation (DEC), and Intel Corporation in the United States. For example, Siemens and Intel formed a joint venture in Oregon in 1988 to manufacture computers designed to be crashproof for mission-critical markets in which system failures have catastrophic consequences.[15] Siemens has few direct ties to the strong triangular associ-

Figure 3-1
Siemens Information Technology Network, 1985–1989 (Data adapted and reprinted with permission from Elsevier Science Publishers.)

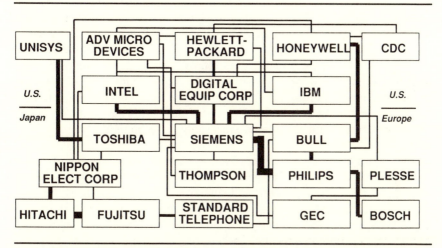

Source: John Hagedoorn and Jos Schakenraad, "Leading Companies and Networks of Strategic Alliances in Information Technologies," *Research Policy* (February 1992): 170.

Note: Number of Agreements ▬ Over 6 ▬ 5–6 ▬ 3–4

ation among Japan's Nippon Electric Corporation (NEC), Hitachi, and Fujitsu, but there are weak links to them through Intel and Toshiba.

In theory, the agreements in Figure 3-1 are all independent bilateral relationships with careful restrictions on further transfers of specified technologies. In practice, however, such exclusive arrangements must pass subsequent antitrust challenges, and as a matter of physical security and normal intellectual processes, it may be difficult to isolate patterns of information exchange in different technology areas.[16]

While the specific form of strategic alliances differs across industries, the trend toward greater reliance on external agreements and coordination is clear in virtually all of them. The growing importance of coordination among suppliers, firms, and customers provides one explanation for the trend as high-value products are increasingly tailored to specialized needs and international corporations concentrate on their core competencies. The success of the Japanese business group, or *keiretsu,* both in horizontal coordination across industries and in vertical coordination between major producers and a network of supporting suppliers, provides an example for new corporate patterns. But the central force behind the change in the structure of international interaction comes from the revolution in information technologies.

THE INFORMATION TECHNOLOGY REVOLUTION

Information technologies are playing a central role in the emergence of global organizational networks. The new technologies both compel and facilitate integration. They promote modular networking, shorten product cycles, enhance production flexibility, and encourage parallel developments in related technologies. They simultaneously provide the systems required to coordinate and integrate across technologies and traditional organizational boundaries. The impact of the revolution in information technology is still unfolding, but there is little question that the ramifications for integrating new technologies, for dramatic changes in organizational structures, and for the broader political-economic system will be enormous.

The digital chips of the information age are the new engines of broad technological change. Earlier general-purpose engines such as the steam engine and the electric dynamo had similar transforming impacts, because those new technologies could be disseminated in standardized modules and engineering approaches that had broad impacts on virtually every other technology.[17] Computer technology has also become ubiquitous. By compressing the time and space required for information storage and processing, the computer has increased the volume and lowered the costs of communication, revolutionized design and simulation processes, dramatically improved quality control through enhanced precision, and made the interpretation of complex signals routine. The miniaturized integrated circuit and the microprocessor, the key modules of the information technology revolution, have already transformed the way in which machine tools, lasers, fiber optics, radar, and thermal imaging can be used. They have also provided the impetus for innovations like robotics that integrate several of the new technologies. These strategic technologies create follow-on waves of innovation with broad applications in a wide array of processes and products. As the U.S. narrowband analog communications infrastructure shifts to a broadband digital network, the potential for further integration of related technologies will be enormous.

The computer age has advanced so far so quickly that it is surprising how recently the most dramatic innovations took place. At the end of World War II, the ENIAC (Electronic Numerical Integrator and Calculator) computer occupied 3,000 square feet, weighed 30 tons, and included 18,000 vacuum tubes.[18] The vacuum tubes were the problem: they were big, they were hot, they had to be wired together, and they had to be replaced frequently. The invention of the transistor in 1948 and the commercial availability of postage stamp–sized transistors in the 1950s solved many of the problems, but the circuit elements still had to be wired together with tedious, expensive soldering that limited the potential for miniaturization. The key breakthrough to the computer age came in 1958 with the development of the integrated circuit. The idea was that elements of the electric circuit—passive resistors and capacitors and active transistors—could all be made of the same semiconductor material and overlaid on a single surface in a way that required no wiring.

The integrated circuit is constructed by photoengraving elements onto a thin silicon wafer, or chip, which is smaller than a pencil eraser. Silicon, the main component of sand and the second most abundant element behind oxygen, can be heated and cooled to form a cubic crystalline structure that makes it an excellent semiconductor—a material that can either facilitate or block the conduction of electricity depending on how it is treated. Pure silicon is a poor conductor, but adding impurities to selected regions of a silicon wafer converts those regions into excellent conductors. After the photoengraving process places impurities in just the right pattern on the silicon wafer to form the desired integrated circuit, metallic leads are attached and the processed chip is placed in a protective plastic or ceramic package for distribution. The central improvement over earlier transistor technology is that the integrated circuit frees production from the size and reliability constraints imposed by wiring circuit elements together. Processing improvements have produced exponential annual gains in miniaturization and cost reduction over the past 20 years. Advanced chips now contain over three million miniaturized components.[19]

Until recently, huge mainframe computers used by large corporations and research centers contained specialized integrated circuits linked together to form large memory and computational capacities. Smaller computers became possible with the advent in 1971 of the microprocessor—a standardized, general-purpose computer on a chip. The microprocessor integrated circuit included a central processing unit, random-access memory (RAM), read-only memory (ROM), and a shift register, all in a standard configuration that could be programmed for a wide range of applications. The Intel 4004 and 8008 microprocessors, capable of handling information in four-bit and then eight-bit sequences of 1s and 0s used in digital formats, quickly became industry standards in the early 1970s with immediate applications in handheld calculators and then in personal computers. The first microcomputers, essentially microprocessors in a box, incorporated the modular flexibility that remains the hallmark of the information technology revolution with "slots" connected to the microprocessor by a network of wires known as a "bus," which permitted the subsequent addition of more memory and peripheral devices.[20]

The integrated circuit in general and its formulation into standardized microprocessors and memory devices provided the basis for the rapid expansion of the information technology revolution. Hardware designers were free to mold the modular, miniaturized, low-cost microprocessors, controllers, and large memories into personal computers, and software writers could design applications for standardized operating systems. The

Apple computer appeared in 1976, the venerable Apple II emerged in 1977, and IBM offered its first personal computer for sale in 1981 using the Intel 16-bit 8086 chip. By 1991 there were more than 77 million Apple, IBM, and IBM-compatible personal computers in operation worldwide.[21]

Standardized digital components, like the microprocessor, continue to revolutionize information technologies as they displace expensive centralized systems and permit integration with other digital technologies such as microelectronics and the optical information technologies known as photonics. Conventional analog components cannot interact easily because each technology passes information differently, but standardized digital components can be combined into integrated systems as mechanical printing yields to desktop publishing, vinyl records fall to compact disks, and analog telecommunications are replaced by digital fiberoptics. Networking of printers, computers, televisions, fax machines, and photocopiers will become commonplace as each technology shifts to digital formats.[22] Laser light passed through fiberoptic cables, coupled with microprocessors to interpret the signals, has revolutionized fields from medical diagnostics and microsurgery to high-capacity long-distance communications. Fiberoptic communications in turn create new opportunities for products from video phones to high-definition television, all linked by digital components.[23]

Digital components in each of these fields are becoming more standardized, with performance-to-price ratios improving at a remarkable rate of over 25% per year.[24] As a result, large, complex, centralized computer structures are giving way to smaller, standardized, decentralized, more flexible systems. Giant mainframe computers have traditionally contained a main memory with thousands of memory chips and hundreds of expensive, high-speed, customized components, as well as elaborate communication, power, and cooling systems. Modern personal computers now process over 50 times as many instructions per second per dollar as those mainframes.[25] Recent successes by DEC and the Hewlett-Packard Company with mainframe computers based on clusters of microprocessors, rather than the traditional custom-designed integrated circuits, have led IBM to move in the same direction, using parallel processing to let the microprocessors work in tandem. Standardization continues to lower costs and enhance quality.[26]

The increasing capacity of standardized integrated circuits that serve as memory devices symbolizes the rapid transformation of information technologies. RAM provides temporary information storage that increases computer flexibility, and dynamic RAM (DRAM) provides the largest storage capacities. Each new generation of DRAM holds four times as much information as its predecessor, a factor determined by the cubic structure of silicon crystals. Capacity is measured in terms of kilobytes, so a 1K memory holds 1,000 bytes of information. A 1970 DRAM stored 1K of information, three short generations later a 1979 DRAM held 64K, and capacity rose rapidly to 256K in 1985, 4 megabytes (MB) in 1989, and 16 MB in 1991. Each generation after the 1970s, however, has required over twice as much R&D and capital investment as the previous generation, so fewer and fewer firms have been able to compete. IBM and Siemens are pursuing a $2 billion joint venture to develop 64-MB DRAM integrated circuits, which may become commercially available in the late 1990s.[27]

The modular building blocks of the information technology revolution facilitated the emergence of communications networks based on compatible hardware and software standards. The diffusion of computer technology has proceeded through incremental improvements in chip design, an accelerating process of miniaturization, dispersion of smaller computers with greater capacities into general use, interconnection of computers into larger networks, and the merger of information processing technologies with other digital technologies in a widening set of interrelated fields.[28] This diffusion of information technologies has produced a simultaneous increase in the quality of communications and a decline in transmission and processing costs. Distance is less and less a question of location than one of network access. In many important ways, colleagues cooperating on research across continents via computer networks are closer to each other than they are to coworkers down the hall.

The physical information network that passes bits of electronic information has an analog in the network of personal and organizational interrelationships that emerge from the altered communications pattern. As the cost of obtaining and processing information declines, the possibilities for tailoring products to individual requirements increase. Similarly, better information processing creates the potential for cost reductions through tighter inventory management and "just-in-time" purchases of supplies, movement of intermediate goods, and delivery of products. The enhanced potential for the precise management of production systems raises feasible standards of quality and makes quality a more important component of competitive advantage. The resulting internal and external networks of information flow are having dramatic impacts on patterns of work and corporate structures. Those linkages among physical networks, organizational networks, and industrial organization are changing the nature of the productivity cycle.

NETWORK RELATIONSHIPS

A physical, or communications, network is a set of interconnections that permit the passage and processing of a signal. An electronic grid conducting current, a set of stations transmitting television signals, or a system of computers exchanging bits of information would all meet this physical definition of a network. The functions of the physical network include preparation of a signal, transmission, propagation, reception, and interpretation, and networks operate most efficiently when equipment and procedures are standardized to permit smooth interaction across those stages. Network technologies and processes enhance interconnection and interoperability of a physical network.

By analogy, any set of objects connected by a pattern of reception and transmission, such as cities connected by automobile traffic flows, could constitute a network. More broadly, virtually all social systems—markets, organizations, states—might be seen as organizational networks concerned with information flows, and network approaches have been applied in such fields as anthropology, sociology, and political science, particularly in the context of relationships between small familial and community systems to other similar systems or the broader environment.[29] Organizational networks are typically linked by physical networks, so they are more than analogies: organizational networks are also the products of the underlying physical networks. Four types of organizational networks—input-output, research, finance, and policy—are most important for an understanding of the productivity cycle. A brief examination of physical networks and network technologies that are particularly relevant to the information technology revolution will provide a foundation for a more detailed analysis of those organizational networks.

Physical Networks and Network Technologies

As discussed earlier, there are strong parallels between the computer and the electric dynamo, not only in their roles as general-purpose engines with modular hardware and engineering designs that have a transforming impact on other technologies, but also in their common functions as nodes, or points of intersection, of physical networks.[30] The computer and the dynamo are both network technologies in the sense that their full potential can only be realized in network configurations, in part because the cost of establishing the network is large compared with the cost of operating it or expanding the number of nodes. As a result, there are large economies of scale—the output of the network expands more rapidly than increases in the number of nodes. Expansion of the network benefits all the organizations, so the economies of scale depend on the actions of other users outside, or *external* to, each organization. Network externality effects shift issues concerning standardization and interoperability from normal internal operating decisions to strategic issues for interfirm strategy and public policy. For example, computer firms must make vital decisions on whether or not to share proprietary information on operating systems with potential software designers. The risk of sharing is that other manufacturers may clone their systems, but that risk may be dominated by gains from the production of supporting software that adds network benefits to potential users. IBM's decision to license its personal computer operating system, MS-DOS, to other firms did lead to a host of clones that reduced IBM's market share, but it also established MS-DOS as the industry standard.[31]

A simple example illustrates the principle. Apple Macintosh and IBM computers use different operating systems that make it difficult to run software designed for one computer on the other. Owners of each type of computer benefit when others buy the same model, because the larger group of users provides a larger market for software tailored to that standard, and the additional software expands the choices available for all users. In addition, the larger the user group, the easier it is to find someone who can provide advice on operating or repairing the computer. Connecting computers in a physical network is also much easier if users own the same hardware. As a result, computer owners gain a stake in expanding sales in their own model or compatible models. Those benefits are external to the economic market in the sense that there is no way to force computer owners to pay for the benefit they receive from expanded sales of similar computers to other users.

Such externalities have a powerful impact on the evolution of physical networks and network technologies. The externalities mean that past events can have a large impact on current choices, so the evolution of the network becomes path-dependent. Early choices about technical standards or production processes influence subsequent decisions, because the costs of shifting standards and undercutting an existing network can outweigh the benefits of increased efficiency from a new standard. More generally, adoption of one technological standard by some users enhances the benefits to other potential users of adopting the same standard because of improvements through learning by using, network externalities, scale economies in production, better information about established standards that reduces risks, and technical interrelatedness with other technologies and products that grow up around the standard.[32]

Paul David's analysis of the evolution of the typewriter keyboard illustrates the importance of path dependence.[33] The QWERTY configuration of keys, named for the upper-left row of letters on the standard keyboard, emerged around 1867 in an effort to minimize typebar collisions at the point of impact with the ribbon. Despite subsequent design changes that reduced the collision problem, and despite the creation of other, more efficient keyboard configurations that arranged letters based on frequency of use, the QWERTY system remains the industry standard.[34] Millions of touch typists continue to use the inefficient QWERTY system with computer keyboards that have no typebars at all! Network externalities explain that somewhat surprising outcome.

Touch-typing training spread quickly in the 1880s and produced a large pool of users tied to the QWERTY configuration, so technical interrelatedness between the keyboard and touch typing created an interdependent system. Scale economies arose from buying QWERTY keyboards that could exploit the skills of existing typists and lower training costs. Similarly, the trained touch typists benefited from and lobbied for the purchase of QWERTY typewriters. Although it was possible to convert to more efficient keyboard designs, the costs of doing so became more and more significant as technical interrelatedness and scale economies worked to lock in the initial decision. In spite of declines in the hardware costs of adopting new keyboards, the software costs of converting a growing pool of touch typists to a new system increased, ensuring the dominance of the inefficient QWERTY system. The U.S. Navy invested heavily in a more efficient system during World War II, and most computers now have a switch to use that improved system, but few users are tempted. QWERTY reigns.[35]

Network technologies give significant advantages to standards adopted early in the network's evolution. For example, one of the major problems in shifting away from large mainframe computers to microprocessor-based computers and open software is the use of payroll and accounting software configured to the mainframe structure. Conversion requires expensive new software, employee training costs, the risk of errors during the transition, and the abandonment of investments of billions of dollars in integrated hardware and software systems.[36]

As a result, the externalities that grow up around early technical configurations exert strong pressure to standardize to capture network benefits that result from direct physical effects in linking network nodes, from indirect effects such as software availability, and from postpurchase effects, including accessible repair service. Network evolution thus involves convergence on common standards, although the convergence may well proceed erratically because conflicting standards become entrenched in competing networks.[37] While the path to standardization depends on chance and interfirm rivalries, the dynamic forces for convergence on some standard, even if it is not the most efficient alternative, are overwhelming.

Similarly, organizations adopt procedures that permit them to exploit the benefits of network technologies. The QWERTY example illustrates the importance of taking a broad approach in identifying the hardware, software, and organizational interactions that will determine the form of standardization and the longer-term productivity implications of the new information technologies. The full impact of the new physical networks will depend on simultaneous patterns of organizational adaptation.

Organizational Networks

Just as a physical, or communications, network is a set of interconnections that permit the routine passage and processing of signals, an organizational network is a set of organizations and suborganizations linked together across normal organizational boundaries through continuing patterns of information exchange. Organizational networks emphasize shared information in flexible relationships that can be adjusted to meet changing conditions. In contrast, hierarchical, functional organizations can be highly efficient in guarding proprietary information and guiding the repetition of routine actions, but strict functional boundaries and layers of supervisory administration make it more difficult to develop, pass, and respond to new information. The more important adaptation to a rapidly changing environment becomes, the more the enterprise needs to communicate smoothly and continuously with suppliers, customers, and researchers outside the firm. Organizational networks stress horizontal relationships that permit easy communication within the firm and with other organizations.[38]

Organizational networks link independent organizations or suborganizations through the need for continuing joint action in cases where mutual obligations are difficult to capture in conventional contracts. Market relationships center on the exchange of a standardized good or service in a transaction that is quickly followed by a contractual settlement of obligations. A network relationship is more likely when continuous sharing of information is vital to the transaction, when, for example, the exchange must be tailored to the individual user, elements of the transaction are hard to price, and both parties have an interest in continuing exchanges in the future.[39] Network relationships lie between arms-length market interactions and the entangling embrace of legal merger. Network alliances, both formal and informal, often permit firms to reposition themselves to offset new exposure, or to gain new competitive advantages in periods of rapid technological or structural change, without the expense and rigidity of formal organizational integration.[40] Such alliances are not without risks, particularly given the inevitable temptations for opportunism to exploit the relationship for short-term gain, so their success hinges on factors that increase the long-term benefits of cooperation.

The efficient passage of information frequently requires longer-term arrangements to ensure adequate compensation in the form of a return flow of future information. In this sense, an organizational network for passing information on technology, production processes, organizational design, likely future government regulations, market assessments, and so forth, depends in large measure on confidence that participants will contribute to and benefit from future exchanges. The cost of failure to contribute may simply be denial of future access to the network. Long-term relationships among participants in the network help to solve the difficulties of adequate compensation, because the participants can carry over impressions of the value they have received from one interaction to the next.

More broadly, organizational networks are social systems—systems

Table 3-2
Kumon's Classification Scheme for Social Systems

Dimension One	Dimension Two	
Interaction Orientation	Actor (Organizational)	Non-Actor (Societal)
Threat	Modern Sovereign State	Modern States-System
Exchange	Modern Industrial Firm	Modern World Market
Consensus	Network Organizations	Societal Networks

Source: Based on Shumpei Kumon, "Japan as a Network Society," in *The Political Economy of Japan, Volume 3: Cultural and Social Dynamics,* ed. Shumpei Kumon and Henry Rosovsky (Stanford, Calif.: Stanford University Press, 1992), 117–122.

composed of actors linked by regular forms of interaction—that emphasize communications flows and consensual relationships. As Table 3-2 indicates, Shumpei Kumon classifies social systems in two dimensions. The first dimension concerns the dominant form of interaction, which he identifies as either threat, exchange, or consensus relationships.[41] In his scheme, states emphasize threats constrained by the limits of international law, modern industrial firms stress exchange based on property rights, and modern network organizations develop consensus-oriented relationships based on information rights.

Kumon's second dimension concerns whether the social system is itself an actor.[42] If it is an actor, he calls it an organization, and if it is not, he defines it as a "societal system." States, modern industrial firms, and network organizations are actors; they are, respectively, parts of societal systems that are not actors—the modern states-system, the modern world market, and societal networks.

Kumon's distinction between a modern world market and a societal network emphasizes the dominant form of interaction among the constituent organizations. He is laying out pure forms in order to clarify the classification scheme. More generally, there is a continuous spectrum between the market and the societal network along a product-information continuum, with the market exchanging pure products and the societal network exchanging information whose full value cannot be captured in traditional markets. Moving from the market toward the societal network, both exchange and consensus are common forms of interaction, and transactions cover mixed bundles of products and information in organizational networks. Organizational networks are becoming more global as the information technology revolution changes the underlying physical networks and the commodities being exchanged become less standardized and more tailored to individual demands. In fact, an increasing share of international exchanges now take the form of information services that can be transmitted through physical global networks.

Organizational networks may be distinguished by the goal of the coordination, and four types are particularly important for analysis of the productivity cycle. Input-output networks, at the product end of the product-information continuum, differ from pure markets in the longevity of relationships among suppliers, producers, and consumers and the extent to which product designs, production processes, and delivery systems are jointly determined. R&D networks, near the information end of the product-information continuum, are becoming more and more important in the coordination of science, technology, and production know-how. Finance networks involve virtually pure information flows and shift funds rapidly to exploit shifts in perceived risks and returns in different markets. Finally, policy networks emphasize communications flows and consensus building among firms, policy analysts, and political actors who have overlapping policy interests. An understanding of the nature of input-output, R&D, finance, and policy networks is crucial to an appreciation of the complexity of the productivity cycle.

Input-Output Networks. An input-output network is an organizational network in which the critical exchange of information concerns coordination of supply, production, and sales-related processes. A series of coordinated activities add value to a product in a "value chain," which includes "primary activities" of logistics, operations, marketing and sales, and after-sale service, and by "support activities," such as finance, planning, human resource development, technology development, and procurement.[43] The fact that inputs and outputs flow between industries or firms does not necessarily imply relationships that go beyond the arms-length interactions of a normal market. In some cases, however, firms form longer-term relationships based on the coordination of information as well as product flows that meet the criteria for an organizational network. In an input-output network, the information concerns coordination over an extended period of time of production processes, including tailored specifications, integrated design, delivery schedules, and so forth. The participants in such a network surrender some flexibility in purchasing from other suppliers or selling to other users in order to gain the benefits of coordination.[44]

Consider, for example, Sun Microsystems' decision at its founding in 1982 to concentrate on designing hardware and software for workstations and to limit manufacturing to prototypes and final assembly of components produced by contract suppliers. One key advantage in this network arrangement with suppliers is the flexibility to exploit innovation in component design within the constraints of system compatibility. Another advantage is the speed with which new product configurations can be designed and marketed. Sun is free to concentrate on its core competencies in design, assembly of final systems, and the improvement of critical technologies, while spreading the risks of product development throughout its supply chain. Although Sun began by integrating standard components, it now exploits unique capabilities of specialized suppliers that work together more like partners in a joint design, development, and production process.[45] Similarly, Apple Computer has licensed out its new Newton handheld computing system—controlled by a stylus rather than a keyboard—to Motorola, Siemens, Kysushu Matsushita, and others to develop a family of Newton-based applications with custom chips produced by Cirrus Logic and LSI Logic.[46]

One key distinction between an input-output network and an organization lies in the legal status of the participants and the dominant governance forms. Organizations emphasize hierarchy and leadership, while networks stress collaboration and cooperation.[47] In fact, the central principle of the organizational network is self-organization—the ability of the participants to modify their relationships in ways that more effectively meet their common goals and so maximize their individual utility.[48] Formal contracts are typically less important in such relationships than good working relationships and mutual trust.[49]

An individual firm's value chain is tied to similar value chains of its suppliers, distributors, and customers, and a firm's ability to sustain competitive advantage increasingly depends on its ability to master its role within this overall "value system."[50] The sustainable sources of competitive advantage in an integrated global economy depend on factors that cannot be shifted internationally from one market to another. Specialized personnel skills, close customer relationships, costs to customers of changing suppliers, the ability to tailor products to customer needs, and constant adjustment to differentiate products from competitors, for example, all help to sustain competitive advantage over extended periods.[51] That kind of specialized coordination is the forte of input-output networks, and as a result they have been growing in importance. At the same time, the information technology revolution has lowered the cost and enhanced the quality of communications and rapid analysis needed for input-output network coordination.

Input-output networks are often superior to arms-length market relationships when there are network economies of scale or scope, when there are high risks, when a firm wants to penetrate new markets, when production processes are highly interdependent, and when transaction costs are high. Increasing economies of scale arise when expansion in the size of an activity produces more than a proportional increase in output. Economies of scope occur when there is a synergy among a set of activities, so that increasing all the activities together produces a more than proportionate rise in output. If the economies of scale or scope come from the firm's own activities, the internal economies work to expand the size of the firm. When the economies come from the activities of all the firms in an industry or a network, the economies of scale or scope are external to the firm. The external economies raise the importance of interconnections among firms and strengthen the role of organizational networks. External economies of scale and scope work together: external economies of scale increase the size of the industry, and external economies of scope strengthen the importance of cooperation across the firms in the expanding industry.[52]

In addition to exploiting external economies of scale and scope, the input-output network also provides flexibility in adjusting production relationships in the face of uncertain supply or demand relationships. Coordination provides better information on the changing environment and permits rapid adjustments in production levels and product quality. Moreover, the long-term benefits of network relationships may work to smooth production requirements over the business cycle, perhaps by adjusting profit margins to ensure continuity in supplier or customer relationships. Similarly, networks can reduce the risks of penetrating new markets by working through other network firms to gain connections with local suppliers or retail outlets, to bypass entry barriers, and to adapt to administrative regulations and tax codes.[53] Rapid access to markets may be particularly important in industries such as microelectronics, robotics, and telecommunications, in which product life cycles are becoming shorter.[54]

Increasing complexity of trade in goods and services also makes input-output networks more important because processes become interdependent. The more products must be tailored to different users or markets and the more important the services component of the bundle of goods and services being delivered, the more important networks become.[55] For example, one of the characteristics of the new network structures is the tailoring of products for specific customers or locations, and the information technology revolution has made limited production runs for such targeted markets feasible. Robotics, for example, permits flexible manufacturing processes that make smaller production runs more efficient and increase the number of feasible product variations. At the same time, the software provided by information technologies makes it possible to tailor bundles of products and services for different markets.[56]

Greater interaction with customers, rapid product changes, and increased variety in the form of goods and services increase the premium on incremental, continuous adjustment to the market, and networks can be adapted to provide the immediate feedback needed to stay abreast of market conditions.[57] The more standardized the technology and the more stable the product line, the less important continuous adjustment will be. As discussed below, one might anticipate an organizational adaptation tied to the trajectories of the principal technologies in the industry, with greater reliance on input-output networks in early stages of rapid product revision and, subsequently, more standardization and greater emphasis on formal market relationships as the technology, products, and organizations mature. Finally, input-output networks can provide a useful balance between the recurrent transaction costs of pure market relationships and the diseconomies of scale that can arise from management and control problems as an organization grows larger.[58]

Evidence on network complexity is difficult to obtain or interpret, because so much of an input-output network's effectiveness depends on the transmission of information that is not recorded in transactions. Available evidence on recorded transactions does, however, suggest the increasing importance of U.S. input-output networks. Transactional activities such as accounting, legal services, and consulting have been increasing as a proportion of total output, along with spending for communications in general.[59]

The key advantages of input-output networks—capturing external economies of scale or scope, spreading the risks of operations in cyclical or new markets, facilitating coordination of interdependent processes, and reducing transaction costs—are most important in the face of rapid technological change. The information technology revolution has increased the importance of input-output networks both by creating the rapid change to which organizations must adjust and by providing new physical networks for coping with that change. Competitive advantage will be determined by the ability of firms to adapt to the increasing importance of global input-output networks. It will also depend on access to scientific research, technological development, and product and process innovation in international R&D networks.

Research and Development Networks. R&D coordination through global organizational networks is transforming the nature of international cooperation and competition. A recent study of roughly 2,000 firms in Holland, for example, showed that over 25 percent of firms were engaged in some form of R&D cooperation with other domestic firms, and over 10 percent had similar arrangements with foreign firms. The agreements were spread uniformly across major industrial categories, and not surprisingly the tendency for international collaboration was larger in firms with substantial exports.[60]

R&D activities lend themselves to network coordination because it is difficult for any organization to appropriate, or capture, the benefits of its own research. Patent restrictions do help restrict access to product or process design in some cases, but patents are often hard to enforce, particularly in international markets, and ideas are sometimes too generic for such protection. As a result, R&D has many of the characteristics of a public good in that users cannot be excluded from using the resulting information. In such cases, a competitive market will tend to provide too little R&D from a public perspective because any firm's assessment of the benefits it can appropriate to itself will understate the full benefit to all potential users. A network provides a better, but still imperfect, means for capturing the benefits, because the promise of future access to the network may induce users to contribute to the R&D process by sharing information.

The information technology revolution provides the physical network for detailed R&D coordination, and it has also contributed to the scale and complexity of R&D projects. For example, few firms have the resources required for the development of new 64-MB DRAM, and fewer still could absorb the financial impact of entering the competition and failing. In addition, many technological advances now come not from pushing forward in one technical speciality, but from combining related technologies in a variety of fields in new ways.[61] The cost of staying at the cutting edge in each relevant technology is prohibitive, but the cost of missing out on a new product line because of limited access to related technologies can be even greater. R&D networks help to spread risks of major projects, to ensure access to new technologies in a period of rapid technological change, and to facilitate greater coordination in production and marketing.[62]

R&D networks are at the pure information end of the organizational network product-information continuum. Such networks are most useful when the interaction is not an exchange to be settled immediately, but a part of a longer-term pattern of interaction based on highly subjective debits and credits that are harder to quantify or capture in a formal contract. Firms may have strong incentives to participate in such R&D networks, even with other firms who may be rivals in product markets, when the research has broad benefits for an industry and no firm can restrict access to the results—for example, in establishing industry standards for grading and testing raw materials.[63]

The proliferation of strategic alliance agreements among information technology firms has been particularly striking. The cooperative agreements and technology indicators (CATI) information system now contains records on roughly 10,000 cooperative agreements in all fields by some 3,500 parent companies. Of those, roughly 4,000 concern R&D relationships, with roughly 1,700, or 42 percent, of those strategic technology alliances in information technologies.[64] John Hagedoorn and Jos Schakenraad compare the actual number of R&D links across information technology firms with the total number of possible connections. In the first half of the 1980s, 23 percent of the possible connections had already been made, and by the late 1980s the ratio had risen to over 40 percent.[65]

During the period from 1985 to 1989, several very strong clusters of tightly networked information technology firms were apparent. As shown in Figure 3-1, a U.S.-European cluster linked IBM, Intel, and DEC in the U.S., and Siemens, Cie Generale d'Electricite, and Philips on the continent. A European network linked Philips, Siemens, and Thompson, while a separate set of agreements, not shown in Figure 3-1, established a U.S. network between AT&T and Sun Microsystems. A European-Japanese network linked Standard Telephone in the United Kingdom with Fujitsu and Hitachi in Japan, and a purely Japanese network, also not shown in Figure 3-1, connected Nippon Electric, Mitsubishi, and Mitsui.[66]

Seven firms—Siemens, IBM, Philips, Fujitsu, Nippon Electric, and AT&T—stand out as leaders in network relationships in several subfields of information technology, although they often are most active outside their central areas of market leadership. Germany's Siemens has been most active in the widest array of fields, including industrial automation, chips, software, and telecommunications.[67] IBM also has a wide array of alliances designed to strengthen different competitive niches, including arrangements with Ferranti to expand markets for the PS/2 operating system, with Toshiba to gain access to liquid crystal display technologies, with DEC, Apollo, and Hewlett-Packard for workstation development, with Microsoft for joint software development, and, as noted earlier, with Siemens to develop the 64-MB DRAM.[68]

The data suggest that firms may be reluctant to share information on their core competencies, but they are more willing to enter network arrangements in other related technologies.[69] They also indicate that while networks have strong regional bases, they also have global reach. These network relationships reflected in formal joint ventures and corporate alliances are supplemented by a much broader, and more difficult to document, set of more informal network connections. They are also supported by a number of public programs aimed directly at building more effective regional networks, such as the coordinating role of the Ministry of International Trade and Industry (MITI) in Japan, Sematech in the United States, and the European Community's ESPIRIT, Eureka, BRITE, Erasmus, RACE, and SCIENCE programs.[70]

Finance Networks. International brokerage houses and exchanges have long been networked together by the telephone and the telex, but the revolution in information technologies has accelerated and simplified the process. All of the world's securities markets use either an order-driven system in which orders to buy and sell are matched at a central point, a quote-driven system in which dealers try to find the best price available for their customers, or some hybrid of the two.[71] Electronic trading can now perform both functions 24 hours a day across integrated systems that link London's International Stock Exchange, the Tokyo Stock Exchange, the New York Stock Exchange, the Chicago Mercantile Exchange, the Chicago Board Options Exchange, the Chicago Board of Trade, and a host of other securities markets to trading houses and institutional investors around the world. As a result, information about risks and returns can be shared more quickly and transactions costs are reduced. The process of factor creation now takes place in an environment in which integrated financial networks can act quickly and efficiently to exploit different potential returns in alternative markets.

As in other network forms, financial networks converge on common standards for passing information. U.S. accounting rules are now widely accepted worldwide, because access to many financial markets requires disclosure in that format. German firms had long refused to provide the information required for listing on the New York Stock Exchange, but it appears that the benefits of network access have now overcome concerns about disclosure. Daimler Benz, for example, recently decided to break with other German companies and publish financial results in accordance with U.S. principles.[72] Global organizational networks create enormous pressures for convergence on network standards in local structures and procedures.

Policy Networks. Robert Keohane and Joseph Nye have defined "international regimes" as a set of government arrangements for regulating and controlling transnational and interstate relationships through "procedures, rules, or institutions for certain kinds of activity."[73] In their terminology, the distribution of resources across nations determines the power structure of the international system, and the regime establishes the "norms, rules and procedures" within which political bargaining takes place on a certain set of issues, such as aid to less developed countries, international telecommunications policy, or international trade. Keohane and Nye argue that the realist model of world politics—with its emphasis on states as coherent units and dominant actors, force or threatened use of force as the most effective instrument of policy, and a hierarchy of issues headed by the "high politics" of military security that dominates the "low politics" of social issues and economics—no longer provides an adequate explanation of regime changes.[74]

Instead, they propose a model of "complex interdependence" with the following characteristics: multiple "transgovernmental" and "transnational" channels of interaction across different levels of government and outside formal government institutions, no clear hierarchy of issues, and limited effectiveness of force in dealing with other states that are tied by mutual interdependence. Complex interdependence suggests that the ability of states to influence outcomes will vary across different issues, that the ability to set the political agenda will therefore be more important in determining the influence of different states, and that coalitions can be formed with actors in other jurisdictions in ways that blur distinctions between domestic and international politics.

In such a world, governments are linked by direct formal ties, by international organizations, by networks of intergovernmental and transgovernmental relationships, and by generally accepted norms. Keohane and Nye use the term "international organization" to describe patterns of interaction that extend beyond specific regimes to include patterns of "elite networks" and formal institutions that are nested in higher and higher levels of policy coordination. In their example, the Bretton Woods international monetary regime defined norms for financial interaction. The international organization of monetary issues included that regime as well as formal institutions like the International Monetary Fund and elite banking and treasury networks. Monetary organization in turn was part of broader international organization under formal institutions like the United Nations and network linkages across governments in general and OECD members in particular.[75]

The model of complex interdependence fits the concept of policy networks very well, except that the networks may or may not be operating under state control or direction. A policy network is an organizational network whose objective is to influence or coordinate government policies. Such networks connect different levels of government and related private and nonprofit organizations within a nation and across national boundaries. The network perspective emphasizes the increasing ease of direct communication among all the participants and patterns of continuing interaction, rather than a more traditional view that would emphasize administrative hierarchies operating at arms length with other hierarchies.

For example, when U.S. automobile manufacturers threatened to file unfair trade practice suits against Japanese and European producers for selling cars below cost in the United States, foreign governments began to pressure the U.S. government, but foreign producers also used their input-output network relationships to pressure U.S. producers. The *New York Times* reported that the head of Toyota, which has a joint venture with General Motors (GM) building small cars in Fremont, California, called the head of GM to lobby for an end to the suit, which was subsequently dropped.[76] Such policy network relationships are a natural outgrowth of input-output and research network connections and the ease of modern communications. Video conferencing and electronic mail networks will increasingly link all participants in international policy networks and provide for new lines of information and influence outside normal organizational channels.[77]

The policy coordination that flows from network relationships will focus more and more on the standardization required to make input-output, research, finance, and policy networks more effective. The European Community (EC), for example, might be seen as a policy network whose goal is to develop externalities from improved interaction by standardizing legal processes, contracting, tax codes, financial regulations, government procurement procedures, and so forth. The gains from standardizing on one policy approach may well be more important than the specific standard that is adopted. Although the formal procedures of the EC are important, the direct policy network interaction of nongovernmental actors and of governmental organizations at all levels will be just as important in determining ultimate network standards.[78]

From a network perspective, regions might be defined more in terms of overlaps among input-output, research, finance, and policy networks than in terms of physical geography. Regional competition would then center on the tension between the benefits of network extension and the potential dislocation from coordinating conflicting network standards. The key insight here is that traditional commercial concerns focused on product movements may now be less important than frictions caused by inconsistent network standards. International policy networks will be instrumental in dealing with the frictions of network evolution.

As organizational networks expand and change over time, they will generate network externalities that benefit all participants, but they will also redistribute access, influence, and power. The positive externalities from working together on a common network standard must be weighed against the transition costs of moving toward that standard. This is the essence of cooperative competition. Cooperation in network expansion creates potential benefits for all participants, but some participants will be able to exploit the possibilities of the new networks more effectively and gain a larger share of the growing pie. Organizations can conform to the new network standards or become less and less effective over time.

THE TRANSFORMATION OF WORK AND ORGANIZATIONS

The emerging organizational networks are both cause and effect of the changing structure of occupations and organizations reflected in new patterns of work within corporations. The evolution of networks and the changing internal structure of organizations both result from the declining cost of information, the need to tailor products to user specifications, and the requirement to coordinate various phases of production as part of an integrated system.

Work Patterns

Large firms engaged in the mass production of standard products have traditionally been organized around the concept of specialized individuals completing independent, routine, repetitive tasks to specification. That structure continues to dominate in some industries, but an increasing number of organizations have shifted to a team structure in which a group of workers with a mix of relevant skills cooperate to provide a product or service to other teams or to ultimate users. Advantages of the horizontal coordination implicit in the team structure include the ability to pass relevant information quickly, the potential to design and modify products and processes simultaneously based on feedback from users, and the stimulus decentralization gives to creativity. The team structure also facilitates coordination across traditional organizational boundaries, so the work group can work directly with suppliers and users without the friction of passing information up and down through administrative layers. To some extent, these U.S. practices have been copied from successful Japanese competitors, but in other cases they are a natural outgrowth of the information technology revolution. The trend toward connected teams of workers can be observed at all levels, from mass-production firms to formerly dispersed service, crafts, and professional activities.[79]

For example, since IBM sold Lexmark International in 1991, the computer printer manufacturer achieved great success by streamlining its organization into worker teams. Lexmark pared its workforce from 5,000 to 3,000 with deep cuts in management and manufacturing, but then added 1,000 workers to international sales. The restructuring reduced the number of layers between the chief executive officer and an assembly line worker from eight to four. Within this more horizontal structure, Lexmark established hundreds of teams with representatives across several departments. The changes cut the total time for developing new products in half by devoting more time to the concept phase of the design stage—increasing consultations with manufacturing and finance departments as well as customers—and then reducing time for subsequent revisions.[80]

Competitive advantage now flows less from the production of standardized items, and more from the ability to adapt products to sophisticated consumer needs. Global firms can quickly shift production of standardized items to low-cost producers based on changes in wages or government regulations, but the production of more advanced bundles of goods and services requires access to educated, flexible workers who can adapt to rapidly changing technologies. Education has become a more important factor in determining competitive advantage, not just in the sense of formal schooling, but also in the sense of facilitating the exchange of information needed to keep workers abreast of new processes. Effective workers do not simply apply the results of research produced elsewhere: they learn continuously and modify processes as parts of integrated teams designed to handle larger and larger information flows.[81]

In more horizontal organizations designed around work teams, middle management positions are declining and differentiation in the kind of work done at various levels in the organization is decreasing. The role of the manager is to serve as a broker, coordinating and modifying teams and providing liaison with other organizations. Workers with narrow, specialized skills are being replaced by those who can use new information technologies to perform a wider range of related tasks. One result is that career patterns are becoming more diverse, with fewer rungs on the ladder and more points of entry. Another result is that work teams become part of an overlapping network that builds from within the organization and extends beyond it.[82]

According to Robert Reich, three kinds of skills are becoming more and more important in high-value enterprises: "problem-solving" skills in finding innovative solutions for putting things together, "problem-identi-fication" skills in defining and matching customer needs to customized products, and "strategic broker" skills in bringing problem identifiers and problem solvers together. All of these skills have to do with "symbolic-analytic" services that exploit the potential of the information technology revolution for manipulating symbols to simulate problems, design solutions, and communicate results.[83]

The rapid expansion of information technology has been reflected in the changing structure of the U.S. workforce. Over the period from 1960 to 1980, the number of workers classified in jobs as "knowledge producers" grew from roughly 7 to 9 percent of total employment, and the number of "data workers" who used that information grew from 36 to 43 percent. Those two groups together accounted for over 50 percent of total employment.[84] Almost half of those information users and producers, some 20 percent of the U.S. workforce, qualify as problem solvers, problem identifiers, and strategic brokers.[85]

This core of information users and producers, and the top tier of problem solvers, problem identifiers, and strategic brokers, constitutes a specialized workforce with strong links to those performing similar functions in other organizations. Indeed, sophisticated information processors may need frequent exchanges with comparable workers elsewhere in order to stay abreast of rapid technological changes within their specialties.[86] Such links are not new, but the amount of time spent in establishing network relationships outside the organization with suppliers, customers, researchers, and even counterparts in competitor organizations is now substantial and similar in time and scope to internal organizational relationships.[87] These changes in skill requirements and work relationships are reflected in comparable changes in organizational patterns.

Organizational Patterns

As Alfred Chandler's studies conclude, U.S. entrepreneurs virtually invented the large managerial enterprise at the end of the nineteenth century to exploit economies of scale in capital-intense industries and to control the large domestic and international distribution systems needed to build markets large enough to sustain efficient levels of production. Improved transportation and communications systems permitted the coordination of supplies, production, and delivery required to sustain mass production, and new managerial hierarchies emerged to coordinate those complex activities. Multinational operations arose as the large managerial enterprises used their advantages in mass production, distribution, and management to extend operations into other countries. The development of the large managerial enterprise and multinational operations was the result of rapid market growth, new technologies that transformed production techniques, and new communications and transportation capabilities that made it possible to sustain large-scale operations.[88]

Market growth and new technologies are once again shaping the structure of multinational operations, but this time the advantages accrue less from control of operations emanating from a central headquarters and more from network integration of globally dispersed activities. Consider three alternative approaches to international operations: national, global, and transnational. A national strategy would emphasize dispersed production and semiautonomous local operations to meet unique local demands, reduce production lead times, tailor practices to local government regulations, lower transaction costs within the enterprise, and keep management operations simple. Marketing, sales, and service costs typically vary with the scale of national operations, in contrast to technology development, where large fixed costs argue for a global scale of production.[89] A global strategy would exploit the following advantages: economies of coordination in applying technological know-how, management skills, and marketing systems throughout global markets; economies of scale in production; and economies from spreading high R&D costs over larger production runs.[90] A transnational strategy would balance both approaches by attempting to capture global scale economies while still responding to national conditions.[91]

Convergence in economic performance across the developed economies and the dissemination of new information and process technologies have now made transnational strategies more feasible and more effective. As a result, network organizations needed to implement transnational strategies have become more important. The information technology revolution has created the means for more flexible manufacturing and more creative, tailored packaging of products and services. Companies across a wide spectrum of industries are now placing greater emphasis on coordinating operations in different national markets to exploit the potential and demand for differentiated products.

More companies have been forced to develop transnational organizations that use internal diversity to provide better sensing of a rapidly changing environment, to coordinate geographically dispersed management and assets, and to integrate internal processes. The transnational organization becomes an integrated network in which the dispersed units all contribute knowledge, skills, and insights, with some locations taking the lead in different aspects of research, production, or marketing and sharing the results with the rest of the network organization. In such a network organization complexity in balancing centralized efficiencies with needs for national diversification is enormous and uncertainty is rampant, so the requirement for smooth, quick, decentralized information flows increases and the viability of formal, line management systems decreases.[92]

The growing importance of transnational management has increased the advantages of horizontal "Toyota"-style structures, which emphasize coordination of work teams and task forces, in contrast to the hierarchical, functional structure of mass-production firms known as "Fordist" organizations. Although few firms have pure Toyota or Fordist structures, the distinction does suggest an important range of organizational differences in terms of management-employee relationships, investment for long-term returns, on-time delivery, total quality management of the entire engineering-production-sales-service system, and the interrelationship of suppliers, producers, and customers in an integrated value chain. The distinctions are not simply in the internal structure of the organization, but in the way linkages are formed with other organizations. The hierarchical structure can achieve economies of scale and scope, but it may be difficult to sustain focus on the nuances of quality and technical adaptation required to keep a competitive advantage.[93] Independent horizontal structures may also encounter difficulties in coordination unless there are mechanisms developed for that purpose. Network structures permit the integration of focused subunits in ways that retain flexibility in adjusting to shifting market conditions while still capturing the economies of scale and scope.[94]

Toyota-style organizations emphasize decentralized decision-making, the accumulation of on-the-spot knowledge by workers in subunits, and sharing of information across teams, all factors that are reinforced by lifetime employment. In contrast, traditional Fordist organizations have emphasized more specialization and standardization leading to compartmentalization within the firm and the need for integration through middle-level management. Patterns of exchanging information within the firm influence organizational structure and the way in which production techniques are developed and disseminated. Fordist firms emphasize a vertical flow of R&D transmitted in formal designs, while Toyota firms stress continuous modifications based on direct coordination between researchers and work teams, with greater attention paid to intangible skills and processes. The Fordist system may well be superior in generating new technologies and spinning them off into new subunits or an entirely new subsidiary, but the Toyota approach may be better in commercializing new technologies, diversifying within the firm, or coordinating across semiautonomous subunits.[95]

In the current global environment, functional Fordist organizations are giving way to new network structures because of the growing importance of such factors as quality, convenience, and speed, which flow from new technological capabilities and more sophisticated demands.[96] The test of success is delivery of a quality product, on time, at competitive prices. Network organizations use flexible work teams to meet those global standards by more effectively tapping the potential of workers with high-value information skills.[97]

The internal network structure reinforces the emergence of input-output and research organizational networks. Such relationships have always existed to some extent, but the intensity and complexity of global competition and the integrating potential of new information technologies have made the linkages tighter and more important to the networked firms. Success in international competition is now more contingent on the effectiveness of the entire network. The core corporation is itself a strategic broker, tying together disparate activities all over the world in integrated input-output networks and working to create new factors of production in research networks. The corporation's real strategy is to develop and exploit the specialized knowledge needed to arrange, alter, and manipulate global networks.[98]

NETWORKS AND PRODUCTIVITY

The changes in the structure of the workplace, the growing importance of information skills, the evolution of organizations as networks of teams, and the development of input-output, research, finance, and policy organizational networks can be traced directly to the revolution in the underlying physical network generated by new information technologies. The new network structures play a pivotal role in determining the pace and structure of productivity growth.

The essence of network relationships is the central role of communications. Input-output networks have emerged to coordinate supply, design, production, and customer service in response to the rapid change in technologies and to meet competition that is based more and more on quality. Horizontal organizations are needed to pass information quickly among teams within the enterprise, to develop connections with related teams in other enterprises, and to tailor packages of services and products to user needs. Research networks respond to the requirement to integrate multiple technologies in new products and production processes, to spread the risks of high investment in new technologies, and to ease access to new global markets. Finance networks quickly and continuously pass information concerning shifting patterns of risk and return in different markets. Policy networks draw together analysts from a variety of overlapping jurisdictions whose agendas focus more and more on administrative inconsistencies that block efficient network operations.

Network relationships are difficult to capture in conventional productivity measures because of the multiple dimensions of interactions, including subtle quality distinctions, response time, rapid shifts in product lines, coordinated delivery schedules, and other coordination factors that help supply, production, and after-sale services mesh smoothly. Productivity properly measured should capture those subtle outputs, but, in practice, output measures typically trail well behind performance in periods of rapid technological and organizational change.[99] The MIT Commission on Industrial Productivity traced many U.S. problems in the manufacturing sector to difficulties in adapting to the new network environment. Their list of behavioral patterns that weaken productive performance includes the following culprits: reliance on mass production and standardized products, short time horizons for investment, technological weaknesses in refining process technologies through adaptation down the learning curve as part of production, insufficient on-the-job retraining in new skills, failures in cooperation with other firms concerning collective goals and within firms across different functions, and antitrust attitudes that block coordination between firms with regard to industry standards, R&D, education, and training.[100] In short, the kinds of network workplace practices, internal network organizations, and external network linkages described in this chapter are the key to more productive performance in manufacturing.

Input-output, R&D, finance, and policy networks all have global dimensions. As a result, the key factors that drive productivity growth are now determined not by national firms drawing on national technologies influenced by national policies and national financial conditions, but by global networks of activities drawing on international technologies influenced by the international financial situation and the interplay of local, national, regional, and international policies. Regions are no longer defined by geographical borders, but by patterns of interconnection in network segments that have settled on common standards. Nations and regions still matter, but their impact is primarily on the structure of the competition for the nodes of global networks, on the evolution of network standards, and on the specialized local factors that determine the home bases for global enterprises. Those network concepts can now be applied to a more detailed examination of how the interaction of innovation, factor creation, and competitive advantage influences the location of global organizational network nodes and the rate of productivity growth.

NOTES

1. For example, see Richard N. Cooper, *The Economics of Interdependence* (New York: McGraw-Hill, 1968), for a pioneering work in this area and his *Economic Policy in an Interdependent World* (Cambridge, Mass.: MIT Press, 1986) for a more recent overview.

2. Robert B. Reich, *The Work of Nations: Preparing Ourselves for 21st Century Capitalism* (New York: Alfred A. Knopf, 1991), 114.

3. Paul Mariti and Robert H. Smiley, "Co-Operative Agreements and Organization of Industry," *Journal of Industrial Economics* 31 (June 1983): 437–451.

4. Philippe Gugler, "Building Transnational Alliances to Create Competitive Advantage," *Long Range Planning* 25 (February 1992): 90.

5. Strategic alliances do not include formal acquisitions, although alliances often lead to actual merger. The number and value of cross-border mergers and acquisitions continue at historically high levels. See Joel Bleeke, David Ernst, James A. Isono, and Douglas D. Weinberg, "The New Shape of Cross-Border Mergers and Acquisitions," in *Collaborating to Compete: Using Strategic Alliances and Acquisitions in the Global Marketplace,* ed. Joel Bleeke and David Ernst (New York: John Wiley & Sons, Inc., 1993), 92, 95.

6. Michael E. Porter and Mark B. Fuller, "Coalitions and Global Strategy," in *Competition in Global Industries,* ed. Michael E. Porter (Boston, Mass.: Harvard Business School Press, 1986), 317.

7. Organization for Economic Cooperation and Development, *Globalization of Industrial Activities, Four Case Studies: Auto Parts, Chemicals, Construction, and Semi Conductors* (Paris, 1992), 11–12.

8. Francois Chesnais, "Multinational Enterprises and the International Diffusion of Technology," in *Technical Change and Economic Theory,* ed. Giovanni Dosi et al. (London: Pinter Publishers, 1988), 516.

9. Richard W. Stephenson, "A First Step Toward an 800-Seat Jet," *New York Times,* January 28, 1993, p. D3.

10. OECD, *Globalization of Industrial Activities,* 13.

11. Chesnais, "Multinational Enterprises and the International Diffusion of Technology," 519.

12. Joel Bleeke and David Ernst, "The Way to Win in Cross-Border Alliances," in *Collaborating to Compete,* ed. Bleeke and Ernst, 17–19, 22, 25.

13. Gian Carlo Cainarca, Massimo G. Colombo, and Sergio Mariotti, "Agreements Between Firms and the Technological Life Cycle Model: Evidence from Information Technologies," *Research Policy* 21 (February 1992): 53.

14. For more detail, see John Hagedoorn and Jos Schakenraad, "Leading Companies and Networks of Strategic Alliances in Information Technologies," *Research Policy* 21 (April 1992): 163–190.

15. Ralinda Lurie, Ben Huston, and David B. Yoffie, "Intel Corporation 1988," Harvard Business School Case 9-389-063, in *International Trade and Competition: Cases and Notes in Strategy and Management,* ed. David B. Yoffie (New York: McGraw-Hill, 1990), 439.

16. Gugler, "Building Transnational Alliances to Create Competitive Advantage," 93.

17. Paul A. David, "General Purpose Engines, Investment and Productivity Growth: From the Dynamo Revolution to the Computer Revolution," in *Technology and Investment: Crucial Issues for the 1990s,* ed. Enrico Deiaco, Erik Hornell, and Graham Vickery (London: Pinter Publishers, 1990), 141–154.

18. Clifton F. Berry, *Inventing the Future: How Science and Technology Transform Our World* (New York: Brassey's, Inc., 1993), 23–24.

19. For example, the new Intel Pentium chip—the fifth generation in the 8086, 286, 386, 486 family—contains over 3 million transistors. See John Markoff, "Newest Chip from Intel Will be Hard to Copy," *New York Times,* March 23, 1993, p. D4.

20. Richard N. Langlois and Paul L. Robertson, "Networks and Innovation in a Modular System: Lessons From the Microcomputer and Stereo Component Industries," *Research Policy* 21 (August 1992): 306.

21. Berry, *Inventing the Future*, 26–33, and Gene Bylinski, Charles O'Rear, and Lawrence Bender, *Silicon Valley: High Tech Window to the Future* (Hong Kong: Intercontinental Publishing Corp., 1985), 35.

22. Charles H. Ferguson, "Computers and the Coming of the U.S. Keiretsu," *Harvard Business Review* 68 (July-August 1990): 60.

23. Berry, *Inventing the Future*, 66–69.

24. Ferguson, "Computers and the Coming of the U.S. Keiretsu," 57.

25. Ibid., 56–57.

26. John Markoff, "A Remade I.B.M. Reinvents the Mainframe," *New York Times,* January 29, 1993, pp. D1, D15.

27. OECD, *Globalization of Industrial Activities,* 135, and Ferguson, "Computers and the Coming of the U.S. Keiretsu," 57, 67.

28. See U.S. Congress, Office of Technology Assessment, *Miniaturization Technologies* (Washington, D.C.: U.S. Government Printing Office, November 1991).

29. Shumpei Kumon, "Japan as a Network Society," in *The Political Economy of Japan, Volume 3: Cultural and Social Dynamics,* ed. Shumpei Kumon and Henry Rosovsky (Stanford, Calif.: Stanford University Press, 1992), 112–113.

30. David, "General Purpose Engines, Investment and Productivity Growth," 142.

31. Langlois and Robertson, "Networks and Innovation in a Modular System," 307.

32. W. Brian Arthur, "Competing Technologies: An Overview," in *Technical Change and Economic Theory,* ed. Giovanni Dosi et al. (London: Pinter Publishers, 1988), 591.

33. Paul A. David, "Clio and the Economics of QWERTY," *American Economic Review* 75, *Papers and Proceedings* (May 1985): 332–337.

34. Ibid., 334.

35. Ibid., 334–336.

36. Steve Lohr, "Mainframes Aren't All That Dead," *New York Times,* February 9, 1993, p. D6.

37. Michael L. Katz and Carl Shapiro, "Network Externalities, Competition, and Compatibility," *American Economic Review* 75 (June 1985): 424–425.

38. For similar views on the evolution of organizational networks, see David Ronfeldt, "Cyberocracy is Coming," *The Information Society* 8 (1992): 275–277.

39. See Oliver E. Williamson, *Markets and Hierarchies: Analysis and Antitrust Implications, A Study in the Economics of International Organization* (New York: Free Press, 1975).

40. Porter and Fuller, "Coalitions and Global Strategy," 329.

41. Kumon, "Japan as a Network Society," 118.

42. Ibid., 118–119.

43. Michael E. Porter, *The Competitive Advantage of Nations* (New York: Free Press, 1990), 40–42.

44. For a discussion of the role of information technologies in linking firms, suppliers, and clients, see Organization for Economic Cooperation and Development, *Information Networks and New Technologies: Opportunities and Policy Implications for the 1990s* (Paris, 1992), 26–29. For an illustration of these rela-

tionships in a logistics alliance, see Donald J. Bowersox, "The Strategic Benefits of Logistics Alliances," *Harvard Business Review* 68 (July-August 1990): 36–37, 41–42.

45. AnnaLee Saxenian, "The Origins and Dynamics of Production Networks in Silicon Valley," *Research Policy* 20 (October 1991): 425–427.

46. John Markoff, "In a Shift, Apple Licenses a System," *New York Times,* March 25, 1993, p. D3.

47. Michael Storper and Bennett Harrison, "Flexibility, Hierarchy, and Regional Development: The Changing Structure of Industrial Production Systems and Their Forms of Governance in the 1990s," *Research Policy* 20 (October 1991): 411.

48. Ken-ichi Imai, "Japan's Corporate Networks," in *The Political Economy of Japan, Volume 3: Cultural and Social Dynamics,* ed. Shumpei Kumon and Henry Rosovsky (Stanford, Calif.: Stanford University Press, 1992), 223.

49. See Saxenian, "The Origins and Dynamics of Production Networks in Silicon Valley," 428–435, for interesting examples.

50. Porter, *The Competitive Advantage of Nations,* 42.

51. Ibid., 51–52.

52. Storper, "Flexibility, Hierarchy, and Regional Development," 409.

53. Anthony Patrick Carnevale, *America and the New Economy: How Competitive Standards Are Radically Changing American Workplaces* (San Francisco, Calif.: Jossey-Bass Publishers, 1991), 214.

54. David C. Mowery and Nathan Rosenberg, *Technology and the Pursuit of Economic Growth* (Cambridge: Cambridge University Press, 1989), 249. See also Saxenian, "The Origins and Dynamics of Production Networks in Silicon Valley," 424–425, for a discussion of the impact of shorter product cycles on the evolution of networks.

55. Albert Bressand, "European Integration: From the System Paradigm to Network Analysis," *The International Spectator* 24 (January-March 1989): 25.

56. Christopher A. Bartlett, "Building and Managing the Transnational: The New Organizational Challenge," in *Competition in Global Industries,* ed. Michael E. Porter (Boston, Mass.: Harvard Business School Press, 1986), 376.

57. Carnevale, *America and the New Economy,* 96–100.

58. Christopher Freeman, "Japan: A New National System of Innovation?" in *Technical Change and Economic Theory,* ed. Dosi et al., 338.

59. Carnevale, *America and the New Economy,* 90.

60. Alfred Kleinknecht and Jeroen O.N. Reijnen, "Why Do Firms Cooperate on R&D?: An Empirical Study," *Research Policy* 21 (August 1992): 350–351.

61. For an elaboration of this point, see Nathan Rosenberg, "Technological Interdependence in the American Economy," *Technology and Culture* 20 (January 1979): 25–49.

62. David J. Teece, "Technological Change and the Nature of the Firm," in *Technical Change and Economic Theory,* ed. Dosi et al., 278–279. See also Thomas M. Jorde and David J. Teece, *Antitrust, Innovation, and Competitiveness* (New York: Oxford University Press, 1992), for a discussion of joint ventures and research consortia and an argument that U.S. antitrust policy needlessly restricts such horizontal arrangements. For a more complete listing of the motives for technology collaboration and a useful guide to the literature, see Luc Soete, "National

Support Policies for Strategic Industries: The Strategic Implications," in *Strategic Industries in a Global Economy: Policy Issues for the 1990s,* Organization for Economic Cooperation and Development (Paris, 1991), 67.

63. Richard R. Nelson, "Institutions Supporting Technical Change in the United States," in *Technical Change and Economic Theory,* ed. Dosi et al., 319.

64. Hagedoorn and Schakenraad, "Leading Companies and Networks of Strategic Alliances in Information Technologies," 163.

65. Ibid., 186.

66. Ibid., 171.

67. Ibid., 183.

68. Edward Krubasik and Hartmut Lautenschlager, "Forming Successful Strategic Alliances in High-Tech Businesses," in *Collaborating to Compete,* ed. Joel Bleeke and David Ernst (New York: John Wiley & Sons, 1993), 61.

69. James D. Thompson, *Organizations in Action* (New York: McGraw Hill, 1967), and W. Richard Scott, *Organizations: Rational, Natural, and Open Systems* (Englewood Cliffs, N.J.: Prentice Hall, 1967), describe buffering strategies to protect core interests and bridging strategies to coordinate in areas of more peripheral interests.

70. Bressand, "European Integration," 25.

71. "Automating Financial Markets," *The Economist* (March 10, 1990): 19.

72. Floyd Norris, "Daimler-Benz Paves the Way for Other German Companies," *New York Times,* March 31, 1993, p. D8.

73. Robert O. Keohane and Joseph S. Nye, *Power and Interdependence,* 2nd ed. (New York: Harper Collins Publishers, 1989), 5.

74. Ibid., 20–21, 23–34.

75. Ibid., 24–25, 30–35, 55.

76. Keith Bradsher, "Big Three Won't Seek Car Tariffs," *New York Times,* February 10, 1993, pp. D1, D2.

77. David Ronfeldt, "Cyberocracy Is Coming," 276, suggests that the rise of multiorganizational networks is particularly important in nongovernmental organizations that use such linkages to strengthen their impact on government and business.

78. Bressand, "European Integration," 27.

79. Carnevale, *America and the New Economy,* p. xvii.

80. Steve Lohr, "For New I.B.M. Chief, Spinoff May Be a Model," *New York Times,* March 29, 1993, pp. D1, D10.

81. Carnevale, *America and the New Economy,* 96–100.

82. Ibid., pp. xviii, 86.

83. Reich, *The Work of Nations,* 84, 85, 177.

84. William J. Baumol, Sue Anne Batey Blackman, and Edward N. Wolff, *Productivity and American Leadership* (Cambridge, Mass.: MIT Press, 1989), 158.

85. Reich, *The Work of Nations,* 179.

86. Imai, "Japan's Corporate Networks," 219.

87. Bressand, "European Integration," 25.

88. Alfred D. Chandler, Jr., "The Evolution of Modern Global Competition," in *Competition in Global Industries,* ed. Michael E. Porter (Boston, Mass.: Harvard Business School Press, 1986), 421–425.

89. Porter and Fuller, "Coalitions and Global Strategy," 322.

90. Pankaj Ghemawat and A. Michael Spence, "Modeling Global Competition," in *Competition in Global Industries*, ed. Michael E. Porter (Boston, Mass.: Harvard Business School Press, 1986), 63.

91. Bartlett, "Building and Managing the Transnational," 369, 372.

92. Ibid., 377–382, 394. See also Jay R. Galbraith, *Organization Design: An Information Processing View* (Reading, Mass.: Addison-Wesley, 1974), for an argument that rising uncertainty increases information processing requirements and hence the need for networking.

93. Carnevale, *America and the New Economy*, 94.

94. Masahiko Aoki, "Horizontal vs. Vertical Information Structure of the Firm," *American Economic Review* 76 (December 1986): 981–982.

95. Carnevale, *America and the New Economy*, 210.

96. Motorola's reorganization is typical of this trend. For a quick summary, see David B. Yoffie and John Coleman, "Motorola and Japan," in *International Trade and Competition: Cases and Notes in Strategy and Management*, ed. Yoffie (New York: McGraw-Hill, 1990), 354–356.

97. Carnevale, *America and the New Economy*, 212.

98. Reich, *The Work of Nations*, 81, 84.

99. Michael L. Dertouzos, Richard K. Lester, Robert N. Solow, and the MIT Commission on Productivity Growth, *Made in America: Regaining the Productivity Edge* (Cambridge, Mass.: MIT Press, 1989), 32.

100. Ibid., 44–105.

4 Economic Systems, Networks, and the Productivity Cycle

U.S. national strategy must adjust to the two central changes in the international economic environment: convergence in the productivity performance of the three major economic regions and the emergence of global organizational networks grounded in the information technology revolution. Convergence and global networks have transformed the nature of the productivity cycle and reshaped the ways in which public policies influence productivity and growth. The processes of factor creation and innovation, which interact with the shifting structure of comparative advantage across industries and competitive advantages of firms within industries to determine changes in productivity, now take place in the context of global networks that link technological developments, factor markets, and product markets within and across national borders. Moreover, governments, policy institutes, interest groups, private organizations, and multinational organizations interact at local, national, regional, and even global levels in complex global policy networks that have an impact on each part of the productivity cycle.

But while firms, products, and technologies are losing their national identities in global organizational networks, differences in national cultures, public policies, and external economies of scale and scope still shape the location of different activities within those networks. As a result, competition to attract high-value activities to local, national, or regional network nodes is becoming more, not less, important. That competition could be a powerful force for greater efficiency and productivity growth if it is channeled toward enhanced innovation and factor creation, or it could slow productivity growth by generating policies designed to shield local producers from the transitions caused by global networks.

Chapter 3 argued that the pieces of the productivity cycle depicted in Figure 2-1—innovation, factor creation, and the structure of competitive advantage—have international dimensions through global networks. This chapter begins with an analysis of how combinations of national attributes lead to alternative approaches to productivity in market, indicative, and network systems. It then examines the impact of systemic differences in national economies on the integrated processes of factor creation, competitive advantage, and innovation, with special emphasis on the role of technological change. Finally, the chapter explores the interaction of global networks and local conditions that lead to regional differences in productivity performance. Chapter 5 then examines the policy implications of the shifting balance between global networks and national systems.

ECONOMIC SYSTEMS

The characteristics of different national economic systems, reflected in slowly evolving social and political attitudes, habits, customs, traditions, and institutional relationships, define the environment for innovation, factor creation, and industrial competition. Social and political stability; property rights; the structure of capital, labor, and product markets; labor-management relationships; the education system; science and technical infrastructures; and attitudes toward innovation shape behavioral patterns that define the economic system.

National Attributes and the Productivity Cycle

Social and political stability permit the development of long-term relationships needed to mobilize resources and provide investments in human and physical capital required for productivity growth. The erosion of social order and the concurrent collapse of the economic system in the former Yugoslavia, Liberia, Somalia, Ethiopia, Zaire, and Cambodia are grim reminders of this pivotal relationship. Social and political stability are underrated treasures in economic discourse, but they define the potential for broad economic advance.

Stability can come from tyranny as well as democracy, but events in Eastern Europe and the former Soviet Union in the late 1980s certainly suggest that long-term stability relies more on open participation than on compulsion. The information revolution has transformed access to communication and made it far more difficult to control informed populations by fiat. As participation becomes a more global value, civil society—the buffer between the individual and the state in the form of groups, associations, clubs, and so forth—has become a more important source of social and political stability, and a necessary, if not sufficient, condition for democracy.[1] Variations in national attitudes toward participation, civil society, and democratic institutions shape long-term social and political stability and provide the ultimate foundations for sustained economic growth. In many regions, successful management of issues related to ethnic minorities may be the most critical determinant of long-term productivity improvements.

If social and political stability provides the context for the mobilization of economic resources, attitudes toward property rights—rights that establish how property can be used and who receives the income—define the form. An emphasis on private property confirms an owner's right to use, retain the income from, deny access to, or transfer rights to property. In contrast, state property assigns those use, income, and denial rights to the government, and communal property assigns use and income rights to the public at large.[2] Property rights, reflected in attitudes toward independence in economic decisions, as well as in formal rules for property ownership, shape expectations concerning contracts, future income, and risk, which in turn have a direct impact on the processes of innovation and factor creation.

The structure of capital, labor, and factor markets follows from attitudes toward property rights and income distribution. If property rights are private and the rewards and risks of using property accrue to individuals, society is more likely to leave decisions in capital, product, and factor markets to individuals. If the risks of property use are seen as interdependent, however, society is more apt to restrict property rights or regulate market activities. For example, in Japan, banks and corporations hold large stock positions in each other through interlocking business group, or *keiretsu,* structures. This interdependence means that business failures have large potential ripple effects in bank failures, so corporations, banks, and government coordinate actions to offset interlocking risks. Similarly, German business groups, centered on the dominant position of banks that hold equity in corporations, create incentives for cooperation among government, industry, and the financial sector. In the United States, commercial banks cannot own common stock and antitrust laws limit mergers in related activities, so risks are less interdependent and markets are freer of government intervention. Differences in national attitudes toward risk, interdependence, and market intervention constrain individual rights in making decisions about property use and retaining the profits that flow from those decisions.

Attitudes toward property rights and interdependent risks spill over into labor-management relationships. In the United States, labor has traditionally been viewed as an input to production rather than an integral part of the corporation itself, and high wages are seen as a cost of business rather than an appropriate reward for high productivity. U.S. attitudes follow in part from the potential for labor mobility in a large, integrated national market in which workers can move to markets where they are most productive and command the highest possible wage. In Germany, where labor mobility has traditionally been more restricted, labor-management relationships have been less confrontational, with workers typically represented on corporate boards. In Japan, "lifetime" employment in one corporation, membership in a company union whose interests are inexorably linked to overall corporate performance, and bonus payments tied to corporate profits work to create a long-term partnership between management and labor.

Labor-force turnover rates, in turn, influence attitudes toward education. The United States led the way in broad public education, but postwar investment in education in Europe and Japan have produced elementary and secondary systems that now achieve superior results by most standards. The strongest difference is in education for those in the bottom half of the income distribution, and here the European and Japanese lead is convincing. In contrast to Japan and Europe, there is no organized postsecondary educational system for those who do not go to college. The German apprentice system and Japanese training programs for lifetime employees provide more systematic approaches to continuous worker training, while in the United States there is greater emphasis on individual responsibility for education and training.[3] The U.S. approach focuses resources at the top end of the education spectrum and has produced the world's best university system, but the emphasis on individual responsibility for education has been less successful at other levels.[4]

These differences in education are reflected in unique national scientific and technical infrastructures. U.S. technology policy has traditionally emphasized work at scientific frontiers in research universities and government laboratories, with specific applications left to the corporate sector. Defense R&D still accounts for over 30 percent of U.S. R&D spending. Other countries have placed R&D emphasis further downstream, with larger proportionate expenditures on manufacturing in general, and on systems engineering and process technologies in particular. While the U.S. spends 70 percent of its private R&D funds on products, Japan spends 70 percent on processes.[5] Japanese R&D institutions developed around the need in the 1950s and 1960s for reverse engineering—deducing design and production processes by examining products—so engineers and managers developed techniques for using the factory as a laboratory. MITI has targeted specific industries such as semiconductors for rapid development, in contrast to more generic and less industry-specific U.S. approaches.[6]

Finally, societal attitudes toward innovation have a large impact on the productivity cycle. In the United States, the Schumpeterian view of the entrepreneur as the champion of technical and economic progress has had a positive impact on attitudes toward change. From this perspective, the heroic entrepreneur takes the risks needed to break away from established norms of production, introduces new products and techniques, and generates surges in economic growth.[7] Schumpeter believed that over time, however, the entrepreneurial function would be opposed by a society that grew hostile to the iconoclastic disruptions of entrepreneurs, innovation would become a more routine function of large, formal organizations, and capitalism would fade into socialism. Indeed, socialist countries have typically taken a dim view of the disruptive entrepreneur, and Russian attitudes against innovators and the profit motive that drives them are a stumbling block to the successful transformation to a market system.

Those key attributes of national systems—social and political stability, property rights, the structure of capital, labor, and product markets, labor-management relationships, the education system, science and technical infrastructures, and attitudes toward innovation—provide the context for the processes of innovation and factor creation that determine competitive advantage and productivity growth. Testing the relationship of any of these attributes to productivity growth is clearly complicated by the wide range of characteristics and the difficulty of aggregating them into appropriate categories for comparison. The information technology revolution suggests a new emphasis on communications patterns as the central principle for describing the aggregation of characteristics into economic systems.

Classifying Economic Systems

Discussions of political economy typically focus on the interaction between the state's emphasis on compulsion, borders, and allegiance and the market's stress on contracts, open interaction between buyers and sellers, and material gain.[8] Traditional classification schemes organize state-market relationships into three dominant patterns—capitalism, socialism, and communism—but these terms are not very useful for describing modern economic systems because they are heavily value-laden, and they focus almost exclusively on property ownership. An improved formulation stresses key differences across major economies in addition to property rights, including levels of decision making, the mechanisms for passing information and coordinating activity, and incentive systems.[9]

Capitalism might then be defined as an economic system characterized by decentralized decision making, market provision of information and coordination of activity, private property rights, and material incentives. Market socialism would include decentralized decision making, a combination of indicative planning—planning that "indicates" expected future directions and provides nonbinding, indirect incentives for compliance— and market coordination, a mixture of state and collective property rights, and a combination of material and moral incentives. Planned socialism would emphasize centralized decision making, coordination through an enforced plan, state property rights, and both material and moral incentives.[10] These new definitions of capitalism, mixed socialism, and planned socialism are more precise and somewhat less normative than the old capitalism, socialism, and communism categories, but the levels of aggregation within the new definitions are still not very helpful in describing important nuances within mixed socialism, and the "socialism" label itself remains distracting.

The key distinctions among economic systems now lie in more subtle variations between capitalism and market socialism, variations that follow from the way information is passed and coordinated. An increased emphasis on the pattern and nature of communications provides a richer under-

Figure 4-1
Information Flows and Economic Systems

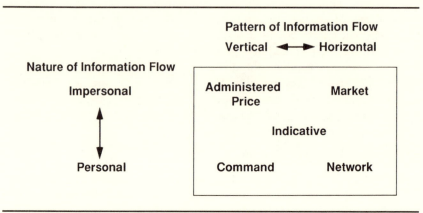

Source: Richard L. Carson, *Comparative Economic Systems* (New York: Macmillan Publishing Co., Inc., 1973), 33–40. Carson discusses the "nature" and "pattern" of information exchanges in market, indicative, command, and administered-price systems. He does not discuss network relationships.

standing of the range of distinctions in countries like the United States, Japan, Germany, France, and the United Kingdom.[11] The patterns of information flow may be vertical across levels of a hierarchy or horizontal among actors at the same level. The nature of messages may be impersonal, with the same implications for all receivers and responses based solely on the content of the message, or personal, with different implications for various receivers and responses based on the identity of the sender as well as content.[12] In this framework, economic systems would be classified by the predominant pattern and nature of communications about transactions.

For example, a market system would emphasize the use of prices to convey information about exchanges. As Figure 4-1 illustrates, in a pure market, price messages are impersonal and horizontal, applying to all potential buyers or sellers and directly linking consumers and producers. In a command system, the messages concerning production and deliveries would be personal and vertical, directed to specific actors from a higher to a lower level within the hierarchy. A combination of vertical information flows and impersonal messages, shown at the upper left of Figure 4-1, would be an administered-price system, with prices set by a plan but production and consumption decisions left to individuals. The problem with such a system, of course, is that the market might not clear at the administered price, so some other mechanism would be needed to deal with surpluses or allocate shortages.[13]

At the lower right of the figure, horizontal information flows and personal messages would be characteristic of a network system. Coordination would occur directly among consumers and producers through negotiated packages based on price, quantity, quality, time of delivery, and so forth in the context of continuing relationships.[14] Indicative systems would lie at the center of this array, emphasizing the combined use of impersonal prices in some markets and personal messages down through the hierarchy to selected groups. These market, network, indicative, administered-price, and command categories are pure types, and any actual economic system would to some extent make use of all of these patterns of exchanging information on production decisions.

In practice, the major modern economic systems now cluster along the market-indicative-network triangle in Figure 4-1, with each system containing some of each characteristic. The United States arguably lies closest to the market corner of the triangle; France, with state-owned companies that still account for roughly a third of industrial production, lies closer to the indicative corner; and Japan is nearer to the network corner. Germany, with its business groups anchored by major banks that work closely with the government, may lie near the center of the triangle. This system for classifying economies based on the nature of communications lends itself to an analysis of the impact of the information revolution on the productivity cycle and productivity growth. Moreover, different national policy approaches that may appear to be confrontational from some perspectives may well be easier to understand and coordinate if they are understood in the market-indicative-network context.

For example, neither the hierarchical planning model of the state nor the decentralized decision processes implied by a market structure seem to fit Japan.[15] Japan has often been called a "network state" or a "network society" to emphasize the mutual exchange of information among government, industry, and labor in a horizontal rather than a vertical relationship, as distinguished from a hierarchical "developmental state" model that would stress more hierarchical indicative planning.[16] The network description is appropriate because the Japanese system deemphasizes coercion and the legal enforcement of contracts and stresses consensus and inducement through reciprocation in networks of organizations designed to share information within stipulated rules.[17] In this case, planning and coordination may proceed in network structures in which government is just one of many participants.[18]

An emphasis on information flows provides important insights into the structure of national economic systems. An information perspective also permits a better understanding of the challenges nation states face in controlling economic relationships. Traditional schemes for classifying economic systems stress the role of government and property ownership, so network systems, which emphasize information rights and view government as one of many actors linked by horizontal information flows, do not emerge as an important category. An emphasis on patterns of information exchange, however, unlocks important new relationships.

In the information age, standardized information flows easily across national borders through organizational networks. But differences in economic systems still matter because of important distinctions in the way less standardized forms of information pass among institutions. As we shall see, those differences have important implications for patterns of innovation and productivity growth. The following discussion of the interaction of factor creation, competitive advantage, and innovation in the productivity cycle draws on the distinctions between market, indicative, and network systems.

FACTOR CREATION

As Figure 2–1 illustrates, national attributes in general and the orientation of the economic system along market, indicative, or network lines in particular have important impacts on the interrelated elements of factor creation, innovation, and the industry structure of competitive advantage that are linked in the productivity cycle. Labor productivity depends on labor skills, the quantity and quality of capital workers can use, the technology available for combining capital and labor inputs in production, and managerial skill in coordinating the entire process. A country's labor, capital, technology, and managerial skills will determine relative costs of production compared with firms in other countries and establish the relative competitive advantage of firms in each industry. Firms exist as part of a value chain of suppliers, producers, and providers of customer services, so competitive advantage is more accurately seen as the advantage of a value chain in one country over the value chain in another. By influencing the processes of factor creation, innovation, and the formation of value chains in different industries, national attributes and economic systems have a strong impact on the industry structure of competitive advantage and productivity growth.

Traditional theories of economic specialization and trade stress the importance of national endowments of labor, capital, and natural resources in determining the industries in which a country would have a comparative advantage. "Comparative advantage" refers to national cost advantages at the industry level, while "competitive advantage" refers to additional "firm-specific" advantages that make some firms or groups of firms within the industry lower-cost or higher-quality producers than others.[19]

The Heckscher-Ohlin-Samuelson theory, for example, argues that the relative abundance of natural resources in each country would lead to specialization in industries that used the abundant factors most intensively. As a result, the United States with relatively abundant capital would be expected to export capital-intensive steel, while labor-abundant India would export labor-intensive textiles. Over time, if countries were able to save from current income and invest in new capital, capital abundance would increase and comparative advantage would shift into more capital-intensive industries. This model would explain the U.S. shift from heavy manufacturing into more capital-intensive aircraft production, the Japanese shift from light manufacturing to cars, the newly industrialized countries' (NIC) movement from textiles to light manufacturing, and the specialization of countries with less capital abundance in textiles. Attempts to quantify the Heckscher-Ohlin-Samuelson hypotheses have produced some paradoxical findings, including Wassily Leontief's conclusion that the capital-abundant United States seemed to import capital-intensive goods, but most of the paradoxes can be resolved by recognizing the existence of different types of capital and labor with various skill levels. When those adjustments are made, the model continues to explain patterns of interindustry trade and specialization in standardized products quite well.[20]

The factor endowment model does not work as well in describing intraindustry trade in which differentiated products, such as competing brands and models of automobiles, are both imports and exports between two countries. When the European Community was established in 1957 and internal tariff barriers among the members were reduced, economists following the factor endowments model anticipated that industries would tend to concentrate in different countries, with heavier industry shifting toward capital-abundant Germany. In fact, trade volume expanded sharply, but much of the increase was in intraindustry trade, with countries exchanging similar, but differentiated goods. Volkswagen sales to France and Italy increased, but so did Simca and Fiat sales to Germany. Apparently, groups of consumers in each country preferred the style, reputation, or performance characteristics of the other country's cars. In addition, by concentrating production on particular models, each country could exploit economies of scale that lowered unit costs. Factor endowments still determined the general industrial structure of comparative advantage, but tastes and scale economies determined patterns of specialization within each industry. Trade among countries with similar factor endowments would understandably be dominated by those patterns of intraindustry specialization.[21]

An increasing percentage of international trade is in intraindustry trade in differentiated goods, where basic resources are less important determinants of cost than sophisticated skills, advanced technologies, and scale economies. Indeed, the concept of trade among nations in end items may have limited relevance in modern markets, where firms in different countries specialize in phases of production rather than in specific final products. The pattern of multinational firms and global input-output networks acquiring resources, producing, and selling in many countries, with constant adjustments to changes in cost factors, has produced a globalization of activity. As global markets and networks become more efficient at moving natural resources, capital, and basic technologies across national borders, cost advantages must be determined by factors that are not easily moved, so high productivity levels depend on production advantages that are hard to replicate elsewhere. Advantages in high-productivity industries depend on labor skills, infrastructure, and sophisticated technologies that are unique to particular locations.

As a result of increased global mobility of basic factors of production, there is a hierarchy of sources of competitive advantage, with low labor or raw-material costs at the bottom, scale economies from sources available to competitors near the bottom, and proprietary access to technology, brand names, customer relationships, and costs to customers of changing suppliers near the top. These more sustainable sources typically require specialized personnel skills, close relationships with customers, an accumulation of physical facilities tailored to key processes, and experience gleaned from experimentation in research, production, and marketing techniques. In short, the factors most critical to competitive success in integrated global markets are created, not inherited.[22]

The idea of factor creation through investment, education, and technological change has always been central to models of economic growth. More recent studies, however, emphasize the kind of factor creation required to gain competitive advantage in high-value industries in the face of global factor mobility. Basic factors of production that are either endowed or the result of very modest investment and general factors that can be used in a wide variety of industries are less likely to yield sustainable competitive advantage because they can be easily replicated elsewhere. On the other hand, advanced factors that require sophisticated training and infrastructure and specialized factors that can be used in a narrow range of industries or just one application are not easily recreated or moved, so they provide the building blocks for longer-term competitive advantage in high-productivity sectors.[23]

In a market system, government is in a weak position to guide the processes of advanced and specialized factor creation, because it does not have the close ties with industry needed to obtain information and make timely decisions in the face of rapid shifts in technologies and market demand. Market decisions have the advantage of permitting decentralized responses to shifting conditions by those with direct information on specific industries and strong incentives for efficiency, but they may suffer from a limited ability to coordinate simultaneous actions in several sectors or to provide infrastructure at an efficient scale. In an indicative system, the hierarchical processes for coordination between government and industry are in place, but there is a risk that bureaucratic incentives might not always focus on efficiency or that bureaucratic layers can distort information flows. In a network system, coordination across different parts of the value chain is simplified and there are long-term incentives to cooperate in establishing the required education, training, and research infrastructures needed to sustain competitive advantage. As a result, differences in national economic systems influence the types of industry in which firms are more likely to gain competitive advantage.

Markets are very efficient in passing standardized information and delivering standardized products, but they are somewhat less efficient in handling the specialized kinds of information needed to coordinate the production of sophisticated differentiated products. Global organizational networks have evolved to provide precisely that kind of information exchange, needed for more complete integration of research and production. Countries like Japan, with sophisticated national research and input-output networks, have been very successful in using those same approaches in global organizational networks.

INDUSTRY STRUCTURE OF COMPETITIVE ADVANTAGE

In a global trading system, national characteristics might be expected to have a limited impact on the nature of the industries that successfully meet foreign competition, because free flows of capital, labor, and technology would overcome distinctions among national systems. Porter's data on 10 nations and over 100 industries suggest, however, that leaders in industries and niches within industries are often regionally concentrated in a small number of countries, and they retain leadership for long periods of time. Specific regions or nations persist as the home bases for leading firms because competitive advantages arise from two sources, those growing out of unique benefits provided by location and those that arise from the global integration and coordination of activities. Global advantages emanate from high-value activities in the home base where the firm sets its strategy, develops its core products and process technologies, and sustains its most sophisticated production. In short, the home base provides the core activities of the global firm, which are then brokered into broader advantages through global networks.[24]

Home-base advantages in particular industries arise from four critical, interactive attributes that Porter calls the "national diamond": factor conditions, demand conditions, related and supporting industries, and firm strategy, structure, and rivalry.[25] These conditions determine the external economies of scale for a given industry and the pressure that is placed on firms to develop creative solutions that lead to competitive advantage. For example, insurance firms operating in Hartford, Connecticut, gain home-base advantages from the development of specialized labor skills and a sophisticated computer network infrastructure; from an informed, demanding set of individual and corporate customers who have needs similar to those that develop in international markets; from the development of a set of supporting sales networks, brokerage firms, and banks; and from local competition that drives firms to a level of efficiency high enough to meet global challenges. These factor, demand, supporting firm, and competition conditions are not easily replicated in other locations, and they make Hartford an important, persisting hub in global insurance networks. Competitive advantage develops through clusters of supporting industries forming local input-output networks that can persist in the face of global competition.

Sustainable home-base advantages, then, lie not in the exploitation of static advantages that spring from endowments, but from dynamic forces that give an industry the ability to adapt quickly to new circumstances and to build on external economies of scale and scope. Competitive pressure sustains innovation and factor creation, so home bases that promote competitive adjustment, whether it be through market pressure, indicative guidance, or network coordination, attract high-value activities in global networks. Successful government intervention in this process depends on promoting adjustment to competitive pressure, not on shielding industry from global competition, because persisting home-base advantages rely on innovation and specialized investment in a continuing search for higher-order advantages. Firms in the industry are far more likely to understand the required dynamic adjustments than government agencies, so government is in a weak position to guide the innovation process or to provide the advanced and specialized factors needed for successful competition in sophisticated industries with differentiated products. Government assistance in the provision of generic technologies or basic infrastructure may be useful, but those factors are less critical to the development or maintenance of home-base advantages in high-value industries.

On the other hand, there may be a strategic role for government in providing early assistance to firms in industries with significant external economies of scale or scope, where cost reductions arise from expanding levels of output or coordination of related activities within an industry. The assistance would have to be in a form that phased out over time, so that competitive pressure, not government largess, would ultimately guide development. The logic behind such intervention would be that the initial location of an activity may be a chance historical event, but subsequent developments are then path-dependent, with strong pressures for related activities to grow in the same area. This suggests a potential role for government in nurturing the early development of particular industries and then standing back and letting the dynamics of external economies of scale and scope take over in sustaining home-base advantages. The problems would lie in selecting industries that had such external economies, in phasing out support, and in potential retaliation from other governments in support of their own firms.

Consider the subsidies provided to the Airbus Industrie consortium by European governments. Suppose that both Boeing and Airbus are considering entry into a new aircraft market in which demand is limited, and that Boeing is the most efficient producer. There are economies of scale in production, so costs per unit decline as more planes are produced. Based on anticipated airline demand, only one producer would be able to make a profit at estimated future prices and output levels. Government subsidies permit Airbus to take a risk and enter the market first on the hope that Boeing will be deterred from entering.[26] If Boeing is deterred, Airbus gains the market and reaps the additional benefits from the development of supporting industries that give it advantages in future competition. If Boeing is not deterred, both Boeing and Airbus will lose, but Airbus will still get some external economies as European aircraft production expands. If the subsidies last long enough and there are significant external economies of scale and scope, the gamble may ultimately pay off.

Strategic trade theorists have shown that in many market circumstances where there are opposing monopolies or oligopolies in different countries or regions, subsidies or taxes can be used to increase the profits of the home industry by more than the subsidy or tax. For example, if the subsidy causes the home oligopolistic firms to expand production, and that leads the foreign oligopolistic firms to cut back on production, profits for the home firms might expand.[27] The success of most strategic trade actions, however, depends on detailed information on cost structures and on accurate predictions of the nature of the opponent's response, information that may not be available in practice. Moreover, even when all the required information is available, there is little evidence that the gains from strategic trade policies are worth the effort. In fact, Elhanan Helpman and Paul Krugman, two of the most prolific writers on strategic trade theory, conclude that there is no evidence of large gains in the industries they have examined.[28]

In sum, the industry structure of competitive advantage depends on the interaction of a number of factors that give the industry home-base advantages in a particular location. Many of those factors are external to the decisions of individual firms, relying on patterns of concentration that develop from the availability of advanced and specialized factors of production and from the simultaneous development of supporting industries. In that sense, firms compete as part of extended value chains that often take the form of integrated input-output organizational networks.

Because external economies of scale and scope are important in determining location advantages, government has a potential role in trying to influence those advantages and capture high-value activities in global networks. Indicative systems may have advantages in generating support for private corporations in exploiting those external economies. Government, however, may be in a weak position to provide the kinds of specialized and advanced factors needed in particular industries. Moreover, strategic trade programs that potentially might be effective require more information than is usually available and promise less help than might be anticipated. Network systems may have significant advantages in coordinating actions to exploit economies of scale without relying on the more hierarchical intervention of indicative systems, because networks can respond more quickly to new information and integrate planning and investment without the level of direct government intervention that might trigger retaliation.

INNOVATION NETWORKS

Competitive advantage in high-value industries depends on the ability to use home-base advantages in responding to pressure for greater efficiency in global markets. Low costs of basic factors are less important sources of competitive advantage in high-value industries than the patterns of innovation driven by environmental conditions and national attributes, which are hard to replicate elsewhere. Innovation occurs in the context of integrated input-output networks that link elements of the value chain, so innovations that enhance the creation of advanced and specialized factors, improve coordination with supporting firms, respond to shifting demand conditions that anticipate global patterns, and adjust to competitive pressures from rivals are more likely to contribute to sustained competitive advantage.

Innovation concerns the development and dissemination of information on improved technologies and better ways of coordinating processes throughout the value chain, so it has technological, organizational, and network dimensions. The technological dimension includes generic knowledge about how processes work, ways of dealing with current constraints, and techniques for handling typical problems, as well as more specific techniques, or artifacts, that provide the know-how for applying generic knowledge in particular circumstances to achieve desired results.[29]

The second dimension concerns techniques for the efficient application of technology in different organizational contexts. Finally, the network dimension addresses the ability to coordinate technical and organizational information in ways that improve the performance of the entire value chain. In this view, innovation takes place across a spectrum of interrelated activities, including scientific inquiry, technical invention, investment, process modification, organizational design, finance, product refinement, marketing, and after-sales services, in a sequence extending from activities in research institutions through the production process to interaction with consumers. R&D expenditures include outlays to improve all those activities, particularly the development of new products and the refinement of production processes.

R&D outlays, then, are one way of measuring formal efforts to improve productivity through innovation.[30] The correlations between R&D expenditures, subsequent innovation, and ultimate productivity improvement, however, are often difficult to establish because the linkages can have long lead times, particularly in the case of scientific research or technical invention, and the benefits accrue both to processes within an enterprise and products delivered to others. If the innovation increases the quality or performance of the product, and the innovating firm does not have the market power to capture all those benefits in higher prices, the price of the product will not reflect the full social benefit of the R&D. Because these benefits escape measurement in national income accounts, these measures understate R&D contributions.[31]

If the product is itself an input to another production process, the ultimate impact of the R&D will spill over across a range of industries.[32] While data on R&D outlays conducted in various industries are directly available from surveys, evidence on the ultimate distribution of benefits must be deduced from estimates of interindustry flows. The available evidence for the U.S. economy, corrected for interindustry flows, does suggest that basic research and private sector R&D are strongly correlated with ultimate productivity growth, although the yields from federally financed R&D may be somewhat lower.[33] Some studies have found that the direct returns to firms pursuing R&D, not counting spillover benefits to other firms, may be as high as 30 percent, and others estimate that the total return including spillovers may be twice as high.[34] Innovation, then, springs from the interrelated activities of a variety of organizations in complex patterns, including product changes and process refinements, which are ultimately reflected in measured productivity growth.

Technology is a "nonrival" good in that the use by one user does not physically preclude use by another. It is "partially excludable" because it is often difficult for the inventor to force users to pay for the privilege and to exclude those who do not contribute. Excludability includes both legal issues concerning intellectual property rights and physical issues that determine the difficulty of preventing access and hence the ability to enforce rights.[35] As a result, technology markets suffer from market failure because market prices cannot be used to fully capture the benefits that accrue to users.

In some cases the innovations flowing from R&D outlays may be appropriated, or captured, by the firm through patents or "first-mover" advantages, but in other instances patent protection may not be available, and there may be few sustainable advantages from being first.[36] If R&D benefits cannot be appropriated, there may be insufficient motivation for firms to finance R&D efforts. This potential failure of the market to provide an optimal level of R&D creates an incentive for government to intervene and encourage additional R&D spending.

The problem of appropriability also suggests that some market structures, like monopolies, may be more conducive to R&D expenditures because there are no rivals to capture the benefits. Appropriability considerations led Schumpeter to argue that an existing monopoly position could be a stimulus to innovation, defying the conventional view that competition provided the best incentive because those who failed to innovate would risk bankruptcy.[37] There is some evidence that greater market concentration increases R&D levels in sectors with slow rates of technological change, because solid profit positions may be needed to risk large R&D outlays on marginal improvements. In fields with more rapid technological changes, however, there is little evidence to suggest that greater market concentration increases R&D.[38]

In fact, in many cases greater market rivalry appears to increase the pace of R&D outlays. The more urgent the project, the greater the anticipated stream of future benefits, and the larger the first-mover advantages over rivals, the faster the pace of R&D is apt to be.[39] As a result, the structure of competition has an important impact on patterns of R&D, innovation, and the industry structure of competitive advantage. The more dynamic the technology involved, the more important market rivalry is apt to be in promoting higher R&D and more rapid innovation. The nature of the economic system—market, indicative, or network—influences the pattern of appropriability, the form of competition, and hence the interaction of different institutions in innovative processes.

The organizations involved in innovation in each country, including research universities and institutes, government laboratories, and private corporations, are linked in innovation networks. The term "network" once again refers to the emphasis on the continuous exchange of information among these organizations. Relationships in the network are horizontal rather than hierarchical and more informal than contractual in order to facilitate information flows. Contracts are, of course, written for some specific exchanges among these organizations. The essence of the relationships, however, is not the delivery of a single information package, but the continuing exchange of information over extended periods.

Figure 4-2 illustrates the relationships among public and nonprofit research institutions, private corporations, and public technology policies within the U.S. innovation network. Research universities, nonprofit research institutes, and government laboratories typically work at the basic, or "pure," research end of the innovation spectrum developing scientific knowledge. In the United States, over 80 percent of basic research is financed by these public institutions, whose comparative advantage is in the development of generic, generalized information rather than the application of those ideas to process technologies, because processes must respond to market forces and to practical insights obtained in production itself. Although many large corporate laboratories are involved in basic scientific

Figure 4-2
Innovation Networks

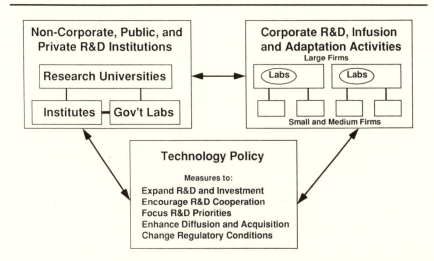

research, the corporate sector in general is more adept at applying scientific knowledge and generic technological information to specific product inventions or new processes. In the United States, industry finances roughly half of applied research and about 56 percent of product and process development. These estimates apply only to formal R&D expenditures and do not capture the substantial "learning-by-using" and adaptation activities by firms that are more difficult to measure.[40]

Table 4-1 shows that the channels for funding R&D differ significantly across leading economies. In the networked Japanese economy, the private business sector generates over 70 percent of all R&D funding. In the indicative French economy, government generates almost half of national R&D finance, with over 40 percent of the government R&D budget going to defense and space programs. The large government share in the U.S. economy has traditionally focused on defense as well, and in 1991 defense and space accounted for almost 70 percent of government R&D outlays. In Germany, defense and space R&D accounted for less than 20 percent of government R&D spending in 1990, and government itself financed less than a third of total national R&D.[41]

Although the financial channels for R&D differ substantially as a result of different emphasis on defense and alternative market, indicative, and network approaches to coordination, Table 4-2 shows that the actual pattern of research performed across different types of organizations is quite similar. German, U.K., and U.S. patterns are virtually identical, with roughly 70 percent of R&D performed by business enterprises, 15 percent

Table 4-1
National Comparisons of Sources of Finance for R&D, 1990 (percent of gross domestic expenditure on R&D) (Reprinted with permission from OECD.)

| | Source of Finance | | | |
Country	Business Enterprise	Government	Other National	From Abroad
France[a]	43.9	48.1	.6	7.4
Germany	65.5	32.5	.6	1.5
Japan[a]	72.3	18.6	9.0	.1
United Kingdom[a]	50.4	36.5	3.2	9.9
United States	49.5	48.2	2.3	.0

Source: Organization for Economic Cooperation and Development, *Main Science and Technology Indicators, 1991,* No. 2 (Paris, 1992), Tables 13–16, pp. 22–23.

Note:
a. 1989.

by research universities, and 13 percent in government laboratories. The indicative French system relies somewhat more on government R&D and less on private business enterprises, and the Japanese system uses university R&D slightly more and government laboratories a bit less than the

Table 4-2
Comparisons of National R&D Expenditures Performed by Different Organizations, 1990 (percent of gross domestic expenditure on R&D) (Reprinted with permission from OECD.)

| | Type of Organization | | | |
Country	Business Enterprise	Higher Education	Government	Non-Profit
France	61.6	14.3	23.3	.8
Germany	73.5	13.9	12.0	.5
Japan[a]	69.7	18.0	8.1	4.2
United Kingdom[a]	65.9	15.4	14.5	.2
United States	69.1	15.6	12.4	2.9

Source: Organization for Economic Cooperation and Development, *Main Science and Technology Indicators, 1991,* No. 2 (Paris, 1992), Tables 17–20, pp. 24–25.

Note:
a. 1989.

others. Despite these minor differences, the actual conduct of R&D is far more similar than the sources of finance.

R&D in the private sector is dominated by firms in which research is related to other activities such as manufacturing or marketing that draw on the research results, rather than by firms that specialize in research alone. This linkage is particularly important in exploiting the firm's experience with the problem and in focusing R&D on unique firm strategies and core competencies. The levels and composition of research spending and patterns of searching for improvements tend to follow established routines in different firms in order to reduce the extraordinary levels of uncertainty in research activities. Institutional traits both in arrangements within the firm and in interaction with other firms, universities, and so forth are an important determinant of innovation success.[42] The key role of experience and institutional arrangements in developing innovations has an important consequence. Those factors limit the ease with which innovative techniques or innovations themselves can be imitated by or communicated with other organizations.

A more detailed examination of the large share of national R&D conducted by business enterprises shows important distinctions between the activities of small- and medium-sized firms and R&D programs in large firms. Smaller firms are typically less willing and able to finance large laboratory operations because of the scale required for efficient operations and the high risks of individual research projects. They may, however, develop niche competencies in isolated technologies, particularly those that exploit new scientific discoveries. Larger corporations play a key role in the incremental development and integration of technologies. They have the production facilities, access to finance, and marketing capabilities often required to exploit new innovations.

Recent studies indicate that small firms with their flexibility and large firms with their scale economies have been more innovative than medium-sized firms, and that large and small firms are entering more network agreements to exploit their different competitive advantages.[43] Figure 4-2 reflects this relationship by depicting R&D network ties between larger and smaller firms. The ratio of R&D expenditures to sales does not seem to depend on the size of the enterprise. Despite Schumpeter's conjectures that large firms would be more active researchers and innovators than small firms, there is little evidence to suggest that the ratio of R&D to sales varies by firm size or that large firms are more successful in generating more innovations per R&D dollar.[44]

The innovation network patterns of interaction among research universities, research institutes, government laboratories, and large, medium, and small firms differ across nations and help to create local conditions that favor competitive advantage in particular industries. On the other hand, all these organizations are also linked in global research, input-output, finance, and policy networks that work to break down regional distinctions. An exploration of those competing pressures requires a more detailed discussion of innovation, technological trajectories, strategic technologies, and national innovation patterns.

Innovation

Innovation includes the discovery of technological, organizational, and network improvements; the diffusion of the new information; and the adaptation of the information to unique settings. This Schumpeterian approach to innovation as the commercial exploitation of new approaches is far more relevant to understanding productivity change than a narrower emphasis on invention as a technical insight.[45] For example, when Britain spurted away from its competitors and opened a technological gap in the first industrial revolution, its success was due not only to breakthroughs in science and inventions in the textile and iron industries, but also to new ways of organizing, financing, and marketing that merged discovery with entrepreneurship. When Germany and the United States subsequently closed the gap, a key breakthrough in each country was to establish special R&D departments within the corporation and to hire graduate scientists and engineers, not only for research and design, but also for a wide range of management, marketing, and production functions.[46] The vertically integrated U.S. and German firms were more efficient in diffusing new innovations than their British counterparts.[47] In each case, innovation in organization and interconnection were as important as technological discovery in making new products and processes commercial successes. Technical invention, commercially oriented innovation, and investment to create the advanced and specialized factors needed to implement the innovation all interact to produce sustained advances in productivity.

Because technological knowledge deals with products and processes rather than abstract principles, the value of that knowledge is determined in organizational and network contexts. Innovations that make the entire value chain more efficient and respond to shifting market trends will have the greatest impact on sustainable competitive advantage. The result of innovation is a flow of new or better products, services, and processes that meet market tests for efficiency. The true test for innovation, then, is not the novelty of the approach or the complexity of technology but the commercial applicability of the breakthrough, and that means innovation that meets global standards.

Wherever it may occur, innovation involves the discovery or creation of a new solution that could not be deduced through the routine application of an established algorithm. In technological innovation, the problem solver applies scientific principles to a material technology, drawing on an accumulated knowledge base that includes both "public" and "tacit" dimensions. Public knowledge, easily captured as information, is readily available to all potential problem solvers, but tacit knowledge is typically ill-defined, unpublished, and easily shared only with those who have had common experiences.[48]

Scientific knowledge produces the premises, theorems, and principles (summarized in equations, experimental results, and blueprints) that lie behind technologies. But while scientific theories can be captured with precision and clearly stated in standardized notations, technologies have other tacit aspects that are more difficult to communicate. Technological knowledge is often obtained through the learning curve of experience that makes processes more efficient and lowers costs as production expands. That experience, captured in the accumulated skills and insights of workers and institutions, provides an external benefit for all local firms in the same or related industry.[49] Because innovation can provide benefits that are not easily transferable, it becomes a basis for the industry structure of competitive advantage.

The technological innovation process normally follows an established pattern of solution or technological paradigm. The paradigm involves the development or refinement of a model of technical relationships following existing prototypes, scientific principles, established search techniques, and an economic context. As a result of the persistence of dominant technological paradigms, technological innovation typically follows a trajectory in which new breakthroughs proceed in a sequential pattern determined by earlier discoveries.[50] As Giovanni Dosi has suggested, the semiconductor is a technological paradigm that draws on advances in solid-state physics, chip manufacturing and testing knowledge, and programming logic. The patterns of innovative search within this paradigm focus on submicron electronic flows, improvements in hardware for miniaturized engraving on chips, and advances in programming logic. The semiconductor paradigm replaced an active electrical components paradigm in which heat loss was a major factor in the technological trajectory and launched a new trajectory centered on miniaturization. A shift in the technological paradigm changes the relevant constraints and launches a whole new technological trajectory.[51]

Technologies follow their own trajectories, which become path-dependent because of the impact of external effects on subsequent patterns of competitive advantage. In other words, prior success in a technology creates patterns of specialization that make future success more probable. Some of the new technologies may be "strategic" in the sense that they have a broad impact on a range of products and processes and have a transforming impact on innovation patterns. Institutions grow around new technologies and mature with them, creating distinct national approaches to innovation that change slowly over time.

Technological Trajectories

Technological innovation has been the driving force behind capitalism, with new approaches—embodied in physical capital, techniques, and organizations—creating whole new industries and destroying old industries in a dynamic process Schumpeter described as "creative destruction."[52] Technological trajectories typically pass through five stages from their launch at creation through replacement by other technologies in their ultimate destruction. Although the stages overlap, they can be divided for discussion purposes into the processes of discovery, experimentation, competition, standardization, and diffusion.

Discovery involves the germination of the initial concept through the development of commercially feasible prototypes. The experimentation stage includes trial and error to determine the best forms, processes, and organizational structure to capture the benefits of the innovation. In the competition stage, the experimental versions of the innovation face market tests of quality and efficiency as production levels expand. The surviving products, processes, and organizational designs then become the standard for broad diffusion of the innovation. As the number of competing versions declines, the scale of production increases even further, and efficiency in producing the standard design becomes the dominant market test. Incremental improvement and process refinement replaces the rapid change of earlier stages as standardization and diffusion reduce profits to normal levels, until a new innovation develops to start the process over again.[53] If these ideas are applied to computer technologies, voice-interactive computers are arguably at the discovery stage, computer-assisted design is at the experimentation stage, personal computers are at the competitive stage, and mainframe and supermini computers would be at the mature stage.[54]

Organizational adaptation tends to follow the stages of the technological trajectory. For example, canal monopolies in the United States in the early nineteenth century gave way to railroad entrepreneurs who experimented with different technical engine, car, and track designs; raised the required capital; and built railway networks that were often parallel to the old canals they ultimately dominated. The process extended over decades and proceeded in fits and starts as financial crises repeatedly interrupted the extension and integration of railway networks, but the pace of technological progress remained impressive.

Construction of the 300-mile Baltimore and Ohio Railroad in 1828 proceeded in the discovery stage, because the locomotive had not yet established itself as a feasible source of power, and only a handful of short mining roads existed.[55] The experimental stage arguably extended through the 1870s, as innovations with different roadbed construction, engine and rolling stock designs, and even track gauges proceeded, and parallel lines vied for developing markets. As late as 1870, the 33-ton American locomotive hauled 11-ton freight cars over iron rail of different gauges, with third rails and car hoists used to accommodate gauge changes.[56] In the competitive stage, in the late 1870s through the 1880s, the transcontinental lines produced truly national railway systems, most of the gauge differences were resolved, and the Vanderbilts, Fisks, Goulds, and Drews vied for financial control of large, integrated, competing rail networks. The financial consequences of the competition were often disastrous, and the banking crisis of 1893 led to a consolidation of lines to rationalize the system. By 1906, seven groups controlled over two-thirds of all mileage and over 85 percent of gross railroad earnings. In this standardization phase, the requirements for network interconnection reduced the number of competing systems as evolutionary improvements in design proceeded. By 1910, 72-ton articulated locomotives, like the Mallet, pulled 18-ton cars over standard-gauge steel rail on integrated national networks.[57]

Railroads passed through the five stages in different periods in different regions of the country, so it would be inappropriate to argue that the national industry passed through a single "life cycle," but each region did follow the same general trajectory. The West clearly borrowed some standardized systems from the East, but there was still considerable technological and organizational adaptation in each stage to compensate for different terrain, longer distances, and divergent market structures. As rail systems spread, they had a transforming impact on related industries and the location of economic activity. For example, the railroads simultaneously created demand for steel for tracks, engines, and cars, and enhanced access to the coal and iron needed for steel production. They also produced new, mammoth holding companies to integrate huge national rail systems. State commissions and the Interstate Commerce Commission emerged to attempt to regulate their behavior, although in practice those agencies typically worked to protect railroad interests.[58] By 1910, railways were in the diffusion stage as standard practices and incremental innovations spread quickly throughout the integrated network, and the ratio of auxiliary track to main track grew rapidly. In ensuing decades railroad dominance gave way to emerging automobile and long-haul truck competition as the process of creative destruction continued.

As a technology moves through the discovery, experimentation, competition, standardization, and diffusion stages, the appropriate organizational structures change. The small, flexible entrepreneurial enterprises that are so effective in adjusting to technological paradigm shifts in the discovery, experimentation, and early competitive stages slowly give way to larger, hierarchical structures as the logic of economies of scale, routine, and incremental adjustment takes over in the standardization and diffusion stages.[59] As a result, firms that dominate at the end of the technological trajectory may be in a poor position to launch new innovations at the beginning of the next trajectory. Established organizations can rarely as-

sume the risks of whole new ventures; abandon their large sunk costs in
people, factories, and equipment; or find ways around the rigidities of bu-
reaucracies designed for routine tasks. New entrepreneurial organizations
typically emerge to launch new technologies.[60]

Recent analyses have altered this traditional picture of technology trajectories in two important, and apparently contradictory, ways. First, global
networks have arguably reduced the sequential logic of a trajectory, because information flows permit firms in one region to bypass stages followed in other regions. This borrowing of technology from advanced areas
has always been possible, and Chapter 2 argued that such technological
transfer was a major contributor to convergence in economic performance
among the three most developed regions. Global research and input-output
organizational networks have shortened that process, however, and made
coordination at each stage more feasible.

More importantly, each type of activity can proceed simultaneously in
specialized organizations within the global organizational network. Activities in different locations can be tailored to perform the functions required
at different stages of a technology's trajectory. As a result, it is no longer
necessary for the enterprise to participate in each stage of a technology's
development. The firm can jump in and out at different levels, or pass
activities to other organizations within the network.[61] If these functions
can be segmented, and participation at one stage is not essential for participation at the next stage, regions would be freed from the logic of their
major technological trajectories and the integration of global networks
would dominate advantages of experience and infrastructure embedded in
particular locations.

Second, however, technological trajectories also reflect factors of tacit
knowledge, institutional routine, locational externalities, and differences in
economic systems that are independent of the universal, generic, and public knowledge that pass easily through organizational networks. Instead,
external economies of scale and scope and learning experience create path-
dependent processes in which future options grow out of prior R&D and
production decisions.[62] In the early stages of a technology's trajectory,
many alternative designs or approaches contend for primacy. QWERTY
keyboard designs competed with other layouts, wide- and narrow-gauge
track coexisted, and Betamax and VHS formats confronted each other in
the VCR market. To some extent, the winning configurations—QWERTY
keyboards, wide-gauge track, and VHS formats in the United States—reflected early decisions driven by unique local conditions. Once a configuration has become entrenched, new alternatives must be very attractive to
convince firms to abandon sunk costs and take new risks.

The technological bets and the resulting innovations follow from past
patterns of R&D experience and the needs of the national community to

which the technology is applied. Subsequent standardization and diffusion provide sustained advantages for those who developed the early lead, because those who pioneered the winning configurations could benefit from external economies of scale and scope as the industry expanded and similar functions could be coordinated across firms. The spillovers from one sector to another then create clusters of technologies that give a region advantages over other locations. In other words, the structure of the local value chain is driven by unique locational factors that influence the evolution of technological trajectories.[63]

Path dependencies that constrain technological trajectories and global organizational networks that break down some of those dependencies offset each other, but they apply with different force to various technologies and regions. When public technical aspects dominate competitive advantage, global networks do make sequential progress through the stages of technological trajectories less important in determining new choices. On the other hand, when externalities and the importance of tacit knowledge create significant path dependencies and competitive advantage is embodied in unique skills and institutions, differences in national innovation patterns can still have a strong impact on the industry structure of competitive advantage.

The global network and national approaches to innovation have sharply different policy implications that come to a head in arguments concerning "strategic" technologies that may have important consequences for regional development. If these technologies are path-dependent, they might be captured by policies that influence their trajectories, particularly in the early stages before standardization occurs. On the other hand, if they are dominated by technical factors that can be captured by global networks, local policies would be ineffective. In any case, the idea of strategic technologies dominates current policy debates.

Strategic Technologies

In an economic sense, "strategic technologies" are those that have great potential for influencing productivity growth because of their spillover impacts on technologies in other sectors or their crucial roles as inputs to a number of other key industries.[64] In the United States, railroads, the electric dynamo, and the computer would all meet both criteria: they are also network technologies that enhance interconnection and interoperability of physical networks. As global research and input-output organizational networks increase in importance, network technologies play a larger strategic role.[65] There is often, however, a long lag between the discovery and experimentation stages for such technologies and their ultimate impacts during the competitive, standardization, and diffusion stages of their technological trajectories. As a result, assessments of potential long-term productivity performance across countries must consider comparative strengths in strategic technologies as well as current productivity results.

The term "critical technologies" has a slightly different connotation, referring not only to strategic technologies with broad economic impacts, but also to those technologies that are important to particular sectors with special policy relevance. The most common usage is in the preparation of U.S. critical-technology lists of capabilities that are critical to provide for future defense, environmental, or energy requirements.[66] Chapter 5 examines the idea of critical technologies in more detail. At this point, the concept of strategic technologies is more central to the linkages between technology and productivity.

Information technologies, composite materials, and biotechnology all meet the criteria for broad potential strategic impacts. New composite materials combine high strength and low weight by embedding fibers in plastic, metal, or ceramic matrices that hold the fibers together, protect them, and distribute loads across them. Biotechnology is based on the discovery and use of the genetic mechanisms that control living organisms. In addition to the obvious medical implications, cells can be used as factories for the efficient synthesis of new materials.[67] These strategic technologies are transforming broad industrial sectors.[68]

The emergence of a new strategic technology can have dramatic impacts on national competitive advantage across a number of interrelated industries. For example, the shift in information technologies from analog to digital formats is changing the basis of competition in related industries from unique functions to price, performance, and interoperability. Electronic hardware markets are already shifting from firms with tailored systems to the producers of standardized components like semiconductors and liquid crystal displays. Digital-component producers, such as Canon and Matsushita, can more easily move downstream to new product applications than analog product producers can shift upstream to DRAM production.

Japanese mastery of component manufacturing and integrated research and input-output organizational networks provide broad advantages in a wide range of industrial applications of the new digital components. As the trajectories of information technologies shift to the standardization and diffusion stages, the early lead in components will work in Japan's favor, raising concerns that policy or industrial structure will restrict the diffusion outside of Japan of those new component technologies.[69] Those concerns underscore the importance of the question of whether global networks will disseminate strategic technologies efficiently, or differences in national innovation systems will work to capture particular technologies at different stages.[70]

National Innovation Networks

Technology policies toward innovation networks clearly differ across economic systems. Governments in market systems, as in the United States, typically focus on the macroeconomic conditions that determine the cost of capital for investment in general, on tax incentives for R&D and investment activities, on diffusion of information to small producers, and on regulations that limit collaboration between the public and private sectors and among private corporations. This general approach is more apt to encourage scientific research or generic technologies than to promote particular technologies or industries. Government intervention in these markets often develops as a spin-off of procurement, as in the defense, space, and nuclear energy programs in the United States.

In network systems, as in Japan, the emphasis is on the continuous refinement of processes and innovation to improve coordinated performance throughout the value chain.[71] Despite the emphasis given to the indicative role of MITI and the Finance Ministry in guiding the R&D process, their impact has been quite indirect since the 1960s. MITI did play a central role in guiding corporations into information technology investments in the 1970s, but MITI's role in most fields has been to facilitate coordination among firms in input-output networks that already existed. Technology policy in Japan has attempted to encourage R&D cooperation and focus R&D priorities, but the approach has become less and less directive over time.

In indicative systems, as in France, new technologies are often championed in enterprises owned or heavily subsidized by the government. Direct assistance to corporate research efforts is more consistent with general attempts to guide the economy into specific new technologies and product lines and to coordinate the development of supporting industries. In France, as in Britain, R&D efforts also flow from sophisticated military production and procurement, including nuclear systems.

In a different framework, Britain, France, and the United States have been described as "mission-oriented" countries, which seek to extend technological applications at the frontiers of scientific knowledge. On the other hand, "diffusion-oriented" countries, such as Germany, Sweden, and Switzerland, emphasize dissemination of new approaches and best industrial practices throughout their economies, with less emphasis on basic research. Finally, "producer-oriented" countries, like Japan, Korea, and Taiwan, stress a balance between cutting-edge developments in selected industries and broad dissemination of best practices through all sectors.[72] These distinctions follow from national attributes and the unique histories of the interaction between science, technology, and commercial enterprise in each country.

ECONOMIC SYSTEMS AND THE PRODUCTIVITY CYCLE

Just as global input-output networks have not eliminated home-base advantages in determining the industry structure of competitive advantage, so global research networks have not eliminated the importance of national innovation networks. Global networks are most adept at passing the generic information provided by the basic research that expands scientific knowledge. Transmitting tacit technological information, however, is more difficult because it exists in individuals and institutions more than in blueprints, and because it develops in the context of unique organizations and local input-output networks. Global research networks attempt to resolve those problems through extended coordination and institutional adaptation, but national distinctions persist because the adjustments do take time and effort. These distinctions in national innovation networks provide a potential role for technology policies in capturing the high-value activities of global networks.

The form of interaction among factor creation, competitive advantage, and innovation varies across market, indicative, and network economic systems. The requirements for coordination across the components of the value chain, for tailoring innovation to that entire value system, and for generating the advanced and specialized factors needed for effective competition in high-value markets are common to each system, but there are important distinctions in the way information is coordinated. Each system has unique characteristics that sustain competitive advantage in various industries at different stages of their development. Those system characteristics and external economies of scale and scope tend to make competitive advantage path-dependent and persistent, despite the growing importance of extensive global networks. Global networks have made advantages in the costs of basic and generalized factors or in technical, generic, and standardized forms of technology more fleeting, but they have not yet made regional differences trivial. Indeed, as the next chapter argues, regional differences in technology policies are the most likely area of conflict in emerging national strategies.

NOTES

1. See, for example, James N. Rosenau, *Turbulence in World Politics: A Theory of Change and Continuity* (Princeton, N.J.: Princeton University Press, 1990).

2. Richard L. Carson, *Comparative Economic Systems* (New York: Macmillan Publishing Co., Inc., 1973), 25–26.

3. Lester Thurow, *Head to Head: The Coming Economic Battle Among Japan, Europe, and America* (New York: William Morrow and Co., Inc., 1992), 274–277.

4. See Henry Rosovsky, *The University: An Owner's Manual* (New York:

W. W. Norton and Company, 1990), 29–36, for an argument that the United States has two-thirds to three-quarters of the world's top research universities.

5. Lewis M. Branscomb, "Does America Need a Technology Policy?" *Harvard Business Review* 70 (March-April 1992): 25.

6. Christopher Freeman, "Japan: A New National System of Innovation?" in *Technical Change and Economic Theory,* ed. Giovanni Dosi et al. (London: Francis Pinter, 1988), 335, 342.

7. Joseph A. Schumpeter, *The Theory of Economic Development* (Cambridge, Mass.: Harvard University Press, 1934).

8. For example, see Robert Gilpin, *The Political Economy of International Relations* (Princeton, N.J.: Princeton University Press, 1987), 9–10.

9. Paul R. Gregory and Robert C. Stuart, *Comparative Economic Systems,* 2nd ed. (Boston, Mass.: Houghton Mifflin Co., 1985), 13–23.

10. Ibid., Figure 1.3, p. 23.

11. Carson, *Comparative Economic Systems,* 33–40.

12. Leonid Hurwicz, "Conditions for Economic Efficiency of Centralized and Decentralized Structures," in *Value and Plan,* ed. Gregory Grossman (Berkeley, Calif.: University of California, 1960), 169–170, as cited in Carson, *Comparative Economic Systems,* 35–37.

13. Wage and price controls are forms of administered prices that inevitably suffer from such surpluses or shortages.

14. Network organizational relationships do imply some price discrimination, or at least discrimination across potential buyers based on longer-term considerations of profitability.

15. Shumpei Kumon, "Japan as a Network Society," in *The Political Economy of Japan, Volume 3: Cultural and Social Dynamics,* ed. Shumpei Kumon and Henry Rosovsky (Stanford, Calif.: Stanford University Press, 1992), 110.

16. Ibid., 110–111. Chalmers Johnson proposes the alternative developmental state model in *MITI and the Japanese Miracle: The Growth of Industrialized Policy, 1925–1975* (Stanford, Calif.: Stanford University Press, 1982).

17. Kumon, "Japan as a Network Society," 124, 133, 134.

18. See Jeffrey Hart, *Rival Capitalists: International Competitiveness in the United States, Japan, and Western Europe* (Ithaca, N.Y.: Cornell University Press, 1992). He argues that Japan and Germany outperformed the United States and Britain in the last two decades in the steel, automobile, and semiconductor industries because their state-societal relationships stressed linkages across government, business, and labor that were superior in creating and diffusing new technologies.

19. For a more complete development of this point, see Kamal Abd-el-Rahman, "Firms' Competitive and National Comparative Advantages as Joint Determinants of Trade Composition," *Weltwirtschaftliches Archiv* 127, No. 1 (1991): 83–97.

20. Edward E. Leamer, *Sources of International Comparative Advantage: Theory and Evidence* (Cambridge, Mass.: MIT Press, 1984), 87.

21. For example, see Abd-el-Rahman, "Firms' Competitive and National Comparative Advantages as Joint Determinants of Trade Composition," 90. Also, see Bela Belassa, "Intra-Industry Specialization: A Cross-Country Analysis," *European Economic Review* 30 (February 1986): 27–42, for a more complete analysis of EC trade patterns. See Paul Krugman, "Scale Economies, Product Differentiation, and

the Pattern of Trade," *American Economic Review,* 70 (December 1980): 950–959, for a theoretical explanation of two-way exchanges of differentiated products.

22. Michael E. Porter, *The Competitive Advantage of Nations* (New York: Free Press, 1990), 50, 74. For an application of this argument to high-technology industries and evidence on the correlation of comparative advantage to R&D outlays in those sectors, see Masaru Yoshitomi, "New Trends of Oligopolistic Competition in the Globalisation of High-Tech Industries: Interactions Among Trade, Investment and Government," in *Strategic Industries in a Global Economy: Policy Issues for the 1990s,* Organization for Economic Cooperation and Development (Paris, 1991), 22–27, 32.

23. Porter, *The Competitive Advantage of Nations,* 77–79. See also David Dollar, "Technological Differences as a Source of Comparative Advantage," *American Economic Review* 83, *Papers and Proceedings* (May 1993): 433–434. Dollar also notes the tendency for persistent comparative advantage in high-technology industries.

24. Porter, *The Competitive Advantage of Nations,* 19, 55, 60. See also Michael E. Porter, ed., *Competition in Global Industries* (Boston, Mass.: Harvard Business School Press, 1986), for a series of articles on the balance between the advantages of location and global integration.

25. Porter, *The Competitive Advantage of Nations,* 71–72.

26. For a game theoretic discussion of this Boeing-Airbus rivalry and the impact of subsidies, see Paul R. Krugman and Maurice Obstfeld, *International Economics: Theory and Practice* (New York: Harper Collins Publishers, 1991), 269–272.

27. For example, see James A. Brander and Barbara J. Spencer, "International R&D Rivalry and Industrial Strategy," *Review of Economic Studies* 163 (October 1983): 707–722, for one of the first analyses of strategic industrial policy.

28. Elhanan Helpman and Paul R. Krugman, *Trade Policy and Market Structure* (Cambridge, Mass.: MIT Press, 1989), 186.

29. Giovanni Dosi, "Technological Paradigms and Technological Trajectories," *Research Policy* 11 (1982), as cited in Richard R. Nelson, "Institutions Supporting Technical Change in the United States," in *Technical Change and Economic Theory,* ed. Dosi et al., 314–15.

30. "Endogenous growth models" stress the impact of R&D on innovation and distinguish that process from the imitation of the innovation through other forms of "ordinary" investment. See, for example, Paul Romer, "Endogenous Technological Change," *Journal of Political Economy* 98 (October 1990): S71–S102. For a critique, see Maurice F. C. Scott, "Explaining Economic Growth," *American Economic Review* 83, *Papers and Proceedings* (May 1993): 424–425. Scott argues that the distinction between R&D leading to innovation and "ordinary investment" leading to imitation is not operational.

31. Zvi Griliches, "Productivity Puzzles and R&D: Another Nonexplanation," *Journal of Economic Perspectives* 2 (Fall 1988): 18.

32. See Jacob Schmookler, *Invention and Economic Growth* (Cambridge, Mass.: Harvard University Press, 1966), for estimates from patent evidence of interindustry impacts of R&D.

33. See Frederick M. Scherer, "Interindustry Technology Flows in the United States," in *Innovation and Growth: Schumpeterian Perspectives,* ed. F. M. Scherer (Cambridge, Mass.: MIT Press, 1984), 54–57; Zvi Griliches, "Productivity, R&D

and Basic Research at the Firm Level in the 1970's," *American Economic Review* 76 (March 1986): 141–154; Griliches, "Productivity Puzzles and R&D," 13–16; and Frank R. Lichtenberg, "The Relationship Between Federal Contract R&D and Company R&D," *American Economic Review* 74, *Papers and Proceedings* (May 1984): 73–78.

34. Zvi Griliches, "Research Expenditures and Growth Accounting," in *Science and Technology in Economic Growth*, ed. B. R. Williams (London: Macmillan, 1973); Edwin Mansfield et al., "Social and Private Returns from Industrial Innovations," *Quarterly Journal of Economics* 91 (May 1977): 221–240; and F. M. Scherer, "Interindustry Technology Flows in the United States," 56, all find private returns in excess of 30 percent, and Mansfield and Scherer report social returns twice that large. See Gene M. Grossman and Elhanan Helpman, *Innovation and Growth in the Global Economy* (Cambridge, Mass.: MIT Press, 1991), 13–14, for a quick summary of those findings and the problems with estimating R&D returns.

35. Grossman and Helpman, *Innovation and Growth in the Global Economy*, 15.

36. For an excellent collection of studies on patents and innovation, see Zvi Griliches, ed., *R&D, Patents, and Productivity* (Chicago, Ill.: University of Chicago Press, 1984).

37. Joseph Schumpeter, *Capitalism, Socialism, and Democracy* (New York: Harper & Row, 1942), 110.

38. F. M. Scherer, "Concentration, R&D, and Productivity Change," in Scherer, *Innovation and Growth*, 253–254.

39. For pioneering studies of this tradeoff between timing and cost, see Morton J. Peck and F. M. Scherer, *The Weapons Acquisition Process: An Economic Analysis* (Boston, Mass.: Harvard Business School Press, 1962); F. M. Scherer, "Research and Development Resource Allocation Under Rivalry," *Quarterly Journal of Economics* 81 (August 1967): 359–394; and William D. Nordhaus, *Invention, Growth, and Economic Welfare* (Cambridge, Mass.: MIT Press, 1969).

40. Giovanni Dosi, "Sources, Procedures, and Microeconomic Effects of Innovation," *Journal of Economic Literature* 26 (September 1988): 1123–1125.

41. Organization for Economic Cooperation and Development, *OECD Main Science and Technology Indicators, 1991*, No. 2 (Paris, 1992), Tables 38–43, pp. 35–37.

42. Dosi, "Sources, Procedures, and Microeconomic Effects of Innovation," 1134–1135.

43. For example, see Keith Pavitt, Michael Robson, and Joe Townsend, "The Size Distribution of Innovating Firms in the U.K.: 1945–1983," *Journal of Industrial Economics* 35 (March 1987): 297–319, and Helen Lawton Smith, Keith Dickson, and Stephen Lloyd Smith, " 'There are Two Sides to Every Story': Innovation and Collaboration Within Networks of Large and Small Firms," *Research Policy* 20 (October 1991): 457–468.

44. F. M. Scherer, "Corporate Size, Diversification, and Innovative Activity," in Scherer, *Innovation and Growth*, 237.

45. See F. M. Scherer, "Invention and Innovation in the Watt-Boulton Steam Engine Venture," in Scherer, *Innovation and Growth*, 8–27, for an examination of the differences between the approaches developed in Joseph A. Schumpeter, *The Theory of Economic Development* (Cambridge, Mass.: Harvard University Press,

1934), and A. P. Usher, *A History of Mechanical Inventions* (Cambridge, Mass.: Harvard University Press, 1954).

46. Freeman, "Japan: A New National System of Innovation?" 330.

47. Marvin Frankel, "Obsolescence and Technological Change in a Maturing Economy," *American Economic Review* 45 (May 1956): 94–112.

48. Dosi, "Sources, Procedures, and Microeconomic Effects of Innovation," 1126. For a more detailed discussion of tacit knowledge, see Nathan Rosenberg, *Inside the Black Box: Technology and Economics* (Cambridge: Cambridge University Press, 1982), and Richard R. Nelson, "What Is 'Commercial' and What Is 'Public' About Technology, and What Should Be," in *Technology and the Wealth of Nations,* ed. Nathan Rosenerg, Ralph Landau, and David C. Mowery (Stanford, Calif: Stanford University Press, 1992), 57–71.

49. See Patrizio Bianchi and Nicola Bellini, "Public Policies for Local Networks of Innovators," *Research Policy* 20 (October 1991): 490–491, for an excellent description of the ways in which networks exploit tacit knowledge through social relationships.

50. David J. Teece, "Technological Change and the Nature of the Firm," in *Technical Change and Economic Theory,* ed. Dosi et al. (London: Francis Pinter, 1988), 264–265.

51. Dosi, "Sources, Procedures, and Microeconomic Effects of Innovation," 1127–1130.

52. Schumpeter, *The Theory of Economic Development.*

53. Anthony P. Carnevale describes a similar sequence, which he defines as breakthrough, innovation, installation, competition, and maturity, in *America and the New Economy: How Competitive Standards are Radically Changing American Workplaces* (San Francisco, Calif.: Jossey-Bass Publishers, 1991), 75–76. See also Gian Carlo Cainarca, Massimo G. Colombo, and Sergio Mariotti, "Agreements Between Firms and the Technological Life Cycle Model: Evidence From Information Technologies," *Research Policy* 21 (February 1992): 50. They describe the stages as introduction, early development, full development, maturity, and decline.

54. Cainarca et al., "Agreements Between Firms and the Technological Life Cycle Model," 61.

55. Albert Fishlow, *American Railroads and the Transformation of the Ante-Bellum Economy* (Cambridge, Mass.: Harvard University Press, 1965), 3.

56. James R. Golden, *Investment Behavior by United States Railroads, 1870–1914* (New York: Arno Press, 1975), 14.

57. Ibid., 14, 27–29.

58. Ibid., 34. Also see Carnevale, *America and the New Economy,* 76–77.

59. See Michael Gort and Steven Klepper, "Time Paths in the Diffusion of Product Innovations," *Economic Journal* 92 (September 1982): 634. They argue that typical technological trajectories show an expansion in the number of new products and producers in their first two phases, a leveling in the third phase, and a contraction in the last two phases based on a slowing of related innovations outside the industry, reduced profit rates, and the growing importance of experience to incumbent firms.

60. Teece, "Technological Change and the Nature of the Firm," 273–275.

61. Carnevale, *America and the New Economy,* 217. Also see Elise S. Brezis, Paul R. Krugman, and Daniel Tsiddon, "Leapfrogging in International Competi-

tion: A Theory of Cycles in National Technological Leadership," *American Economic Review* 83 (December 1993): 1218. The authors argue that leading nations or regions may be slow to adopt new technologies when there are large wage differentials, the new technology appears initially less productive than the old, and experience with the old technology is not very important in implementing the new technology. If the new technology is ultimately more productive than the old, these conditions may lead to a "leapfrogging" effect with the backward region or nation surging past the old leader.

62. John Zysman, with Laura Tyson, Giovanni Dosi, and Stephen Cohen, "Trade, Technology, and National Competition," in *Technology and Investment: Crucial Issues for the 1990s*, ed. Enrico Deiaco, Erik Hornell, and Graham Vickery (London: Pinter Publishers, 1990), 187.

63. Ibid., 188–189.

64. Michael L. Dertouzos, Richard K. Lester, Robert N. Solow, and the MIT Commission on Productivity Growth, *Made in America: Regaining the Productivity Edge* (Cambridge, Mass.: MIT Press, 1989), 33.

65. See Stephen S. Cohen and John Zysman, *Manufacturing Matters: The Myth of the Post-Industrial Economy* (New York: Basic Books, Inc., 1987), 102–106, and Martin C. Libicki, *What Makes Industries Strategic* (Washington, D.C.: The Institute for National Strategic Studies, National Defense University, November 1989), 19–33.

66. Air Force Institute of Technology, *Critical Technologies for National Defense* (Washington, D. C.: American Institute of Aeronautics and Astronautics, Inc., 1991), 3–11.

67. Ibid., 13, 268.

68. See Zysman, "Trade, Technology, and National Competition," 185, for a similar assessment.

69. Charles H. Ferguson, "Computers and the Coming of the U.S. Keiretsu," *Harvard Business Review* 68 (July-August 1990): 61–62.

70. Zysman, "Trade, Technology, and National Competition," 186.

71. Ken-ichi Imai, "Japan's Corporate Networks," in *The Political Economy of Japan, Volume 3: Cultural and Social Dynamics*, ed. Kumon and Rosovsky (Stanford, Calif.: Stanford University Press), 222.

72. H. Ergas, "Global Technology and National Politics," paper prepared for U.S. Council on Foreign Relations, New York, 1989, as quoted by Zysman, "Trade, Technology, and National Competition," 206–207.

Part II   Toward a Strategy of Cooperative Competition

5 Global Networks, National Systems, and Strategic Policies

Part I considered the central role of productivity growth in determining a country's ability to meet national needs and sustain national influence; explored the pattern of convergence in the productivity performance of Japan, Europe, and the United States; and emphasized the interaction of factor creation, innovation, and the industry structure of competitive advantage in determining productivity growth through a cyclical, path-dependent process. Those elements of the productivity cycle are all linked in global input-output, finance, and R&D networks that have become more integrated as a result of the revolution in information technologies. Improvements in communication have made close coordination more possible and linkages across technologies have made coordination more important. At the same time, differences in economic systems and external economies of scale and scope make the path of technological development dependent on past events as well as the current environment. Path dependence provides opportunities for national or regional policies to influence the location of high-value activities within global networks.

Part II applies those findings in an assessment of government policies designed to achieve strategic national advantages both in sustaining high and growing levels of productivity and in reaching other national security objectives. Government interventions in complex economic systems almost always have unintended consequences, and that is particularly true in network systems where the range of potential adaptations to local policies is enormous. Global networks are shifting the competition for strategic advantages in both the commercial and defense sectors. This chapter uses a network perspective to examine the efficacy of various national policies to achieve commercial advantage, Chapter 6 explores the impetus for a new U.S. technology policy, and Chapter 7 examines the prospects for a revised U.S. military technology policy. Chapter 8 then summarizes the implications and presents an argument for a strategy of cooperative competition as an integrating framework for policies to promote productivity growth and pursue other national security objectives.

The basis of commercial policy designed to influence patterns of international trade is changing. Attempts to lower the costs of basic and general factors of production through tax preferences or trade restrictions no longer provide sustained advantages, because global networks can easily shift the location of activities that use those factors. Instead, strategic advantage in high-value activities depends on the ability to influence patterns of innovation and the creation of advanced and specialized factors—patterns and factors that are enmeshed in local institutions and the tacit knowledge of local workers. Although commercial policies can be used to influence those patterns, they are blunt instruments with unpredictable and often damaging side effects. Technology policies designed to influence domestic factor creation have greater potential for achieving subtle impacts on innovation at critical points in the trajectories of strategic technologies. As a result, technology policies have become more important, and more controversial, strategic instruments.

Technology policies designed to enhance or develop national or regional industrial advantages must rely on differences in national innovation networks to produce enduring results. As the last chapter argued, standard knowledge is easily passed through global networks, but tacit knowledge and unique local institutions can be used to capture sustained local advantages. Disputes over the relative effectiveness of various technological policies, and debates over the strategies being pursued by regional competitors, focus more and more on complex differences in economic systems and institutional structures that influence the ability to attract and sustain high-value activities, particularly high-technology industries.

In the 1980s, U.S. high-technology output increased as a share of total manufacturing production from 20 to 30 percent and as a share of GDP from 4.3 to 5.4 percent, and high-technology employment rose by 12 percent from 1972 to 1989, while manufacturing employment rose only 3 percent in the same period. At the end of that period, high-value technology jobs commanded wages that were roughly twice as high as wages in the overall private nonfarm sector.[1] The rapid pace of growth and the high wages in the high-technology sector has made it the focal point of efforts to capture high-value activities in the nodes of global networks.

As a result, the central international issues now focus more and more on policies and practices that influence factor creation, innovation, and sustainable competitive advantage. Disagreements over these policy issues pose the greatest challenge to sustaining a liberal international economic regime and the largest potential for regional economic conflict. To the extent that differences in national innovation systems create advantages that cannot be shifted through global organizational networks, those unique local conditions provide room for government policies to influence the location of high-value network activities. Differences in national systems of innovation and the relative effectiveness of various systems in dealing with new technological paradigms could provide a basis for policies designed to develop sustainable competitive advantage.

In order to explore those possibilities, this chapter defines the concept of national systems of innovation, applies the concept to an analysis of the evolution of U.S. innovation networks, and then assesses the relative advantages and disadvantages of the U.S. system in capturing technologies at various points in their trajectories. Having defined the idea of national systems and the characteristics of U.S. networks, the discussion proceeds to an examination of the relative effectiveness of alternative policies in exploiting systemic differences and developing sustainable competitive advantage in high-value industries.

That examination of policy options begins with a review of commercial policies from the perspective of the tension between globalization and localization of economic activity. The analysis concludes that commercial policy instruments are becoming less important in influencing long-term sources of competitive advantage. Next, an examination of strategic-trade policies highlights the complexity of unintended consequences from strategic- and managed-trade policies in a world of global R&D, finance, and input-output networks. An overview of the semiconductor industry in general, and DRAMs in particular, illustrates the problems of managed-trade approaches. A closing section argues that technology policies may be more effective strategic instruments than commercial policies in influencing activities within global networks.

NATIONAL INNOVATION NETWORKS

The U.S. national system of innovation is changing in the face of the wave of information technologies and the organizational adjustments required to deal with those new technological relationships. The changes open dramatic new possibilities for expanding productivity growth and new avenues for public policy, but they also challenge traditional institutional arrangements and constrain the effectiveness of traditional policy approaches. National innovation systems evolve in a path-dependent process that is tied to the impact of waves of technological development and institutional adaptation. An understanding of the national innovation systems therefore requires an appreciation for patterns of national adaptation to different types of technology. The next sections clarify the concept of national innovation systems, present a framework for examining the organizational implications of technological shifts, and show how the U.S. national innovation system has evolved in response to shifts in the underlying technological paradigms.

Systems of Innovation

In the late 1970s and 1980s, public officials in the United States and Europe became concerned with the increased competitiveness of Japanese manufacturing in general, and high-technology industry in particular. As Japanese shares of world automobile and information technologies markets grew, and Japanese trade surpluses persisted, studies of Japanese commercial, industrial, and technology policies proliferated. The OECD in Paris, with representation from the three critical regions, emerged as a clearing house for ideas on innovation policy, including the following: measures related to R&D and investment through grants or government programs, tax incentives, or measures to channel funds to higher-risk small- and medium-sized enterprises; measures related to the acquisition and diffusion of technological know-how such as education, databases, and government extension services; and measures related to general conditions of competition, including antitrust, government procurement, patents and licenses, and other regulatory policies.[2]

A group of researchers working with OECD developed the idea that innovation "systems" differed across nations as a result of not only divergent government policies, but, more importantly, different patterns of interrelationships among firms, government, and the broader national economic environment. Writers in the OECD school noted that national economies provide unique advantages for interactions between producers and users, including proximity; common language; culture; social organization; government standards, regulation, and intervention; and unique technological capabilities that result from the history and form of "national systems of innovation." These systemic differences, reinforced by the limited mobility of skilled labor, provide limitations to the international transfer of learning and technology and constrain the potential for international cooperation.[3]

The OECD studies and other work on differences in national approaches to innovation highlighted three unique analytical traditions. The U.S.-British perspective tends to view national economies as a set of fairly distinct and independent industrial sectors, while the French approach emphasizes vertical interrelationships through *filieres* linking stages of production from basic resources through ultimate products, and the Japanese stress horizontal relationships across firms that coordinate activities to obtain mutual long-term advantages.[4] These conceptual approaches follow from the distinctions among market, indicative, and network economic systems presented in Chapter 4. The national-system approaches to innovation attempt to show how these broader systemic differences translate into alternative innovation network relationships among firms, research universities, and government agencies, as portrayed in Figure 4-2.

National Innovation Systems and Technological Trajectories

Short and long cycles in economic activity have fascinated economists for some time. Swings in growth rates are driven by shifts in aggregate demand and aggregate supply, and explanations for cycles typically center on monetary factors that produce fluctuations in demand or on investment

Figure 5-1
Coupling, Complexity, Technology Types, and Organizations

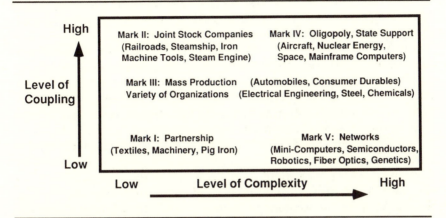

Sources: Christopher Freeman and C. Perez, "Structural Crisis of Adjustment: Business Cycles and Investment Behavior," in *Technical Change and Economic Theory*, ed. G. Dosi et al. (London: Francis Pinter, 1988), 50–53, and Herbert Kitschelt, "Industrial Governance Structures, Innovation Strategies, and the Case of Japan," *International Organization* 45 (Autumn 1991): 468–475.

Note: Approximate Time Periods—Mark I 1770–1840; II 1830–1890; III 1880–1940; IV 1930–1990; V 1980–?.

spurts that change capital stocks and hence supply. From the supply perspective, the opportunities for new investment follow technological innovation, and arguments for periodic surges in economic activity depend on factors that explain interrelated waves of discovery and diffusion. One possible explanation, promoted by Joseph Schumpeter, is that waves of innovation spread from industry to industry as a new technological paradigm is fully absorbed, and growth spurts again as a new paradigm is discovered.[5] Whether or not one supports the idea of regular economic "cycles," there is substantial evidence that groups of technologies do tend to emerge in clusters that have similar production characteristics.[6] Figure 5-1 depicts five technological clusters, or what Herbert Kitschelt calls "Marks," that emerged in different periods.[7]

As Kitschelt argues, any technology arguably has two important dimensions: "coupling" and "complexity." The extent of coupling refers to the requirement for spatial or temporal links between different production steps. If the steps must be done at the same location or at the same time, they are tightly coupled, but if they can be done in any sequence at any location, they are loosely coupled. For example, computer technologies are loosely coupled because the components can be produced separately. The complexity dimension refers to the importance of feedback among production stages that is required to keep the whole process on track. Linear systems that proceed from one stage to the next without feedback are not complex, but those that are iterative and interactive are more complex.[8] For example, computer technologies tend to be highly complex because the components interact with extensive feedback.

Kitschelt shows that complexity and coupling influence the efficiency of different governance structures in managing information flows.[9] Tight coupling requires close supervision in order to contain problems that might otherwise spread quickly to other processes, and loose coupling permits less centralized control. For example, loosely coupled computer components can be produced by decentralized, independent firms.

Complex systems produce large information requirements to manage the intricate flow of connections across processes, but large communications flows overload the capacity of centralized governance structures. As a result, complex systems favor decentralized production units coordinated through network connections. For example, standards for the components of complex, integrated computer systems must be closely coordinated to ensure compatibility in network configurations. Technological processes that are more sequential, and less interactive, have fewer information requirements and are therefore more amenable to centralized control.

Although the combination of coupling and complexity of a technology do not determine a uniquely optimal governance structure, they do constrain the efficient possibilities. Mark I technologies of the late eighteenth century such as textiles and light machine tools, with low coupling and low complexity, provided a wide range of organizational possibilities because there were few complexity constraints on centralization and few coupling advantages of larger scale. As shown in Figure 5-1, the Mark I technologies lent themselves to small firms, typically organized as partnerships, and to competitive market structures.

Mark II technologies that applied steam engines and exploited iron and steel had higher levels of coupling, producing greater economies of scale and larger capital requirements that were met by joint stock companies. Mark III technologies of the late nineteenth and early twentieth centuries with moderate coupling and complexity gave rise to a wide variety of organizational structures. Automobile and consumer-durable-good production processes were moderately complex and tightly coupled, a combination that produced large economies of scale and hence large corporations with Fordist structures. Electrical engineering and chemical processes were more complex, requiring subtle production controls, but the extent of coupling varied from close integration in chemicals, leading to large vertical organizations, to looser coupling in electrical engineering applications, fostering network configurations of medium-sized firms.

Postwar development of Mark IV nuclear systems, aircraft, space systems, and large computers involved very tight coupling and highly complex interactive processes, creating levels of scale and risk that produced various forms of government assistance and regulation. Finally, the more recent Mark V technologies, such as software, microprocessors, and genetic engineering, combine loose coupling with substantial complexity and uncertainty that are best exploited in network structures. Network organizations provide an effective structure for decentralizing production of distinct components while still ensuring effective integration.

Coupling and complexity may arise from demand as well as supply conditions. Components may be produced separately because they have unique production requirements or because consumers prefer to mix and match the components in various product designs. For example, some products—such as automobiles or lawnmowers—may have components with large minimum efficient scales of production and clusters of common demand characteristics that lead to standardized packaging. Other products may actually be loosely coupled modules—as in the components of sound systems—that can be mixed and matched to suit individual preferences. Sound-system modules are loosely coupled, but their integration into an effective system may be complex. Such loosely coupled and highly complex modular systems are typical of Mark V technologies that often lead to network configurations,which are organized around network compatibility standards permitting decentralized innovation and flexible integration.[10]

As patterns of coupling and complexity have shifted over time, so have the forms of industrial organization and the broader economic systems that are most conducive to exploiting those technologies. Different combinations of technological coupling and complexity lead to problems in defining property rights and structuring contracts that make some systems more successful than others in dealing with that technology.

Market contracts might not be able to anticipate or capture all relevant dimensions of transactions involving technologies that are tightly coupled or highly complex. In tightly coupled technologies, the value of assets depends on the way in which they are integrated with other assets, so placing separate prices on components may be difficult. In highly complex technologies, it may be difficult to anticipate all the feedbacks that must be covered in the contract.

As a result, a market system with its emphasis on clear property rights and standard contracts may be very successful in dealing with loosely coupled, noncomplex technologies where innovation can be uncoordinated, decentralized, and incremental. Under tightly coupled technological systems, however, market contracts and clearly defined property rights might break down, and there would be a tendency toward larger organizations, greater concentration, and oligopolistic market structures. With complex technologies and tight coupling, a stronger government role might be needed to deal with required coordination under high levels of uncertainty.

Chapter 4 described this pattern of government-industry interaction as an indicative system. Finally, technologies that are loosely coupled and highly complex might favor organizational network structures that are decentralized to exploit flexibility in sequence and location, but coordinated through trust and reciprocity to deal with high levels of uncertainty.[11]

Kitschelt argues that as technologies shifted from Mark I to Mark V types, the favored structure for innovation adjusted from individual inventors (Mark I), to R&D in networks of corporate laboratories (Mark II), to state planning of R&D (Mark IV), and to innovation networks and public R&D infrastructure (Mark V), with the Mark III technologies spread across different categories.[12] In terms of broader national economic systems, this would correspond to shifts from pure market (Mark I), to a market dominated by corporate oligopolies (Mark II), to a more indicative system (Mark IV), and to a network system (Mark V).

Patterns of innovation may also vary from one technological paradigm to the next. For example, the traditional "breakthrough" pattern of innovation, in which basic research in a single technology leads to a series of new products, may not be appropriate for Mark V processes where loose coupling permits easier integration across technologies. Product innovation in such technologies frequently takes the form of a more dynamic system of "technology fusion," creating new hybrids from related technologies.[13] Organizations designed for breakthrough innovation in one technological area may be poorly structured for fusion activities.

The optimal organizational structure varies from industry to industry as well as between technological waves. As a result, no one economic system is apt to position a country to exploit the frontiers of all technologies at any one point in time. As a country adjusts to each new technological wave, it will be more efficient at capturing technological systems whose organizational requirements match existing institutional capabilities.[14]

To the extent that national institutions and systems adjust to the patterns of the dominant technologies, adaptations to one cluster can produce paths of experience that shape and constrain adjustments to the next wave of technologies. As a result, national innovation networks may well differ in their ability to deal with various technologies because of the lingering impacts of earlier production patterns. These national differences provide scope for policies to exploit advantages inherited from earlier experience or to assist in promoting transitions to new institutions that are more consistent with emerging technologies.

Patterns of adaptation to technological changes influence the relationships among the components of national innovation systems and the interaction of organizations in national innovation networks. From this perspective, technological change helps to explain the structure of U.S. innovation networks and the forces that are redefining them.

U.S. Innovation Networks and the Productivity Cycle

The U.S. postwar innovation network has been centered on three institutions: the industrial research laboratory, the research university, and government agencies coordinating research programs tied primarily to defense and nuclear energy procurement. As shown in Tables 4-1 and 4-2, government and industry each provide roughly half of national R&D funding, but private firms perform an overwhelming majority of the actual R&D.[15] This system, however, was not typical of innovation patterns at the end of the nineteenth and the beginning of the twentieth centuries, but evolved in response to path-dependent adjustments to new technologies.

In the nineteenth century, growth in manufacturing productivity relied on what has been called the "American system of manufactures," which drew on the benefits of a large, protected national market to exploit advantages in transportation, agriculture, mineral extraction and refining, and the mass production of consumer goods. Innovation centered on the adaptation to the American system of European technology, facilitated by machinery imports and the immigration of skilled workers.[16] Formal research efforts, such as Thomas Edison's Menlo Park industrial laboratory in the 1870s and 1880s, were typically independent of manufacturing firms.

By the end of that century and the beginning of the twentieth, research laboratories were brought in-house, and the relative importance of stand-alone laboratories declined through the twentieth century.[17] The Sherman Antitrust Act encouraged firms to look inward for new sources of competitive advantage, and the new Mark III chemical and electrical technologies provided the economies of scale needed to exploit central research facilities. In-house laboratories dominated contracted research because they provided a means for protecting unique firm knowledge, facilitated freer exchanges of ideas than contracts permitted, and took advantage of interaction between technical, market, and manufacturing insights.[18] Corporate laboratories were clustered in regions to exploit pools of skilled workers and supporting infrastructure, including links to academic research centers in an expanding state university system. Although in the pre-1940 period, few U.S. universities were as strong as their European counterparts in scientific research, the U.S. system was very effective in training large numbers of scientists and engineers and diffusing ideas, which helped U.S. firms catch up with advanced European techniques.[19]

In the prewar period, the heart of the U.S. system of innovation was the industrial laboratory centered on adaptation and diffusion of innovations, and business funded and conducted almost 70 percent of all R&D. The emergence of Mark IV (nuclear, aircraft, space, and large computer) technologies, with their tightly coupled and complex characteristics and military relevance, and Mark V (software, microprocessors, genetic engineering) technologies, with their loose coupling and high complexity, altered the U.S. innovation system in two different ways.

First, the federal government assumed a new role as the principal funder of academic and industrial research, financing half of national R&D, primarily to support military procurement and exploit the economies of scale in Mark IV technologies. Most federal R&D funding is tied to government procurement interests through the agencies with applied missions, such as the Department of Defense, the Department of Energy, and the National Institutes of Health, rather than through the general mission of the National Science Foundation.[20]

Second, although large firms continued to dominate in Mark IV technologies, small firms played a major role in commercializing Mark V technologies, particularly in semiconductors and biotechnology. The new, small firms were able to exploit basic R&D completed by the larger firms and to tap scientific breakthroughs in a research university system that became a world leader in the postwar period.[21] Military procurement practices that channeled funds to smaller firms, an active private venture-capital market, and strict U.S. antitrust policy also worked to support the growing importance of new firms in the postwar period.[22]

As indicated in Table 5-1, the postwar trends produced a shift in the pattern of R&D funding that reflected a fundamental realignment in each set of institutions that make up the innovation network. At the research university level, the U.S. emerged from the war as the world leader in science and basic research, and funds were channeled there through federal government programs rather than local government or independent private sources. University research has been particularly important to technical advances in computer science, materials science, metallurgy, chemistry, and in some specialties in biology.[23] Business funding declined as a source of R&D at the commercial level as large firms with major research laboratories sustained their positions in Mark IV technologies, but surrendered market share to smaller firms who were very successful in exploiting commercial applications of basic research in Mark V technologies. Finally, the federal government assumed an expanded role in channeling R&D funds to areas that supported public procurement, particularly in the defense sector.

The two central trends—federal government funding to support procurement and the rising importance of new, smaller firms in commercializing innovations—may now, however, be reversing as defense budgets drop in the post-cold war period and small firms struggle to sustain the level of financing needed to meet global competition.[24] In the immediate postwar period, the commercial spin-offs of military R&D in aircraft, semiconductors, and computers were impressive, but more recently there have been fewer comparable examples, and the case for military R&D as the center-

Table 5-1
Sources of U.S. National R&D Funding, 1930–1990 (percent of national funds
to each category)

	Business	Federal Government	Other
1930–1940[a]	67	16	17
1953–1960	38	60	2
1961–1970	35	63	2
1972–1980	45	51	4
1981–1989	49	47	4

Sources: 1930–1940—National Resources Planning Board, *Research—A National Resource* (Washington, D.C.: U.S. Government Printing Office, 1942), 178, as cited in David C. Mowery, "The U.S. National Innovation System: Origins and Prospects for Change," *Research Policy* 21 (February 1992): 132; 1953–1989—National Science Foundation, *National Patterns of R&D Resources, 1989* (Washington, D.C.: 1987), as cited in Mowery, "The U.S. National Innovation System," 135.

Note:
a. Mowery gives the 1930–1940 federal funding figure a range from 12 to 20 percent over the decade. The table takes the midpoint of that range as the average and treats the other funding category as a residual. An alternative computation of the industry share of national "scientific research expenditures" for 1930 to 1940 produced an estimate of 68 percent using data from the Office of Scientific Research and Development, *Report of the Committee on Science and the Public Welfare* (Washington, D. C.: April 16, 1945) as reproduced in National Science Foundation, *Vannevar Bush: Science—the Endless Frontier* (Washington, D.C.: 1990), 86.

piece of national policy has diminished. Commercial technologies may now be more sophisticated than military requirements, with more spin-ins from civilian R&D to military applications than spin-offs in the other direction.[25] Antitrust attitudes that supported the surge in smaller firms have also weakened. For example, the 1984 National Cooperative Research Act has made it more possible to collaborate on precommercial research. Finally, small firms may find it harder to develop new technologies in the current environment. For example, the Semiconductor Chip Protection Act of 1984 helped to tighten protection for intellectual property rights, making it more difficult for small firms to adapt proprietary information.

In the face of high R&D costs, the independent industrial research laboratory is being supplemented by broader cooperation in university-corporate research ventures, research alliances with other foreign and domestic firms, and cooperative research programs sponsored by public agencies.[26] Although state and local public funding has been used to promote university-corporate collaborative R&D, public funding has been used only in exceptional cases, such as Sematech and the National Center for Manufacturing Sciences, to support private research consortia.[27] For example, the State of North Carolina established the Microelectronics Center with both public and private funds linked to research universities and Stanford University established the Center for Integrated Systems to link university research with commercial needs. The university-industry links have been strongest in basic research in computers, semiconductors, and pharmaceuticals.[28] As a result, independent efforts by small firms may be giving way to greater integration in research networks.

The shift in the structure of U.S. innovation networks reflects changes in the organizational requirements of Mark IV and Mark V technologies as they pass through different points in their technological trajectories. The postwar system was arguably best configured for the large-scale requirements of the complex and tightly coupled Mark IV technologies, where public demands claimed a large share of industry outputs. The system also had sufficient flexibility, however, to permit the innovation of new structures more conducive to the early stages of discovery and experimentation in Mark V technologies. As the Mark V technologies shift into the competitive and standardization stages, however, new R&D and input-output networks are becoming a more important component of the innovation system.

In sum, the U.S. system of innovation is adjusting to two fundamental changes. First, the shift away from cold war priorities is reducing emphasis on government funding of Mark IV technologies that are now in the standardized or mature stages of their technological trajectories. Second, the new technological paradigm of Mark V technologies has increased the relative importance of cooperative R&D and input-output networks.

GLOBALIZATION, LOCALIZATION, AND POLICY FORMULATION

The transition from the prominent position of government-supported Mark IV technologies to more diffuse Mark V technologies with their network linkages poses major policy problems for the United States. The accumulated organizational and infrastructure advantages the U.S. enjoyed in centralized, large-scale production do not necessarily translate into success in competition for high-value activities in the value chains of Mark V technologies. Strengths in basic research do not provide clear advantages in the flexible application of innovation in rapidly developing process technologies. The challenges provided by required adjustments to the new technologies, organizations, and innovation networks will not be resolved by recasting commercial policy in a more strategic role, but by combining the strengths of flexible market forces with enlightened technology policy.

Commercial Policies

Global networks have increased the level of international interaction in finance, R&D, and input-output organizational networks in ways that alter patterns of trade and pose dilemmas for commercial policies. The challenges go beyond traditional concerns over the standard fare of trade disputes over tariffs, quotas, subsidies, procurement practices, and dumping. The new, more complex issues concern the national attributes, the nature of the economic system, interaction of the components of the productivity cycle, and specific government policies that determine the industry structure of competitive advantage and influence relative productivity growth. In a sense, then, the struggle for competitive advantage in high-value industries—the competition for network nodes—is itself a competition among complex economic systems in general, and among alternative innovation networks in particular, and their ability to adapt to new technological relationships and new global linkages.[29]

The traditional GATT system—founded on the principles of reciprocity, nondiscrimination, and transparency—is poorly equipped to handle the complex set of structural issues that are at the heart of modern commercial competition. "Reciprocity" means that a concession to open a country's markets should be met by a return concession of equal magnitude. "Nondiscrimination" applies the most-favored nation (MFN) principle that no country or group of countries should be given preferential treatment over others. "Transparency" means that any trade restrictions should be converted into tariffs, which are less harmful than other types of nontariff barriers such as quotas, and then bound at a ceiling that can become the focus of negotiations. These principles worked well enough through the 1970s, but their application to new structural issues has been less successful. GATT now struggles because domestic industrial and R&D policy structures are uniquely intertwined in broader systemic differences, they inherently favor local firms, and they are far from transparent.

The Bretton Woods planners in 1944 wanted to establish a more binding regime with enforcement teeth through the International Trade Organization (ITO), but the charter for such an autonomous and powerful body could not be ratified. Instead, the interim, nonbinding GATT structure was established by treaty and embedded in a small secretariat in Geneva that monitors the trade policies of the roughly 100 member states and coordinates rounds of negotiations that seek to lower trade barriers. The "interim" period has now stretched to five decades. A series of GATT negotiation rounds succeeded in lowering average tariffs on manufactured goods from 40 percent in 1947 to under 10 percent by the end of the 1970s as the volume of world trade expanded by roughly 500 percent compared with output growth of about 220 percent.[30] The GATT structure had difficulties in forcing nontariff barriers into the tariff structure, but it clearly worked remarkably well for its first four decades.

Since the late 1970s, the ratio of trade volume growth to GDP growth, although still greater than one, has dropped substantially. One explanation for the decline in the rate of trade growth may be the proliferation of voluntary export restraints (VER) created by pressure on exporters to "voluntarily" restrict sales to the protected market or face retaliation. Such agreements—roughly 300 exist for textiles, cars, consumer electronics, and other items—avoid the letter, if not the spirit, of GATT restrictions.

The justifications for such protection are that governments may be subsidizing exports and foreign firms may be dumping their products at prices below costs of production, as indicated by export prices that are below domestic prices. Most countries pursue retaliation against dumping and impose countervailing duties to offset foreign subsidies, and the United States alone initiated 427 antidumping and 371 countervailing duty cases between 1979 and 1988.[31] The threat of initiating such actions becomes the lever behind VERs.

Although Article 19 of GATT does provide an escape clause to permit temporary protection for industries threatened by rapid import expansion, VERs threaten the GATT framework because they challenge the principles of transparency and reciprocity, are rarely temporary, usually apply to a few targeted trade partners, and work to limit trade expansion. Bilateral efforts to pressure other countries to open their domestic markets to imports are also outside the GATT framework because they threaten increases in protection in the short run, even when the ultimate objective is trade expansion.

Under the U.S. Omnibus Trade and Competitiveness Act of 1988, Section 301 gives the President broad powers to retaliate against foreign practices that limit specific U.S. exports, and "Super 301" provisions can be used to respond to countries that are accused of pursuing a wide range of policies that close their domestic markets. Pressure from these provisions contributed to the opening of Structural Impediments Initiative negotiations in 1989 between the United States and Japan over some 200 issues, including Japan's retail distribution system, government contracts, household savings practices, and so on. More recently, the United States and Japan announced a 1993 agreement on a new trade "framework" of principles for lowering the Japanese trade surplus with the United States through subsequent negotiations covering specific industries and practices, including government procurement, regulations that impede market access, economic harmonization of investment limitations, implementation of existing trade accords, and other major sectors, such as automobiles.[32] This kind of bilateral pressure on "unfair" trade practices extends well beyond traditional commercial topics into an examination of fundamental differences in economic systems.

The Uruguay round of GATT negotiations initiated in 1986 is also pressing beyond traditional tariff questions to complex agreements on agricultural subsidies, intellectual property rights, and manufacturing subsidies that focus negotiations on basic differences in economic structures.[33] The risk is that GATT will prove to be ineffective in producing real solutions to structural impediments to trade and that competitive trade practices will drive North America, Europe, and the Asia-Pacific region centered on Japan into rival trading blocs. While traditional free-trade theory argues that all regions would gain from more open trade and reconciliation of structural differences that impede it, strategic-trade and technology arguments have arisen to challenge that conclusion. The central issue is whether nations or regions can exploit structural differences to gain local outcomes that are superior to free trade.

Traditional arguments do admit three important exceptions to the fundamental principle that open trade permits exploitation of national comparative advantages, benefits all participants, and provides the best incentives for efficiency and growth. First, a country might have a large enough presence in a particular market to create market leverage by using a domestic tariff to shift international prices in its favor. For example, by placing a tariff on automobile imports, the U.S. might expand domestic production, lower world prices of cars, and raise the relative price of U.S. exports compared with cars in world markets. This shift in the relative prices, or terms of trade, could conceivably lead to a net benefit to the United States, although foreign retaliation might wipe out those benefits.[34] A tariff would only work to improve the terms of trade if a country had a significant share of the relevant world markets and supply and demand curves had appropriate shapes, or elasticities.

Second, infant industries may need a boost because many of the benefits of launching into a new field may be external to the pioneering firm, but important to the whole economy.[35] Protection could allow the industry to get started and develop economies of scale and scope that would increase efficiency, lower production costs, and subsequently allow the industry to compete in world markets without protection.

Third, some industries may be so vital to national security that domestic sources must be sustained even if they are inefficient, because of the risk of interrupted access. U.S. tradition has treated each of these arguments with caution, noting that retaliation can eliminate potential advantages from tariff manipulation, that infant industries are hard to wean from protection, and that the national security argument can be extended to areas of dubious importance and vulnerability.

Most arguments for alternatives to free trade turn out to be variants of the terms-of-trade, infant-industry, and national-security exceptions, or else attempts to redistribute income to some favored industry, group, or region. The redistribution and national-security arguments presumably accept lower national economic welfare as an acceptable cost to reach other objectives. The terms-of-trade and infant-industry arguments, on the other hand, suggest that total national income might be improved through government intervention. Whether that increase in income would lead to an unequivocal increase in welfare would depend on the way in which the gains were distributed.

Alternative views on the relative importance of each objective and the ability to influence the behavior of trading partners lead to different policy orientations that can be labeled free trade, protectionism, fair trade, managed trade, and strategic trade. "Free trade" is simply a preference for the GATT approach of negotiating the elimination of trade restrictions through reciprocity, nondiscrimination, and transparency. The term "protectionism" is often applied to any government intervention to alter free-trade patterns, but the term is used here to describe support of existing industries in order to prevent industry, regional, or labor-force dislocations, even though such protection would lower national income and would be in clear violation of the GATT process. Other forms of intervention are proposed as techniques for actually raising national income.

"Fair trade" endorses the objective of open markets, but suggests that actions to restrict trade can be justified to counter protectionist practices by foreign governments and create a level playing field. Section 301 provisions, countervailing duties, and the Structural Impediments Initiatives illustrate fair-trade principles. Advocates of "managed trade" begin with the premise that markets are so contaminated by structural impediments, government intervention, and oligopolistic firms that it is impossible to create the level playing field envisioned by free-trade or fair-trade theorists, so government pressure should be used to negotiate the outcome of trade patterns rather than attempt to influence trade practices. The management may include VER or "voluntary import expansion" (VIE) agreements to establish quantitative trade targets, often reinforced by involuntary coercion in the form of threatened tariff or quota retaliation.[36]

As in the large-country terms-of-trade case, managed- and fair-trade arguments suggest that a country can use its large market shares to influence the behavior of its trading partners. In the tariff case, the country alters its imports to shift the terms of trade and hence trade patterns. In the managed- and fair-trade cases, the country threatens tariff retaliation unless the target takes actions to shift the terms of trade.

In theoretical terms, managed trade is a significant departure from fair trade because managed trade endorses a regime with substantial, sustained government intervention, while fair trade would envision limited, intermittent intervention. The managed-trade targets could be set at levels that might prevail in a free market, or they might be set at arbitrary levels to suit a variety of national interests. Moreover, managed trade would inevitably involve government coordination of industry pricing and quotas in order to meet trade targets, while fair trade would focus on regulating industrial practices. The distinctions, however, are greater for the target country than for the initiator, because in each case the form of pressure on the target might be the same, but the expected response would be different. For example, Section 301 provisions could be used to press for reduced impediments to trade under a fair-trade strategy or for a specific share of a target country's market under a managed-trade approach.

The U.S.-Japanese 1991 semiconductor agreement, discussed in more detail below, illustrates the managed-trade principles. It included an expectation that the foreign share of the Japanese domestic market would reach 20 percent in 1992, although there were no binding commitments to enforce the target. In early 1993, the U.S. Advisory Committee for Trade Policy and Negotiations recommended temporary market-share targets for U.S. exports to Japan because of Japan's low percentage of manufacturing imports compared with other countries.[37]

Finally, "strategic-trade" arguments suggest that trade policies should be applied in order to support sectors that provide unique national advantages either to offset such actions by others or to simply improve national welfare. These arguments figure prominently in current debates over future directions for trade policy, and they demand more detailed discussion.

Strategic Trade

Strategic-trade proposals derive from variations of the terms-of-trade, infant-industry, and national-security exceptions to free trade, although those distinctions have unfortunately been lost in a generic strategic-trade soup that lumps all of the categories together because they call for government intervention to support specific industries. The distinctions, however, are important to make sense of policy implications, so it is worth a moment to lay out the three different groupings of strategic arguments, labeled S1, S2, and S3 for easy reference.

S1 Arguments—Variations of the Terms-of-Trade Case. The first set of strategic-trade arguments focuses on the market power that a country may have in industries that are not perfectly competitive. For example, in the aircraft industry there are large economies of scale that drive the market toward a small number of producers, or oligopolistic market structures. When there are only a few large firms in a market, they typically make above normal profits or "rents," because new firms have difficulty entering the industry and capturing those profits. In such markets, government might intervene with export subsidies to help domestic firms shift their outputs and prices in ways that increase profits at the expense of foreign firms.[38] A commitment to support a domestic firm with subsidies might itself be sufficient to deter foreign firms from entering a particular market.[39]

This is a new twist on the terms-of-trade argument, because the market power comes not from the scale of national purchases in competitive markets, but from the ability to influence decisions in noncompetitive markets. S1 arguments essentially call for policies that help domestic firms compete for rents in oligopolistic international markets. According to that approach, if international markets are controlled by oligopolies, the nation might as well support its own oligopolistic firms and keep the profits from flowing elsewhere.[40]

S2 Arguments—Variations of the Infant-Industry Case. A second set of arguments expands on the general idea of infant industries by emphasizing the possibility of internal economies of scale and technological spillovers from one industry to another. The *internal* economies of scale argument introduces the possibility that unit costs may decline within a firm as output expands because of large initial R&D outlays or because of gains from learning by doing as cumulative output increases. Normally, firms do not require government assistance to capture internal economies of scale as long as capital markets are working well and firms have access to sufficient capital to reach efficient output levels, but governments might intervene if those conditions do not hold. In cases where economies of scale produce a small number of firms in world markets, import protection might permit firms to expand domestic production, move down their learning curves, lower unit costs, and actually increase exports.[41]

Technological spillovers provide additional justification for S2 strategies. For example, suppose that there are no internal economies of scale in DRAM production, but as all firms increase R&D and output, they generate knowledge that spills over to other types of semiconductors or even other related industries. Because each firm cannot charge other firms for those spillover benefits, market DRAM prices would not reflect the broader benefits to the entire economy, so the market might require stimulus from government to reach the optimal level of DRAM R&D and production. In this case, a subsidy to DRAM producers could be used to entice them to produce the socially optimal output, and society would gain the spillover benefits in the form of lower cost or higher quality of other products. Strategic technologies, as defined in the last chapter, with their broad impacts on a number of other sectors, might have particularly large spillover benefits in a variety of industries.

The S2 arguments for internal and external economies of scale suggest policies to protect selected industries through trade impediments or support for R&D. R&D support might not favor local firms if innovations flowed quickly to all firms linked in global R&D networks, but some of the results might provide tacit knowledge that could be captured by local workers, institutions, or supporting infrastructure in ways that favored domestic firms.

For example, suppose firms in different countries of equal size compete in R&D, that the R&D produces competitive advantages that can be captured in product markets, that one country has a knowledge lead based on prior R&D, and that the knowledge generated is learned by local workers but cannot be exported. In other words, even though a firm cannot appropriate all the advantages provided by R&D, the spillovers are limited to other firms in the same country, so the general knowledge created by R&D is a "local public good"—it is readily available in one area but not in other countries.

Gene Grossman and Elhanan Helpman show that in such a world the country with the initial lead in knowledge will accumulate new information more quickly than its rival, and will therefore sustain and perhaps even increase its productivity lead. As a result, R&D subsidies may produce policy "hysteresis:": a policy applied for a short time may have permanent impacts. Such policies, however, may lead to retaliatory policies, because R&D subsidies in the rival country can reverse the lead and give the rival a sustainable advantage.[42]

If the prospects for effective retaliation are limited, government may have an S2 strategic role in promoting R&D and hence innovation and productivity. This R&D argument is similar to the infant-industry trade argument to the extent that domestic innovation can shift the industry structure of competitive advantage. That conclusion is contingent on the assumption that the knowledge generated by the R&D stays within the country, but in many cases global organizational networks can easily shift technologies outside national borders. Generic technologies are arguably the easiest to export, so the S2 arguments for internal and external economies of scale apply most forcefully to those more unique aspects of technology that are not easily transferable.

S3 Arguments—Variations of the National Security Case. A third set of strategic arguments points to the importance of technologies that are critical to high-priority national objectives, particularly national security. Intervention to protect such technologies might be warranted if it were critically important, there were substantial risks of interrupted access to the technology, and the relative costs of alternatives to domestic production, such as stockpiling, were high.

Theodore Moran correctly emphasizes the importance of market concentration in assessing the extent of vulnerability to foreign blackmail, denial, or pressure, and he suggests that if the largest four firms or countries control more than 50 percent of a "critical" market, they may pose a real threat to national security.[43] In practice, of course, any such rule quickly explodes into a tangle of national and global contractors and subcontractors, so a "50–4" principle or its equivalent would have to be refined in any specific application to make it an operational policy instrument. Edward Graham and Paul Krugman argue that tests similar to Moran's should be applied during reviews of foreign takeovers of U.S. firms under the Exon-Florio amendment to the 1988 Omnibus Trade and Competitiveness Act. They suggest that in cases where the takeover poses a national security threat the government should block the takeover, take actions to ensure sufficient U.S. national presence in the market, or impose domestic content requirements on production and R&D.[44]

The S1 competition for favorable terms of trade, the S2 cases of internal and external economies of scale, and the S3 concerns regarding critical technologies and supply clearly apply with different force to various technologies and industries. The overlaps across all three cases are perhaps strongest in the Mark IV nuclear, aircraft, space, and mainframe computer sectors, with significant economies of scale, oligopolistic market structures, and substantial public R&D support. Newer Mark V software, microprocessors and genetic engineering have fewer scale economies and more competitive market structures, but they may have substantial technological spillovers. They do have important national security impacts, but their vulnerability to international leverage may be more limited than in sectors with greater market concentration. In short, the S1, S2, and S3 arguments apply with different force to disparate technologies at various points in their technological trajectories.

The S1, S2, and S3 strategic-trade arguments are quite different, and the types of evidence required for an evaluation of public policy vary in each case. The available evidence suggests that the potential gains from S1 intervention to shift terms of trade are quite small.[45] The arguments about S2 spillovers or S3 vulnerability are inherently dynamic and far more difficult to quantify, so the evidence there tends to draw on descriptive case studies rather than tighter analytical models. Some studies have, however, found that knowledge spillovers from R&D outlays can be very significant, contributing up to half of the total social return on R&D expenditures.[46] An analysis of the semiconductor industry illustrates applications of the terms-of-trade, internal and external economies of scale, and critical-technology arguments, and demonstrates the enormous difficulties of evaluating the impacts of such policies when unintended consequences are magnified by global networks.

THE CASE OF SEMICONDUCTORS

The United States dominated the early stages of the semiconductor trajectory, but in the mid-1980s Japanese firms gained a larger share of the worldwide semiconductor market.[47] The reversal was most apparent in the market for DRAM chips, where Japan pulled ahead of the United States in 1981 and 1982 and gained 80 percent of the world market by 1986. The United States lost and then recovered the lead in erasable programmable read-only memory and logic circuits (EPROM), and it retained a dominant position in microprocessors and application-specific integrated circuits (ASIC). By 1991, Japanese firms held just under 50 percent of the worldwide semiconductor market and U.S. firms contributed roughly 40 percent of worldwide sales.[48]

The semiconductor case has been widely studied because of the intense competition between the United States and Japan in a strategic technology, the differences in national systems of innovation suggested by shifts within the industry, and the clash of Japanese industrial policies and U.S. managed-trade efforts beginning in 1986.[49] The conclusions drawn from various studies are highly dependent on the time period examined, the sector of the semiconductor industry selected for emphasis, and the relative weight given to measures of industry performance, such as price behavior, production levels, world trade shares, ownership or location of fabrication facilities, and the impact on semiconductor-using, or "downstream," industries. For example, an emphasis on the DRAM market paints the worst picture of U.S. performance and the strongest case for the effectiveness of Japanese industrial policy, while relative U.S. success in the microprocessor and ASIC markets tells a somewhat different story. Similarly, an emphasis on price behavior and the impact on downstream industries presents a dismal view of U.S. managed-trade efforts, but a focus on U.S. trade shares presents those policies in a somewhat more favorable light.

A review of the evidence across the various semiconductor sectors and through the longer swings of the last two decades suggests that the fundamental shifts in the industry structure have had far more to do with underlying stages of technological trajectories and systemic differences in innovation networks than with narrowly defined U.S. or Japanese trade policies. As a result, efforts to manage market shares produce unintended and often undesirable side effects. Technology policies targeted more directly on the creation of the advanced and specialized factors needed for effective competition in the industry had larger, more sustainable impacts on competitive advantage and market shares.

Semiconductors as a Strategic Sector

All the strategic-trade arguments have been used extensively by both Japan and the United States in their policies toward the semiconductor industry. In Japan, MITI viewed the sector as a classic S2 strategic industry with large spillovers to other sectors, and it supported semiconductor development through preferential procurement of computers and telecommunications equipment with Japanese chips. In the United States, the S3 national security arguments dominated, and defense R&D and procurement contracts played a central role in the industry's evolution. Virtually all the industry's output went to defense in the early years, and as much as 40 percent of output was still going to the military in the late 1960s. Federal sources financed about 50 percent of the industry's R&D from 1958 to

1970.[50] Because each country placed such strategic emphasis on semiconductor production, Japan's large gains in market share in the 1980s, particularly in memory chips, posed a direct challenge to U.S. national technology policy.

The DRAM semiconductor played a critical role as a "technology driver" in semiconductor evolution.[51] Although DRAM semiconductors accounted for only 20 percent of total semiconductor sales in the late 1980s, their relative simplicity and long product cycle provided a stable source of earnings, and technical experience gained in developing the DRAM could then be applied to more complex chips. Different DRAM designs provided various levels of speed, power consumption, and reliability, but all designs met industrywide standards that permitted users to choose among different suppliers. As a result, there were few demand-side marketing constraints to limit new entrants to the DRAM market.[52]

There were, however, significant supply-side advantages in gaining a large share of the market because of the steep learning curve and the substantial reductions in unit costs as production expanded. As a rule of thumb, every doubling of volume lowered production costs per unit by roughly 30 percent, primarily because of the high percentage of defective chips, or low "yields," in the early stages of each new product.[53] The steep learning curve and the sensitivity of unit costs to volume led many firms to set aggressive "forward prices," prices computed from the lower costs anticipated at higher volumes of production, in order to gain market share.[54] The demand for DRAM chips was very sensitive to quality, because the cost of the chips was generally a small part of the total cost of the systems in which they were packaged, but DRAM failures could have a large impact on system performance.

The growing demand for DRAM chips in the early 1980s, the steep learning curve, the spillover benefits, the national security implications, the importance of quality differences, and aggressive pricing practices all combined to make the sector a centerpiece of strategic competition. U.S. firms initially pulled out to a clear lead in the competition, drawing on a strong science and R&D base that was important in the early stages of the DRAM trajectory.

Only U.S. firms produced the 1K DRAM, introduced in 1972. As output expanded from 5 million per year in 1972 to 20 million in 1975, prices fell from about $10 to $3 a kilobyte. The top 10 producers of the 4K DRAM that appeared in 1975 were also all U.S. firms.[55] U.S. firms moved down steep learning curves with each new DRAM generation, retained large shares of the world market, and developed production techniques that provided large advantages for the next DRAM generation and for the manufacture of other chips. As late as 1978, the United States still held over 70 percent of the worldwide DRAM market.

Despite the advantages of that early lead, by 1986 Japan had captured almost 80 percent of the worldwide DRAM market as the U.S. share dropped below 20 percent.[56] Japanese firms NEC, Hitachi, and Toshiba joined the top 10 producers with the 1978 introduction of the 16K DRAM, Fujitsu entered with the 1981 launch of the 64K DRAM, and when the 256K DRAM came to the market in 1983, virtually all of the major producers were Japanese.[57]

The Japanese entry to the top ten producers at the 64K DRAM level corresponded to a technological discontinuity between the large-scale integration (LSI) production techniques used in manufacturing 4K and 16K chips and the very-large-scale integration (VLSI) techniques employed for 64K, 256K, and 1-MB DRAM chips. A similar break subsequently occurred between the 1-MB generation and the ultra-large-scale integration (ULSI) techniques for the 16-MB DRAM and the 64-MB DRAM still to be developed. The technological discontinuities also produced sharp increases in the level of investment needed to enter each new DRAM market. Relatively small firms were able to dominate LSI technologies, but larger firms were more important at the VLSI level, and even larger firms have dominated ULSI technologies.[58]

The growing Japanese market share at the 64K level and Japan's move to dominance at the 256K level also corresponded to important shifts in the applications of DRAM chips. While the 16K chips had been used primarily in mainframe computers, minicomputers, and graphics applications, the 64K chip became a mainstay of the rapidly expanding personal computer market as well, all areas in which U.S. firms had strong positions. The 256K chip introduced a much broader range of applications, including robotics, which played more directly to Japanese electronics strengths.[59]

The critical crossover point in the competition came in 1985 when the bubble of expanding 256K DRAM sales burst, the industry faced large excess capacity, and DRAM prices dropped dramatically. Japanese producers lost roughly $4 billion, and U.S. producers lost some $2 billion. In the face of those losses, most U.S. producers dropped from the market, but Japanese firms actually expanded output to gain market share.[60] The Japanese share of world DRAM exports rose from 39 percent in 1980 to 74 percent in 1988, as the U.S. share fell from 60 to 16 percent. In the face of that Japanese expansion, only Texas Instruments and Micron Technology continued DRAM production as seven of the nine U.S. producers left the market.[61] The Japanese were left with a large share of a depressed market, but the subsequent rebound in DRAM prices, helped significantly by the U.S. pressure on Japanese producers discussed below, gave Japanese firms enormous profits and ample sources for continued investment.

Overcoming the Early U.S. Lead

The Japanese performance parallels the Grossman-Helpman S2 spillover model in which government protection permitted Japanese firms to capture technological spillovers and overcome the U.S. lead. Although Japanese firms were arguably higher-cost producers of semiconductors than their U.S. competitors through the late 1970s, they benefited from various forms of domestic protection, including high tariffs, quotas, import registration requirements, MITI's intervention in buying and diffusing foreign technology, formal restrictions on foreign investment, cooperative R&D efforts across major firms that were excluded from antitrust restrictions and supported by MITI, Nippon Telephone's (NTT) procurement preferences, and the domestic supply preferences of Japanese electronics producers. In particular, the cooperative VLSI project, established by MITI and NTT in 1975, accounted for some 15 percent of semiconductor R&D in the late 1970s and allowed Japanese firms to reach competitive levels in DRAM production.[62]

The Japanese industrial policies imposed significant costs on both Japanese and U.S. consumers. Baldwin and Krugman examined the 16K DRAM chip market that existed from roughly 1976 to 1983 to see if the apparent Japanese restrictions on imports, which amounted to the equivalent of a 26-percent tariff rate in their model, improved Japanese welfare. They used an S1 model designed to see if the Japanese were able to shift the terms of trade and capture "rents" from U.S. firms.

According to the Baldwin-Krugman simulation, the protection did permit Japanese firms to expand output, lower their own unit costs, and gain 86 percent of their domestic market. The improved cost position of Japanese producers allowed them to gain 19 percent of the U.S. market. As Japanese firms expanded output, U.S. firms were unable to capture the lower unit costs they would have obtained from higher levels of production in an open market. As a result, Japanese protection increased the total number of U.S. and Japanese producers, reduced the average size of a production run, increased average costs per chip, and drove up the price of the 16K chip in both markets compared to what it would have been under free trade. The higher chip prices reduced the welfare of consumers in each country. Baldwin and Krugman argue that protection did not increase corporate profits in Japan, because the free entry of new firms held profits at normal levels. The net effect of the protection, then, was a gain in Japanese market share, but a loss of net national welfare in both Japan and the United States, because costs of production and chip prices rose, ultimately hurting consumers, and producers did not capture any excess profits. Baldwin and Krugman's simulation also shows that retaliation by the United States would have lowered welfare in both countries even further.[63]

The Baldwin and Krugman emphasis on capturing rents follows the logic of S1 strategic competition for the excess profits of oligopolistic firms. The focus on capturing rents does not, however, address the S2 spillover dynamics that may have been created by the Japanese intervention. Japanese protection of the 16K chip may have been a failure from the perspective of current profits, but it also had an impact on future generations of chip production. According to the Baldwin-Krugman model, those advantages did not come from high Japanese semiconductor profits that could be poured into research, because free entry held profits down to normal levels. The dynamic Grossman-Helpman model, however, suggests that there may have been significant spillover benefits from improvements in process technologies that produced more sustained increases in competitive advantage.

National Innovation Networks

The differences in the financial structures of U.S. and Japanese chip producers explain a great deal about the divergent responses to the collapse of the semiconductor market in 1985. U.S. chip manufacturers include two groups. First, merchant producers specialize in making semiconductors for use by other firms. Second, chip-producing subdivisions of parent electronics firms sell in the broader market only after the parent company's needs are met. In the mid-1980s, the smaller U.S. merchant companies with erratic earnings and limited R&D lost out to captive subdivisions, of AT&T and IBM for example, who could draw on their parents for steady markets and R&D support.[64]

The Japanese semiconductor industry was dominated by large, vertically integrated electronics firms that could provide similar support for their semiconductor subdivisions.[65] Reliable sources of finance became more and more important with each generation of DRAM as the complexity of production processes increased, the investment required for each new generation rose, the share of the total market required for an adequate return on investment increased, and earnings became captive to cyclical fluctuations in demand.[66] As a result, the vertically integrated Japanese firms that produced a wide range of electronics provided more stable sources of financing than were available to most U.S. firms.[67] The Japanese also exploited a domestic market for semiconductors, which was expanding more quickly than the U.S. market in the mid-1980s. Faster domestic market growth was particularly important because ASICs were becoming a larger part of the market, and customized chip manufacturers benefited from close associations with domestic users.[68]

In addition to the advantages of vertical integration, a rapidly expanding domestic market, and access to patient capital, the Japanese semiconductor industry also benefited from a traditional emphasis on adapting foreign technology and improving it through incremental process improvements and tight quality controls. These advantages of Japanese innovation networks proved to be particularly important as DRAM technology moved beyond the discovery and experimentation stages, in which the U.S. system excelled, to the competition, standardization, and diffusion stages, in which quality and incremental process improvements were more important.

U.S. Strategic-Trade Responses

Two of the trade weapons in the U.S. arsenal in the mid-1980s included the antidumping and Section 301 provisions of the Trade Act of 1974, renewed in the 1988 U.S. Omnibus Trade and Competitiveness Act discussed earlier. In 1985, a number of related actions were initiated under those provisions to block the growing Japanese share of U.S. semiconductor markets and to gain a larger foreign share of Japanese markets. The Semiconductor Industry Association (SIA) submitted a Section 301 petition charging limited access to Japanese markets, Micron Technology lodged a complaint against Japanese firms for dumping 64K DRAM chips in the United States below prices in Japan, three firms initiated a dumping charge against Japanese producers of EPROM memory devices, and the U.S. Department of Commerce charged Japan with dumping 256K and 1-MB DRAM chips. A preliminary positive finding on the dumping suits early in 1986 prescribed retaliatory duties of up to 188 percent on EPROMs and 108 percent on 256K and 1-MB DRAM chips. All of the pending actions were merged in negotiations to avoid the imposition of duties and reach a compromise settlement.[69]

In August of 1986, the United States and Japan announced the compromise five-year Semiconductor Trade Agreement (STA), amplified by related company negotiations, under which Japan would end dumping and help foreign firms toward a goal of doubling their share of Japanese semiconductor markets to 20 percent. Under the agreements, the Department of Commerce set a "foreign market value" for the minimum prices Japanese firms could use in international markets. The price floors varied for each company based on estimates of the firm's average production costs. MITI agreed to help enforce the pricing restrictions by monitoring export prices of selected semiconductor products, and the United States agreed to suspend the dumping and Section 301 suits.[70] In short, the United States used the threat of tariff retaliation against Japan as leverage to obtain a managed-trade agreement and assurance that MITI would coordinate efforts by Japanese firms to achieve the target level for foreign sales to Japan.

The first year of the agreement ended with U.S. charges that Japan was not living up to the provisions on market access and that prices of semiconductors in third markets were below agreed levels. In April 1987, Presi-

dent Reagan imposed $300 million in retaliatory tariffs on Japanese elec-
tronics imports.[71] Subsequently, foreign market shares in Japan began to
rise, price differentials in third markets narrowed, and the Department
of Commerce removed half of the sanctions. The shift involved tighter
coordination by MITI to include export allocations, price floors for various markets, and reviews of investment plans to avoid oversupply. From
1986 to 1991, the foreign share of Japanese semiconductor markets did
rise from roughly 8.5 to just over 14 percent, due primarily to larger U.S.
sales, but they fell short of the 20 percent target level. As agreed, Japanese
semiconductor prices in the United States remained above the negotiated
foreign market values.[72]

Assessing Strategic-Trade Impacts

By many measures, the consequences of the agreements were disastrous
for the United States and a windfall for Japanese producers. The higher
DRAM prices set to restrict dumping actually led to soaring Japanese
profits when demand increased in the late 1980s. The requirements to control prices and coordinate semiconductor imports reinforced and legiti-
mized natural tendencies for collusion among Japanese producers. The impact on opening the Japanese market to foreign firms is somewhat more
ambiguous. Although foreign firms did gain a larger share of the Japanese
market, most of the arrangements were coordinated through global network arrangements that increased fabrication of chips by U.S.-owned firms
but did not necessarily expand production or promote other high-value
activities within the United States.

Higher Prices and Collusion. MITI's efforts to coordinate firm output
and prices reinforced normal tendencies for coordination among government and firms in Japan's network economy. Laura D'Andrea Tyson argues that after Japan achieved a dominant position in the DRAM market
in the mid-1980s, coordination among firms under MITI's direction would
have been a natural response to exploit market power even in the absence
of a semiconductor agreement.[73] At any rate, the STA certainly facilitated
coordination and made it more legitimate from an international perspective. As semiconductor demand increased in the late 1980s, Japan's cartel-
like output restrictions and pricing coordination succeeded in driving up
world DRAM prices from $2.25 for a 256K DRAM in early 1986 to $3.50
by mid-1989. Given the huge industry excess capacity in 1985, that reversal was remarkable. All DRAM producers benefited, but because Japanese
firms had such a dominant market position they benefited the most, recov-
ering losses from the overexpansion early in the decade and establishing
large reserves that permitted continuing R&D at levels much higher than
those of U.S. producers.[74]

The increase in international semiconductor prices hurt U.S. electronics producers and provided a competitive advantage in downstream applications for the vertically integrated Japanese electronics firms. In the oligopolistic DRAM market, the agreement limited output, drove up prices, and increased profits for Japanese producers, Texas Instruments, Micron Technology, and the Motorola-Toshiba joint venture. The U.S. share of the world DRAM market stopped declining and stabilized at about 20 percent. Korean Samsung and German Siemens, both supported by government R&D programs, also benefited from the higher DRAM prices. In fact, Korea's share of the world DRAM market rose from virtually nothing in 1984 to 18 percent in 1991, a surge that reduced Japan's world market share from roughly 84 to 57 percent in the same period.[75]

The antidumping efforts of the STA were arguably counterproductive because they encouraged cartel-like coordination in Japan to limit output and raise prices, they set price targets based on average costs that were too high compared with marginal or average variable costs that more correctly reflect predatory behavior, they placed U.S. computer producers who had to buy high-priced semiconductors at a disadvantage, and they attempted to control prices for third parties who were not part of the agreement.[76] If the goal was to support domestic semiconductor production, direct R&D subsidies would have had a more direct impact with fewer unintended consequences, although even R&D support probably would have been partially diffused in global R&D networks.

Global Network Arrangements and U.S. Fabrication. Managed-trade arrangements imply substantial government intervention to alter market outcomes. In the Japanese case, the semiconductor agreement reinforced traditional patterns of close interaction between MITI and the *keiretsu* and pushed firms into more extensive global organizational network relationships to meet import targets. As a result, the STA strengthened the trend toward closer global R&D and input-output networks.

For example, the semiconductor agreement accelerated and expanded an R&D alliance between Motorola, a leader in microprocessors, and Toshiba, a leader in DRAM technology. Motorola reentered the DRAM market through its joint venture with Toshiba, producing 1-MB DRAM chips in Japan and Scotland. A number of other U.S. firms entered arrangements to design chips for Japanese electronics systems producers, including cooperative projects on compact discs, camcorders, and automobiles. Fujitsu and Advanced Micro Devices (AMD) formed an alliance in 1992 to produce EPROM memory devices in Japan.[77] The STA also increased Japanese investment in foreign facilities as a hedge against trade retaliation. Mitsubishi, Nippon Electric, Hitachi, and Fujitsu all added "greenfield" (start from scratch) chip fabrication facilities in the United States after the 1986 agreement, and Japanese firms pursued 51 acquisitions of U.S. firms in the semiconductor industry between October 1988 and April 1992.[78]

Although those organizational network arrangements between U.S. and

Japanese firms arguably strengthened the U.S. share of the Japanese domestic market, they did not necessarily shift high-value design activities to the United States. The net impact on the location of fabrication plants is also ambiguous. In the Motorola and AMD case, for example, a large share of the expanded production actually took place in Japan. Similarly, Texas Instruments expanded its semiconductor output in Japan, Taiwan, and Italy.[79]

The major shift in the international DRAM market came not from the reentry of U.S. firms, but from increased competition from Korean firms that expanded output during the price surge of the late 1980s triggered in large part by the STA. Korean firms remain competitive at the lower end of the DRAM technology spectrum, and their expanded output, particularly of 1-MB chips, has worked to lower international DRAM prices. Korean Samsung emerged as the world's largest 1-MB DRAM producer in 1992, and fifth largest memory producer overall, despite the continuing Japanese grip on the upper-end 4-MB and 16-MB DRAM technologies.[80]

The managed-trade agreement in semiconductors increased tendencies for cartel-like cooperation in Japan, strengthened global R&D networks, and arguably increased semiconductor production outside Japan, although not necessarily in the United States. Modifications to the agreement in 1991 eliminated some of the more egregious pricing impacts, set a clear target for foreign shares of Japanese markets, and eliminated the third-country price controls. The new five-year semiconductor agreement relaxed antidumping restrictions, suspended sanctions that were still in place, and explicitly recognized the target of a foreign share of 20 percent of the Japanese semiconductor model. The modified antidumping rules eliminated the foreign market price targets, but required Japanese firms to maintain data that would be needed in the event of a dumping suit. The curtailed price restrictions were a response to complaints from the U.S. computer industry and from European chip importers over the increased price of semiconductors at the end of the 1980s.[81] Figures for 1992 indicate that the foreign share of the Japanese semiconductor market still fell short of the 20-percent target for the entire year, but hit the target for the fourth quarter before falling back below 20 percent in the first half of 1993.[82]

The net impact of STA attempts to open Japanese semiconductor markets to foreign sales is difficult to assess. Because the VIE target of 20 percent applied to all foreign producers, it avoided some of the more blatant anticompetitive aspects of a national VIE, and in the DRAM case both Korean and European producers may have benefited from improved access. It is far more difficult to assess whether or not this global R&D and input-output networking has made the market more competitive or has favored "U.S." firms. It is clear, however, that managed-trade initiatives have complex spillover impacts through R&D, finance, and input-output networks that are difficult to assess in terms of conventional measures of national imports and exports.

Semiconductors and Strategic Policies

MITI's efforts to support the semiconductor industry through the 1970s did lead to advantages that were potentially self-sustaining through the 1980s. The deep pockets of vertically integrated Japanese electronics firms, the *keiretsu* structures that provided additional patient capital and favored purchases from Japanese suppliers, the technological trajectory of the DRAM chip, and the financial weaknesses of the U.S. market structure all contributed to Japanese success.[83] The ability to expand market share in declining markets through pricing below average costs, sustained by favorable financing and the expectation of learning-curve advantages, gave Japanese producers a dominant position in the DRAM market in the mid-1980s.

The hostile U.S. reaction to the Japanese gains in market share, centered on the charges of dumping and restricted access to Japanese domestic markets, calls the long-run efficacy of strategic-trade policies into question. There is little evidence that the clash of innovation systems can be effectively managed through trade policies. Global organizational networks can easily bypass local trade restrictions by shifting patterns of investment and production without altering the location of the high-value activities that really drive competitive advantage. On the other hand, there is considerable evidence that managed trade can lead to sharp short-term dislocations in prices with unintended and potentially disastrous consequences. Arguably, the U.S. share of the semiconductor market would have rebounded more quickly if the STA had not bailed out Japanese firms by driving up prices in a period of high excess capacity, and U.S. electronics systems producers would have been able to sustain a more competitive position with Japanese rivals.

If the STA did not benefit the United States, it did send a clear signal to Japan that national strategic-trade policies can trigger international retaliation. As a result, a new framework is needed to deal with clashes in national innovation systems that will increasingly focus on competitive technology policies. The negative side effects of using trade policies to deal with those systemic differences are potentially too great to risk, both in terms of short-term dislocations and long-term stability of the international trading regime. Instead, a new framework is required for managing the competitive technology policies more directly.

Activist commercial and industrial policies seek to alter market outcomes in order to obtain perceived national advantages. Regardless of their intended purposes, they are apt to suffer from unintended consequences as markets seek ways around the restrictions, either by "black market" transactions to illegally bypass the restraint or by shifting transactions to other forms that are less restricted. To the extent that national commercial and industrial policies succeed in favoring national firms over international competitors, they create additional incentives for international collaboration to bypass the restraint. The expansion in international R&D and input-output networks is at least in part a response to constraints on other forms of market access. The sharing of technology in international collaboration may be an end in itself in some industries, particularly when one partner benefits from government R&D subsidies. In other sectors, technology transfer may be a way of cementing agreements that permit sales in protected markets.[84] As a result, trade and industrial policies have a direct impact on technology policy.

The form of international collaboration in general and R&D transfers in particular, then, depends on the broader structure of commercial and industrial policy. Although consensus is expanding through the GATT process against the most blatant forms of discrimination against foreign firms, strategic policies are often pursued through subtle adjustments in economic structure that are more difficult to regulate. As the DRAM discussion demonstrated, sustainable improvements in competitive advantage now depend less on basic and general factors of production and more on advanced and specialized factors that are nurtured by structural differences in economic systems. Trade disputes, particularly in high-technology areas, now focus less on imports and exports of final products by national firms and more on the pattern of integration of R&D and related high-value activities in global networks. Commercial policies are blunt instruments for dealing with the subtle differences in economic structure that influence network behavior, so technology policy is rapidly becoming a centerpiece of national and regional economic policies to improve productivity performance, and differences in technology policies have become a critical area for regional competition.

STRATEGIC POLICIES AND NATIONAL SYSTEMS

Managed-trade policies are a politically understandable, but economically inefficient, response to the new trade relationships. The central problem is that global networks will shift the location of generic economic activities regardless of the form of national agreements, and trade restrictions have little impact on creating the tacit forms of knowledge and the local infrastructure that can capture high-value activities. National innovation systems will have more direct impacts on those sources of sustainable competitive advantage, and the U.S. system is in the midst of a fundamental transition to adapt to the new challenges.

Current U.S. innovation networks have strengths in basic research that can be captured in early stages of technological trajectories and in the integration of large complex systems, but they are still adjusting to the complexities of coordination required to exploit new information technologies. Access to patient capital may be particularly important in the case of technologies that are passing from the competitive to standardization stages of their trajectories, when scale economies become a more important factor and learning curve reductions in costs per unit give large advantages to first-movers who can rapidly expand output. Speculative venture capital is vital in the early stages of the technological trajectory, but access to patient capital is more critical in the later stages. The U.S. system may be highly adept at diffusing venture capital to small firms where risks are high, but potential returns over short periods can be substantial, and somewhat less successful in pooling private capital for the long haul. The loss of market share in DRAM technologies, for example, had a great deal to do with the greater ability of Japanese firms to sustain high levels of funding in the weak market of the mid-1980s.

The U.S. system is also adjusting to the increased coordination required across global input-output and R&D networks. Japanese and European systems, with their traditional emphasis on coordination through business groups and a more relaxed approach to antitrust restrictions in industries facing international competition, have important advantages in facilitating network operations.

It is quite clear that the U.S. system will be moving away from its strong orientation on government procurement as an organizing principle for R&D outlays. Defense budgets will be declining through the 1990s, and production runs will stretch out as the military services draw on systems fielded in the 1980s. Nuclear energy remains a questionable alternative for the future, and the procurement of nuclear weapon systems will decline. Government laboratories have already begun to shift emphasis toward dual-use technologies with broader industrial applications and closer coordination with the private sector. As the spin-offs to the private sector from government R&D decline, the pace of spin-ons from the private sector to public military, energy, and environmental programs is increasing. The role for public sector R&D outlays, then, will shift from an emphasis on procurement to support of the diffusion and adaptation of technologies developed in the private sector.

The U.S. policy structure and innovation networks are not well organized to implement strategic policies outside the area of S3 critical technologies. The orientation on defense R&D with its controls on classified materials and export restrictions does provide a basis for regulating access to critical technologies, although global network structures are clearly making such control more difficult. The framework for S1 competition for international rents exists in the Mark IV industries that benefited from large government R&D and procurement outlays, but that leverage is declining along with government expenditures. The government's ability to use S2 spillover strategies is particularly weak because of the limited role of business groups, antitrust restrictions on collaboration, and the strong tradition against direct government subsidies for individual industries outside the defense and energy sectors.

As a result, the ability to pursue strategic technology policies in the United States depends on a confluence of the S1, S2, and S3 arguments for a particular technology at a given point in its development. U.S. government intervention may only be feasible when those three arguments reinforce each other, generate sufficient political support to overcome the inherent bias against such approaches, and provide access to the instruments needed to pursue strategic policies. Semiconductors and aircraft are widely cited candidates for such policies because they appear to meet the criteria for each argument, and there is a history of strong government involvement in those sectors. They are clearly atypical, however, and few other industries have the same position in terms of strategic impacts or policy tradition.

Those structural limitations on strategic policies are reinforced by the patterns of U.S. innovation networks. U.S. advantages at the science and basic research levels are more difficult to translate into strategic advantages given the nature of global networks. The United States does, however, have a major advantage in a large, prosperous national economy, which gives it substantial leverage in deterring or constraining foreign strategies, so its comparative advantage is the strategic defense. For all their implementation problems, the deterrent value of instruments such as the Section 301 provisions against unfair trade practices or dumping restrictions is substantial.

A common counterargument to this pessimistic assessment of the potential for offensive strategic policies is that the United States should adjust its economic system to be more like Japan or Europe and, in Lester Thurow's terms, compete "head to head." [85] Charles Ferguson argues that the U.S. should adopt a *keiretsu* structure to deal with the complexities of information technologies and compete in the expanding market for integrated digital components. [86] Some adaptation in the U.S. system will certainly be required for more effective competition, and global networks are already producing substantial changes in organizational structure. It is unlikely, however, that changes in the U.S. system over the next decade will alter the relative ability of the United States to pursue offensive strategic policies. The changes in technology policy discussed in the next chapter, however, should work to improve the effectiveness of U.S. defensive strategies.

NOTES

1. Alison Butler, "Why High-Tech Is at the Center of the Industrial Policy Debate," *National Economic Trends,* The Federal Reserve Bank of St. Louis, May 1993, 1. There is no consensus on what defines "high technology," but most definitions do emphasize research intensity.

2. Organization for Economic Cooperation and Development, *Innovation Policy: Trends and Perspectives* (Paris, 1982), 151–158.

3. Bengt-Ake Lundvall, "Innovation as an Interactive Process: From User-Producer Interaction to the National System of Innovation," in *Technical Change and Economic Theory,* ed. Giovanni Dosi (London: Francis Pinter, 1988), 360–361. Also see the following: Bengt-Ake Lundvall, *Product Innovation and User-Producer Interaction* (Aalborg, Denmark: Aalborg University Press, 1985); Christopher Freeman, "Japan: A New National System of Innovation?" in *Technical Change and Economic Theory,* ed. Dosi et. al. London: Francis Pinter, 1988), 330–348; and OECD, *Technology Policy and Economic Performance* (Paris, 1987).

4. Lundvall, "Innovation as an Interactive Process," 361, and Ken-ichi Imai, "Japan's Corporate Networks," in *The Political Economy of Japan, Volume 3: Cultural and Social Dynamics,* ed. Shumpei Kumon and Henry Rosovsky (Stanford, Calif.: Stanford University Press, 1992), 198–230.

5. Joseph A. Schumpeter, *The Theory of Economic Development* (Cambridge: Harvard University Press, 1934).

6. For example, David S. Landes, *The Unbound Prometheus: Technological Change and Industrial Development in Western Europe from 1750 to Present* (London: Cambridge University Press, 1969), 249–323, discusses the overlapping impacts in the nineteenth century of innovations in new materials (particularly steel and chemicals), new sources of energy and power (steam and electricity), and various principles of mechanization.

7. Herbert Kitschelt, "Industrial Governance Structures, Innovation Strategies, and the Case of Japan: Sectoral or Cross National Comparative Analysis," *International Organization* 45 (Autumn 1991): 453–493.

8. Ibid., 461.

9. This section summarizes ibid., 460–468. Kitschelt examines the kinds of market contracts and property relations that might be most efficient for various technological systems.

10. Richard N. Langlois and Paul L. Robertson, "Networks and Innovation in a Modular System: Lessons From the Microcomputer and Stereo Component Industries," *Research Policy* 21 (August 1992): 298–302.

11. Kitschelt, "Industrial Governance Structures," 464–468.

12. Ibid., 471–475.

13. Fumio Kodama, *Analyzing Japanese High Technologies: The Techno-Paradigm Shift* (London: Pinter Publishers, 1991).

14. Kitschelt, "Industrial Governance Structures," 475, 492–493.

15. Business enterprises perform almost 70 percent of the actual R&D, with research universities contributing 16 percent, government laboratories 12 percent, and nonprofit institutes only 3 percent.

16. David C. Mowery, "The U.S. National Innovation System: Origins and Prospects for Change," *Research Policy* 21 (February 1992): 126–133.

17. David J. Teece, "Technological Change and the Nature of the Firm," in *Technical Change and Economic Theory*, ed. Dosi et al., 256.

18. Ibid., 263–264, and David C. Mowery and Nathan Rosenberg, *Technology and the Pursuit of Economic Growth* (Cambridge: Cambridge University Press, 1989), 6.

19. Mowery, "The U.S. National Innovation System," 135, makes this point, but he notes that U.S. work in physics was gaining rapidly on European standards in the 1930s.

20. Richard R. Nelson, "Institutions Supporting Technical Change in the United States," in *Technical Change and Economic Theory,* ed. Dosi et al. (London: Francis Pinter, 1988), 322.

21. Teece, "Technological Change and the Nature of the Firm," 276.

22. Mowery, "The U.S. National Innovation System," 135–137.

23. Nelson, "Institutions Supporting Technical Change in the United States," 320–321.

24. Mowery, "The U.S. National Innovation System," 125–126.

25. John Zysman with Laura Tyson, Giovanni Dosi, and Stephen Cohen, "Trade, Technology, and National Competition," in *Technology and Investment: Crucial Issues for the 1990s,* ed. Enrico Deiaco, Erik Hornell, and Graham Vickery (London: Pinter Publishers, 1990), 203.

26. Mowery, "The U.S. National Innovation System," 140.

27. David C. Mowery and Nathan Rosenberg, *Technology and the Pursuit of Economic Growth* (Cambridge: Cambridge University Press, 1989), 239.

28. Nelson, "Institutions Supporting Technical Change in the United States," 319, 321.

29. Laura D'Andrea Tyson, *Who's Bashing Whom?: Trade Conflict in High-Technology Industries* (Washington, D.C.: Institute for International Economics, 1992), 31.

30. Robert Gilpin, *The Political Economy of International Relations* (Princeton, N.J.: Princeton University Press, 1987), 190–203, and "Survey of World Trade," *Economist* (September 22, 1990): S-7.

31. "Survey of World Trade," S-8, S-11.

32. Andrew Pollack, "A Trade Agreement Born of Political Necessity: A New Approach to Old Problems," *New York Times,* July 12, 1993, pp. D1–D2.

33. Jadish Bhagwati, "Jumpstarting GATT," *Foreign Policy* 83 (Summer 1991): 105–115.

34. See Robert E. Baldwin, "Are Economists' Traditional Trade Policy Views Still Valid?" *Journal of Economic Literature* 30 (June 1992): 809–812, for a more complete discussion.

35. For a history of the idea, see Douglas A. Irwin, "Retrospectives: Challenges to Free Trade," *Journal of Economic Perspectives* 5 (Spring 1991): 202–205.

36. Jadish Bhagwati, *Protectionism* (Cambridge, Mass.: MIT Press, 1988), 83.

37. Keith Bradsher, "Big Three Won't Seek Car Tariffs," *New York Times,* February 10, 1993, pp. D1, D2.

38. See, for example, James A. Brander and Barbara J. Spencer, "International R&D Rivalry and Industrial Strategy," *Review of Economic Studies* 163 (October

1983): 707–722, and Brander and Spencer, "Export Subsidies and International Market Share Rivalry," *Journal of International Economics* 18 (February 1985): 83–100, for a follow-on study. See Baldwin, "Are Economists' Traditional Trade Policy Views Still Valid?" 819–820, for qualifications to their argument.

39. For an application of this idea to the Boeing-Airbus competition, see Avinash K. Dixit and Albert S. Kyle, "The Use of Protection and Subsidies for Entry Promotion and Deterrence," *American Economic Review* 75 (March 1985): 139–152.

40. For an excellent survey of the theoretical arguments behind competition for oligopoly rents and summaries of case studies that show limited practical gains from such policies, see Elhanan Helpman and Paul R. Krugman, *Trade Policy and Market Structure* (Cambridge, Mass.: MIT Press, 1989).

41. Baldwin, "Are Economists' Traditional Trade Policy Views Still Valid?" 820–821.

42. Gene M. Grossman and Elhanan Helpman, *Innovation and Growth in the Global Economy* (Cambridge, Mass.: MIT Press, 1991), 206–233.

43. Theodore H. Moran, *American Economic Policy and National Security* (New York: Council on Foreign Relations Press, 1993), 43–46. See also, Moran, "International Economics and National Security," *Foreign Affairs* 69 (Winter 1990/1991): 74–90.

44. Edward M. Graham and Paul R. Krugman, *Foreign Direct Investment in the United States,* 2nd ed. (Washington, D.C.: Institute for International Economics).

45. Baldwin, "Are Economists' Traditional Trade Policy Views Still Valid?" 822–823.

46. See, for example, Adam B. Jaffe, "Technological Opportunity and Spillovers of R&D: Evidence from Firms' Patents, Profits, and Market Value," *American Economic Review* 76 (December 1986): 994. Also, see Jeffrey I. Bernstein, "Costs of Production, Intra- and Inter-industry R&D Spillovers: Canadian Evidence," *Canadian Journal of Economics* 21 (May 1988): 324–347.

47. Tyson, *Who's Bashing Whom?* 105.

48. Ibid., 105, 108, 127.

49. Studies include the following: Tyson, *Who's Bashing Whom?* 85–154; OECD, *Globalisation of Industrial Activities: Four Case Studies: Auto Parts, Chemicals, Construction, and Semi Conductors* (Paris, 1992); David T. Methe, "The Influence of Technology and Demand Factors on Firm Size and Industrial Structure in the DRAM Market: 1973–1988," *Research Policy* 21 (February 1992): 13–25; and Richard Baldwin and Paul R. Krugman, "Market Access and International Competition: A Simulation Study of 16K Random Access Memories," in *Empirical Methods for International Trade,* ed. Robert Feenstra (Cambridge, Mass: MIT Press, 1988), 171–197.

50. Tyson, *Who's Bashing Whom?* 88–89.

51. As discussed in Chapter 3, integrated circuits consist of miniature electronic circuits imprinted on thin silicon semiconductor chips. For an excellent summary of the chip market structure in the mid-1980s, see David B. Yoffie, "The Global Semiconductor Industry, 1987," in *International Trade and Competition: Cases and Notes in Strategy and Management,* ed. David B. Yoffie (New York: McGraw-Hill, 1990), 390–391, Exhibit 2, p. 404.

52. Tyson, *Who's Bashing Whom?* 89, 97. See also Yoffie, "The Global Semiconductor Industry, 1987," 391.

53. Yoffie, "The Global Semiconductor Industry, 1987," 393.

54. Forward pricing is often attributed to Japanese firms, but Tyson argues that Texas Instruments pioneered the strategy. Tyson, *Who's Bashing Whom?* 89.

55. Alexis Jacquemin, "Strategic Competition in a Global Environment," *Trade, Investment and Technology in the 1990s* (Paris: OECD, 1991), 23.

56. Tyson, *Who's Bashing Whom?* 106.

57. Jacquemin, "Strategic Competition in a Global Environment," 23.

58. Methe, "The Influence of Technology and Demand Factors on Firm Size and Industrial Structure," 17–18.

59. Ibid., 22.

60. Jeffrey A. Hart, *Rival Capitalists* (Ithaca, N.Y.: Cornell University Press, 1992), 82. Also see Jacquemin, "Strategic Competition in a Global Environment," 22. Jacquemin argues that the surge in Japanese investment in DRAM chips led to a combined U.S.-Japanese 256K DRAM capacity that was fully 2.5 times larger than world demand in 1985.

61. Tyson, *Who's Bashing Whom?* 26, 101, 106.

62. OECD, *Globalisation of Industrial Activities*, 152. Tyson, *Who's Bashing Whom?* 93–98.

63. Baldwin and Krugman, "Market Access and International Competition," 171–197, and Helpman and Krugman, *Trade Policy and Market Structure*, 169–174.

64. Eliot Marshall, "U.S., Japan Reach Truce in Chips War," *Science* (August 15, 1986), reproduced in *Japan and the U.S.*, ed. Robert E. Long (New York: The H. W. Wilson Company, 1990), 54, and Daniel I. Okimoto, "Outsider Trading: Coping with Japanese Industrial Organization," in *The Trade Crisis: How Will Japan Respond?* ed. Kenneth B. Pyle (Seattle, Wash.: Society for Japanese Studies, 1987), 97.

65. See Dennis J. Encarnation, *Rivals Beyond Trade: America Versus Japan in Global Competition* (Ithaca, N.Y.: Cornell University Press, 1992), 127. He argues that MITI played a role in blocking the entry of small manufacturing firms into the semiconductor industry and promoting the entry of large, diversified electronics companies.

66. Yoffie, "The Global Semiconductor Industry, 1987," 394.

67. See Okimoto, "Outsider Trading," 97, for an argument that the Japanese firms also had important technical advantages.

68. Yoffie, "The Global Semiconductor Industry, 1987," 394, 396.

69. John J. Coleman, "The Semiconductor Industry Association and the Trade Dispute With Japan," in *International Trade and Competition*, ed. Yoffie (New York: McGraw-Hill, 1990), 415–420.

70. Ibid., 420–422.

71. George Russell, "Trade Face-off," *Time* (April 13, 1987), as cited in *Japan and the U.S.*, ed. Long, 57.

72. Tyson, *Who's Bashing Whom?* 111, 118–119.

73. Ibid., 120.

74. Hart, *Rival Capitalists*, 83, 274, and Tyson, *Who's Bashing Whom?* 117. Howard K. Gruenspecht, "Dumping and Dynamic Competition," *Journal of Inter-*

national Economics 25 (November 1988): 225–248, and Robert W. Staiger and Frank A. Wolak, "Discretionary Trade Policy and Excessive Protection," *American Economic Review* 77 (December 1987): 823–837, demonstrate how antidumping laws in general can promote collusion among foreign and domestic producers.

75. Tyson, *Who's Bashing Whom?* Figure 4.2, p. 106.

76. Ibid., 136–141. European complaints about MITI's control of semiconductor prices in third markets led to a 1988 GATT panel finding that the export restrictions were inconsistent with GATT, and MITI subsequently amended its third-country monitoring system. See OECD, *Globalisation of Industrial Activities*, 153.

77. Tyson, *Who's Bashing Whom?* 112–113, 125.

78. Ibid., 143–145.

79. Ibid., 126.

80. Ibid., 127.

81. "Survey of World Trade," 21, and Tyson, *Who's Bashing Whom?* 130–131.

82. See Andrew Pollack, "Japan Gets New Demands on Chip Imports," *New York Times*, March 24, 1993, pp. D1, D17, and Keith Bradsher, "Share of Foreign Chips in Japan's Market Slips," *New York Times*, September 23, 1993, p. D2.

83. Okimoto, "Outsider Trading," 92, illustrates the point.

84. Mowery and Rosenberg, *Technology and the Pursuit of Economic Growth*, 255.

85. Lester Thurow, *Head to Head: The Coming Economic Battle Among Japan, Europe, and America* (New York: William Morrow and Co., Inc., 1992).

86. Charles H. Ferguson, "Computers and the Coming of the U.S. Keiretsu," *Harvard Business Review* 68 (July-August 1990): 55–70.

6 U.S. Technology Policy

U.S. postwar technology leadership was driven by a superior technological infrastructure and exploited by vertically structured corporations that translated technological leadership into competitive advantage through long product cycles. That leadership has now given way to technological parity and intense regional competition fueled by organizational networks designed to exploit short product cycles. The competition focuses on the ability to design and create advanced and specialized factors of production needed to develop and sustain advantage in high-value activities.

Technology, industrial, and trade policies are the key national instruments for influencing that competition. Those policies are clearly interconnected, and there are no commonly accepted definitions or clear organizational boundaries that separate them, but in broad terms, technology policy focuses on patterns of innovation, industrial policy emphasizes the sectoral or regional composition of production, and trade policy influences the impact of national border restrictions on relative domestic and international prices. In the United States, technology and industrial policies have been more implicit than explicit, with programs and responsibilities scattered through a wide range of agencies. While some critics might argue that the United States does not or should not have coordinated technology or industrial policies, most would certainly agree that federal policies have enormous impacts in both areas.

Trade, industrial, and technology policies might be viewed as overlapping circles with important intersections. Industrial and technology policies come together when the objective is to provide support for innovation processes in a particular region or industry. Trade and technology policies overlap when the purpose of a trade restriction is to promote innovation, or when the objective of a technology policy is to provide a trade advantage. All three policies intersect in cases such as the Semiconductor Trade Agreements discussed in the last chapter, where an important objective was to use managed-trade targets to ensure access to Japanese markets, expand U.S. market share, and gain the technological spillover benefits of DRAM production by U.S. firms. Although the three policy approaches do intersect, the distinctions among the policy objectives are important and the international organizations and regimes for dealing with each policy area do differ.

U.S. technology policy includes government efforts at the local, state, and national levels to influence innovation networks in support of national strategy. Because the government laboratories, research universities, research institutes, private corporations, and government agencies that interact in the innovation network all have international links through formal agreements and informal relationships, technology policy has important international dimensions. Indeed, the desire to develop an integrated U.S. technology policy in the last decade has come largely in response to perceived challenges from foreign technology policies.

Note that the definition of technology policy suggests a spectrum of techniques for "influencing the activities" of a wide array of public and private organizations. Technology policy is certainly reflected in budget outlays by government agencies, but it also includes a host of impacts on the cost of capital and regulatory requirements that influence innovation. The focus on innovation suggests that technology policy covers a wide range of activities beyond a traditional emphasis on the creation and dissemination of scientific, engineering, and technical knowledge, to include policies that shape organizations and their operating environments.

Technology policy will clearly play an important and controversial role in the competition for high-value activities. Used correctly, such policies can target sources of market failure and increase economic efficiency. As earlier chapters have argued, markets tend to underfund R&D because many of the advantages spill over to other firms in the industry. Capital markets may not work efficiently in channeling funds to new technologies where risks are perceived to be high because of uncertainty over future national or international policies. Small firms may not have adequate access to new technologies, because economies of scale in obtaining that information favor larger organizations. All of these market failures provide arguments for government intervention, but there are also important arguments against government involvement.

First, government might be biased toward inappropriate means for correcting the market failure. For example, direct subsidies to firms for specific types of R&D outlays might be an appropriate remedy to promote an optimal level of basic research, but government may find it difficult to make such expenditures line-item budget entries in a period of severe fiscal constraints. Instead, the government might turn to blunt, indirect forms of support, such as trade protection to drive up prices, increase profits, and thus expand the pool of funds that could be applied to R&D. The side effects, or "deadweight losses," of such inefficient policies might well outweigh the potential benefits.

Second, government might find it difficult to target only sources of market failure. For example, if there is a market failure in the diffusion of information on new machine tool technologies to the small firms that dominate that sector, the government might design an appropriate demonstration and extension program to correct the problem. The political dynamics of establishing such a program to help one group of producers may, however, create enormous pressure to assist other industries in which there is no similar market failure. This danger exists, of course, in any government program, but it is perhaps more difficult to contain in technology policy where the sources of market failure are subtle and differ from industry to industry.[1]

Third, there may be a fundamental problem in designing government agencies that can act as effective entrepreneurs in correcting market failures in rapidly developing technological areas. Effective management requires an understanding of the technology, the shifting structure of consumer demands, the underlying structure of the industry, and the policies that can be most effective in responding to market forces. The private sector has superior information and incentives for dealing with market signals, and it may be reluctant to share that information with the government because of the potential loss of advantage over commercial competitors.[2] Government should arguably be relatively more effective at the basic and precompetitive levels of R&D, where rapid reaction to market shifts is not as crucial, and less effective at the level of applied and competitive R&D, where responsiveness to market forces is critical. Government's ability to develop effective R&D policies also varies across industries. Government policy arguably has a greater chance for success in technological areas such as semiconductors, nuclear energy, or aircraft, in which agencies have developed expertise as a result of earlier government R&D or procurement.

Fourth, government programs may simply displace private initiatives. For example, providing matching grants to private firms to induce R&D on new network technologies may simply shift funds from alternative, less risky projects or free the R&D funds for other purposes. Effective programs must be designed to draw new funds into targeted R&D areas rather than simply providing windfalls for those already engaged in such activities.

Fifth, global R&D networks may exploit local or national R&D subsidies and shift the impact elsewhere. Procedures that limit participation in such projects to national firms, as in the case of SEMATECH discussed below, have limited effectiveness. Global network relationships and the potential for foreign acquisition diffuse the benefits of national subsidies.[3] Government programs targeted at the creation of tacit knowledge or infrastructure that can be exploited by local firms have the best chance of developing sustainable competitive advantages. Those specialized skills, institutional relationships, and infrastructure are most important at the competitive level in general and in process technologies in particular. Unfortunately, U.S. institutional relationships among industry, research universities, and government are less developed in the areas of process technologies, so tailoring government programs that are responsive to market pressures at the process level is a major challenge.

Despite those significant obstacles to an effective technology policy, there is enormous pressure for broader U.S. government intervention in technology markets beyond the traditional levels of support for science, basic research, and government procurement. As noted in Chapter 5, the strategic arguments for intervention to shift terms of trade and gain oligopoly rents, to capture spillovers from enabling technologies with broad impacts on other industries, and to ensure access to critical technologies important to national security all support some form of intervention. Although Japanese and European Community technology policies have had mixed results, their success in some key areas makes a case for some U.S. response.[4] Although subsidies by foreign governments to their high-technology sectors may help the U.S. economy by lowering the prices of imported goods for U.S. consumers, there is enough uncertainty about the dynamic impacts of those subsidies in shifting comparative advantage to warrant concern. Moreover, the United States has had an implicit technology policy through its defense R&D and procurement system, so the real challenge is to manage the transition in R&D policies in the context of active technology policies by other regions.

THE SCOPE OF U.S. TECHNOLOGY POLICY

Although many U.S. agencies pursue policies that have an impact on innovation, no single agency has the clear lead in this area. Until very recently, efforts to integrate, or even monitor, overlapping programs have been limited. Just listing budgeted technology initiatives in different agencies is a difficult task, and assembling information on the impact of various government regulations on technology is even more challenging. A review of the current structure of U.S. R&D expenditures, government efforts to influence the allocation of R&D outlays, and procedures for coordinating government R&D programs suggests the scope of the challenge in establishing and implementing a coherent national technology policy.

R&D Expenditures

In 1991, total U.S. R&D outlays were $152 billion, more than the combined R&D expenditures of Japan, West Germany, France, and the United Kingdom. The share of GNP allocated to R&D in each country, however, was remarkably similar, at 2.7 percent in the United States, 3.0 in Japan, 2.9 in West Germany, and 2.3 percent in France and the United Kingdom. Despite the similar shares of GNP allocated to R&D, the composition of the R&D outlays differed substantially across countries, primarily because of the large defense R&D expenditures in the United States. In 1991, U.S.

Table 6-1
U.S. R&D in 1991 by Category, Source (S), and Performer (P) (billion nominal dollars)[a]

	Basic Research		Applied Research		Development	
	(S)	(P)	(S)	(P)	(S)	(P)
Federal Government	14.5	2.8	13.1	4.1	38.5	9.5
Industry	4.9	5.1	19.7	23.9	53.5	79.5
Universities and Colleges	2.9	11.1	1.7	5.2	.4	.9
U&C FFRDCs[b]	2.6	.0	.7	.0	1.6	.0
Other Nonprofits	1.3	2.0	.9	1.5	.4	1.3
Total	23.5	23.5	35.4	35.4	92.8	92.8

Source: National Science Board, *Science and Engineering Indicators—1991,* 10th ed. (Washington, D.C.: U.S. Government Printing Office, 1991), 309–311.

Notes:
a. Details may not add to totals because of rounding.
b. FFRDCs administered by universities and colleges. Those administered by industry and nonprofit institutions are included in the totals for their respective categories.

nondefense R&D outlays constituted only 1.9 percent of GNP compared with 3 percent in Japan.[5] This dramatic difference in commercial R&D has become a major focus in reviewing U.S. technology policy.

One way of tracing the dimensions of national technology policy is to track the flow of R&D funds from their sources to actual R&D providers. Table 6-1 divides the total U.S. 1991 R&D outlay of $152 billion by source of funds and performer across the major categories of basic research, applied research, and development. The National Science Foundation defines basic research as efforts to develop knowledge "without specific applications in mind," and basic research by industry as "research that advances scientific knowledge but does not have specific commercial objectives." Applied research focuses on a specific need, and development uses knowledge from research for "the production of useful materials, devices, systems, or methods, including design and development of prototypes and processes."[6]

Industry provides the largest share of funds for applied research and development, and it performs the lion's share of R&D in each of those areas. The federal government's primary role is to channel R&D funds to actual providers, with the largest net flow going to industry for development, particularly in the defense sector. Federal programs play a critical role in funding over 60 percent of all basic research, primarily by channeling resources to universities and colleges. Funding for R&D by state and local government remains a very small part of R&D outlays, accounting for roughly 1.5 percent of national expenditures.[7]

Federal Sources and Channels for R&D Funds

The federal share of national R&D funding has declined from a peak of 63 percent in the 1960s to under 50 percent in the 1980s and an estimated 44 percent in 1991. Nonetheless, the federal government retains the dominant position in funding basic research. In addition, federal technology expenditures exert enormous influence over national R&D priorities by supporting roughly one-third of outlays for applied research and over 40 percent of development expenditures.[8]

Recent budgets provide insights into the main actors at the federal level and the most important agencies for channeling R&D funds to ultimate users. Table 6-2 presents data from President Clinton's fiscal year 1994 budget submission to Congress and provides a quick overview of budget authority for the conduct of R&D by federal department and R&D category. The Departments of Defense (DOD), Energy (DOE), and Health and Human Services (HHS), and the National Aeronautics and Space Administration (NASA) claim most of the available funds.

Defense R&D has taken up over 50 percent of federal obligations since 1981, rising through the defense expansion under President Reagan to roughly 64 percent of federal R&D expenditures by 1986.[9] Since 1987 defense R&D has declined in terms of constant dollar outlays and as a share of federal expenditures, dropping to about 55 percent of federal obligations in President Clinton's proposed 1994 budget. Because some 90 percent of defense R&D has historically gone to development activities, total federal expenditures for development have been declining along with defense outlays, and the relative emphasis on basic research has been increasing.[10] Although real military R&D continues to decline, it still dominates the federal government's efforts in applied research and development.

HHS, NASA, and DOE together account for over 35 percent of federal R&D. HHS and its National Institutes of Health provide some 40 percent of federal funds for basic research.[11] Funding for Space Station Freedom has figured prominently in NASA's recent R&D obligations, accounting for over 25 percent of its proposed 1994 budget.[12] HHS and NASA out-

Table 6-2
Federal Conduct of Research and Development, 1992–1994 (budget authority in
millions of nominal dollars)

	1992 actual	1993 estimate	1994 proposed	Change (%) 1993–1994
By R&D Category:				
Basic Research	12,984	13,701	13,940	2
Civilian	11,838	12,306	12,688	3
Defense	1,146	1,395	1,252	-10
Applied R&D	55,069	56,602	58,153	3
Civilian	16,132	16,389	17,427	6
Defense	38,937	40,213	40,726	1
Subtotal	68,053	70,303	72,093	3
R&D Facilities	3,903	3,259	3,498	7
Total	71,956	73,562	75,591	3
By Agency[a]:				
DOD	37,418	38,793	39,301	1
HHS[b]	10,138	10,378	10,704	3
NASA[c]	7,712	8,007	8,667	8
Energy	5,954	5,981	5,877	-2
NSF[d]	1,846	2,069	2,221	7
Agriculture	1,335	1,336	1,365	2
Commerce	545	562	731	30
Transportation	540	656	727	11
EPA[e]	494	508	548	8
Education	165	166	176	6
All Other	1,906	1,846	1,777	-4
Total	68,053	70,303	72,093	3

Source: U.S. Office of Management and Budget, *Budget of the United States Government,
Fiscal Year 1994* (Washington, D.C.: U.S. Government Printing Office, April 8,
1993), 44.

Notes:
a. Excludes facilities.
b. Health and Human Services.
c. National Aeronautics and Space Administration.
d. National Science Foundation.
e. Environmental Protection Agency.

lays have been expanding in real terms since the early 1980s, while DOE
R&D budgets have been declining in constant dollars over the same period
and will continue to decline under President Clinton's proposed budget.[13]
    Federal agencies have become quite specialized in channeling funds to

Table 6-3
Estimated Federal Obligations for R&D, by Selected Agency and Performer,
Fiscal Year 1991 (billion nominal dollars)

Agency	Total	In-House	Industry	FFRDCs[a]	College/ Univers.	Other[b]
DOD	36.9	9.0	25.4	1.2	1.1	.3
HHS	8.9	1.9	.4	.1	4.9	1.6
DOE	6.0	.4	1.0	4.0	.4	.2
NASA	8.3	2.6	4.3	.7	.5	.2
NSF	2.0	.2	.1	.1	1.5	.1
DOA[c]	1.2	.8	.0	.0	.4	.0
Other	2.8	1.6	.4	.1	.4	.4
Total[d]	66.1	16.4	31.5	6.3	9.2	2.8

Source: National Science Board, *Science and Engineering Indicators—1991*, 10th ed. (Washington, D.C.: U.S. Government Printing Office, 1991), 318.

Notes:

a. Industry-administered FFRDCs received $2.062 billion, university-administered FFRDCs $3.654 billion, and nonprofit-administered FFRDCs $0.482 billion.

b. Includes nonprofit organizations ($2.3 billion), state and local government ($0.2 billion), and foreign sources ($0.3 billion).

c. Department of Agriculture.

d. Details may not add to totals because of rounding.

particular R&D performers and categories. Table 6-3 shows how R&D disbursements by each agency were divided over various recipients in 1991. Defense dominated federal in-house R&D, with over 85 percent of those DOD outlays going for development. DOD and NASA played the central role in channeling funds to industry, and HHS provided over half of all federal funds to universities and other nonprofit organizations. DOD, DOE, and HHS all play a significant role in federally funded research and development centers (FFRDC), administered by corporations, universities, or nonprofit institutions, which account for over 10 percent of federally funded R&D activity. The 10 industry-administered FFRDCs received over $2 billion in 1991, with the bulk of the funding by DOE and DOD.[14] DOE provides most of the funds to university-administered FFRDCs for applied research and development, and DOD funds most of the development expenditures by nonprofit-administered FFRDCs.

The programmatic, specialized orientation of federal R&D programs has made it difficult to provide central coordination of those activities. The dominant role of DOD in channeling funds to industry, particularly for development, has made it the central player in what has amounted to a de facto industrial policy. As defense R&D has declined and national technology policy has begun to focus on industrial competitiveness, however, the federal government has made a concerted effort to provide greater coordination of R&D efforts across agencies and to focus initiatives more directly on the industrial sector.

Coordination of National Technology Policy

In the postwar period, federal R&D expenditures have been designed primarily to support government procurement objectives. As a result, decentralization of expenditures across procuring agencies provided a sensible principle for allocating R&D funds. Moreover, federal R&D procurement happened to support technologies that had extensive spillovers to the private sector, so the procurement-oriented R&D strategy had fortuitous commercial impacts without centralized control. Those two conditions arguably held from the 1950s through the 1970s, but they were both called into question in the 1980s. Defense spillovers into the private sector declined, the level of defense and energy procurement dropped by the end of the decade, and foreign technology policies shifted the U.S. emphasis toward the impact of technology on competitiveness. As a result, the policy process began to focus more directly on R&D programs that had dual impacts on federal procurement and industrial competitiveness.

The FCCSET Process. Coordination of technology policy is complicated by the wide array of congressional committees and executive agencies with responsibility for oversight and implementation. Seventeen authorizing committees in the House and Senate have significant legislative authority over R&D expenditures.[15] The Office of Technology Assessment, created by the Technology Assessment Act of 1972, supports those committees with policy reviews, but there is no effective congressional process for integrating policy approaches across the authorizing committees.

Coordination is somewhat better in the executive branch, although integration has not been a high priority until very recently. As shown in Figure 6-1, executive branch technology policy is coordinated within the Executive Office of the President through an interagency Federal Coordinating Council for Science, Engineering, and Technology (FCCSET—pronounced "fixit") chaired by the Assistant to the President for Science and Technology, who directs the Office of Science and Technology Policy (OSTP) and is supported by the President's Council of Advisers on Science and Technology. The Office of Management and Budget (OMB), the National Security Council (NSC), and the newly organized National Economic Council (NEC) all play critical roles in linking technology decisions to other national priorities. The key issue in the coordination process is how budget outlays will be allocated across and within departmental programs.

Figure 6-1
Executive Branch Technology Policy Coordination

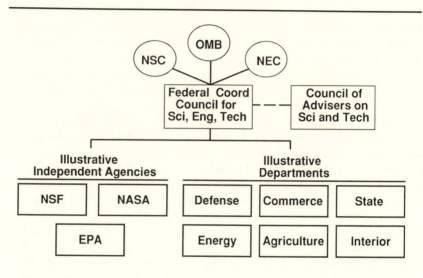

The FCCSET, a cabinet-level committee including representation from the Environmental Protection Agency (EPA), NASA, National Science Foundation (NSF), Veterans Affairs, OMB, and the NSC, was established by statute in 1976 to address science and technology issues that cut across agencies. Until recently, the FCCSET had no formal role in the budget process and the influence of the OSTP on spending priorities depended on informal relationships between the science adviser and the director of OMB.[16] Since the late 1980s, FCCSET has been used to review each agency's planned R&D budget submissions, identify overlaps, and provide recommendations to OMB for funding priorities. Although the FCCSET meets as a full committee only a few times a year, it has an elaborate structure of subcommittees that meet almost continuously. During President Bush's administration, major committees included the following: Earth and Environmental Sciences; Education and Human Resources; Food, Agriculture, and Forestry Research; International Science, Engineering, and Technology (CISET); Life Sciences and Health; Physical, Mathematical, and Engineering Sciences; and Technology and Industry. CISET, for example, reviews international policy matters that cut across agency boundaries, advises on U.S. policies and positions in multilateral organizations, and drafts an annual report to Congress, *Science, Technology, and American Diplomacy.*[17]

The FCCSET process has focused on the identification of critical technologies to guide national R&D priorities and on the identification of overlaps and redundancies within, but not across, departmental programs. Since the fall 1990 publication of *U.S. Technology Policy,* authored by President Bush's Science and Technology Advisor, Allan Bromley, the coordination of technology policy has taken on new directions. In Bromley's words, the federal government has a responsibility "to participate with the private sector in precompetitive research on generic, enabling technologies that have the potential to contribute to a broad range of government and commercial applications." [18] But despite this emphasis on the integration of private and public efforts, no clear methodology has yet emerged for linking the process of establishing national priorities to sources of market failure that create the need for government intervention. The critical-technology approach, in and of itself, does not provide useful criteria for evaluating national priorities. It could, however, serve as a valuable means for evaluating federal programs if it were linked to an assessment of the sources of market failure in each technology area.

The Critical-Technology Approach. Lists of critical technologies proliferated in the late 1980s and early 1990s in attempts to identify technologies that would serve as enabling technologies with large spillover benefits to other sectors and would be most important to future military capabilities. The *1990 DOD Critical Technologies Plan* designated 20 key technologies for reaching military goals of deterrence, military superiority, and affordability. The plan divided those 20 technologies into three categories: technologies with the highest priority for sustaining current capabilities, enabling technologies offering the most immediate advances in weapon system capabilities, and emerging technologies with uncertain, but potentially important, future impacts. [19] In a parallel report, *Emerging Technologies: A Survey of Technical and Economic Opportunities,* also released in the spring of 1990, the Department of Commerce identified emerging technologies expected to contribute to competitiveness by the end of the century and assessed U.S., Japanese, and European Community positions in developing those technologies. [20] In the spring of 1991, a panel appointed by the director of OSTP reviewed those efforts and generated an integrated list of 22 national critical technologies important to economic strength and national security. [21] Table 6-4 presents the national critical technologies identified in that report.

The high level of aggregation in such lists makes them cumbersome guides to priorities within specific technological areas. [22] The major problem with the critical-technology approach, however, is deeper than reaching agreement on the crucial technologies of the future and specifying those technologies in sufficient detail to guide policy decisions. The key issue is whether the private sector will allocate resources to those technologies proportionate to the total return to society of those investments. To argue that semiconductors are a critical enabling technology, or even more specifically that DRAM lithography is critical, for example, provides little

Table 6-4
National Critical Technologies

Materials
  Materials synthesis and processing
  Electronic and photonic materials
  Ceramics
  Composites
  High-performance metals and alloys

Manufacturing
  Flexible computer integrated manufacturing
  Intelligent processing equipment
  Micro- and nano-fabrication
  Systems management technologies

Information and Communication
  Software
  Microelectronics and optoelectronics
  High-performance computing and networking
  High-definition imaging and displays
  Sensors and signal processors
  Data storage and peripherals
  Computer simulation and modeling

Biotechnology and Life Sciences
  Applied molecular biology
  Medical technology

Aeronautics and Surface Transportation
  Aeronautics
  Surface transportation technologies

Energy and Environment
  Energy technologies
  Pollution minimization, remediation, and waste
    management

Source: Air Force Institute of Technology, *Critical Technologies for National Defense* (Washington, D.C.: American Institute of Aeronautics and Astronautics, 1991), 8.

insight into public policy. A persuasive case for government intervention requires evidence that a market failure exists and that an available policy response can effectively target and correct the failure.

Dimensions of Technology Policy. These two policy dimensions, the importance of the technology and the nature of the market failure, provide a starting point for evaluating federal technology policy. Sources of market failure vary significantly across technologies based on their coupling and complexity, the stage of the technological trajectory, and the domestic and international market structure. Market failures in diffusing information on new technologies through the small firms that make up the machine tools sector, for example, would be very different from the high risks of foreign government subsidies and large economies of scale in the aircraft sector. As a result, technology policy should address varying sources of market failure across different sectors. The case for market failure arguably becomes weaker as technology shifts from basic, to applied, to developmental, to diffusion levels, because it is easier for the firm to capture the full benefits of expenditures that are targeted on acquiring specific capabilities rather than general knowledge.

The emergence of global organizational networks suggests yet another important dimension for examining national technology policy. Even if policymakers could identify key points of intersection between important technologies and significant market failures, the remedies might not lead to more high-value activities within national borders or even by national firms. Government policies that support basic research, where market failures are most obvious, are also most likely to improve the world's store of knowledge through global networks. Such policies may have a laudable impact on international efficiency, but they should have limited impacts in favoring local high-value activities over international competition.

The potential for capturing local benefits from government R&D assistance is greatest in applied and developmental efforts, particularly work on process technologies, which create the infrastructure and tacit knowledge that are hard to pass through global networks. Traditionally, the case that market failures exist at those levels has been more difficult to establish than that for the basic research, because firms are more likely to capture the benefits of outlays on applied research and development. A more complete analysis of network behavior, however, suggests that market failures in innovation extend through the organizational problem of linking information across researchers, suppliers, producers, and consumers. Organizational networks can help to resolve those linkage problems, but there may be obstacles to forming such networks. Impediments to coordination may then provide important sources of market failure even at the applied research and development levels.

Global organizational networks have therefore reinforced the role of basic research as an *international* public good. Applied research, development, and local diffusion activities are more likely to provide regional or national advantages, although some of that information will also be captured by global networks. As a result, the impacts of various policies fall on different government jurisdictions at the global, federal, state, or local level. Technology policy should therefore be designed so that the level of government most likely to capture the benefits would have the lead, because lower levels of government would undersupport R&D and diffusion activities that spill over to other jurisdictions. At the basic research level, a coordinated international technology policy is required to offset the general market failure where individual firms or countries cannot capture the full benefit of the general knowledge they produce. The further one moves from broad general research down to local diffusion of information, the more the comparative advantage of public institutions in correcting market failures shifts from multinational organizations to national government to state and local institutions.

Just as different levels of government vary in their competence to assess and respond to different forms of market failure, the structure of organizations equipped to merge the patience of government with the responsiveness of the private sector will also vary. In general, government is best equipped to allocate funds for basic research, because the scale of projects may exceed the capacity of the private sector, there is sufficient time to overcome the slow reactions of the public sector, and there is less need to tailor projects to market feedback. At the applied, development, and diffusion levels, however, responsiveness to the market is more important, and the level of detail required for timely decisions often exceeds the capacity of the public sector. Unfortunately, although feedback from the private sector is crucial in designing and implementing effective development and diffusion programs, firms face a moral hazard in cooperating with government. Information from the private sector may be biased because firms will understandably act in their own best interests. Programs at the applied and diffusion level must therefore give firms a vested interest in providing accurate information. One technique for accomplishing that objective is to ensure that public outlays reinforce substantial private investment, so that firms have a clear stake in the success of the project.[23]

The science in technology policy is in assessing the importance of different technologies and identifying sources of market failure. The art is in designing organizations and programs that create incentives for the accurate exchange of information, for targeting efficient responses on precise market failures, and for appropriate adjustments based on market feedback. The actual structure of technology policy, of course, depends at least as much on balancing political interests as on the analytical tradeoffs across critical technologies, market failures, and global network flows. Despite those complexities, the four criteria for assessing technology policies—the critical nature of the technology, the source of market failure, the potential for diffusion through global networks, and the possibility of designing programs that elicit accurate market feedback—provide a useful framework for assessing priorities, evaluating programs, and highlighting policy trends.

REFORMING U.S. TECHNOLOGY POLICY

U.S. technology policy is in an important period of transition. Informed choices will require an understanding of the evolution of current U.S. innovation networks, an appreciation for the impacts of economic convergence and global organizational networks, an understanding of the central transforming role of information technologies, an evaluation of the different sources of market failure in developing various critical technologies, and appropriate adjustments to the heightened importance of adapting to foreign technological breakthroughs and meeting international competition in commercializing new technologies. In particular, U.S. technology policy should focus on achieving the following central tasks: (1) strengthen coordination across agencies, (2) expand levels of private R&D and investment, (3) promote cooperative international technology regimes, (4) increase emphasis on market-oriented programs targeted on dual-use technologies, (5) improve diffusion and acquisition of new process technologies, (6) enhance network integration, and (7) preserve access to critical technologies.

Policy Coordination

Despite recent attempts to improve integration, the federal government's efforts to develop a coordinated technology policy have been largely ineffective. That is not to say that various agencies have failed in their own missions, or that there have been no improvements in coordination across programs, but rather that no effective principle for establishing and pursuing technology goals has been adopted. The FCCSET process has produced clear improvements in the focus on critical technologies, but it has not provided a systematic emphasis on sources of market failure or an effective framework for enforcing tradeoffs across programs.

President Clinton's new program described in his February 1993 booklet, *Technology for America's Economic Growth, A New Direction to Build Economic Strength,* addresses many of the weaknesses. The booklet identifies the government's "key role helping private firms develop and profit from innovations," and presents the following directions for the new technology policy: improving industrial competitiveness and creating jobs; creating an environment that supports business innovation and investment; improving coordination of technology management within government; forging ties across the public and private sectors; focusing on critical industries such as "information and communication, flexible manufacturing, and environmental technologies"; and reaffirming the central role of basic science.[24]

These "new directions" would shift the emphasis of technology policy away from support of government procurement toward a more active role in developing commercial technology. The initial proposed budget adjustments shown in Table 6-2 do reflect some shifts in that direction, particularly the large percentage increase for the Department of Commerce, but the momentum of current programs ensures that the actual composition of R&D outlays will change slowly. The most significant impacts of the new policy directions are apt to come not in the levels of aggregate spending across programs, but in the relative priorities within agency programs. President Clinton's budget proposals show the civilian share of federal R&D outlays rising from some 41 percent in 1993 to over 50 percent by 1998, so defense R&D outlays will continue to account for a majority of federal R&D until almost the end of the decade.[25] Because most federal R&D funds will continue to flow through defense programs, the new technology policy's emphasis on dual military- and civilian-use DOD R&D programs could have the largest near-term impact on the structure of federal R&D priorities.

The "new directions" support the following three technology goals articulated in President Clinton's policy statement: "long term economic growth that creates jobs and protects the environment; a government that is more productive and responsive to the needs of its citizens; world leadership in basic science, mathematics, and engineering."[26] The scope of these goals suggests a broad view of technology policy as a centerpiece of national strategy. The proposed policy components include the following: lowering the federal deficit and interest rates, tax credits for research, "open but fair trade," regulatory policy that "encourages innovation and achieves social objectives efficiently," education and training, R&D funding to offset market failures, outlays on "R&D centers and manufacturing extension centers," assistance in developing national telecommunications and information infrastructures, federal purchasing policies that enhance innovation, strong support for basic science, development of cooperative international science and technology projects, funding for dual-use R&D projects, and use of "national user facilities" to provide advanced tools for "a variety of research organizations."[27]

The scope of this list, encompassing fiscal policy, trade policy, regulatory policy, education policy, R&D priorities, and international science and technology objectives, is impressive. The organization of these ideas under the framework of technology policy represents a revolutionary departure in the way the federal government envisions linkages across policies and the central thrust of those policies. The coordination of this broad technology policy will clearly require a new level of integration within the FCCSET process and a critical role for the new National Economic Council in harmonizing fiscal, trade, and regulatory policies in support of the technology goals. President Clinton's technology policy statement does not elaborate on the trade and regulatory components, but it presents the fiscal and R&D components in some detail.

In addition to general deficit reduction to lower interest rates, the fiscal proposals include permanent extension of the research and experimentation tax credit, incentives for high-risk, long-term venture capital investments in new enterprises and other small firms, a permanent tax credit for incremental investment in equipment by small firms and a temporary credit for large firms, and a review of proposals to encourage long-term asset ownership.[28] The technology policy emphasizes cost-sharing with private firms, peer review, and merit-based competition as criteria for selecting investments to improve competitiveness. As suggested in the policy, in the summer of 1993 Congress reformed the National Cooperative Research Act of 1984 to include joint production as well as joint research efforts.[29]

Specific technology areas singled out for special emphasis in the policy proposals include learning and teaching technologies, school access to communications networks, manufacturing engineering, advanced manufacturing technology, automobiles with new fuel and propulsion systems, the high-performance computing and communications program, national communications infrastructure, mass transit, high-speed rail, "smart" highways, civil aviation, public infrastructure rehabilitation, government applications of information technology for public services, energy-efficient retrofits of public buildings, and research instruments such as synchrotron radiation and neutron beam tools.[30] The FCCSET process has articulated these priorities in terms of "six cross-cutting budget initiatives" in the following areas: advanced manufacturing technology, high-performance computing and communications, global change research, advanced materials and processing, biotechnology research, and mathematics and science education.[31] These major initiatives will presumably be coordinated by a committee process reporting through the FCCSET structure to the NEC.

President Clinton's technology policy also highlights the following specific roles for various agencies: the Advanced Technology Program in the Department of Commerce grows; the Defense Advanced Research Projects Agency (DARPA) loses the "Defense" prefix, reverts to its pre-1972 name of ARPA, and expands its program in dual-use technologies; DOE programs encourage private sector R&D consortia focused on reductions in pollution; the SEMATECH industry consortium for developing semiconductor manufacturing technology continues to receive DOD matching funds in fiscal year 1994; DOE, NASA, and DOD laboratories devote 10 to 20 percent of their budgets to industry partnership agreements; the Telecommunications and Information Administration of the Department of Commerce provides matching grants to schools, libraries, and local government for computer networking; Commerce also creates a national network of manufacturing extension services and provides seed funds for regional technology alliances; and the Department of Labor coordinates assistance in improving management and work processes.[32] These initiatives represent a very small part of the federal R&D budget, but taken together they provide a wide range of highly visible cooperative experiments between government and business and across different levels of government.

The new technology policy is very consistent with the major findings in earlier chapters on the importance of capital costs, education, infrastructure, manufacturing processes, and organizational networks to the development of sustainable competitive advantages in high-value industries. The policy keeps government programs at the levels of basic, generic, and precompetitive research in most cases, moving cautiously beyond that with cooperative ventures with the private sector, such as SEMATECH, and perhaps including an AEROTECH initiative in the aircraft sector. Although the policy has few references to specific market failures, the ideas of high U.S. capital costs, the need for patient capital, the large investments required to create adequate infrastructure, the high risk levels facing small firms, and the need for improved diffusion of technology to small firms permeate the document.

Despite the policy's stated emphasis on basic research, there is also careful reference to international cooperation in that area and the need for collaboration to address global problems.[33] The emphasis on international cooperation in basic research and the increase in the relative emphasis on manufacturing technologies are both very consistent with the findings presented earlier on the impact of global networks. Basic research results are easily absorbed by global networks, but R&D in process technologies is more likely to create sustainable national advantages. The dual-use emphasis in the policy is also very consistent with the argument that the federal government is more likely to develop effective programs in areas in which earlier procurement has produced a bureaucracy experienced in a particular technology.

The strength of the proposed technology policy lies in the clear articulation of guiding principles for the FCCSET process and the emphasis on using government policy to support private-sector initiatives. The inability to articulate specific sources of market failure to be corrected by government policy continues to be a weakness. Without such a perspective, government task forces in particular policy areas will find it difficult to set the limits of government intervention or explore alternative approaches to correcting the market failure. The policy correctly emphasizes the complex dimensions of technology policy and the need to coordinate them, but more complete articulation of the use of trade and regulatory policies will be required to permit task forces to look across all the available policy options.

Private R&D and Investment

Investment varies sharply over the business cycle as firms adjust their capital stocks to stay in balance with anticipated sales. R&D varies somewhat more gradually because of its long-term payback, but the availability of funding does have a strong influence on R&D outlays. As shown in

Table 6-5
National Trends in Business Enterprise R&D, 1975–1990 (percent per year)
(Reprinted with permission from OECD.)

Country	1990 R&D Billion $[a]	Compound Real Growth Rates 1975– 1979	1979– 1985	1985– 1990
France	13.0	3.8	5.1	4.8
Germany	20.9	8.2[c]	3.9[c]	4.8
Japan	40.2[b]	6.6	12.0	9.6[d]
United Kingdom	12.2[b]	5.0	2.1	2.2[d]
United States	104.2	4.5	6.7	1.0

Sources: 1975–1985—Organization for Economic Cooperation and Development, *Science and Technology Indicators No. 3: R&D, Production and Diffusion of Technology* (Paris, 1989), Table 60, as cited in Gene M. Grossman and Elhanan Helpman, *Innovation and Growth in the Global Economy* (Cambridge, Mass.: MIT Press, 1991), Table 1.2, p. 9; 1985–1990—Organization for Economic Cooperation and Development, *Main Science and Technology Indicators, 1991,* No. 2 (Paris, 1992), Table 22, p. 26, and Table B, p. 71.

Notes:
a. National currencies converted to dollars using OECD purchasing power parity estimates.
b. 1989.
c. Natural science and engineering only.
d. 1985–1989.

Table 6-5, business R&D rose slowly in the late 1980s as weak overall economic performance forced firms to cut costs.

Table 6-5 also shows interesting regional patterns in R&D growth. The differences between the United States and Europe may simply reflect cycles around long-term trends, with somewhat higher European rates in 1975 to 1979 and 1985 to 1990 and a higher U.S. rate in 1979 to 1985. The consistent disparity between the United States and Japan, however, is striking, particularly in the 1980s. The higher cost of capital to U.S. firms provides one explanation. The cost of capital depends on the source of funds, including the use of retained earnings or the sale of bonds or equity, and the tax treatment of the expenditure. The primary means for expanding private investment and R&D lies in lowering the after-tax cost of capital to the firm through policies that lower real interest rates, improve the tax treatment of investments through rapid depreciation schedules or tax credits, or expand after-tax corporate earnings.

As discussed in Chapter 2, real interest rates depend on the level of national savings, particularly the government deficit, and the supply of foreign capital. High real interest rates drive up capital costs, but so do government tax policies that reduce the returns on long-term investment. Perfect international capital markets should ideally equalize the cost of finance across different countries, but in practice, local tax policies and patterns of industrial organization create large disparities in financing costs.[34] For example, Japanese capital costs are low not only because of the high national savings rate, but also because there is no capital gains taxation of long-term investments. Moreover, the firm's measure of the cost of capital must include an assessment of the risk associated with the investment, and government policies can have a large impact on perceived risks.[35] R&D expenditures are very risky, so they should be particularly sensitive to expectations about the level of support foreign governments might provide to their national champions.[36]

The short-term focus of the U.S. venture capital structure is effective in providing seed funds for small firms, but far less effective in generating the patient capital needed to shift from the prototype stage to full production. For example, the review of the semiconductor industry in Chapter 5 suggested that the lack of patient capital was an important explanation for the exit of several U.S. firms from the industry in the mid-1980s. Capital market conditions also contributed to the exit of U.S. firms from the computer display market and to the failure of U.S. firms to exploit the growth potential of the VCR market.[37]

Technology policy must therefore work to lengthen the time horizons of U.S. firms by lowering real interest rates, reducing the after-tax costs of finance, and lessening perceived risks. President Clinton's proposed technology policy recognizes the key role of the cost of finance and provides several fiscal initiatives mentioned earlier in addition to an emphasis on deficit reduction, although proposed increases in corporate tax rates clearly lower investment incentives. The permanent research and experimentation tax credit enacted in 1993 should reduce the after-tax costs of R&D projects, help to offset the international differential in capital costs, and work to correct the market failure created by R&D spillovers. The proposed incremental investment tax credits, providing tax relief for firms that expand equipment purchases, are somewhat more controversial because they would tend to favor firms that cut back investment in the recession. Moreover, in a period of severe fiscal constraints, the negative impact on investment of other tax increases may well offset the positive impact of investment tax credits, so a more comprehensive assessment of the net impact of the tax package is required. The objective, however, of lowering the after-tax costs of investment financing is clearly appropriate.[38]

The National Academy of Sciences has proposed a more direct and controversial solution to the problem of channeling funds to risky high-technology R&D and investment. It recommends a privately operated, publicly funded, Civilian Technology Corporation that could take a longer-term view of the full returns to the nation of such expenditures and lower the cost of capital to firms.[39] President Clinton's technology policy paper commits only to a review of such proposals.[40] Although the Civilian Technology Corporation concept does address a real market failure caused by tax distortions of capital costs and uncertainty over government policies, the devil in such a solution lies in the details of targeting funds only on critical industries and in preventing the crowding out of private funds. Moreover, the more direct solution is to address the source of the market failure through the creation of appropriate tax incentives for R&D and other forms of investment.

International Technology Regimes

International technology policy coordination has grown out of the more mature GATT regime for managing reductions in barriers to international trade. Trade policies also provide the most readily available levers for dealing with foreign structural impediments, discriminatory policies, or technology subsidies that might hinder the development of U.S. industries. As discussed in Chapter 5, U.S. Trade Act Section 301, Super 301, and antidumping restrictions have been used extensively to open foreign markets to U.S. goods. Article VI of GATT permits countervailing duties in response to "injurious" subsidization, and the United States has been the most active country in seeking relief under that provision.[41] The key issue is how that trade leverage will be applied in the context of broader technology policy.

President Clinton's technology policy paper provides some hints by arguing for a "trade policy that encourages open but fair trade" and promotes "full access to overseas markets and effective protection of intellectual property rights" through "multilateral and bilateral negotiations" and "enforcement of existing agreements" in a structure that is "consistent with a vigorous public research and development program." [42] Despite this somewhat vague wording, the focus on opening markets, intellectual property rights, bilateral negotiations, and enforcement does suggest how the link between trade and technology policy might evolve.

Laura D'Andrea Tyson, chairperson of President Clinton's Council of Economic Advisers, argues that there are four important dimensions for assessing trade policy. Trade policies can focus on aggregate patterns or particular sectors, they can be negotiated in bilateral or multilateral frameworks, they can focus on rules or outcomes, and they can seek to promote or restrict trade. She argues that in the high-technology area, U.S. policy will often be required to focus on bilateral agreements designed to open markets in particular sectors, because the GATT process is not yet capable of dealing with many of the key issues. She suggests that in such cases "aggressive unilateralism" and "selective reciprocity" provide useful principles for defining U.S. trade policy.[43]

"Aggressive unilateralism" refers to the sector-specific, bilateral, out-come-oriented, trade-promoting actions pioneered in the 1980s to address foreign trade practices and structural impediments not specifically covered by GATT. The Semiconductor Trade Agreement of 1986, for example, exploited the leverage provided by Section 301 and Super 301 to gain wider multilateral access to Japanese markets. Similarly, the Commerce Department used the Semiconductor Chip Protection Act of 1984 to obtain reciprocal agreements with foreign firms to protect original chip designs.[44] In these areas of structural impediments and intellectual property rights, GATT has been relatively unsuccessful in defining and enforcing multilateral rules that can apply across product areas. Tyson argues that in such cases aggressive unilateralism is required to deal with the specific countries and sectors involved in most disputes over high technology.[45]

"Selective reciprocity" would tie foreign access to a national market for a specific product to comparable access to the foreign market. This principle clearly conflicts with the GATT principle of broad reciprocity, which emphasizes equal access across a wide range of goods and trading partners. Again, Tyson believes that selective reciprocity is required because most of the important issues involve particular countries and industries. This principle appears to be at the heart of the July 1993 trade agreement between the United States and Japan, which provides a framework for negotiating steps to open Japanese government procurement and major sectors such as automobiles and parts to freer trade. Progress will be evaluated using specific objective criteria, and the United States has been pressing for a standard that would compare foreign shares of Japanese markets to similar ratios in other countries.[46]

Aggressive unilateralism and specific reciprocity provide powerful tools for targeting individual industries and technologies, and they can serve as short-run solutions to problems that should ultimately be solved by multilateral agreements on competitive policies, antitrust provisions, and guarantees for intellectual property rights. The central concern with such actions, however, is that they can undermine the broader GATT principles required to reach ultimate multilateral agreements. Tyson argues that as long as arrangements focus on voluntary import expansion in response to real foreign impediments and extend to all trading countries in a nondiscriminatory manner, as was the case in the Semiconductor Agreement, they will not undermine the long-term multilateral process.[47]

In the context of Tyson's earlier arguments, President Clinton's technology policy emphasis on opening markets, protecting intellectual property rights, bilateral negotiations, and enforcement may well signal a more aggressive U.S. trade policy in support of high-technology sectors. Movements in that direction must obviously be carefully balanced with desired progress toward a successful conclusion of the Uruguay Round of GATT negotiations. An expanded emphasis on federal subsidies for private sector

R&D will also raise issues for GATT, because subsidies of any kind have clear trade implications.

GATT regulations prohibit export subsidies and many other subsidies that impose material injury on industry in another country. When injury can be demonstrated, the normal remedy is the imposition of a countervailing duty. The countervailing duty, however, is often an ineffective deterrent that produces undesirable side effects. In the case of subsidies for investment, there is a long interval between the subsidy and any harm to another country. As a result, any countervailing duty is unlikely to reverse the long-term advantage of a shift in market share. Moreover, the ultimate imposition of the duty creates higher prices in the injured country, which may hurt domestic industries that use the import. For example, duties on foreign semiconductor producers would drive up U.S. semiconductor prices and hurt U.S. electronics producers. In addition, the imposition of countervailing duties is an aggressive action that runs the risk of spiraling retaliation.[48] As countries shift toward subsidies for R&D and other investment to increase market share in strategic industries, the risk of protectionist reactions increases.

For example, in early 1992 a GATT ruling supported U.S. claims that European subsidies to Airbus violated GATT regulations, but the U.S. tried to avoid the imposition of countervailing duties that would weaken other agreements on aircraft trade. Instead, bilateral negotiations led to a July 1992 U.S.-European Community agreement to limit aircraft subsidies to 33 percent of development costs on future programs.[49] Unfortunately, there are persuasive arguments for using subsidies to offset market failures in R&D, so it would be extremely difficult to develop any clear, general rules for setting subsidy limits across industries. Uruguay Round proposals to permit precompetitive R&D subsidies will not produce much improvement because of the inherent problems of defining basic, precompetitive, and applied research in terms that would be enforceable. In Tyson's view, the appropriate alternative is further bilateral, industry-specific negotiations to limit subsidies.[50]

Given the difficulties of establishing clear, enforceable multilateral guidelines on R&D and other investment subsidies, and the weaknesses of countervailing duties in responding to injurious subsidies, Tyson proposes the use of countervailing subsidies as a remedy when foreign subsidies threaten material injury to U.S. industry.[51] Countervailing investment subsidies would avoid the price island effects of countervailing duties, and they would be less confrontational than production subsidies. Most importantly, they could act as a deterrent because they could be imposed before any impact on market share actually took place.

On the other hand, movement toward a unilateral preemptive strategy would be fraught with other difficulties. First, the countervailing subsidy would respond to the foreign subsidy rather than its demonstrated impact, so the process would be very vulnerable to domestic firms claiming potential, not actual, injury. Second, unilateral judgments on potential harm would move the process outside the existing GATT subsidy regime. Third, subsidies designed to offset foreign subsidies might divert scarce funds from other, more critical sectors where market failures were more significant. Fourth, as Chapter 5 argued, the effectiveness of subsidies in capturing rents for domestic firms depends on the market structure. In some cases, subsidies can lead to a loss of market share depending on the pricing behavior of foreign firms. Moreover, there is little evidence from available case studies that the gains from such subsidies will be large, even when they shift market shares toward domestic firms.

The main advantage of a unilateral countervailing subsidy strategy would be the leverage provided for negotiating limits to subsidies in different technologies, but the risks of undermining multilateral approaches and of diverting funds from more efficient uses outweigh that potential advantage. Despite Tyson's cautious tilt toward aggressive unilateralism and specific reciprocity as useful defensive instruments in high-technology areas where multilateral agreements have not yet emerged, her central conclusion is that trade policies are very blunt instruments for influencing domestic growth, for "what emerges from the preceding discussion of trade policies is not their strengths but their weaknesses."[52] That central conclusion is correct, and it should be the pillar of U.S. trade policy in this area. Indirect trade instruments provide weak alternatives to direct domestic policies.

Investment subsidies and intellectual property rights provide the greatest challenge for the international trading regime. Unlike more traditional instruments of commercial policy, they can have significant impacts on the location of high-value activities within global R&D and input-output organizational networks. The challenge is to develop multilateral approaches to these difficult issues to avoid protectionist measures that can isolate regions from the benefits of those global networks. As a result, the central thrust of trade policy as a component of broader technology policy should be the development of cooperative international regimes to constrain aggressive unilateral behavior. Aggressive unilateralism and specific reciprocity may be appropriate in some sectors as long as agreements emphasize trade expansion and nondiscrimination, but such tactics should not be allowed to undermine broader progress toward consensus on effective multilateral rules. The thrust of U.S. technology policy should be to enhance U.S. competitiveness within that cooperative framework.

Global R&D networks have also increased the international spillovers of science and basic research and reduced the narrow national advantages generated by such projects. As a result, funding for basic research projects could well decline as national governments shift funds toward more applied research that can enhance competitive advantage. "Big science" projects like the superconducting supercollider, Space Station Freedom, and the unmanned exploration of the solar system face termination or sharp budget constraints. New international regimes for science and basic research will be needed to sustain adequate funding for such efforts in proportion to the benefits received by all of the developed regions.

U.S. international science and technology activities are coordinated by the Bureau of Oceans and International Environmental and Scientific Affairs (OES) in the Department of State, which manages some 34 government-to-government science and technology umbrella agreements that outline broad areas of cooperation. More specific agreements are directly administered by technical agencies through over 650 detailed memoranda of understanding covering 20 different technical areas, including earth sciences, nuclear energy and safety, biomedical sciences, transportation, and space and aeronautics. The agencies administering the most agreements in 1992 included the Departments of Interior (138 agreements), Health and Human Services (79), Energy (78), Commerce (67), Defense (43), and Transportation (37), as well as the Nuclear Regulatory Commission (72) and NASA (47).[53]

Several of those projects have such great scope and impact, require such large investments, and necessitate such large-scale collaboration that they have been named "megascience" or "megaprojects."[54] Recent experience with such projects has not been promising. After $2 billion had been spent on a proposed superconducting supercollider, designed to accelerate particles in a circular tunnel with a circumference of over 50 miles in Texas, the project was canceled in 1993 because of budget constraints, cost overruns, and a dearth of international support.[55] NASA's Space Station Freedom and the U.S. Global Change Research Program, designed to provide an interdisciplinary review of the physical and biological processes that regulate and change the Earth system, face similar budget constraints. U.S. diplomatic efforts to expand international participation in these projects has met with mixed results, in part because of concerns over technology transfers with large potential private sector impacts and security implications.

The need for international collaboration extends beyond cooperation on specific projects to the maintenance of the broader environment within which innovation proceeds. Global organizational networks and trade liberalization have made competition through science and technology policies more appealing, but perhaps also less possible. In the open trading regime, intervention to create the public goods of science and basic research is acceptable, but nations find it difficult to appropriate the returns from those investments. Direct subsidies to firms might help to capture high-value activities in some sectors, but such intervention contradicts GATT principles by imposing harm on trading partners, and the administration of such direct subsidies violates open market principles. Similarly, local purchasing practices to favor domestic firms violate the GATT principles of nondiscrimination, and as a practical matter global networks can shift structures to offset such policies.

Global organizational networks increase the importance of harmonizing fiscal incentives for R&D and sharing the costs of providing international public goods. Within that cooperative framework, competition will focus on the development of a national climate that favors innovation and on the interaction of national, local, and private sector programs that can translate that climate into real competitive advantage. The heart of technology policy in this framework lies in dual-use technologies, the diffusion of process technologies, and network integration. An open international trading regime provides the correct environment for the efficient operation of global networks, and national policies that promote market-led innovation offer the best prospects for capturing high-value activities within those networks.[56]

Dual-Use Technologies

As national technology policy shifts from an overwhelming emphasis on federal R&D in support of defense and energy procurement toward an increased focus on correcting market failures in critical technology areas, there will be a corresponding shift toward support of technologies with dual defense and commercial uses or direct commercial applications. In order to ensure responsiveness to market forces, such programs will require closer collaboration between government agencies and private firms.

Tyson's criteria for allocating government funds to such programs are right on the mark. Government and industry should share the costs of projects to ensure efficiency in design and implementation. Projects should be initiated by private firms to ensure responsiveness to market forces. Government funding decisions should be based on a merit review by an independent panel, and agency decisions on individual projects should be shielded as far as possible from budget and political pressures.[57] Several projects are fostering greater network integration between public institutions and private firms, including Cooperative Research and Development Agreements (CRADA) between federal laboratories and the private sector, National Science Foundation initiatives, the Advanced Technology Program matching grants for industry projects, and the collaborative efforts of the federal government with semiconductor manufacturers in SEMA-TECH. Although those programs constitute a very small part of the federal R&D effort, they are expanding under President Clinton's technology policy and a review of their advantages and weaknesses provides important insights into collaborative technology efforts between government and industry.

Table 6-6
Number of CRADAs by Department, 1987–1990

Department	1987	1988	1989	1990
Agriculture	9	51	98	128
Commerce	0	9	44	82
Defense				
Air Force	0	2	7	13
Army	2	9	32	80
Navy	0	0	2	20
Energy	0	0	0	1
Environmental PA	0	0	2	11
Health and Human Serv	22	28	89	110
Interior	0	0	1	12
Transport	0	0	0	1
Veterans' Affairs	0	0	1	2
Total	33	99	276	460

Source: National Science Board, *Science and Engineering Indicators—1991*, 10th ed. (Washington, D.C.: U.S. Government Printing Office, 1991), 103.

Cooperative Research and Development Agreements. The federal government devotes roughly $22 billion per year to in-house research and development in some 726 laboratories it owns or operates, ranging from the large facilities at Oakridge, Brookhaven, Argonne, and Ames, to the extensive Lawrence Livermore, Los Alamos, and Sandia Defense Program Laboratories operated by DOE, to much smaller operations with a few researchers. The 21 large DOE laboratories with an annual budget of roughly $9 billion employ some 70,000 people, and DOD laboratories with 60,000 employees spend $7 billion each year.[58] The Federal Technology Transfer Act of 1986 authorized most of those laboratories to reach CRADAs with private firms. The agreements specify in advance how the results of the research would be divided between the firms and laboratories, including a five-year exclusive-use provision for the participants.[59] The National Competitiveness and Technology Transfer Act of 1989 extended that authority to the Defense Program laboratories as well.[60] The Federal Laboratory Consortium for Technology Transfer provides information on the CRADA process to the private sector.[61] As shown in Table 6-6, the number of CRADA agreements got off to a slow start but grew rapidly in 1989 and 1990, particularly in agriculture and health and human services.

The CRADA process has received mixed reviews in the early years of implementation, primarily because of the time required to reach agreements, patent rights disputes, and the initial emphasis on pushing accumulated laboratory research into the private sector rather than shifting research toward commercial application.[62] In other words, the network relationships between the commercial market, producers, and laboratories were not yet fully developed. The technology transfer typically required extensive modification after being brought into the company's system before it could be made commercially useful.

Funding has also been a problem. Laboratories have been slow to shift resources to cooperative agreements, often because of greater emphasis on traditional missions by parent agencies. In the fall of 1992, the private Council on Competitiveness called for DOE and NASA laboratories to allocate at least 10 percent of their budgets to technology transfer.[63] President Clinton's 1993 technology policy calls for all federal laboratories to target 10 to 20 percent of their budgets on R&D partnerships with private industry.[64]

Although commercial firms clearly carry the burden of commercializing R&D efforts, federal laboratories could do more to bridge the gap between research, product adaptation, and marketing. For example, the creation of internal cells to pursue licensing arrangements and locate funds and partners for joint ventures, or affiliation with nonprofit organizations for the same purpose, would enhance network relationships. Such network linking functions would correspond to trends in the private sector to coordinate processes across the value chain. The Center for Advanced Technology Development (CATD), affiliated with Iowa State University and Ames Laboratory, for example, provides one example of how such linking functions might be organized.[65] The earlier that commercialization considerations can be inserted in the research process, the more likely it is that the technology transfer will survive the critical test of timely responsiveness to market forces.

Technical Area Coordinating Teams (TACT) have now been established in the DOE Defense Program laboratories to recommend priorities, facilitate project development, and coordinate with industry on work in materials, photonics, precision engineering, advanced manufacturing, and computer applications. The success of such internal laboratory organizational efforts, however, critically depends on broader outreach efforts with industry, personnel exchanges, and simplified contracting procedures. The 10 to 18-month contracting process common in negotiating CRADAs is clearly excessive given the rapid pace of technological advance.[66] In other words, effective linkage between federal laboratories and industry requires the same kind of network relationships and rapid response to shifting market conditions and technological advances that are found in R&D organizational networks in the private sector.

National Science Foundation Initiatives. As shown in Table 6-2, funding for NSF represents only 3 percent of federal R&D outlays, but those programs have important impacts on basic science and engineering, education, and critical research and technology priorities. Under President Clinton's budget proposals for fiscal year 1994, NSF's budget would increase by 7 percent, in part to cover new research initiatives in five "strategic" areas covering "high performance computing and communications, manufacturing, materials, global change, and biotechnology."[67] The programs focus on partnerships among government, industry, and universities to accelerate the creation and deployment of new technologies in those fields.

NSF disperses funds to researchers through an elaborate grant system based on evaluation by program officers and advice from reviewers concerning these factors: the merit of the proposed research, the competence of the principal investigator, the relevance of the research, and the impact of the work on the science and engineering infrastructure.[68] The NSF grant system has been criticized for the complexity of the proposals, the evaluation workload, and the constraints the review system places on taking risks with innovative projects.[69] The flexibility of the grant structure and the emphasis on merit review, however, make the NSF structure a useful model as other agencies shift from an emphasis on procurement toward more direct roles in cooperative arrangements with private firms.

For example, the NSF Engineering Research Centers augment private funding with public funds subject to an extensive review process and 11-year sunset provisions.[70] The Small Business Innovation Research (SBIR) Program, operated in 11 federal agencies under the SBIR Program Reauthorization Act of 1992, attempts to expand the role of small businesses in federal R&D. The NSF-SBIR program directs funds toward small firms to foster basic research in high-risk areas, stimulate private technological innovation, and increase the commercial application of NSF-supported research.[71] Such programs provide seed funds that can strengthen the network relationships needed to focus public programs on market forces.

Advanced Technology Program. The National Institute of Standards and Technology (NIST) in the Department of Commerce is the only federal laboratory with the primary mission of providing support to U.S. industry. NIST's budget authority of $247 million in 1992 will rise to $535 million in 1994 under President Clinton's proposed budget.[72] NIST grew out of the 1988 Omnibus Trade and Competitiveness Act as a compromise with congressional pressures for a new civilian version of DARPA. Instead, the old Bureau of Standards was given a new name and a new mission.

NIST's Advanced Technology Program (ATP) provides grants to companies to develop and commercialize precompetitive generic technologies with a specific objective of promoting "cooperative and strategic alliances in U.S. industry," similar to SEMATECH.[73] ATP proposals must pass through a merit review process, including technical and business evaluations. In 1992, 27 projects were funded in technologies ranging from optical computer switches to new car plastics.[74]

ATP represents a tentative testing of the waters for new directions in technology policy, but despite the recent budget increases, the experiment is more interesting as a design model than as a serious redirection in national priorities. The ATP formula of private-sector initiative, cost sharing, and merit review is well designed, but the concept continues to suffer from a fundamental problem in defining the market failures needing to be corrected by public policy. High risk in and of itself does not necessarily reflect a market failure or a case for government intervention.

ARPA has been very successful in designing cooperative projects with the private sector, but it has had the enormous advantage of focusing on perceived requirements for future defense technologies.[75] That ultimate procurement focus provided a clear rationale for filling gaps in available commercial technologies. Without that procurement focus, it is far more difficult to define market failures in particular technologies that warrant attention through programs like ATP. Such programs require an unusual government agency that can combine an entrepreneurial sense of market direction with an appreciation for the need to keep government R&D programs focused on market failures. ARPA developed an organizational culture that encouraged that kind of entrepreneurship and it benefited from a huge defense market and an enormous R&D establishment for direction and expertise. It remains to be seen whether NIST can perform as effectively in a completely different organizational context.

SEMATECH. The Semiconductor Research Consortium, SEMATECH, provided a model for the ATP initiatives by using public funds to focus industrial efforts on semiconductor technologies. In response to the dramatic loss of U.S. world semiconductor market share in the mid-1980s, particularly in memory devices, legislators began drawing up plans in 1987 for what ultimately became a consortium headquartered in Austin, Texas, of some 14 major U.S. semiconductor manufacturers. SIA pressed for a multifirm collaborative project to provide a laboratory and prototype facility for member firms. National Semiconductor took the lead in the project with strong support from IBM.[76] The federal government began funding the consortium through a five-year program established in 1988 in which DARPA provides $100 million per year and consortium members contribute an equivalent amount. President Clinton's technology policy extends federal matching funds through fiscal year 1994. The policy cites SEMATECH as a model for federal consortia for other critical technologies, such as the "development of a new automobile, new construction technologies, intelligent control and sensor technologies, rapid prototyping, and environmentally-conscious manufacturing."[77]

The specific objectives of SEMATECH are to develop new semiconductor process technologies in order to keep U.S. producers in the industry and sustain competitive markets. SEMATECH's own fabrication facility was able to produce batches of chips in 1991 with a 0.5-micron resolution (a human hair is roughly 100 microns wide), equaling the Japanese standard.[78] SEMATECH critics note, however, that without production for sale and the advantages of moving down the learning curve as output expands, SEMATECH's contributions to actual production processes have been limited.[79] SEMATECH's real focus has not been on developing new production processes, but on strengthening the roughly 130 companies that produce tools for critical photolithography, chemical etching, and molecular epitaxy processes, and on promoting closer supplier-buyer partnerships. In fact, building these input-output and research network relationships may well be SEMATECH's greatest contribution. The consortium's efforts in developing new Micrascan lithography technology have been particularly effective, and IBM's access to Micrascan may have influenced the decision for Toshiba, Siemens, and Toshiba to go forward with a new DRAM joint venture.[80]

Although SEMATECH may be helping to build local network relationships, there have also been several problems with the new concept. A central concern relates to the ability to limit access to technologies developed by SEMATECH to member firms or at least to U.S. firms. In an attempt to contain such leakages, SEMATECH has been open only to U.S. firms, despite European objections. The Joint European Submicron Silicon (JESSI) program did admit IBM because of its joint ventures with Siemens and its European chip production facilities, but SEMATECH has remained closed to non-U.S. firms.[81]

Nonetheless, U.S. member firms have extensive global network relationships and international production facilities that can exploit SEMATECH developments. In addition to the IBM-Siemens connection, SEMATECH member AT&T has semiconductor links with Japan's NEC and Mitsubishi Electric, Intel has similar arrangements with NMB Semiconductor and Matsushita in Japan, and Texas Instruments has fabrication plants in Japan and Taiwan.[82] Licensing arrangements within SEMATECH constrain transfers, but the central point is that new technology developments feed into global networks that do not necessarily pursue fabrication in the United States. Moreover, the potential foreign acquisition of small suppliers cooperating in SEMATECH provides an even more direct form of technology transfer.[83]

SEMATECH should be judged not by its technological breakthroughs, but by its ultimate impact on the location of high-value semiconductor activities. Even by that more stringent criterion, SEMATECH may well have helped to create some of the ingredients that lead to sustainable competitive advantage, because global networks find it more difficult to shift the infrastructure, the expertise captured in process technologies, and the closer linkages between suppliers and producers encouraged by SEMA-TECH. On balance then, despite the inevitable risk of leakages of SEMA-TECH's technology innovations to non-U.S. firms and to foreign plants of U.S. firms, the design of the project does provide an interesting model for supporting dual-use technologies through cooperation between government and private firms in a format that responds to market forces and captures important benefits for local networks.

Diffusion of Process Technologies

Economic convergence and global organizational networks have increased the importance of expertise in assimilating technological information from other sources outside firms and outside the country.[84] Competitive advantage increasingly relies on the adaptation of that information in the development of process technologies that are integrated with suppliers and responsive to rapid shifts in market conditions. The market may fail to disseminate such information effectively if there are large economies of scale in tapping external sources. Moreover, venture capital markets oriented toward quick returns and new products may not generate the patient funds needed for incremental innovation in process technologies. For example, Japanese firms allocate two-thirds of R&D to improvements in process technologies, while U.S. firms devote only one-third to process improvements.[85]

The MIT Commission on Productivity noted that the U.S. still leads the world in basic research, but other countries are as good or better at applying that research to production.[86] In particular, U.S. firms spend more time refining technologies before moving into production, while Japanese firms begin production with low-risk prototypes and then improve on the design as they expand output.[87] In a period of rapid changes in technology and markets, that ability to adjust processes during production and to react to external ideas becomes more important. For example, Eric von Hippel estimates that three-quarters of innovations in scientific instruments in the 1980s came from users rather than producers.[88]

In such an environment, government restrictions on cooperation across firms can block the dissemination of information on process technologies that have become an important component of effective competition. The MIT Commission found that such information flows were important in innovation and productivity advances in Europe and Japan.[89] To the extent that U.S. antitrust restrictions reduce the dissemination of information on process technologies across firms, the government may have an increased rationale for intervening to assist in technology diffusion.

The federal government is pursuing a number of initiatives designed to improve the dissemination of information on new technologies in general, and process technologies in particular. The Technology Transfer and Outreach Program under NIST includes the Manufacturing Extension Program, which will create over 100 manufacturing technology centers by 1997.[90] The first seven manufacturing extension centers managed by NIST under the 1988 Trade Act are already operating in Ohio, New York, South Carolina, Kansas, Louisiana, Minnesota, and Michigan. For example, the Great Lakes Manufacturing Technology Center in Cleveland demonstrates the operation of advanced metal-working machines. The center receives combined support from Ohio, 100 local companies, and the Department of Commerce. Under current procedures, the manufacturing extension centers must become self-sufficient within six years, so there is a clear incentive to respond effectively to market requirements.[91]

For such centers to be most effective, they should be targeted on areas with concentrations of small manufacturing firms in industries that draw substantial inputs from other manufacturing firms and have strong local input-output network linkages. Such locations are most likely to develop the external economies of scale and scope required to exploit the technological spillovers extension programs can provide.[92] In an analysis of locations with concentrations of linked manufacturing firms, an Industrial Technology Institute study finds that the seven initial manufacturing technology centers have been located in the right states, but not necessarily in the correct metropolitan areas or with the correctly targeted service areas.[93]

State and local governments may be in a position to focus extension services more effectively than the federal government. They are not immune from political pressure on the location of such services, but they are closer to the information needed to target resources. Many states provide technical field services, but only a dozen provide traveling agents who provide on-the-spot assistance to manufacturers.[94] Such state programs are consistent with the principle that support for R&D should be managed by the level of government corresponding to the area within which technological spillovers are expected to occur.

Network Integration

Technology programs are most effective when they focus on the creation of the advanced and specialized factors that can be captured in local organizational networks or local nodes of global networks. Physical information technology networks have a special role in this process, because they facilitate the emergence of organizational networks so important to exploiting interconnections through the value chain. The appropriate role for government in this process is difficult to define, however, because "information highways" differ substantially from the mammoth physical transportation systems conjured up by the metaphor.

Government must certainly adjudicate access to different frequency bands over public airways, but aside from assisting in the evolution of system standards and evaluating the competitive implications of various physical network designs, it is not at all clear that government should play a major role in constructing or operating information networks.[95] The government has been appropriately active, however, in promoting network linkages in the defense and education sectors.

In 1968, ARPA initiated the development of packet-switching technology that initially tied four computers together in a network that grew into ARPANET.[96] By the mid-1980s, DOD had moved its military operations to a separate military network (MILNET), leaving ARPANET for researchers. In 1990, ARPANET was dissolved and its functions were taken over by the National Science Foundation Network (NSFNET). NSFNET is a part of the INTERNET system of nearly 10,000 autonomous, interconnected networks that adhere to open protocols and defined standards. INTERNET connected a million computers and some 4 million international end users in 1992 and is expected to reach 10 million computers by 1996. In true network fashion, no single organization manages INTERNET, although the nonprofit INTERNET Society formed in January 1992 promotes collaboration and integration. INTERNET permits file transfers, remote computer access, electronic mail exchanges, and public access to areas such as electronic serial publications.[97]

In 1991, the High-Performance Computing Act authorized federal funds to support the National Research and Education Network (NREN) and the High-Performance Computing and Communications (HPCC) Program. The NREN goal is to link research and education network components through one gigabit-per-second (billion-bit) transmissions, providing dramatic improvements in collaborative research and a testbed for new technologies that will have broader impacts on general-purpose communications. The enhanced computational capacity obtained by linking large computers through NREN will support other "grand challenge" goals of the HPCC, such as predicting climate changes, determining atomic structures, and understanding biological macromolecules.[98] Another critical goal of the HPCC is to improve commercial productivity by helping to make "computing and network technologies an integral part of the design and production process."[99]

The 1992 Information Infrastructure and Technology Act provided a five-year program of $1.15 billion for 1993 to 1997 to develop and deploy new network applications for education, libraries, manufacturing, and health care. The act allocated funds to tie primary and secondary schools to the NSFNET, gave the NIST at the Department of Commerce responsibility for developing networking technology for manufacturing, and charged NSF and NASA with building digital libraries for use on nets like NSFNET.[100]

In the past few years, there has been an explosion in physical network capabilities. For example, NSFNET, which connects state governments, NSF, and 650 colleges and universities, grew from 200 million to 15 billion packets a month between 1988 and 1992.[101] The NSFNET already permits communication links at the rate of 45 megabits per second (Mbps), and NREN will soon allow rates of one gigabit per second (Gbps) using asynchronous transfer mode (ATM) switching technology.[102] Local-area network (LAN) connections of computers are common, cellular telephones are expanding rapidly, high-density television proposals have shifted from analog to digital formats, and client-server computing is replacing centralized mainframe operations. These changes mean that a fiberoptic backbone network with access from fiber, copper, and radio connections will give individuals voice, data, and image access to a global public network. That network will have gigabit linkages, permit the networking of supercomputers to solve "grand challenge" problems, and translate computers, workstations, televisions, and facsimile devices into networked, interactive, multimedia systems. The implementation of such integrated network systems, however, still requires control mechanisms to support connections operating at a wide range of link speeds, internetworking protocols, and high-speed gateways to merge transmissions from LAN and NSFNET networks into the NREN system.[103]

President Clinton's technology policy statement argues that government has an important role in accelerating the introduction of new high-speed communications systems.[104] The policy calls for an interagency task force within NEC to examine the need for a stable regulatory environment and identify policies to speed implementation of a "national information infrastructure." Specific proposals include the creation of an information infrastructure technology program to assist industry in applying networking technology, the provision of matching grants to local government and nonprofit organizations for networking connections, and the promotion of more efficient dissemination of federal information.[105] As long as such initiatives do not involve the government in designing or operating information networks, they seem appropriately targeted. Supporting those physical network connections will promote the organizational network integration required for sustained productivity improvements.

POLICY IMPLICATIONS

U.S. technology policy is clearly shifting from a traditional emphasis on procurement to a broader role in dual-use technologies. The limits of the shift and the rationale for precise levels of involvement in different industries are still evolving. A clearer philosophy and closer coordination across agencies will be required to avoid the tendency to spread scarce resources over a wide range of technologies and to resist inevitable pressures to support special interests rather than to correct real market failures. Policies that focus on critical technologies, target specific sources of market failure, create tacit knowledge and infrastructures that create local competitive advantage, and emphasize responsiveness to market feedback have the best chance for success. U.S. national technology policy should stress cooperation in developing efficient global organizational networks and competition through aggressive national policies to stimulate innovation. Such policies do not involve market intervention so much as the creation of an environment that supports entrepreneurial initiative.

The program outlined in this chapter moves in those directions. A more tightly coordinated national policy will provide a better focus for the allocation of scarce resources across and within agencies, and help to target the most critical technologies and the most egregious sources of market failure. Emphasis on lowering the real cost of capital through deficit reduction and tax incentives for R&D and investment will keep the policy focused on exploiting the potential of dynamic market forces. The promotion of cooperative international technology regimes will help to keep competition away from costly subsidies and to focus policy on open international markets. Emphasis on dual-use technologies will provide an effective transition from a procurement-based national technology policy to one that is more fully integrated with commercial market forces. A new focus on technology diffusion and process technologies will help to correct systemic market failures and reinforce the development of organizational networks that are more attuned to global competition. Efforts to smooth the process of physical network integration will be useful as long as government does not become directly involved in building or administering those networks, because the nature of the technologies is inconsistent with hierarchical control.

Finally, military technology policy will continue to play a central role in national technology policy despite the reorientation toward the commercial sector. The information technology revolution has already had a dramatic impact on military systems and organizations, and the logic of global organizational networks poses new challenges to traditional thinking about security issues. Chapter 7 extends the broader context of national technology policy to a more detailed consideration of military technology policy.

NOTES

1. For illustrations, see Linda Cohen and Roger Noll, *The Technology Pork Barrel* (Washington, D.C.: The Brookings Institution, 1991).

2. Industry cooperation is essential for the effective formulation and administration of government programs. See Richard R. Nelson, *High Technology Policies: A Five-Nation Comparison* (Washington, D.C.: American Enterprise Institute, 1984), 12–13.

3. For example, in 1991 the Japanese firm Nippon Sanso purchased the Semi-Gas Systems division of U.S. chemical producer Hercules. Semi-Gas had been a supplier to SEMATECH of ultrapure gases used in semiconductor fabrication and a collaborator in R&D.

4. Nelson, *High Technology Policies*, 68–72, provides a good, quick summary of Japanese and EC policies and their impacts.

5. National Science Board, *Science and Engineering Indicators—1991*, 10th ed. (Washington, D.C.: U.S. Government Printing Office, 1991), 108, 341.

6. Ibid., 91.

7. National Science Board, *Science and Engineering Indicators*, 105–107, 340.

8. See Table 5–2.

9. National Science Board, *Science and Engineering Indicators*, 315.

10. Ibid., 94, and Table 6–2.

11. National Science Board, *Science and Engineering Indicators*, 94.

12. U.S. Executive Office of the President, *Budget of the United States Government, Fiscal Year 1994* (Washington, D.C.: April 8, 1993), A-1003.

13. National Science Board, *Science and Engineering Indicators*, 94.

14. Ibid., 91.

15. U.S. Congress, Office of Technology Assessment, *Federally Funded Research: Decisions for a Decade, Summary* (Washington, D.C.: U.S. Government Printing Office, May 1991): 13.

16. Organization for Economic Cooperation and Development, *Choosing Priorities in Science and Technology* (Paris, 1991), 43.

17. U.S. House of Representatives, Committee on Science, Space, and Technology, *Science, Technology and American Diplomacy, 1993: Fourteenth Annual Report Submitted to the Congress by the President Pursuant to Section 503(b) of Title V of Public Law 95–426* (Washington, D.C.: U.S. Government Printing Office, May 1993), pp. vii-ix, 12–13.

18. U.S. Office of Science and Technology Policy, *U.S. Technology Policy*, as cited in Eliot Marshall, "U.S. Technology Strategy Emerges," *Science* (April 5, 1991), 23.

19. U.S. Department of Defense, *DOD Critical Technologies Plan* (Washington, D.C.: March 15, 1990), as cited in Air Force Institute of Technology, *Critical Technologies for National Defense* (Washington, D.C.: American Institute of Aeronautics and Astronautics, 1991), 2–4.

20. U.S. Department of Commerce, *Emerging Technologies: A Survey of Technical and Economic Opportunities* (Washington, D.C., Spring 1990).

21. U.S. Office of Science and Technology Policy, *National Critical Technologies* (Washington, D.C., March 1991).

22. See Air Force Institute of Technology, *Critical Technologies for National Defense*, 9.

23. The traditional U.S. consensus has been that development is best left to the private sector, although exceptions have been made to compensate for high risk in agriculture and national security interests in defense and energy sectors. See Frank Press, "Technological Competition and the Western Alliance," in *A High Technology Gap?: Europe, America and Japan*, ed. Andrew J. Pierre (New York: Council on Foreign Relations, 1987), 17, 19.

24. President William J. Clinton and Vice President Albert Gore, Jr., *Technol-*

ogy for America's Economic Growth, A New Direction to Build Economic Strength (Washington, D.C.: U.S. Government Printing Office, February 22, 1993), 1.

25. Ibid., 8.

26. Ibid., 3.

27. Ibid., 3–4.

28. Ibid., 12–13.

29. Ibid., 5, 12.

30. Ibid., 14–19, 31–33.

31. Federal Coordinating Council for Science, Engineering, and Technology, FCCSET Initiatives in the FY 1994 Budget (Washington, D.C.: Office of Science and Technology Policy, April 8, 1993), 1–3.

32. Clinton and Gore, Technology for America's Economic Growth, A New Direction to Build Economic Strength, 8–10, 32.

33. Ibid, 4.

34. Various estimates show that Japanese capital costs are 36 to 63 percent below U.S. levels. See J. Poterba, "Comparing the Cost of Capital in the U.S. and Japan: A Survey of Methods," Federal Reserve Bank of New York Quarterly Review (Winter 1991): 30.

35. See Michael T. Jacobs, Short-Term America: The Causes and Cures of Our Business Myopia (Boston, Mass.: Harvard Business School Press, 1991), 194–197, for a more complete discussion of the reasons for high perceived investment risks in the United States. See also B. Douglas Bernheim and J. B. Shoven, "Comparing the Cost of Capital in the United States and Japan," in Technology and the Wealth of Nations, ed. Nathan Rosenberg, Ralph Landau, and David C. Mowery (Stanford, Calif.: Stanford University Press, 1992), 165–172.

36. Michael L. Dertouzos, Richard K. Lester, Robert N. Solow, and the MIT Commission on Productivity Growth, Made in America: Regaining the Productivity Edge (Cambridge, Mass.: MIT Press, 1989), 57–66.

37. Michael Borrus and Jeffrey Hart, "Display's the Thing: The Real Stakes in the Conflict Over High-Resolution Display," BRIE Working Papers 52 (Berkeley, Calif.: Berkeley Roundtable on the International Economy, 1992), as cited by Laura D'Andrea Tyson, Who's Bashing Whom?: Trade Conflict in High-Technology Industries (Washington, D.C.: Institute for International Economics, 1992), 286, and Dertouzos, Made in America, 54–55.

38. Clinton and Gore, Technology for America's Economic Growth, 12.

39. National Academy of Sciences, Committee on Science, Engineering, and Public Policy, The Government Role in Civilian Technology (Washington, D.C., 1992), 94.

40. Clinton and Gore, Technology for America's Economic Growth, 13.

41. "A Survey of World Trade: Nothing to Lose But its Chains," Economist (September 22, 1990), 11.

42. Clinton and Gore, Technology for America's Economic Growth, 3, 12–13.

43. Tyson, Who's Bashing Whom? 255–263.

44. Ibid., 258.

45. Ibid., 256.

46. Ibid., 261–263, and Andrew Pollack, "A Trade Agreement Born of Political Necessity," *New York Times,* July 12, 1993, pp. D1, D2.

47. Tyson, *Who's Bashing Whom?* 265.

48. Ibid., 281–282.

49. The aircraft industry global input-output network covers many U.S. suppliers of parts to Airbus, including General Electric and Pratt & Whitney who provide jet engines. Even U.S. aircraft producers Boeing and McDonnell Douglas may not want to push too hard against Airbus subsidies, because they are pursuing network arrangements with subsidized foreign firms. See Richard W. Stevenson, "Latest Airbus Flight Into the Storm," *New York Times,* March 4, 1993, p. D5.

50. Tyson, *Who's Bashing Whom?* 284–285.

51. Ibid., 285–286.

52. Ibid., 286.

53. U.S. House of Representatives, Committee on Science, Space, and Technology, *Science, Technology and American Diplomacy, 1993,* 18–20.

54. The Organization for Economic Cooperation and Development's Megascience Forum conducted its first meeting in July 1992 to exchange views on potential forms of improving coordination. For a summary of major collaborative projects, see U.S. House of Representatives, Committee on Science, Space, and Technology, *Science, Technology and American Diplomacy, 1993,* 50–106.

55. Gary Taubs, "The Supercollider: How Big Science Lost Favor and Fell," *New York Times,* October 26, 1993, p. D1.

56. Chris DeBresson and Fernand Amesse, "Networks of Innovators: A Review and Introduction to the Issue," *Research Policy* 20 (August 1991): 372–373.

57. Tyson, *Who's Bashing Whom?* 292.

58. Clinton and Gore, *Technology for America's Economic Growth,* 8; Atlantic Council of the United States, *Transfers of Technology to Industry from the U.S. Department of Energy Defense Programs Laboratories* (Washington, D.C., July 1992), p. i; National Science Board, *Science and Engineering Indicators,* 102; and Edmund L. Andrews, "Swords to Plowshares: The Bureaucratic Snags," *New York Times,* February 16, 1993, D-1.

59. National Science Board, *Science and Engineering Indicators,* 102, and Atlantic Council, *Transfers of Technology to Industry,* 9.

60. Atlantic Council, *Transfers of Technology to Industry,* 2.

61. National Science Board, *Science and Engineering Indicators,* 102.

62. Atlantic Council, *Transfers of Technology to Industry,* 15. See Andrews, "Swords to Plowshares," D4.

63. Council on Competitiveness, *Industry As a Customer of the Federal Laboratories* (Washington, D.C., 1992), 14.

64. Clinton and Gore, *Technology for America's Economic Growth,* 9.

65. Atlantic Council, *Transfers of Technology to Industry,* 13.

66. Ibid., 17–20.

67. National Science Foundation, *Promoting the Progress of Science and Engineering, Budget and Program Strategy Fiscal Year 1994* (Washington, D.C., March 1993), 6.

68. National Science Foundation, *Report of the Merit Review Task Force* (Washington, D.C., August 23, 1990), 5.

69. Ibid., 6–16.

70. "American Technology Policy: Settling the Frontier," *Economist* (July 25, 1992), 23.

71. National Science Foundation, *Small Business Innovation Research (SBIR) Program Solicitation*, (Washington, D.C., Closing Date, June 14, 1993), 1.

72. U.S. Executive Office of the President, *Budget of the United States Government, Fiscal Year 1994*, A-66.

73. Ibid., A-1218.

74. "American Technology Policy," 22.

75. ARPA and the Office of Naval Research have been particularly successful in providing support for innovative breakthroughs in the semiconductor and computer fields. See John Markoff, "Not Everyone in the Valley Loves Silicon-Friendly Government," *New York Times*, March 7, 1993.

76. John J. Coleman, "The Semiconductor Industry Association and the Trade Dispute With Japan," in *International Trade and Competition: Cases and Notes in Strategy and Management*, ed. David B. Yoffie (New York: McGraw-Hill, 1990), 423.

77. Clinton and Gore, *Technology for America's Economic Growth*, 9.

78. Marshall, "U.S. Technology Strategy Emerges," 23; Brink Lindsey, "DRAM Scam," *Reason* (February 1992); 42, and Raymond Y. Chiao, Paul G. Kwiat, and Aephraim M. Steinberg, "Faster Than Light?" *Scientific American* 269 (August 1993): 53.

79. Lindsey, "DRAM Scam," 44.

80. Tyson, *Who's Bashing Whom?* 153.

81. Ibid., 150.

82. Robert B. Reich, *The Work of Nations: Preparing Ourselves for 21st Century Capitalism* (New York: Alfred A. Knopf, 1991), 160–161.

83. For example, as noted earlier, the Japanese firm Nippon Sanso purchased Semi-Gas Systems, a SEMATECH member, in 1991.

84. David C. Mowery and Nathan Rosenberg, *Technology and the Pursuit of Economic Growth* (Cambridge: Cambridge University Press, 1989), 291.

85. Edwin Mansfield, "Industrial R&D in Japan and the United States," *American Economic Review* 78, *Papers and Proceedings* (May 1988): 223.

86. Dertouzos, *Made in America*, 68.

87. Ibid., 74–75.

88. Eric von Hippel, *Sources of Innovation* (New York: Oxford University Press, 1988), 4, as cited in Dertouzos, *Made in America*, 102.

89. Dertouzos, *Made in America*, 105.

90. U.S. Executive Office of the President, *Budget of the United States Government, Fiscal Year 1994*, A-1218.

91. Philip Shapira, *Modernizing Manufacturing: New Policies to Build Industrial Extension Services* (Washington, D.C.: Economic Policy Institute, 1990).

92. Patrizio Bianchi and Nicola Bellini, "Public Policies for Local Networks of Innovators," *Research Policy* 20 (October 1991): 491.

93. Daniel Luria, Roland J. Cole, and Alan Baum, with Edith Wiarda, Carey Treado, and Martin Grueber, "Fixing the Manufacturing Base: The Allocation of Manufacturing Extension," *Journal of Policy Analysis and Management* 12 (Fall 1993): forthcoming.

94. See John Holusha, "Traveling High-Tech Agents Help Update Small Factories," *New York Times,* February 16, 1993, p. D8.

95. The American National Standards Institute, a private, non-profit organization, works as a clearing house for roughly 400 private sector standards organizations, including trade associations and professional societies. The U.S. federal Government has played virtually no role to date in supporting the voluntary standards process. Federal standards have been imposed primarily through the Department of Defense and agencies administering environmental, health, and safety laws. See U.S. Congress, Office of Technology Assessment, *Global Standards: Building Blocks for the Future* (Washington, D.C.: U.S. Government Printing Office, March 1992), 49–58.

96. Packet-switching technologies exploit digital formats and capture information bundles, or packets, of varying lengths from a transmission stream and redirect them in a one-step process. Newer ATM technologies split information into smaller, 53–byte cells that can be captured and processed simultaneously. ATM formats are at the heart of the revolution permitting rapid transmission of video and voice as well as text. See Josh Hyatt, "In the Fast Lane," *Boston Globe,* July 25, 1993, 73–74.

97. U.S. Department of Defense, *Defense Science and Technology Strategy* (Washington, D.C.: Director of Defense Research and Engineering, June 1992), I-14, and A. Lyman Chapin, "The Internet Board and the Future," *Educom Review,* 27 (September/October 1992): 42.

98. U.S. Federal Coordinating Council for Science, Engineering, and Technology, Office of Science and Technology Policy, *Grand Challenges 1993: High Performance Computing and Communications, The FY 1993 U.S. Research and Development Program,* A Report by the Committee on Physical, Mathematical, and Engineering Sciences (Washington, D.C.: Office of Science and Technology Policy, 1992), 2, 18.

99. Ibid., 3, and "The Internet," *Higher Education Product Companion* 2 (January/February 1993): 20–21.

100. Albert Gore, Jr., "The Information Infrastructure and Technology Act," *Educom Review* 27 (September/October 1992): 28–29.

101. James J. Duderstadt, "An Information Highway to the Future," *Educom Review* 27 (September/October 1992): 38.

102. As noted earlier, ATM technologies split information into cells that can be captured and processed simultaneously.

103. National Science Foundation, *Researching Priorities in Networking and Communications* (Washington, D.C., April 1992), 4, 6–7.

104. Clinton and Gore, *Technology for America's Economic Growth,* 16.

105. Ibid., 17.

7   Military Technology Policy

Military technology policy lies at the crucial nexus between national security strategy and national economic policy. From a defense perspective, military technology policy should support the national military strategy as a component of broader national security strategy. From an economic perspective, military technology policy plays a central role in national technology policy, not only because defense R&D commands such a large share of national R&D assets, but also because defense procurement contributes a substantial share of final demand for high-technology industries that have large impacts on the commercial sector. As national military strategy adjusts to post-cold war challenges and national technology policy shifts in the direction of more direct support for generic, pre-competitive R&D with commercial applications, military technology policy will play a major role in both adjustments.

The information technology revolution, convergence in the economic performance of the developed regions, and the growing importance of global organizational networks will have enormous impacts on military technology policy for a number of reasons. Those trends are shaping the ways in which military strategy will be pursued, altering the nature of the competition in defense industries, shifting the relative importance of various military technologies, changing the nature of the relationship between R&D and procurement, and raising new questions about regional interdependence in military technology.

This chapter begins with an examination of military technology policy as a component of national technology policy, building on the framework established in the last chapter. It then examines the impact of the information technology revolution on the relationship between technology and military strategy, including impacts on warfighting, R&D, and procurement. The following two sections explore the impact of networks on defense R&D and procurement in more detail, with emphasis on the evolving U.S. defense science, technology, and acquisition strategies, and the emergence of defense global input-output and R&D networks. A final section then examines the implications of global organizational networks for access to critical technologies.

MILITARY TECHNOLOGY AND NATIONAL
TECHNOLOGY POLICIES

National technology policy includes government efforts at the local, state, and national levels to influence the activities of the organizations that make up the national innovation network. Military technology policy includes efforts primarily at the federal level to influence innovation in the technologies, production processes, and distribution systems that contribute to defense capabilities in support of military strategy. Because defense outlays have dominated national R&D in the postwar period, military technology policy has driven national technology policy. As the priority given to other national technology policy goals increases, the coordination of military technology policy as a component of overall national strategy becomes more important. One key question is how military and commercial goals and programs will be balanced in the area of dual-use technologies with both military and commercial applications. Another central issue is how the need for hierarchical defense organizations, designed to safeguard sensitive information, can be reconciled with horizontal organizational structures required to participate in the new flow of technology through global networks.

The dominant role of military technology policy was established in the immediate aftermath of World War II. NSF, established in 1950, grew out of the wartime Office of Scientific Research and Development, whose task had been to mobilize civilian science in support of the war effort. The surge in cold war defense R&D outlays shifted the control of policy toward the departments, particularly the newly organized DOD, and NSF assumed a less central role in establishing overall technology policy priorities. Instead, NSF focused on basic research outside the mission areas of other agencies.[1]

DOD assumed control of funding for military technology and a large share of the nation's basic scientific research. In 1949 and 1950, 90 percent of federal R&D funds went to the new DOD and the Atomic Energy Commission. Well over half of the defense R&D budget in that year went to fund industrial laboratories, including some 15 percent of the Bell Telephone Laboratory budget, and a substantial sum went to university laboratories. The Korean War brought a surge in defense spending and in defense R&D outlays, and by 1953, DOD was funding roughly half of the transistor research at Bell Laboratories, defense research employed some two-thirds of the country's scientists and engineers, and defense and atomic energy contracts contributed almost 40 percent of industrial and academic research outlays. An Executive Order in 1954 ratified the relative roles of NSF and the other agencies, leaving the overwhelming majority of federal R&D funds targeted on agency missions.[2]

As Table 7-1 indicates, DOD obligations have dominated the federal

Table 7-1
Department of Defense R&D Share of Government R&D Obligations by Category of R&D, 1980–1991 (percent)

	1980	1985	1990
Total R&D	46.9	61.6	59.6
Basic Research	11.6	11.0	8.4
Applied Research	24.9	27.7	24.8
Development	64.3	82.6	81.4

Source: Computed from National Science Board, *Science and Engineering Indicators—1991,* 10th ed. (Washington, D.C.: U.S. Government Printing Office, 1991), Appendix Table 4–8, pp. 313–314.

government's total R&D expenditures, particularly outlays for development. The DOD share in both categories rose through the early 1980s during the buildup associated with President Reagan's tenure and then leveled off for the rest of the decade. By 1990, DOD contributed roughly one-quarter of federal efforts in applied research but less than 10 percent of basic research.

The major role of U.S. defense R&D in terms of government or national priorities is striking. In comparison, OECD data on R&D outlays show Japan spent a negligible share of government R&D on defense in 1990, Germany allocated roughly 14 percent of government R&D to defense,

Table 7-2
Defense Budget R&D as a Share of Gross Domestic Product, 1971–1989 (percent)

Country	1971	1975	1980	1985	1989
France	.4	.3	.4	.5	.5
Germany	.2	.1	.1	.1	.1
Japan	.0	.0	.0	.0	.0
United Kingdom	.6[a]	.6	.7[b]	.7	.4
United States	.7	.6	.6	.8	.8

Source: Computed from National Science Board, *Science and Engineering Indicators—1991,* 10th ed. (Washington, D.C.: U.S. Government Printing Office, 1991), Appendix Tables 4–26 and 4–27, pp. 341–342.

Notes:
a. 1972.
b. 1981.

Table 7-3
U.S. National Defense-Related R&D Support, 1980 and 1989 (billion nominal dollars)

Source of Defense-Related R&D Outlays	1980	1989
Non-Federal (Industry and State) Defense-Related R&D Investments	16.2	43.9
Federal Programs		
DOD RDT&E[a]	13.4	37.5
Technology Base[b]	2.3	3.5
Advanced Technology Development[c]	.6	5.8
Strategic Programs	2.2	6.4
Tactical Programs	5.2	13.0
Intelligence and Communications	1.2	4.5
Defense-Wide Mission Support	1.9	4.2
DOE Defense R&D	1.1	2.6
IR&D with Potential Military Relevance[d]	1.7	3.8
Reimbursed As Overhead on Contracts	.9	2.3
Not Reimbursed	.9	1.4

Source: National Science Board, *Science and Engineering Indicators—1991*, 10th ed. (Washington, D.C.: U.S. Government Printing Office, 1991), Table 4–3, p. 100.

Notes:
a. Research, Development, Test, and Evaluation.
b. Fundamental research funds (DOD category 6.1) and exploratory development funds (DOD category 6.2). See text for an elaboration of funding categories.
c. DOD category 6.3A.
d. Independent Research and Development Program. A "fair" share of overhead for IR&D with military relevance is reimbursed through payments on federal contracts.

France 37 percent, the United Kingdom 45 percent, and the United States 63 percent.[3] Table 7-2 shows a similar pattern in defense R&D outlays as a share of GDP over the period from 1971 to 1989.

Those estimates of defense R&D outlays provide a general impression of the scope of U.S. military technology policy, but a focus on DOD budget outlays does not present the whole story. As Table 7-3 indicates, private sector and state R&D efforts that support defense missions are larger than the DOD budget for research, development, test, and evaluation (RDT&E). Independent research and development (IR&D) funds, which partially offset the cost of private R&D done in anticipation of government space or defense requirements, contribute an additional amount equal to roughly 10 percent of budgeted RDT&E expenditures.[4] The DOE defense laboratories also contribute to defense nuclear weapon programs and some NASA R&D has military applications. As a result, in 1989, DOD RDT&E expenditures accounted for only about 43 percent of national defense-related R&D support.

DOD clearly influences national technology policy through the scope of its in-house R&D programs and its impact on commercial R&D and procurement contracting. The emphasis on development pushes its programs further into the commercial sphere than most other government efforts, producing an elaborate web of R&D and procurement regulations and highly standardized funding procedures. As a result of the need for budgetary control and secrecy, a central objective of military technology policy has been to provide clear boundaries between military R&D and procurement practices and commercial operations.

Funding for technologies with dual military and civilian uses poses unique challenges in properly allocating corporate R&D and other overhead charges to defense contracts. In order to comply with accounting and security requirements, most defense contractors in dual-use industries operate completely separate R&D facilities and production lines for defense projects.[5] In addition to its commercial contracts, DOD operates an extensive arsenal system to produce munitions and other standardized equipment. Contractors and arsenals producing defense products and DOD and DOE laboratories have traditionally operated in hierarchical structures that emphasize vertical information flows and limited horizontal interaction with other organizations or even other divisions within their own organizations.

Defense R&D is conducted in a closely scrutinized sequential process with carefully defined funding categories. Research program funds in category 6.1 are used to foster basic research, tap worldwide scientific knowledge, and support defense, academic, and nonprofit laboratories with defense relevance. DOD's annual outlays of roughly $1 billion in this area emphasize electrical engineering, materials science, applied mathematics, and computer science. Those expenditures contribute some 8 percent of federal and 5 percent of national funding for basic research. Exploratory development funds in category 6.2 support experiments that evaluate concepts, including modeling and simulation. Advanced development program funds in category 6.3a bring new systems to the prototype level in order to provide information for subsequent production decisions.[6] Budget categories 6.3b and 6.4 fund the development of systems up to the point of actual procurement. Table 7-3 shows the dramatic increase in funding for advanced technology development in the 1980s as development funds expanded and prototype reviews became more important in procurement decisions.

DOD's central mission of fielding forces in support of military strategy produces an understandable emphasis on development and ultimate procurement of systems. Decisions to fund particular technologies have been based on military requirements, not potential commercial applications, and spin-offs to the commercial sector have been serendipitous rather than planned. ARPA, discussed in more detail below, has been quite successful in funding dual-use technologies with large commercial spin-offs. ARPA's emphasis on generic and pre-competitive technologies, however, came from its extended view of future defense applications rather than from any special expertise in forecasting commercial trends.

Several factors are now forcing fundamental adjustments from the traditional national technology policy emphasis on maintaining technology leadership in East-West competition. The increasing focus on dual-use technologies and more direct support of pre-competitive R&D will place significant pressure on defense R&D institutions designed for more narrowly defined mission support. Competition for scarce R&D funds between new dual-use priorities and traditional defense missions is creating new tensions both within DOD institutions and in the FCCSET process discussed in the last chapter. Military technology policy is also adjusting to the information technology revolution, which is having important impacts on the battlefield of the future, on R&D and procurement processes, and on the context of national security and military strategies.

INFORMATION TECHNOLOGY AND MILITARY STRATEGY

In many ways, the 1991 Gulf War with Iraq marked a turning point in the relationship between technology and military strategy. Systems designed in the 1970s and fielded in the 1980s, such as the M1 Abrams tank, the M2/3 Bradley fighting vehicle, the AH-64 Apache and UH-60 Black Hawk helicopters, multiple launch rocket systems (MLRS), Patriot air-defense missile systems, and joint surveillance target attack radar systems (JSTARS) dominated the battlefield. They did so with precision munitions and command, control, communications and intelligence (C^3I) systems designed around information technologies that already lag far behind current commercial computer system and network integration capabilities.[7] The cold war systems that served so well in Desert Storm should continue to meet conceivable challenges for some time, but those systems will drop behind potential military technologies very quickly. In a period of budget austerity, the challenge will be to field a force capable of meeting current requirements while continuing to develop new, more effective systems that can exploit rapid technological advances. The new technological requirement is not to keep pace with a sophisticated peer opponent, but to design a replacement strategy that will move the force structure toward the greater mobility, accuracy, and control necessitated by declining budgets, demanded by evolving military strategy, and facilitated by the revolution in information technologies.

The information technology revolution is driving commercial economic strategy and military strategy in several parallel ways. Industrial relationships are adjusting to the enhanced capabilities for technology transfer in global organizational networks, to the advantages of real-time communications throughout the R&D and production processes, to improved precision and flexibility in controlling production, and to the enormous potential for system integration throughout the value chain. Similarly, military organizations are adapting to the transfer of defense technologies in global defense networks, to dramatically improved communications, to revolutionary advances in munitions control and precision, and to the enhanced capacity for integration across units and services. Those capabilities will place increasing importance on the integration of combined arms operations and on the simultaneous development of technologies, force designs, and force structures. In other words, network integration across force structures and through the procurement, training, and deployment of forces will be just as important in the military sphere as it has become in the commercial sector.

Technological advances have always had a major impact on the nature of strategy, and the information technology revolution is no exception. In *Technology and War*, Martin van Creveld argues that the industrial revolution expanded the meaning and scope of strategy from the narrow realm of the maneuver of military forces to include broader issues of the allocation of national resources between the front and the rear. This "grand strategy" required the coordination of the nation's resources in support of the military strategy for deploying units as part of the battle campaign. At the end of the nineteenth century and the beginning of the twentieth, the emergence of telegraph and rail networks developed new military capabilities, transformed patterns of military competition, and created a revolution in grand strategy.[8] Just as transportation and rail networks transformed grand strategy in that period, the information technology revolution is changing the nature of the battlefield, the procurement process, and the direction of military strategy.

The ongoing revolution in military affairs includes a new framework for the application of network concepts to doctrine and organization, enabling capabilities that permit enhanced access to information and command and control, and a series of new precision strike systems and platforms. The framework, enabling capabilities, and precision strike systems interact in ways that are having revolutionary impacts on the nature of modern warfare.[9] The three main battlefield impacts of the revolution in information technologies are enhanced precision and rates of fire, instantaneous integration of intelligence sources and maneuver elements, and virtual simulation in training that provides a more seamless transition to actual combat.

Precision

Military applications of information technologies are improving the ability to acquire, track, and engage targets at increasing ranges with accurate munitions. Army Chief of Staff General Gordon Sullivan describes the main components of the military technical revolution (MTR) as "lethality and dispersion, volume and precision of fire, integrative technology, mass and effects, and detectability." [10] Lethality in delivery systems produces dispersion in military units. Dramatic increases in the lethality and range of modern systems have led to exponential increases in the area occupied by a force of 100,000 troops from some 248 square kilometers in World War I, to 2,750 in World War II, to 4,000 in the 1973 Arab-Israeli War, to 213,200 in the 1991 Gulf War.[11]

Not only are new munitions more lethal per round, but the rate of fire and the precision of delivery systems have also expanded sharply. Integrative technologies exploit the capability of dispersed forces to deliver increased volumes of fire with high first-round hit probabilities. Improved physical network connections highlighted in the "digitization of the battlefield" are providing near-real-time communications among intelligence, maneuver, fire, and logistical support systems, allowing commanders to focus accurate, lethal, high-volume fires on targets dispersed throughout the battle area. This pattern also creates a new relationship between "mass and effects." Smaller units can achieve decisive results through improved combined arms integration, more rapid maneuvering, and increased invisibility made possible by greater range in surveillance and delivery systems and improved electronic countermeasures.[12]

At the same time that greater precision and range in weapon delivery systems have become more possible, they have also become more important. U.S. operations in Grenada, Panama, and the Gulf War, for example, all emphasized the need for rapid termination of hostilities, limited casualties for U.S. forces, and minimal collateral civilian damage. In the post-cold war environment, those conditions will almost certainly apply to any commitment of U.S. forces in situations with limited objectives. Given the proliferation of highly destructive conventional munitions, improved range and precision in engaging such systems will be increasingly important. Further improvements in range, accuracy, and control will be driven in the short term not by competition from peer opponents with systems as sophisticated as U.S. systems, but by the need to refine U.S. capabilities to meet requirements for speed, safety, and precision.

Command, Control, and Communications

The National Research Council committee's 1992 study of strategic technologies for the Army (STAR) of the next century, widely known as

STAR 21, links eight technology forecast assessments with their expected impacts on systems to win the information war, provide integrated support for soldiers, enhance combat power and mobility, improve air and missile defense, and strengthen combat services support.[13] The study stresses the central role of C³I and RISTA (reconnaissance, intelligence, surveillance, and target acquisition) through a highly networked system including an array of sensor devices on robot vehicles, rapid processing of enormous information flows, battlefield management software, interservice network interoperability, and rapid, unambiguous IFFN (identification of friend, foe, or neutral) for ground as well as airborne systems.[14] Virtually all of the advanced system concepts identified as having the highest potential payoffs for the Army draw on continuing advances in the information technology revolution. Those systems include robot vehicles, network architectures, "brilliant" munitions with sensors and guidance systems that ensure high accuracy even in indirect fire, lightweight indirect fire weapons, integrated theater air and missile defense, and simulation systems for R&D and training.[15] The four technologies identified as having the highest priority for the Army—multidomain smart sensors, high-speed electronics, secure wideband communications, and battle management software—have the most direct impact on C³I and RISTA capabilities.[16]

The technology trends that will increase dispersion and improve integration of information will increase the scope for interservice networking. For example, the JSTARS carried by aircraft in Desert Storm and used to detect moving ground systems will be supplemented by an array of mobile, ground-based systems with programmable processors capable of translating radar signals into reports on moving targets. The reliability and survivability of communications linking the military services will become more and more important. The military satellite communications architecture for the next century will feature extremely high-frequency capabilities, wideband techniques, and autonomously adaptive antennas to reduce susceptibility to jamming and improve covert communications.[17] Enhanced, secure physical network capabilities will make relationships across military units more horizontal and emphasize the network organizational relationships that have been growing in importance in the commercial sector.

Simulation

Simulation technologies have transformed military training. Electronically monitored exercises at the Army's National Training Center at Fort Irwin, California, allow units to train realistically for operations like Desert Storm. Individual simulators for crew training on jet fighters and other sophisticated weapon systems permit extensive practice in scenarios that cannot be replicated with the primary systems. The Army simulation network (SIMNET) has been used effectively in combat training centers to train individuals and crews in the context of realistic battle scenarios. Expanded use of sensors on remote systems and integration of input from multiple sources can create a seamless "virtual reality" for the repetitive exercise of procedures that would otherwise be too costly or risky to practice.

For example, a proposed Army close combat tactical trainer will train mechanized infantry, cavalry, and tank units for combined arms operations by the end of the century using over 400 simulators at fixed sites on 11 installations and over 100 mobile simulators for reserve units away from the fixed sites.[18] Complex joint exercise simulation systems can construct battles using equipment and units that are programmed to fight according to a specified doctrine, permitting realistic command-post exercises for large units.[19] Those simulation capabilities permit the simultaneous evolution of interfaces between soldiers and equipment, links among weapons and control systems, and doctrine for employing integrated systems on the battlefield. They will also make it possible for units to coordinate actions prior to combat, perhaps even while they are en-route to the theater of operations.

As system integration becomes more and more important on the battlefield, the gap between simulation and actual practice is narrowing. The Army's Louisiana Maneuvers (LAM) program, established in May 1992 and named for the 1941 maneuvers in preparation for World War II, is designed to merge simulation and modeling technologies in testing new weapons and concepts and developing doctrine in theater-level war exercises. The concept has already been integrated in the conduct of regular command-post and field exercises.[20] Future large-scale wargaming simulations may in fact employ the same systems used in the conduct of actual warfighting. As a result, wargaming exercises can provide realistic insights into the advantages and shortcomings of current integration capabilities. Advanced techniques have already given the United States a long, sustainable lead in simulation that could provide major advantages in future conflicts.[21]

NETWORKS AND DEFENSE SCIENCE, R&D, AND PROCUREMENT

Just as shifts in technology are producing a military technical revolution, they are transforming the defense R&D and procurement process. Commercial advances are outrunning the ability of military planners to specify new requirements. The technology flow has reversed from the old pattern of defense innovations finding civilian application, to a new relationship with military technologies adapting to civilian breakthroughs. As a result, access to global networks has become increasingly important as a source of technologies with military applications.

The new technologies have spawned horizontal structures designed to pass information more efficiently both inside and outside the firm. Hierarchical organizations designed to grind out incremental changes in standardized products have given way to network industrial firms that emphasize continuous product innovation, just-in-time production, shorter production cycles that keep pace with sophisticated consumer preferences, and a focus on the next product line. Military procurement practices and R&D organizations will increasingly reflect the characteristics of those network industrial firms.

Defense science, R&D, and procurement organizations evolved in an environment in which perceived defense requirements exceeded the capacity of commercial technology. Through the required operational capability (ROC) system, services established requirements for new capabilities and the R&D and procurement process sought to fill them, primarily by funding the development of new systems to meet advanced defense specifications. That process no longer does justice to the real pattern of innovation in many defense-related technologies. In the semiconductor and computer area, for example, commercial capabilities are expanding more rapidly than the ROC process can capture them. The prices of commercial semiconductors designed for comparable environments and durability standards are dramatically lower and their reliability rates are higher than for military equivalents.[22] The central problem is not to promote the development of new technologies to meet military requirements, but to identify commercial trends and adapt evolving commercial capabilities to military applications.

One key aspect of these new relationships is the potential of simulation to compress the time required to move from the requirement to prototype to full development stages. By resolving design flaws early in the process and testing doctrine for deploying the systems before extensive production, the procurement process can become far more efficient and responsive. As a result, there is a pressing need for more flexibility in the ROC process and for new horizontally structured organizations designed to tap breakthroughs that occur in the private sector, and increasingly in foreign firms, and apply them in the defense sector.[23]

Goals

The relative roles of DOD and the services in defining acquisition goals and implementing programs have changed dramatically over time. The puzzle is how to balance the desire for centralized control of priorities against the benefits of exploiting service expertise on specific systems. Not surprisingly, new administrations tend to redress the perceived problems of the last administration, so the balance cycles between centralization in DOD and decentralization to the services.

The 1958 Defense Reorganization Act centralized control of DOD re-source allocation and technology management that had largely been dele-gated to the services. That centralization provided the foundation for the planning, programming, and budgeting system (PPBS), introduced in the 1960s to emphasize tradeoffs across services in terms of contributions to output-oriented programs. Reforms to the system in 1970 returned the initiative in identifying needs and producing systems to the services, leav-ing the Office of the Secretary of Defense (OSD) to monitor the system through the Defense Acquisition Board (DAB). The board approves the beginning of a development system and makes subsequent decisions on full-scale development. The undersecretary of defense for acquisition, an office established under the Defense Reorganization Act of 1986 to cen-tralize control of the process, chairs the DAB.[24]

The current process gives DOD the dominant role in setting goals and strategy and in monitoring projects through a milestone review process, but the individual services retain the initiative in proposing, developing, acquiring, and supporting new systems. The secretary of defense's July 1989 Defense Management Report to the President strengthened the un-dersecretary for acquisition's broad control of the acquisition system, in-cluding authority to direct DOD component heads on acquisition matters and to withhold funds if milestone criteria are not met. The director of defense research and engineering (DDR&E), who serves as the chief scien-tific adviser to the secretary of defense, plays a key role in development programs, particularly in the early formative stages. OSD defines the broad defense goals and strategy for development and procurement through the Defense Planning and Resources Board and the DAB. The Joint Chiefs of Staff help articulate military needs and validate performance goals through the Joint Requirements Oversight Council. The procurement commands of the individual services—for example, the Army Materiel Command—have responsibility for the development, acquisition, and support of specific sys-tems. Each service has a clear, short, direct acquisition supervisory chain flowing from a service acquisition executive at the assistant secretary level through a set of full-time program executive officers, who manage a lim-ited group of projects, to a program manager for each project.[25]

Within that general organizational framework, DOD science and tech-nology strategy has been responding to the new requirements of military strategy, the expanding potential of information technologies, the need to develop improved organizational network relationships, and the increased importance of dual-use technologies in national technology policy. In July 1992, the DDR&E published a new *Science and Technology Strategy* that stressed improved information flows between the science and technology community and warfighters, the revolution in information technologies, and the prominent role of advanced technology prototype demonstrations in a more austere procurement environment.[26]

The acquisition strategy emphasizes rapid war termination with limited casualties and the need for technological superiority in order to enhance deterrence, provide a range of options for commanders, bolster the confidence of allies in U.S. capabilities, and strengthen combat effectiveness.[27] In DOD's terms, the science and technology "drivers," or conditions that set directions for required technological improvements, include the following: the shift from one main adversary to regionally diverse challenges and the concomitant adjustment from a struggle for national survival to an emphasis on regional conflict; a reduced tolerance for extended conflict and for both military and civilian casualties because survival is not at stake; an increased requirement for rapid deployment, intense firepower, and emphasis on coalition warfare because of the shift away from forward basing outside the United States; and the expanded threat of facing Western-quality equipment even in regional conflicts.[28]

New Defense Science, Technology, and Acquisition Strategies

Those goals and technology "drivers" produce an expanded emphasis on precision, control, and integration as a focus of acquisition strategy, dimensions that have also become increasingly important in the acquisition process itself. The DOD process now emphasizes exploiting the information technology revolution, providing realistic and extensive demonstrations of new systems, and continuing interaction between participants in R&D and field commanders.[29] The requirement for enhanced network integration in adapting civilian technologies to military applications and coordinating throughout the process across suppliers, producers, and warfighters has increased. As a result, emphasis on information technologies and integration across organizations is both a goal for military systems and for the acquisition process itself.

Fiscal austerity means that adjustments in military systems and acquisition processes will have to take place without the benefit of the continuing large-scale procurement of incrementally improved systems that characterized the cold war period. Instead, R&D will have to focus on continued improvements in prototypes, and decisions to press on to full procurement will be more important and less frequent. The Office of Technology Assessment has urged an interesting "prototyping-plus" approach that would push the prototype process beyond the design stage, exploiting flexible manufacturing techniques to keep production capabilities "warm," provide sufficient systems for field testing, and maintain key manufacturing skills.[30]

Current DOD policy stresses the importance of technology demonstrations as validations of engineering and manufacturing development stages, with increased emphasis on designing families of systems for standard platforms, improving manufacturing processes, and using electronic battlefield

Figure 7-1
Key Defense Technology Areas and Systemic Thrusts

Area \ Thrust	Computers	Software	Sensors	Communications Networks	Electronic Devices	Environmental Effects	Materials and Processes	Energy Storage	Propulsion and Energy Conversion	Design Automation	Human-System Interfaces
Global Surveillance & Communications	O	O	●	*	●	O	O	O	O	O	O
Precision Strike	O	*	●	●	O	O	O	O	O	O	O
Air Superiority and Defense	●	O	*	O	●	O	O	O	O	O	O
Sea Control and Undersea Superiority	●	O	*	O	O	O	O	O	O	●	O
Advanced Land Combat	O	O	●	●	O	O	*	O	O	O	O
Synthetic Environments	O	O	O	O	O	O				●	*
Technology for Affordability	O	●		O	O		●			*	O

Source: U.S. Department of Defense, *Defense Science and Technology Strategy* (Washington, D.C.: Director of Defense Research and Engineering, June 1992), 1–23.

Key: ✢ Highest Priority ● Priority Effort ○ Very Important

simulations to develop doctrine, tactics, and force structure.[31] The new process builds on many of the same network practices that have become so dominant in the private sector, including interaction throughout the value chain, simulation, and simultaneous development and control of system components.

The 1992 *Science and Technology Strategy* sought to extend the critical technologies framework by showing how 11 key technology areas were related to seven leading defense priorities, or "thrusts." The strategy identified the following seven thrusts for technology initiatives: global surveillance and communications, precision strike, air superiority and defense, sea control and undersea superiority, advanced land combat, simulation, and affordable technology, including integrated product and process design, flexible manufacturing systems, information management systems for control and cost reduction, and engineering environments that apply integrated software capabilities.[32]

Figure 7-1 shows the relative importance of the eleven designated technologies—computers, software, sensors, communications networking, electronic devices, environmental effects, materials and processes, energy storage, propulsion and energy conversion, design automation, and human-system interfaces—in contributing to the seven thrusts. The study concluded that sensors, networking, and design automation had the highest-priority impacts on several different key outputs. In short, the study targeted the revolution in information technologies as the driving force in the highest-priority areas for evolving defense systems.[33] Note that these key technologies are process technologies, rather than product technologies, and they have dual-use applications in both military and commercial sectors.[34]

The overlap of key technologies with several high-priority defense thrusts highlights the problems of coordinating the management of R&D soley by either technology area or by program goals. Network linkages across both technologies and programmatic thrusts are needed. In the new defense management structure, each thrust has a leader who reports to DDR&E, coordinates all service and agency programs across technologies, emphasizes coordination of advanced technical demonstrations, and ensures that the demonstrations are linked to goals for that thrust. There is also a need to coordinate within each technology area and ensure that advances are applied to all thrusts. Each key technology area has a senior technologist who performs that role and reports to the deputy director of defense research and engineering for science and technology. In addition, 16 project reliance panels integrate efforts among services and joint directors of laboratories to encourage the transfer of technologies. The senior technologist for each key area works with the related reliance panel.[35]

The complexity of this coordination process and the need to share information across traditionally compartmentalized organizations are best resolved through the development of dynamic organizational networks whose operation cannot be adequately described by hierarchical "wiring diagrams." The thrust, area, and reliance panel framework is at best an illustration of the kinds of interaction that a new defense R&D organizational network environment should encourage. Moreover, the critical interaction may no longer be within DOD organizations, but between elements of those organizations and the commercial sector. The emphasis should be on tracking rapidly evolving civilian technologies, identifying gaps or issues in adapting those technologies to defense purposes, and providing the right mixture of contracting and in-house R&D efforts to create the required linkages. Defense organizations tailored for those tasks will be more horizontally structured and rely on the coordination techniques now common in commercial organizational networks.

Organizational Networks. The DOD thrust and area framework provides an architecture to which subordinate services and agencies can tie their own R&D and procurement strategies. For example, the STAR 21 panel suggested that the Army should link its funding requests to priorities established in OSD, focus R&D resources on high-payoff technologies that were underfunded in the commercial sector, exploit commercial technologies, products, and production capabilities as much as possible, and concentrate on designing systems that are easily adaptable to modular improvement and replacement.[36] The panel recommended steps to improve organizational networking through the following actions: shifting research centers from a narrow focus on individual combat arms to a broader emphasis on capabilities such as C3I, missile systems, and simulation; enhancing the exchange of information with industry; and maintaining a worldwide watch for new technologies.[37]

Building on the STAR 21 analysis, the 1992 Army Technology Base Master Plan and Army Research Laboratory Implementation Plan initiatives realigned the technology base with functional mission areas and modernization plans, consolidated advanced technology programs in a central "flagship" Army Research Laboratory, and formed more efficient clusters from the remaining laboratories. The Army Training and Doctrine Command has established "battle labs" to coordinate planning based on evolving capabilities that can influence "battlefield dynamics" in the following areas: early entry, lethality, and survivability; depth and simultaneous attack; battle command; mounted and dismounted battlespace; and combat service support. Following the network dynamics of the commercial sector, the battle labs are designed to cut across traditional organizational boundaries; define future requirements within the Concept-Based Requirements System; exploit distributed interactive simulation; link users, laboratories, and industry; and promote horizontal integration of technologies for upgrading systems.[38]

Similarly, the Navy is consolidating its R&D efforts into four RDT&E engineering and fleet support centers and one service-wide research facility, all organized around warfighting missions, and the Air Force is consolidating 14 laboratories into 4 "superlabs." Such service initiatives support the broader triservice project reliance efforts to assign the lead in each technology to a single service, to emphasize broader mission goals, and to exploit cross-organizational networking capabilities.[39]

In short, DOD strategy and service implementation of that strategy are moving toward the development and exploitation of the organizational network patterns that have become so important in the commercial sector. Both trends build on the underlying information technology revolution. Seamless simulation of combat scenarios with data entry from instrumented combat vehicles on ranges, workstations, and networked simulators has permitted dramatic improvements in the ability to evaluate weapon systems and doctrine in realistic settings much earlier in the R&D and acquisition cycle. Those same technologies permit extensive modeling of the R&D and acquisition processes themselves, to include simulation of delivery of supplies, manufacturing processes, and product distribution. Enhanced simulation capabilities improve integration of the processes of defining requirements, specifying capabilities, generating prototypes, and testing and fielding produced systems.[40] One perceptive strategy document makes this point: "one could characterize the entire information technology revolution and its application to national security as the creation, maintenance, and operation of an ever-expanding, adaptive network of systems and networks. These range from precision-guided weapons to the factories and design teams that build them." [41] Physical network capabilities are transforming organizational network relationships throughout the defense establishment.

Dual-Use Technologies. DOD technology policy must clearly emphasize adaptation to the organizational logic of the new dual-use technologies. There is less consensus on the appropriate DOD role in the development of those technologies. Nonetheless, funding for dual-use technologies has become an important component of planning for defense conversion. The increased emphasis on network integration, from warfighting to training simulation to R&D and acquisition processes, has heightened the relative importance of several dual-use technologies, particularly those associated with digital integration. At the same time, national technology policy has increased the focus of R&D outlays on dual-use technologies and those defense agencies that have played the largest role in those areas.

For example, President Clinton's technology policy paper notes the need to focus a larger share of the defense R&D budget on dual-use projects similar to those already supported by ARPA, and ARPA has been singled out for a key role in building regional technology alliances. [42] In part, the dual-use strategy is to serve as a component of a broader program of defense conversion during the transition to a smaller defense establishment. The Defense Conversion, Reinvestment and Transition Assistance Act of 1992 created eight DOD programs known collectively as the Technology Reinvestment Project (TRP). The roughly $480 million in those programs for fiscal year 1993 form part of the Clinton administration's announced plans for a five-year, $19 billion program to offset the impact of the defense transition. The TRP and many of the other proposed initiatives are designed to encourage R&D on commercial technologies. The Defense Technology Conversion Council, an interagency group led by DOD (ARPA) and including NSF, NASA, and the Departments of Energy, Transportation, and Commerce (NIST), will direct the dual-use program. [43]

The new emphasis on dual-use technologies raises two key concerns. First, agencies designed to perform roles in the defense procurement process may be poorly equipped for a more direct commercial role. For example, ARPA's extraordinary record of promoting technologies with large spillovers to the private sector has made it a widely cited model of how collaborative technology efforts between the public and private sector might proceed. It has, however, enjoyed a number of advantages in that process that might be difficult to expand or duplicate elsewhere, such as the ability to draw on the expertise of a vast defense R&D establishment, the flexibility to focus a relatively small staff of professionals on a few key technologies, and an orientation on ultimate procurement applications. Attempts to shift R&D allocation decisions from military application to much different considerations of commercial viability would pose an entirely new set of challenges.[44]

The dual-use emphasis also raises important questions for priorities in applying scarce defense R&D funds to meet legitimate market failures. In the early stages of a technological trajectory, there is uncertainty over ultimate applications and risk in appropriating benefits of R&D, so there is a strong case for DOD intervention to reduce uncertainty, ensure the pursuit of alternative approaches, and offset the tendency of the market to underinvest. In later stages of the trajectory, when the form of ultimate products has been clarified and the market has greater incentives to sustain product and process improvements, the case for DOD funding is reduced.

Theodore Moran draws on that general distinction between early and later stages to argue for the following defense R&D priorities: (1) early-stage projects with high potential defense utility but limited commercial application, (2) similar early-stage projects with dual-use applications, (3) later-stage projects with high potential defense utility and limited commercial application, and (4) later-stage projects with dual-use applications.[45] The key is to target funds on market failures and to exploit commercial incentives as much as possible. A shift in defense strategy toward dual-use applications, however, threatens to reverse those priorities and risks spending scarce defense R&D funds on projects that might simply crowd out private investment. Moreover, as Moran notes, later-stage commercialization projects often demand much larger outlays than prototype development by a ratio of roughly three to one, so the shift toward commercialization projects can impose a substantial drain on funds for early-stage R&D.[46]

On balance, then, while a heightened focus on dual-use technologies may be warranted to encourage defense conversion in a transition period, there will be numerous organizational and allocation problems in centering long-run DOD R&D and procurement strategy on dual-use applications. Those problems will be reduced if DOD policy avoids R&D support for later-stage commercialization.

GLOBAL NETWORKS AND DEFENSE RATIONALIZATION AND COPRODUCTION

New information technologies are changing military strategy in general and defense R&D and procurement strategy in particular. They are also transforming global defense markets, although the pace of adaptation there has been slowed by national and regional restrictions on defense integration. Just as the pressure for organizational adaptation to the new technologies has transformed commercial relationships, organizational network relationships are redefining global defense patterns.

In the United States, defense contractors are networked in their relationships with subcontractors, but network relationships across primary contractors or between primary contractors and DOD are constrained by rules designed to keep the bidding process as competitive as possible. Similarly, accounting and security requirements normally force defense contractors to maintain separate divisions and production facilities for defense and civil operations. That structure clearly contrasts with defense R&D and procurement arrangements in Europe and Japan.

In the European case, governments have actively promoted national champions to glean all the available economies of scale from limited defense expenditures. Declining budgets and movement toward a single European market have shifted that process to a new stage. National champions have now become enmeshed in regional networks through an array of strategic alliances.

Despite the limited scale of production in the Japanese defense market, neither national champions nor international collaboration have emerged to the extent of the European model. Instead, Japan has promoted a network of defense producers whose primary markets are in the commercial sector. Those firms achieve economies of scale and scope not from large defense production runs, but by sharing R&D across civil and defense applications. Reliance on the United States for advanced military technologies through coproduction has permitted a concentration of domestic R&D on the incremental development of a broad technology base. Gradual expansion in indigenous defense technology has now made it feasible to codevelop advanced systems with the United States.

U.S. Defense Production Networks

U.S. defense firms fall into three major categories—prime contractors in the first tier capable of sophisticated international ventures, subtier producers that rely on the prime contractors for most or all of their business, and a third tier of diversified suppliers that produce primarily for the nondefense commercial sector.[47] In fiscal year 1992, the leading 100 first-tier defense contractors received some $75 billion, or roughly 62 percent, of the $121 billion awarded in prime defense contracts.[48] The top 10 contractors, listed in Table 7-4 along with examples of their major products, accounted for some $38 billion, or about 31 percent of all prime contracts.

Defense funds flow through a limited number of prime contractors to a wide array of diverse subtier producers that make up, by some estimates, over 70 percent of the companies in the defense production base.[49] The prime contractors and the smaller subtier producers are dependent on contracts for specific major weapon systems, which will become more and more scarce in the defense drawdown. Larger subtier producers are somewhat more diversified across different systems.[50] Teaming arrangements

Table 7-4
Leading U.S. Defense Contractors: Parent Companies Receiving the Largest
Dollar Volume of Prime Contract Awards, Fiscal Year 1992 (billion nominal
dollars)

Company	Awards	Selected Major Products
McDonnell Douglas	5.3	F-18, F-15, C-17, AV-8, T-45, AH-64 Aircraft; Tomahawk, Harpoon Missiles.
Northrop	4.9	B-2 Stealth Aircraft; Electronics, Communications.
Lockheed	4.7	TRIDENT Missile System; Advanced Tactical Fighter; C-130, C-141, C-5 Aircraft.
General Dynamics	4.5	F-16 Fighter; Nuclear Submarines; M-1 Tank; Tomahawk, Stinger Missiles.
General Electric	4.0	TOW, AEGIS, TRIDENT Missile Components; T-700, F-110 engines; Submarine reactors.
General Motors	3.7	AMRAAM, TOW, TRIDENT, MAVERICK Missile Systems; M-1 Tank Components.
Raytheon	2.8	PATRIOT, AMRAAM, TRIDENT, HAWK, RIM 66 Missile Systems and Components.
United Technologies	2.8	F-100, TF-30, TF-33 Aircraft Engines; UH-60, SH-60, CH-53 Helicopters.
Boeing	2.5	A-6, CH-47, KC-135, Aircraft B-1, E3A, and VSX Aircraft Components; Space Vehicles.
Martin Marietta	2.4	TITAN Missile R&D; A-64 Aircraft Equipment; MK-41 Guided Missile Launcher.

Source: Department of Defense, Directorate for Information Operations and Reports, *100 Companies Receiving the Largest Dollar Volume of Prime Contract Awards, Fiscal Year 1992* (Washington, D.C.: U.S. Government Printing Office, 1992), 4–6.

what more diversified across different systems.[50] Teaming arrangements across prime contractors have become more common as the risks and importance of winning the limited number of available contracts increases, and some contractors even participate on several competing teams to increase their chances. For example, Lockheed joined three competing teams in the competition for the Navy's AX attack plane, and Boeing, General Dynamics, and McDonnell Douglas each participated on two teams.[51]

The largest defense contractors do roughly 15 percent of their defense business on an international basis, primarily through exports and licensing or coproduction arrangements, but U.S. operating restrictions keep them from becoming truly global firms.[52] International sales are conducted either through foreign military sales (FMS) negotiated by the Defense Security Assistance Agency or through direct military sales negotiated in commercial channels. Firms must generally follow the FMS process when technology transfer accompanies the sale. FMSs dominated commercial arms deliveries through the early 1980s, but since then direct commercial sales have risen to roughly equal FMS transactions. In either case, licensing for the sale must be approved in the interagency review process directed by the Department of State under the Arms Export Control Act of 1976.[53] Coproduction agreements with foreign firms require a government-to-government bilateral memorandum of understanding (MOU) that sets the terms of cooperation, waives national procurement restrictions, and protects classified information and intellectual property rights.

In a declining defense market with excess capacity, the pressure to expand international sales is enormous. The consolidation of defense production in Europe and the emergence of more sophisticated production capabilities in Japan means that competition for sales in those markets will increasingly require more participation in joint ventures, the acceptance of inefficient production offset agreements, and licensing of technology that is closer to the current technology frontier.[54]

European Defense Production Networks

Network Structure. In Europe as in other defense markets, the anticipation of reduced levels of defense procurement has accelerated the trend toward collaboration. The promise of more integrated regional defense markets under EC92 reforms and the allure of regional economies of scale have dramatically weakened the traditional national champion approach to defense procurement and strengthened intra-European cooperation.[55] New network arrangements center on tight linkages among defense producers in Germany, the United Kingdom, and France in patterns that have strong political overtones.

The European defense market is roughly half the size of the U.S. market in procurement, with some $47 billion for the 13 European members of NATO in fiscal year 1990 compared to $81 billion for the United States. Similarly, the top five European countries had some $60 billion in arms sales in 1988 and 1989 compared to roughly $95 billion for the United States. The gap was even wider in defense R&D, with European outlays of about $13 billion in fiscal year 1990 coming to roughly one-third of the U.S. total of $37 billion.[56] The EC market is divided into three tiers with the relatively self-sufficient and technologically advanced firms in France, Germany, and the United Kingdom; a mixed set of smaller firms in Italy, Spain, Belgium, Norway, and the Netherlands, which rely on collabora-

Figure 7-2
Simplified View of European Defense Production Networks

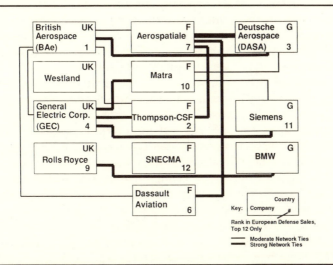

Sources: James B. Steinberg, *The Transformation of the European Defense Industry* (Santa
Monica, Calif.: RAND, 1992), 75–94, and Elisabeth Sköns, "Western Europe: Internationalization of the Arms Industry," in *Arms Industry Limited*, ed. Herbert
Wolf (Solna, Sweden: Stockholm International Peace Research Institute, 1993),
167–188.

tion; and a third tier of firms in Greece, Turkey, Portugal, and Denmark,
which depend more on imports and production under license.[57]

Figure 7-2 provides a simplified view of the major first-tier British,
French, and German arms producers.[58] British Aerospace (BAe), French
Aerospatiale and Dassault Aviation, and Deutsche Aerospace (DASA) are
the major producers of military fixed-wing aircraft. Aerospatiale, DASA
subsidiary MBB, and British Westland are the leading military helicopter
manufacturers. British Rolls-Royce leads in aircraft engines, with DASA
subsidiary MTU and French SNECMA also playing significant roles. Leading missile producers include Aerospatiale, BAe, DASA, and French Matra
and Thompson-CSF. British General Electric and Thompson-CSF are large
producers of avionics and guidance systems. British Vickers, French Giat,
and German Krauss-Maffei, MAK Systems, and Thyssen Henschel, all not
shown in Figure 7-2, are the leading tank producers, and other land systems are dispersed over a number of firms, including BAe and German
Rheinmetall.[59] The largest European defense firms are typically more diversified than their U.S. counterparts. For example, BAe relies on defense
for 40 percent of total sales, Thompson-CSF for 65 percent, Matra 70
percent, and Aerospatiale 44 percent.[60]

Figure 7-2 reflects a significant expansion in the number of interfirm input-output and R&D organizational network relationships within European defense markets. That trend parallels similar adjustments in the nondefense commercial sector. The process of international cooperation is most advanced in the military aircraft sector. French-German collaboration is reflected in a number of agreements between Aerospatiale and DASA in projects such as long-standing Euromissile, 1991 Eurocopter, and 1992 Euro-Hermespace with Dassault. BAe and DASA have also had extensive cooperative experience since 1969 centered on their Tornado Fighter consortium, with Italian Alenia, which is now phasing out production. Their follow-on European Fighter Aircraft (EFA) consortium, formed in 1986 with Spain's CASA, has had an uncertain future since Germany's July 1992 cancellation of anticipated purchases. The BAe ties to DASA and Aerospatiale have been tightened by cooperation on third-generation antitank missiles, work on the Family of Anti-Air Missiles program, and 1992 arrangements for Euroflag to develop a military cargo aircraft and for Europatrol to develop a maritime patrol aircraft. BAe has also been discussing joint R&D with Dassault Aviation for a follow-on to the EFA and Dassault's Rafale, probably anticipating that the European market will only permit one successor to the EFA.[61] The Aerospatiale-DASA connection continues to serve as the core of current cooperative aerospace efforts, with BAe making a number of adjustments in the wake of Germany's EFA decision.

Strategic alliance relationships have also been important in defense electronics. The U.K.-French connection centers on the 1989 Matra-Marconi space joint venture, linking the wholly private Matra missile firm in France and the General Electric Corporation (GEC) of the United Kingdom, which has led to a number of teaming arrangements.[62] GEC has also developed ties to Thompson-CSF through a 1991 GTAR joint venture to develop advanced radar for fighter aircraft. GEC's continental ties include close relationships with German Siemens flowing from their purchase and division of British Plessey and their continuing joint management of Plessey's former aerospace microelectronics.[63] Eurodynamics, a major joint venture that would have strengthened U.K. ties to the continent even further by linking BAe weapon platforms and Thompson-CSF guidance systems, was abandoned in 1991 after contract disputes.[64]

Although the global defense market is still dominated by U.S. firms, European consolidation has allowed several firms to achieve comparable scale. BAe was in a virtual tie with the U.S.'s Lockheed for third place in 1990 defense-related revenues behind the U.S.'s McDonnell Douglas and General Dynamics. Thompson-CSF ranked eighth behind the U.S.'s General Electric, General Motors, and Boeing, and Dassault Aviation and GEC ranked, respectively, eleventh and twelfth behind the U.S.'s Raytheon and Northrop.[65]

European defense firms have also noted the same potential in information technologies, systems integration, and the use of standardized plat-forms with multiple applications that have been stressed in evolving DOD technology policy.[66] The exploitation of those technologies requires a level of standardization and integration of R&D, production, and testing that is difficult to achieve within vertically structured national champions. Technological, economic, and political considerations all support the con-tinued evolution of tighter European defense organizational networks. Eu-ropean governments and multinational defense organizations are reinforc-ing that trend.

Policy Coordination. While economic pressures have forced consolida-tion and integration in the defense sector, the success of government-to-government integration efforts has been more erratic. Coordination of de-fense policy and defense industry has traditionally been beyond the areas of EC "competence." Article 233(b) of the Treaty of Rome permits each EC member to pursue its own defense procurement policies, but Article 30 of the 1987 Single European Act does give the EC new authority in indus-trial-base issues and procurement of dual-use technologies.[67] Coordination of defense programs has been pursued through the NATO cycle of re-viewing national force goals and, since 1966, through the Conference of National Armaments Directors (CNAD). In 1968, the European members of NATO, less France, Portugal, and Iceland, formed Eurogroup to help coordinate and publicize the European commitment to NATO. After Den-mark, Belgium, the Netherlands, and Norway chose coproduction of the U.S. F-16 over the competing French Mirage, France agreed to join an expanded consultative body called the Independent European Program Group (IEPG), which channels recommendations on coproduction and standardization efforts to CNAD.[68]

IEPG has played a central role in pressing for European collaboration projects to enhance standardization.[69] In 1990, IEPG issued a Coherent Policy Document establishing rules for the operation of the common de-fense market, for bidding on procurement projects, and for restricted ap-plication of the inefficient *juste retour* principle of dividing work according to procurement shares.[70] CNAD continues to play a central coordinating role at the transatlantic level with a Conventional Armaments Planning System that seeks to identify potential collaborative projects early in the R&D cycle. The CNAD Task Force on Defense Trade argued in 1991 for a transatlantic code of conduct on acquisition, extensive bilateral purchas-ing agreements, and the creation of a centralized NATO purchasing agency.[71]

Despite those government-to-government efforts at defense integration, however, the market has proven to be a more effective mechanism for coordination and rationalization of European defense markets. The pat-tern of commercial integration in dual-use sectors continues to drive evolv-ing European defense network relationships.

Japanese Defense Production Networks

The network organizational relationships emerging in Europe have long existed in the Japanese defense sector, but on a national rather than a regional scale. Coordination across firms and government agencies is designed first to achieve technological excellence with economic spillover benefits to other sectors, and second to meet military security needs. The broad Japanese view of security, the emphasis on high technology as an objective in itself, and Japan's unique security requirements create a substantially different defense policy process from that found in Europe or the United States. The clear emphasis is on technology management in government and in industry to develop dual-use technologies that will ensure future security in broad terms.[72]

The distinction is particularly apparent in the relationship between the Japanese Defense Agency (JDA) and the senior cabinet level Ministries of Foreign Affairs, Finance, and International Trade and Industry. Officials representing the other ministries have key positions within the JDA itself, and those ministries play a dominant role within the National Security Council process in setting defense policies that reflect primary economic interests.[73] The JDA's R&D and procurement policies are certainly influenced by threat perceptions. The driving force, however, is to develop high-technology capabilities that will reinforce broader national goals and increase the stature of and support for the JDA and the Self-Defense Forces within the government and with the people.[74]

The unique U.S.-Japanese bilateral security relationship, stretching back to the postwar occupation and the subsequent U.S.-Japan Mutual Security Treaty, is reinforced by Japanese policies that preclude participation in collective security arrangements like NATO. Just as Japan has depended on the United States to come to its aid in the event of attack, it has also relied on U.S. military technology, primarily through licensing arrangements that permit production of U.S. systems by Japanese firms. This preferential access to U.S. technology has allowed the Japanese to save R&D costs, while the United States has gained from the recovery of some overhead costs through licensing.[75]

The Japanese defense R&D and procurement process emphasizes purchases from domestic firms. It also stresses closer relationships between government and defense contractors and among defense firms than exist in the United States, relationships that are also typical of the private commercial sector in general. The limited missions assigned to Japanese Defense Forces, the reliance on the United States for advanced military technology, and the emphasis on defense R&D as a component of national industrial policy all reinforce an R&D and procurement strategy that draws technology into defense from the private sector. The Technical Research and Development Institute (TRDI) in the JDA, for example, stresses programs with broad technological impacts rather than targeting state-of-the-art technologies for advanced weapon systems. In comparison with the U.S. system, Japan's strategy places greater emphasis on defense spin-ins from the commercial sector and on total return on investment across all sectors. There is far less policy separation in the treatment of defense and commercial technologies.[76]

TRDI outlays are used to support projects initiated in the private sector, with at least 50 percent of the R&D funds for each project provided by private firms. Close contacts between commercial firms and TRDI ensure that the JDA can track potential defense applications of commercial applications and channel seed funds to worthy projects. Participation of commercial firms in R&D demonstrates competency for the receipt of future procurement contracts, building a pattern of close cooperation and trust extending over the decade required to bring most R&D projects to fruition.[77]

The emphasis on dual-use technologies and the reliance on advanced U.S. military technologies has produced a less specialized defense industry in Japan. Even Mitsubishi Heavy Industries (MHI), which receives roughly one-quarter of the JDA procurement budget each year and ranks as seventeenth in the world in defense contracts, relies on defense for only 15 percent of its total sales. The top six defense contractors—MHI, Kawasaki Heavy Industries, Toshiba, Ishikawajami-Harima Heavy Industries, Mitsubishi Electric Company, and Nippon Electric Company—accounted for over 56 percent of all procurement contracts in 1991, but all are heavily diversified with an overwhelming majority of sales in the commercial sector. The JDA attempts to ensure equitable shares of contracts across a number of firms, regardless of the selection of prime contractor, in order to smooth the impact of variations in sales on any one firm.[78] That process facilitates networking through exchanges of plans and technology across firms, because all firms realize they will be able to share in ultimate defense contracts.

Coproduction and codevelopment efforts with the United States coordinated by the JDA have formalized network relationships within Japan and between Japanese and U.S. producers. Coproduction under U.S. licenses proceeds through bilateral MOUs that provide for the transfer of data on such items as manufacturing processes, component designs, and quality control measures. Most agreements have been for the production of aircraft—the F-86, F-104, and F-4 fighters and the P-2V/7 patrol aircraft early on, and more recently the F-15 fighter and P-3c antisubmarine aircraft—and missiles, including the Nike-J and Hawk and then the Patriot air-defense missile system.[79] The FSX fighter-support aircraft provides a new departure from this pattern, featuring codevelopment of a complete system with Japanese firms in the lead.

MHI was the prime Japanese contractor for the coproduction of the

McDonnell Douglas F-15 fighter, with some 187 aircraft delivered between 1983 and 1994.[80] The components of the F-15 that could not be produced in Japan—the basic airframe technology and the restricted avionics and electronics—became the focal points of TRDI-funded aircraft research, designed to enhance Japan's indigenous capabilities.[81] As the capability for producing an advanced domestic fighter expanded, Japanese firms led by MHI and supported by the JDA pressed for an indigenous FSX fighter support aircraft. The Ministry of Foreign Affairs, however, pushed for coproduction with the United States to reinforce bilateral security relationships and help offset trade imbalances.[82] In the ultimate 1988 compromise, Japan and the United States settled on a controversial codevelopment arrangement that tied design to the General Dynamics F-16C airframe, with Japanese firms receiving 60 percent of the development work and U.S. firms 40 percent.[83] The FSX program has encountered numerous problems in moving toward its anticipated initial deployment in the year 2000. The costs of developing an entire aircraft, even with the head start of an existing airframe, have far exceeded plans, and work on the program appears to be taxing the capacity of the firms involved.[84]

The FSX debate focused attention on a number of key issues for the future of the U.S.-Japanese military technology relationship. Japan has consistently designed defense projects to maximize the potential for spinins from the domestic commercial sector and to absorb U.S. technologies that could strengthen the broad Japanese industrial base. Although the costs of domestic production have been high, with a domestic F-15 costing some $30 to $50 million per plane or roughly twice the U.S. price, the Japanese have remained more concerned with the long-run advantages of technology transfer and with building a foundation for future industrial strength.[85] There are still powerful forces for sustaining the current U.S.-Japanese defense technology and procurement relationship, including the limited scale of Japanese production, the continuing importance of the bilateral security treaty, and more advanced U.S. technologies in many areas. Moreover, as Japanese technologies advance, the potential technological gains to the United States from collaborative projects are expanding.[86] As collaboration moves from coproduction to codevelopment, however, it will also require more difficult integration into Japanese R&D and production networks that will be hard to penetrate, and the earlier pattern of technology transfer on favorable terms will certainly give way to closer scrutiny of the commercial implications of any collaboration.

Globalization of Defense Production

The U.S., European, and Japanese defense firms are linked through cross-border alliances rather than multinational corporations that produce in each region because of continuing national desires to retain defense production capabilities on national security grounds. As technological convergence continues, codevelopment agreements across regions are apt to become more prevalent than earlier coproduction arrangements, just as codevelopment has already come to dominate European R&D and procurement. The General Dynamics collaboration with MHI on the FSX provides a primary defense example of a trend that is now well established in the commercial sector.

International collaborations in commercial ventures by firms with related defense production lines are already becoming more common. Boeing began a shift toward increased subcontracting with the development of the 747, with some 70 percent of the value of the first versions subcontracted primarily to U.S. firms. In 1978, in an attempt to spread the development costs it was incurring on several aircraft, Boeing signed an MOU for the production of the 767 transport with Italian Aeritalia and a consortium ultimately coordinated by the Japan Aircraft Development Corporation (JADC), including Mitsubishi, Kawasaki, and Fuji Heavy Industries, as "risk-sharing subcontractors." The arrangement allowed Boeing to tap subsidies from Italy and Japan, to leverage its own technologies by selective transfer of component design and production, and arguably to expand its access to growing Asian markets.[87] The workshare agreement called for Japan to produce roughly 15 percent of the fuselage and a 1991 contract extension brought expected Japanese production runs on the 767 up to 1,000 units. Boeing entered a follow-on agreement with JADC in 1991 for a 777 transport aircraft under which the Japanese firms will have a 21 percent risk-sharing stake in the program with partial design, development, and manufacturing responsibilities.[88]

Interregional cooperative ventures are also prevalent in engine production. General Electric (U.S.) and SNECMA (France) are pursuing codevelopment of the CFM56 high-bypass jet engine for medium- and short-range aircraft. A complex International Aero Engines V2500 joint venture, involving a Japanese consortium, Pratt and Whitney (U.S.), Rolls Royce (U.K.), Fiat(Italy), and MTU (Germany), has been working on engines for the 150–seat aircraft market.[89]

Similarly, European defense consortia have been adding some U.S. representation, creating the possibility of global defense networks that might compete for contracts across regions. For example, consider the following arrangements: Rockwell-Collins, General Electric, and Honeywell (U.S.) have ties to GEC (U.K.); BAe (U.K.) has links with McDonnell Douglas, Hughes Aerospace, General Dynamics, ITT Defense, and Raytheon (U.S.); Westland (U.K.) has collaborated with Sikorsky, McDonnell Douglas, and IBM (U.S.); and Matra (France) has relationships with Fairchild, General Dynamics, and McDonnell Douglas (U.S.). A consortium including Siemens (Germany), Thompson-CSF (France), Thorn-EMI (U.K.), and General Electric (U.S.) won the competition over two other all-European consortia for the COBRA counter-battery radar to be purchased by Germany, the United Kingdom, and France.[90]

As in the case of the FSX collaboration, however, it is not at all clear how the future balance between the desire for enhanced market access through global networking and the persisting emphasis on national or regional R&D and procurement preferences will be resolved. The networking approach holds out the promise of improved global efficiency in a shrinking defense market. Those advantages, however, may not be sufficient to overcome national linkages between R&D and procurement that lock in contracts well into the future, the principle of *juste retour* with its emphasis on protecting national jobs, and concerns over the broad economic consequences of sharing defense technologies.

The growing emphasis on dual-use technologies and economic security is pushing defense markets into two conflicting directions. On the one hand, the emphasis on commercial technologies presses defense technology, particularly aerospace and electronics, into the environment of global organizational networks which play such a key role in high-technology sectors. That trend should work to promote linkages between commercial and defense collaboration. Tendencies toward interregional defense collaboration early in the R&D cycle and toward buying off-the-shelf systems already in production also work toward greater network integration, because they can break close national ties between development and procurement. On the other hand, efforts to sustain competitiveness in high-technology areas by restricting defense technology transfers work against the commercial trend and limit defense collaboration. The technology transfer issues are particularly complex because of concerns over ownership, control, and access in global networks.

CRITICAL TECHNOLOGY ISSUES: OWNERSHIP, LOCATION, AND ACCESS

Just as new technologies and organizational network relationships have important implications for military strategy, defense R&D and procurement practices, and global defense networks, they have dramatically changed the magnitude and strategic implications of international technology transfer. The potential transfer of technology through defense collaboration is just one piece of a broader issue of national control of technologies that have special strategic characteristics, either in the economic sense of potential spillovers to other sectors or in the military sense of influencing defense capabilities. Because economic and technology trends are clearly moving rapidly toward closer global network relationships to enhance efficiency, the operative policy questions involve whether and how to block that process in strategic sectors.

Arguments for Intervention

Open product and capital markets move resources to their most efficient use, but they do not reflect national concerns over the ownership of firms, the location of particular activities, or access to key resources or products. Global organizational networks compound those national concerns by blurring distinctions among various national and international actors. The arguments for intervention to constrain international mergers and global organizational network relationships include the following: potential interruptions of foreign sources of supply and equal access to the best available technologies, extraterritorial influence over U.S. subsidiaries by foreign governments, loss of commercial or military technological advantages through excessive technology transfer, and the possible erosion of the defense industrial base resulting from a loss of firms that qualify for defense contracts.

Equal Access and Vulnerability to Foreign Sources of Supply. Issues of access revolve around the structure of the market and the ability of a small number of firms, a nation, or a small group of nations to limit output and gain monopoly rents, to delay delivery or give preferential treatment to one set of firms, or to embargo sales to some destinations. These vulnerabilities exist in any market relationship in which there is a limited number of buyers or sellers and substitutes are not readily available. Techniques for modeling such vulnerabilities are well established in game theory in general and in oligopoly theory in particular.

Access becomes an issue when a small number of firms or countries controls a large share of the market. Economists have long used the idea of a concentration ratio—the fraction of total market sales made by some number, typically four, of the largest firms—as a crude measure of potential market power if the firms were to collude. Moran suggests that a similar rule of thumb should be applied for determining whether a foreign acquisition of a U.S. firm could lead to sufficient market power to pose an access risk. If four countries or four firms controlled more than 50 percent of the market for a critical military technology, the 4-4-50 rule, Moran argues there should be a presumption of national security risk.[91]

Tyson argues that the same rule should be applied in evaluating commercial risk in strategic industries, and that liquid crystal displays, some semiconductor equipment and materials, and advanced avionics are already at risk. In her view, that level of concentration provides a justification for Committee on Foreign Investment in the United States (CFIUS) reviews of any further deterioration of the position of U.S. firms in such industries. She argues that such bilateral pressure is justified as an interim form of anticartel insurance until broader international agreements, such as the U.S.-EC. antitrust agreement of 1991, can be reached. She recommends a monitoring system under the National Academy of Engineers or the Office of Science and Technology Policy to track patterns of concentration in strategic industries and provide a database for CFIUS reviews, trade actions, and other steps to generate alternative sources of supply.[92]

Extraterritorial Influence. Moran cites a variety of cases in which the United States attempted to use export controls and constraints on European subsidiaries of U.S. firms to influence "high politics," including denial of an export license to IBM and Control Data for the sale of advanced computers to the French Atomic Energy Commission in the mid-1960s.[93] The risk that foreign governments might turn the tables and use such external influence on U.S. defense capabilities could provide a legitimate basis for concern over the location and ownership of defense suppliers. Moran suggests that even home-owned national champion corporations may be subject to significant external leverage from their global network relationships, as demonstrated by British Petroleum's refusal to shift additional deliveries to the United Kingdom during the OPEC embargo in the early 1970s.[94] On the other hand, as Edward Graham and Paul Krugman note, present political relationships make any serious disruption flowing from international ownership patterns highly unlikely, because roughly 64 percent of total foreign direct investment in the United States is controlled by NATO members and another 21 percent is controlled by Japan.[95]

Technology Transfer. The trend toward global organizational networks and the increasing level of foreign investment in the United States have intensified interest in the transfer of both commercial and military strategic technologies.[96] Processes for controlling product and technology transactions with direct defense relevance are well established. Under the Export Administration Act of 1979, as amended, all foreign sales require an export license. Export permission is automatically given for most products and destinations under a general license, but a formal review process is used for listed products with direct military relevance going to specified destinations. The Department of State coordinates the interagency review process for munitions and the Department of Commerce coordinates the process for other products and technologies. Until it was abolished in early 1994, a Coordinating Committee (COCOM) in Paris, representing Japan and the NATO countries, less Iceland, reviewed national requests for exceptions to an agreed list of restricted exports. Western countries are now discussing a replacement for that cold war institution that might attempt to control sales of arms and dual-use products to outlaw countries.

National procedures for reviewing technology transfer through exports are well developed, but procedures for reviewing transfers through foreign purchases of U.S. firms are still evolving. Technology transfer through the takeover of a U.S. firm by a foreign firm could have substantial implications for specific defense capabilities or the broader defense industrial base.

Although most U.S. observers agree that some limitations on foreign investment in the defense sector are warranted, no U.S. law specifically forbids foreign purchases of defense contractors. Current review procedures do not establish clear grounds for blocking takeovers.[97]

The Exxon-Florio Amendment to the Omnibus Trade and Competitiveness Act of 1988 gave the President limited powers to block foreign mergers or takeovers in cases that threaten national security and are not covered by other statutes. Subsequent presidential regulations revitalized CFIUS, chaired by the secretary of the treasury, which reviews foreign investment for impacts on national security. So far, CFIUS has reviewed over 600 foreign purchases, investigated 13, and blocked only 1. The sole denial blocked the proposed sale of MAMCO, a Seattle-based aerospace company, to China National Aero-Technology Import and Export Corporation, a Chinese government-owned firm. In a few cases, the original investment proposal was withdrawn or approved with conditions. For example, CFIUS permitted the takeover of Fairchild Semiconductor by French private defense producer Matra only after Matra agreed to restructure its export control system.[98] Thompson-CSF of France, 58 percent of which is owned by the French government, withdrew its 1992 offer to buy the missile division of Dallas-based LTV after strong opposition emerged in Congress. The proposed purchase of the missile division was the first attempt by a foreign corporation to purchase a U.S. weapons manufacturer.[99]

Erosion of the Defense Industrial Base. In most cases, DOD policy prevents the award of primary contracts to non-U.S. firms. Foreign-owned subsidiaries seeking defense contracts have traditionally been required to negotiate a special security arrangement or to place control of the subsidiary in a nonvoting trust to ensure appropriate safeguards for classified materials.[100] As a result, the foreign purchase of a potential defense contractor can serve to weaken the defense industrial base, because the costs of participating in defense contracts are greater for those foreign subsidiaries. Those restrictions on foreign subsidiaries serving as primary defense contractors could be relaxed in order to stimulate larger foreign investment and technology flow into the United States. That step to strengthen the defense base by more open contracting, however, would increase concerns over potential leakages of defense technology through foreign firms.[101]

Policy Implications

Policy on technology transfer must weigh the advantages of greater national controls against the efficiencies available through global organizational networks. The nature of the new information technologies and their dual-use applications will make it more difficult to block technology transfers and more costly to limit access to foreign sources of innovation. As a result, policy should be focused on a narrow range of technologies with the most critical impacts.

CFIUS Reviews. Critics of the CFIUS process suggest that the review criteria should be expanded to include economic as well as defense impacts of foreign acquisitions, and that the President's broad discretion on whether or not to take action should be reduced.[102] The center of the controversy concerns the need for criteria that are transparent, precise, and directly related to the issues of access and control. Reviews might consider the impact on potential supply disruptions, potential problems in timely access to the best available technologies, the external impacts of the net technology transfer on other firms and industries, and the employment impacts of any change in production in the United States.

The analysis of the potential for supply interruption or delayed access to new technologies involves issues that are very similar to the normal review of acquisitions for violation of antitrust statutes. Evaluation of the external impacts of net military technology transfer is an extension of the normal MOU process. The review becomes murkier, however, when the impacts on dual-use technology spillovers and shifts in U.S. production patterns are evaluated. Such a review involves more subtle judgments on the size and importance of technological spillovers and on the relative effectiveness of various policies in capturing them, and CFIUS has been understandably reluctant to move into those areas. As broader technology policy shifts toward more direct intervention to capture technological spillovers, however, CFIUS may be pulled into such considerations or other mechanisms may be found for evaluating issues of economic security.

The use of concentration ratios to screen proposed acquisitions may be useful, but such ratios are still very crude guides for actual policy decisions for several reasons. First, the ratios at best only indicate the potential for collusion. Economists have not yet established any relationship between the size of the ratio and actual covert, overt, or tacit collusion.

Second, the application of the ratio requires a clear definition of the market being considered and the substitutes that may be available. For example, concentration ratios would yield dramatically different results if they were applied to semiconductors, semiconductor memory chips in general, DRAM memory chips in particular, or 16-MB DRAM chips even more precisely. Moreover, high-technology products are typically produced through complex input-output organizational networks with primary contractors and a wide array of subcontractors, so meaningful application of concentration ratios requires formulation and maintenance of an enormous database on rapidly shifting network relationships. Levels of concentration would also vary sharply across separate divisions of individual firms, so an aggregated concentration ratio at the corporate level might be very misleading.

Third, most high-technology sectors are already highly concentrated, at least at the primary contractor level, so action based on concentration ratios would imply a dramatic policy shift to extensive intervention. Finally, the Department of Justice is already experienced in the nuances of reviewing mergers for their impacts on potential restraint of trade, so adding similar reviews on broader grounds of economic security may simply add another layer of bureaucracy with overlapping jurisdiction.

Section 232 Reviews. Dependence on foreign suppliers for critical military technologies can result from normal patterns of international specialization as well as from foreign acquisition. Section 232 of the Trade Expansion Act of 1962 allows the President to restrict imports to protect industries that are vital to U.S. national security, without any requirement to show that foreign trade practices have been unfair. For example, Japanese Kyocera Corporation controls over half of the world's market for ceramic casings that house sophisticated semiconductors. Coors Electronics Packaging Company and Ceramic Process Systems Corporation, both U.S. firms, sued for regulatory relief under Section 232, on the grounds that Kyocera and a few other smaller Japanese firms control over 70 percent of the world market and supply 98 percent of the ceramic chip housings for some weapons systems. According to the *New York Times,* the National Security Agency relied on Kyocera for 171 of its 195 customized chips in 1986 and faced delays when Kyocera stopped producing one.[103] A recent Department of Commerce review found that Japanese firms contributed 90 to 95 percent of the ceramics housings used in the Verdin Communications System, the MK-48 Torpedo, and the HARM missile.[104] In August of 1993, the Commerce Department ruled that despite that evidence, the chip-packaging industry did not meet the national security test required by the law, but the Commerce Department nonetheless proposed a number of steps to provide assistance to the industry.[105] The suit illustrated the difficulty of basing such actions on a law that provides no clear definition of national security and emphasizes protectionist responses to complex issues of global networking.[106]

Balancing Access and Vulnerability. Global network organizational relationships provide new challenges to national sovereignty, particularly in their impact on the ownership and location of defense-related activities. On balance, the key in such network relationships is the location of vital activities and the availability of multiple sources of supply rather than national "ownership."

The U.S. industrial base will increasingly rely on global network relationships that are pervasive in the information technologies driving the military technical revolution. In those fields, defense adaptations of commercial technologies will be critical, and key commercial technologies will be developed in global organizational networks. As in the commercial sector, defense technology will draw on breakthroughs emanating from the linkages formed in global networks. As a result, efforts to preserve current defense advantages by restricting foreign investment in dual-use sectors might actually retard future capabilities.

The goal in the defense technology competition is to retain critical defense development and manufacturing capabilities on national soil, while tapping as much of the efficiency and technology access as possible through global networks. The need for balance between those two conflicting objectives requires a narrow emphasis on a clear set of defense technologies with the most critical impacts and a focus on the location of the most important activities associated with those technologies.

In most cases, foreign direct investment in the U.S. high-technology sector should not jeopardize control over the most critical elements of the defense technology base as long as R&D and production facilities stay in the United States. As Graham and Krugman argue, foreign subsidiaries are covered by the Defense Production Act of 1950, which ensures DOD priority deliveries in periods of national emergency, and by the International Emergency Powers Act, that permits the host country to seize the assets of enemy foreign subsidiaries in wartime.[107] If the consequence of restricting direct investment in the United States were the collapse of a U.S. firm or foreign investment elsewhere, the restrictions actually could reduce U.S. control over defense supplies.

Nonetheless, a number of steps suggested by Graham and Krugman would help to ensure a strong U.S. defense industrial base with appropriate ties to global networks. First, the trend within DOD to internationalize the procurement process should enhance the defense base by opening up a wider range of bids to global competition and limiting restrictions on foreign subsidiaries operating in the United States. Second, the development of a short classified list of absolutely critical defense technologies in sufficient detail to guide CFIUS and Section 232 reviews, along the lines of the lists developed for the export control process, would focus the review process on the most important defense technologies. Third, confidential performance and reporting requirements on R&D and content should be imposed on foreign firms acquiring U.S. firms in defense-related industries to ensure that those firms would remain self-sufficient if they were severed from the parent in emergency. Fourth, the U.S. should press for a multilateral framework to limit extraterritoriality, to give precedence to home-country laws, to ensure equal treatment of firms regardless of parent citizenship, and to delineate acceptable performance requirements. Such a framework would expand on and formalize OECD investment guidelines and help to alleviate U.S. concerns over potential vulnerabilities to the industrial base.[108]

FUTURE DIRECTIONS FOR MILITARY TECHNOLOGY POLICY

Military technology policy must now be formulated in a completely new international, technological, economic, and national policy environment. The multiplicity of security challenges requires broad capabilities across a wide range of potential regional contingencies. The military technology revolution creates new possibilities for precision, integration and simulation in R&D, production, and warfighting, but the dissemination of even relatively primitive versions of advanced systems also creates new vulnerabilities to less advanced military forces. At the same time, national concerns for promoting technological advances in commercial sectors, a growing emphasis on dual-use technologies, and declining defense budgets will squeeze defense R&D and procurement funds.

The only feasible response for defense organizations will be to exploit the efficiencies available through organizational networking arrangements made possible by the information technology revolution. Traditional hierarchical organizations, designed to meet defense requirements at virtually any cost and to safeguard technological information, must now transform themselves into the horizontal structures of the commercial sector that are designed to draw in information and adapt it through flexible arrangements with other organizations. That reform process is already well underway, at least in terms of consolidation and management reforms designed to encourage broader interaction within the defense R&D and procurement community and to promote greater reliance on commercial sources.

There is more controversy over efforts to have DOD shift even further beyond adaptation to commercial trends to a larger role in developing dual-use technologies. In the new national policy environment, dual-use technologies are apt to have a high priority in funding. Defense institutions, however, have a limited capacity to develop dual-use technologies in the absence of the active market feedback needed to guide commercial ventures. Moreover, the pressure on organizations like ARPA to sustain mission-critical programs while promoting dual-use technologies will be great. The thrust and key-technology framework provides an important improvement in DOD's ability to target limited funds on technology areas with high potential return and small anticipated commercial investment. The promotion of dual-use activities in those sectors through defense R&D may be a useful transition step during the defense drawdown as long as it remains tightly focused on traditional areas of defense expertise.

The strategic transformation is forcing an important reexamination of the essential characteristics of the defense industrial base in the light of the growing importance of global networks in dual-use and defense technologies. The new network organizational structures mean that the base should be defined less in terms of the ownership of firms, and more in terms of the location of critical defense activities on national soil. The globalization of defense production provides important opportunities to form tighter interregional security linkages through interpenetration of arms markets, but it also imposes heightened risks in controlling critical technologies. Balancing those two trends will require a tighter focus on truly critical defense technologies, a general relaxation of restrictions on most dual-use technologies, and heightened awareness of foreign technology plans and developments.

During the East-West competition, DOD technology policy emphasized technological leadership because the potential results of falling behind were catastrophic. In the new environment, the challenge is not technological leadership narrowly defined, but the ability to adapt doctrine and organizational structures to exploit new technologies that will be generated in global organizational networks. In the commercial sphere, U.S. technological innovation and early dominance in the semiconductor industry was not sufficient to hold off Japanese firms who mastered process technologies and commercialization of new chips. Similarly, the new military technology challenge may be less in promoting technical breakthroughs and more in developing efficient, integrated approaches to emerging technologies through closer linkages across the R&D, procurement, and warfighting communities. In short, new military technology policy will have to exploit the advantages of the organizational network structures made possible by the information technology revolution.

NOTES

1. Daniel J. Kevles, "Principles and Politics in Federal R&D Policy, 1945–1990: An Appreciation of the Bush Report," in *Vannevar Bush: Science—the Endless Frontier,* National Science Foundation (Washington, D.C., 1990), pp. ix-x, xvii-xviii.

2. This paragraph follows Kevles, "Principles and Politics in Federal R&D Policy," pp. xv-xviii.

3. Organization for Economic Cooperation and Development, *OECD Main Science and Technology Indicators, 1991,* No. 2 (Paris, 1992), Table 64, p. 49. The French estimate is for 1989.

4. See National Science Board, *Science and Engineering Indicators - 1991,* 10th ed. (Washington, D.C.: U.S. Government Printing Office, 1991), 98.

5. See Senator Jeff Bingaman, Jacques Gansler, and Robert Kupperman, *Integrating Commercial and Military Technologies for National Strength* (Washington, D.C.: Center for Strategic and International Studies, 1988).

6. U.S. Department of Defense, *Defense Science and Technology Strategy* (Washington, D.C.: Director of Defense Research and Engineering, June 1992), I-9, I-10, I-22.

7. See "The Microchip War," *Economist* (January 26, 1991), 77–79.

8. Martin van Creveld, *Technology and War: From 2000 B.C. to the Present* (New York: Free Press, 1989), 167–171.

9. Michael J. Mazarr, *The Military Technical Revolution* (Washington, D.C.: Center for Strategic and International Studies, March 1993), 16–21.

10. Gordon R. Sullivan and James M. Dubik, *Land Warfare in the 21st Century* (Carlisle, Penn.: U.S. Army War College, Strategic Studies Institute, February 1993), 12.

11. Ibid., 13. Terrain also played a role in those figures, but the trend to greater dispersion is clear even after adjusting for those impacts.

12. Ibid., 16–25.

13. National Research Council, Board on Army Science and Technology, Commission on Engineering and Technical Systems, *STAR 21: Strategic Technologies for the Army of the Twenty-First Century* (Washington, D.C.: National Academy Press, 1992).

14. Ibid., 44–61.

15. Ibid., 43. See U.S. Congress, Office of Technology Assessment, *Miniaturization Technologies* (Washington, D.C.: U.S. Government Printing Office, November 1991), 27–32.

16. National Research Council, *Star 21*, 194–197.

17. Ibid., 132–133.

18. John W. Shannon and Gordon R. Sullivan, *Strategic Force—Decisive Victory: A Statement on the Posture of the United States Army, Fiscal Year 1994* (Washington, D.C.: U.S. Department of the Army, March 1993), 66.

19. Frederick J. Brown, *The US Army in Transition II: Landpower in the Information Age* (Washington, D.C.: Brassey's (US), Inc., 1993), 102–103.

20. Shannon and Sullivan, *Strategic Force—Decisive Victory*, 58–59, and Robert Holzer and Vago Muradian, "Simulations Help Army Plan for Future Battles," *Army Times*, June 21, 1993, 32.

21. National Research Council, *STAR 21*, 100.

22. See Jacques S. Gansler, "The Future Industrial Base," in *1993 American Defense Annual*, ed. Joseph Kruzel (New York: Macmillan, 1993), 206–208.

23. See National Research Council, *STAR 21*, 236–237, for a discussion of the ROC system and the related Concept-Based Requirements System (CBRS). See Brown, *The U.S. Army in Transition II*, 87–98, for a positive assessment of the importance of CBRS in developing Army systems.

24. Daniel J. Kaufman, "The Defense Technology Community: Players and Roles," in *Defense Technology*, ed. Asa A. Clark, IV, and John F. Lilley (New York: Praeger, 1989), 183–189.

25. Dick Cheney, *Annual Report of the Secretary of Defense to the President and the Congress* (Washington, D.C.: Department of Defense, January 1991), 28–29.

26. U.S. Department of Defense, *Defense Science and Technology Strategy*, I-2. See "Strategic Defence: Second Coming" *Economist* (May 22–28, 1993), 31–32.

27. U.S. Department of Defense, *Defense Science and Technology Strategy*, I-2.

28. Ibid., I-2, I-6.

29. Ibid., I-10.

30. U.S. Congress, Office of Technology Assessment, *Building Future Security: Strategies for Restructuring the Defense Technology and Industrial Base* (Washington, D.C.: U.S. Government Printing Office, June 1992), 12–13, 51–75.

31. U.S. Department of Defense, "White Paper on Defense," May 20, 1992, as cited in U.S. Department of Defense, *Defense Science and Technology Strategy*, I-8.

32. U.S. Department of Defense, *Defense Science and Technology Strategy*, I-18.

33. Ibid., I-22, I-23.

34. See Jacques S. Gansler, "The Future Defense Industrial Base," in *1993 American Defense Annual*, ed. Joseph Kruzel (New York: Macmillan, 1993), 205–208.

35. U.S. Department of Defense, *Defense Science and Technology Strategy*, I-24, I-26, I-27.

36. National Research Council, *STAR 21*, 207–8.

37. Ibid., 227.

38. Deputy Assistant Secretary of the Army for Research and Technology, *Army Technology Base Master Plan* (Washington, D.C.: U.S. Department of the Army, November 1992), I-6–I-11, I-26–I-29, and U.S. Department of the Army, *Army Research Laboratory Implementation Plan* (Washington, D.C.: July 15, 1992).

39. Office of Technology Assessment, *Building Future Security*, 44–45.

40. U.S. Department of Defense, *Defense Science and Technology Strategy*, I-12.

41. Ibid., I-14.

42. President William J. Clinton and Vice President Albert Gore, Jr., *Technology for America's Economic Growth, A New Direction to Build Economic Strength* (Washington, D.C.: U.S. Government Printing Office, February 22, 1993), 8.

43. U.S. Executive Office of the President, *Budget of the United States Government, Fiscal Year 1994* (Washington, D.C., April 8, 1993), A-462; Wil Lepkowski, "Dual-Use Program in Science, Technology To Be Run by Five-Agency Group," *Chemical and Engineering News* (March 29, 1993), 21; and Congressional Budget Office, *The Technology Reinvestment Project: Integrating Military and Civilian Industries* (Washington, D.C., July 1993), pp. vii, 2–7.

44. For a pessimistic assessment of the post-World War II experience in blending commercial and military procurement objectives, see Richard R. Nelson, *High Technology Policies: A Five-Nation Comparison* (Washington, D.C.: American Enterprise Institute, 1984), 73.

45. Theodore H. Moran, "The Globalization of America's Defense Industries," *International Security* 15 (Summer 1990): 76–77.

46. Ibid., 78.

47. U.S. Congress, Office of Technology Assessment, *Arming Our Allies: Cooperation and Competition in Defense Technologies* (Washington, D.C.: U.S. Government Printing Office, May 1990), 27.

48. Department of Defense, Directorate for Information Operations and Reports, *100 Companies Receiving the Largest Dollar Volume of Prime Contract Awards, Fiscal Year 1992* (Washington, D.C.: U.S. Government Printing Office, 1992), 9.

49. Defense Systems Management College, *Defense Manufacturing Management: Guide for Program Managers*, 3rd. ed. (Washington, D.C.: U.S. Government

Printing Office, April 1989), chap. 2, p. 5, as cited in Office of Technology Assessment, *Building Future Security,* 80.

50. Office of Technology Assessment, *Building Future Security,* 81–82.

51. Ibid., 92.

52. Office of Technology Assessment, *Arming Our Allies,* 27. Many of these defense firms do a much larger share of their dual-use business in international markets. See U.S. Congress, Office of Technology Assessment, *Global Arms Trade: Commerce in Advanced Military Technology and Weapons* (Washington, D.C.: U.S. Government Printing Office, June 1991), 49.

53. Office of Technology Assessment, *Global Arms Trade,* 56–58.

54. Ibid., 53.

55. The same process is under way in the private commercial sector. See, for example, Roger Abravanel and David Ernst, "Alliance Versus Acquisition: Strategic Choices for European 'National Champions',," in *Collaborating to Compete: Using Strategic Alliances and Acquisitions in the Global Marketplace* eds. Joel Bleeke and David Ernst (New York: John Wiley & Sons, Inc., 1993), 229–248.

56. James B. Steinberg, *The Transformation of the European Defense Industry: Emerging Trends and Prospects for Future U.S.-European Competition and Collaboration* (Santa Monica, Calif.: RAND, National Defense Research Institute, 1992), 8–11.

57. Ibid., p. vi.

58. Figure 7–2 includes only French, German, and British firms. Producers of land systems are not shown in the figure because there are few network connections in that sector. Italian Alenia is Europe's fifth largest defense producer and French Giat is eighth largest. Giat and Alenia are not shown in the Figure.

59. Elizabeth Sköns, "Western Europe: Internationalization of the Arms Industry," in *Arms Industry Limited,* ed. Herbert Wolf (Solna, Sweden: SIPRI, 1993), 169–170.

60. Office of Technology Assessment, *Global Arms Trade,* 39–40.

61. Sköns, "Western Europe: Internationalization of the Arms Industry," 172–176, and Steinberg, *The Transformation of the European Defense Industry,* 79.

62. GEC-Marconi is the defense division of GEC.

63. Steinberg, *The Transformation of the European Defense Industry,* 79–82.

64. Sköns, "Western Europe: Internationalization of the Arms Industry," 177.

65. Steinberg, *The Transformation of the European Defense Industry,* 69.

66. Steinberg, *The Transformation of the European Defense Industry,* 100–101.

67. Ibid., p. ix.

68. See James R. Golden, *The Dynamics of Change in NATO: A Burden-Sharing Perspective* (New York: Praeger, 1983), 58–59.

69. For a history of Franco-German and Franco-British collaborations, see Steinberg, *The Transformation of the European Defense Industry,* 48–53.

70. Ibid., 42–44.

71. Ibid., 47–48, and "NATO: The Fight for Freer Trade," *Economist* (June 5–11, 1993), 57–58.

72. See Michael W. Chinworth, *Inside Japan's Defense: Technology, Economics & Strategy* (Washington, D.C.: Brassey's (US), Inc., 1992).

73. For example, a representative from MITI typically heads the JDA Equip-

ment Bureau, which reviews technical aspects of equipment proposals. See Tetsuya Kataoka and Ramon H. Myers, *Defending an Economic Superpower: Reassessing the U.S.-Japan Security Alliance* (Boulder, Colo.: Westview Press, 1989), 66.

74. Chinworth, *Inside Japan's Defense,* 2–6.

75. Office of Technology Assessment, *Global Arms Trade,* 109–111. Despite the relatively low share of GDP Japan devotes to defense, in comparison with NATO members Japan ranks behind only the United States in total defense outlays.

76. Kataoka and Myers, *Defending an Economic Superpower,* 67–69, Chinworth, *Inside Japan's Defense,* 31–32, 35–36, and Office of Technology Assessment, *Global Arms Trade,* 116–117.

77. Chinworth, *Inside Japan's Defense,* 34–35, 37, 46. The close network relationships between the government and firms involved in defense production are reinforced in a number of ways. For example, The Federation of Economic Organizations, or *Keidranen,* provides an important link between government agencies and firms in each industrial sector. See Kataoka and Myers, *Defending an Economic Superpower,* 67, and Chinworth, *Inside Japan's Defense,* 24.

78. For example, see "Mitsubishi Dominated Japanese Military Contract Awards in 1991," *Aviation Week & Space Technology* (April 20, 1992), 24, and Chinworth, *Inside Japan's Defense,* 57, 190–191.

79. Chinworth, *Inside Japan's Defense,* 197, fn. 46.

80. Ibid., 110.

81. Ibid., 134.

82. Ibid., 141–144, and J. Richard Walsh, "Technonationalism in U.S.-Japanese Security Relations: The FSX Controversy," *Armed Forces and Society* 19 (Spring 1993): 379.

83. Walsh, "The FSX Controversy," 380.

84. Office of Technology Assessment, *Global Arms Trade,* 118.

85. Chinworth, *Inside Japan's Defense,* 58–59.

86. For examples, see Walsh, "The FSX Controversy," 387.

87. "Mitsubishi Expands Commercial Sectors," *Aviation Week & Space Technology* (July 29, 1991), 46.

88. David C. Mowery, "Joint Ventures in the U.S. Commercial Aircraft Industry," in *International Collaborative Ventures in U.S. Manufacturing,* ed. David C. Mowery (Cambridge, Mass: Ballinger Publishing Company, 1988), 79–82.

89. Ibid., 86–89, 93–97; Keith Hayward, *International Collaboration in Civil Aerospace* (New York: St. Martin's Press, 1986), 113–118, 128–137; and Steinberg, *The Transformation of the European Defense Industry,* 87.

90. Steinberg, *The Transformation of the European Defense Industry,* 105, and Sköns, "Western Europe: Internationalization of the Arms Industry," 172–175.

91. Moran, "The Globalization of America's Defense Industries," 82–83.

92. Laura D'Andrea Tyson, *Who's Bashing Whom? Trade Conflict in High-Technololgy Industries* (Washington, D.C.: Institute for International Economics, 1992), 277–278.

93. Moran, "The Globalization of America's Defense Industries," 60–62

94. Ibid., 63.

95. Edward M. Graham and Paul R. Krugman, *Foreign Direct Investment in*

the United States, 2nd ed. (Washington, D.C.: Institute for International Economics, 1991), 95–97.

96. See ibid., 12. According to Graham and Krugman, the share of U.S. manufacturing assets owned by foreign affiliates increased from 5.2 percent in 1977 to 16.8 percent in 1989.

97. Ibid., 95–97, 110–113.

98. Ibid., 125.

99. Eric Schmitt, "Sale of LTV Missile Unit up to the Administration," *New York Times,* May 20, 1992, D1, D20.

100. Moran, "The Globalization of America's Defense Industries," 94–95.

101. Graham and Krugman, *Foreign Direct Investment in the United States,* 115.

102. Tyson, *Who's Bashing Whom?* 277–278.

103. Keith Bradsher, "Industries Seek Protection as Vital to U.S. Security," *New York Times,* January 19, 1993, D1–D2.

104. U.S. Department of Commerce, Office of Industrial Resource Administration, *National Security Assessment of the Domestic and Foreign Contractor Base: A Study of Three Navy Weapons Systems* (Washington, D.C.: U.S. Government Printing Office, March 1992).

105. Keith Bradsher, "U.S. Plans to Offer Aid, Not Protection, in Chips," *New York Times,* August 13, 1993, D1, D6.

106. See Erik Pages, "Coming to Terms With Foreign Dependence in a Global Environment," *Issue Brief* No. 5 (Washington, D.C.: Business Executives for National Security, July 1993), 7–11.

107. Graham and Krugman, *Foreign Direct Investment in the United States,* 152–153.

108. Ibid., 150–159.

8 A National Strategy of Cooperative Competition

The information technologies of the third industrial revolution are forcing fundamental adjustments in U.S. national strategy.[1] That strategy must adapt to new patterns of interaction in global organizational networks, to heightened competition for high-value activities in the regional nodes of those networks, to new relationships between commercial and military technologies, and to an ongoing revolution in military technology, systems, and doctrine. Fortunately, the relatively open U.S. economy provides enormous flexibility in meeting the new challenges, and there are clear reasons for optimism as U.S. institutions shift from the hierarchical structures of the past to the more flexible network relationships of the future.

The Soviet Union collapsed in part because its underlying civilian economy could not adjust to the demands of the new technologies, and its military base faced obsolescence. Future competition for economic and military leadership will come from the advanced economies of Europe, Japan, and others who can make the transformation. That competition need not be confrontational and it need not threaten U.S. interests as long as it proceeds within a cooperative framework. Indeed, the competition will be the source of future U.S. economic and military strength by ensuring that U.S. institutions meet global standards. Continuing U.S. economic and military leadership is vital not only to U.S. well-being and influence, but also to world stability and global progress toward more democratic institutions.[2] U.S. strategy must recognize that economic convergence and the logic of the new technologies have produced an integrated system in which network relationships will determine national prosperity and influence. The challenge to the United States is to use the enormous leverage provided by its current leadership position to craft a framework of cooperative competition that will sustain U.S. leadership in evolving global organizational networks.

ECONOMIC, MILITARY, AND TECHNOLOGY INTERRELATIONSHIPS

Figure 8-1 portrays the key relationships among the commercial industrial base, the military industrial base, the military R&D and procurement structure, and the systems, forces, and doctrine that provide military capa-

Figure 8-1
The Industrial Base and Military Capabilities

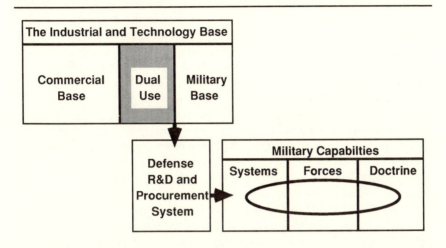

bilities. In the short run, current systems, forces, and doctrine determine the capabilities that underlie security strategy. In an intermediate period that has traditionally spanned 10 to 20 years, the defense technology and industrial base (DTIB) determines the potential flow of new systems that can respond to or permit changes in forces or doctrine.[3] In the longer run, the broader civilian technology and industrial base provides the foundation for sustaining the military industrial base, particularly in dual-use technologies shown in the overlapping, shaded section in Figure 8-1. The information technology revolution, the emergence of global organizational networks, and convergence in economic performance across the three developed regions have had dramatic impacts on each set of relationships in Figure 8-1, altering the nature and relative importance of different linkages. The R&D, production, and maintenance components of the DTIB each have public and commercial elements that are integrated into the broader commercial technology and industrial base and increasingly into global organizational networks.[4]

The Commercial Industrial Base

National strategy responds to a number of important objectives, including economic prosperity and national security, but those goals and the means to reach them are interrelated in complex patterns. In several important ways, economic strength and national security reinforce each other. National security contributes to prosperity by providing a stable environment for private enterprise, and economic vitality provides the means for pursuing national security objectives. Economic strength increases international influence directly through market relationships and bargaining power and indirectly by providing a technological base for military capabilities and funds for defense procurement. At a lower level of importance, there are often important spillover benefits from R&D in military technologies to commercial applications.

On the other hand, the goals of economic well-being and national security conflict with each other through competition for the allocation of scarce national resources. In the short run, funds to provide military capabilities must be obtained from increased national debt, higher taxes, or shifts in public spending. The longer-term consequences of that defense spending depend on just what activities were "crowded out" by the requirement to finance debt, increase taxes, or reduce competing public programs. At the microeconomic level, spending for defense reallocates R&D and science and engineering talent away from commercial applications.

Economic strength and national security are inseparably intertwined, even in isolated national economies. Security policies that ignore economic consequences and economic policies that ignore the need for a secure environment are both dangerous. In globally networked economies, the linkages are even more complex. National security and economic well-being increasingly depend on the performance of networks of international organizations. Congruent economic and security policies are crucial in shaping the operation of those networks to meet vital national interests, to foster democratic institutions, and to sustain international stability.

As Chapters 1 and 2 argued, productivity growth is the best long-term measure of future potential to sustain a vibrant commercial industrial base, meet domestic needs, and sustain international influence. The productivity growth performance of the U.S. economy has declined below long-term trends since the early 1970s, but growth slowed in all major economies in that period, so the sources of the lower growth are not unique to the United States. Moreover, U.S. manufacturing productivity growth did not decline, and the full impact of investment in information technologies has not yet been felt. That record lends little credence to the argument that there are fundamental flaws in the U.S. economy that will lead to continued productivity decline compared either to the historical record or to the performance of other economies. There is, however, clear evidence that the unique sources of the postwar productivity surge based on U.S. dominance in science-based technology and mass markets have now run their course, and that productivity levels in North America, Europe, and Japan are converging.

In that new environment, productivity growth depends on the interaction of factor creation, innovation, and the industry structure of competitive advantage in a dynamic productivity cycle. The information technology revolution has reinforced global dimensions of each part of the productivity cycle by providing a new physical communications network, creating new technological paradigms in strategic industries, and opening extraordinary new opportunities for exploiting technological spillovers across industries. Global input-output, R&D, and finance organizational networks, stimulated in part by the information technology revolution, now link organizations in horizontal communications structures that enhance coordination across all dimensions of the value chain. Network performance, rather than the performance of individual firms, has become a more important determinant of productivity trends.

Despite the integrating force of global networks, local factors remain important in determining the kinds of network activities that will occur in regions or nations. National attributes and differences in economic systems create unique climates that influence potential comparative advantages in various industries. Although some forms of generic knowledge can be communicated easily across networks, other forms of tacit knowledge are embedded in the skills of individual workers, in institutional procedures, and in specialized infrastructures that are not easily transferable. It might be possible to transfer some forms of tacit knowledge by hiring skilled workers from abroad, but it is more difficult to recreate institutional contexts and unique supporting infrastructures. The creation of local advantages in advanced and specialized factors is often path-dependent, with advantages from external economies of scale and learning by doing creating sustainable advantages for future rounds of competition. Those advantages may be concentrated in regions below the national level.

In short, sustaining a commercial industrial base in a period of economic parity and global networking requires policies that emphasize constant adaptation and aggressive support of factor creation. Promoting growth in the commercial industrial base does not mean protecting the status quo, but instead encouraging dynamic adaptation to new global possibilities.

Dual-Use Technologies

The information technology revolution has increased the overlap between the commercial industrial base and the military industrial base shown in Figure 8-1, and that trend should continue. The key technologies driving the military technical revolution through enhanced precision, integration, and simulation are the same ones driving the commercial technical revolution. As a result, there is increased justification for government policy to enhance innovation in high-technology dual-use industries. These are industries with high returns on technology investments in general and with spillover externalities that support some forms of government intervention.

Defense R&D and procurement already embraces dual-use areas, so the federal government has the expertise to make informed judgments on technological developments, at least at the basic and generic pre-competitive levels. On the other hand, there is little evidence of market failure at the level of later-stage commercialization R&D, and DOD has little expertise to share with the private sector in pursuing such projects. In the transitional period as defense spending drops to a new equilibrium level, existing defense R&D facilities can ease the transition by building capabilities for sharing pre-competitive dual-use technologies with the private sector. Similarly, nondefense programs can offset the impact of the transition by supporting R&D with dual-use applications. In a period of limited defense budgets, DOD will have to continue to shift toward greater reliance on dual-use technologies, tighter networking with the private sector, and better adaptation of commercial technologies and products for defense applications.

The growing importance of dual-use technologies also means that defense firms will be increasingly involved in global R&D and input-output organizational network relationships. That process is already well advanced in the divisions of defense firms that produce for commercial markets. Networking is also a fact of life in the European and Japanese defense industries, and the trend toward interregional collaborative projects is increasing at the industry-to-industry level, if not at the government-to-government level. The management of access to those evolving defense organizational networks will be a central strategic issue.

The Military Industrial Base

The corollary to the expansion of the dual-use component of the military industrial base is a decline in the "arsenal" base of government facilities and dedicated defense contractors. Even those organizations that remain in the arsenal system will be different, because the information technology revolution will force adjustments to horizontal structures that are more adept at drawing in commercial technologies and adapting them to integrated military systems. Production runs will be reduced and stretched out over time by exploiting flexible manufacturing processes, with greater emphasis on continuing incremental adaptation of families of platforms and just-in-time inventory control techniques. Prototyping, production management, and training will all stress advanced simulation techniques to increase effectiveness within tighter budget constraints.

Integration of R&D, Procurement, Force Structure, and Doctrine

Military strategy seeks to provide military systems, force structure, and doctrine to meet the contingencies suggested by national security strategy. The challenge has been to integrate the process across services and to provide effective feedback to guide the evolution of systems, forces, and doctrine. The revolution in military technology, systems, and doctrine has made such integration and feedback, illustrated by the horizontal loop in Figure 8-1, more important and more feasible. Mass can now be achieved more than ever before by concentrating fires, rather than forces, through dramatically improved sensing, processing, and coordination of information, and closer integration of delivery systems across services. That higher level of integration is achievable, but it still requires constant training through joint simulations and exercises. The feedback concerning integration problems increasingly raises issues that fall at the boundaries of traditional service responsibilities.

The revolution in military affairs is transforming the kinds of exercises that can be conducted, the rate at which feedback can be achieved, and the potential for modifying systems and doctrine based on the new information. Just as networked firms now conduct R&D, product design, process design, and customer services through a continuous, virtually concurrent process, military R&D and procurement, force structure adjustments, and doctrinal revisions can also proceed in a continuous loop. Exploiting that new process requires changes in organizational practices and procurement procedures.

Commercial firms have adapted to this process by creating teams, focused on clear output goals, that cut across traditional organizational boundaries. The teams can then coordinate back to R&D and product design organizations and forward to customers. The firm becomes a network of teams working at different levels to achieve higher and higher stages of integration. That kind of integration has traditionally been achieved by tailoring force packages within military services using field exercises to evaluate integration problems and provide feedback to service-dominated procurement systems. More recently, increased attention has been focused on the integrating functions of commanders-in-chief (CINC) of joint and combined commands, which include forces from all services. The Goldwater-Nichols Act of 1986 enhanced the roles of the CINCs and the chairman of the Joint Chiefs of Staff (JCS) in the command structure, the budget process, and the procurement process.

The revolution in military affairs has worked both to decentralize combat to smaller, more-dispersed units with greater freedom of action permitted by networking, and to centralize integration functions in the JCS apparatus that cuts across traditional service boundaries. Those trends suggest three broad organizational adaptations to new organizational network relationships. First, simulation permits the continuous exercise of interservice coordination, but greater centralization in procurement may be needed to capture the lessons of those exercises in solving complex integration problems. Second, joint exercises with actual forces tied to larger simulations may become more and more useful in demonstrating to potential

allies and adversaries the enormous force multipliers that emerge from integration. In that way, exercises coordinated with simulations can increase
the deterrent effects of military capabilities. The trend toward integration
across services may heighten the importance of maintaining and exercising
joint task force relationships in peacetime in order to demonstrate and
improve network relationships. Third, because expertise in information
technologies and networking techniques now flows from civilian sources to
military applications and because integration across services has increased
importance, the revolution in military technology, systems, and doctrine
may also lead to a more active role for civilian leadership in DOD further
down in the service-oriented procurement process.[5]

TECHNOLOGY STRATEGY

Those adjustments in the linkages across the commercial industrial base,
the military industrial base, and the integration of military systems, forces,
and doctrine provide a useful perspective for examining the changing roles
of technology strategy and military strategy as components of broader national strategy. The first step in any effective U.S. technology strategy will
be to lower the real after-tax costs of capital by reducing federal budget
deficits and increasing national savings. That step alone, however, will not
overcome structural advantages that give European firms and particularly
Japanese firms access to patient capital that is crucial as companies move
beyond venture capital financing in the later stages of technological trajectories. Government intervention in U.S. innovation networks is justified to
support science and basic research that is underfunded by the private sector, capture externalities from enhanced network connections, and encourage the spillover benefits that flow from R&D in high-technology sectors.

In the United States, roughly half of all R&D is funded by government
and half by the private sector, with about 70 percent of R&D performed
by private firms, 16 percent by universities, 3 percent by nonprofit organizations, and 12 percent by government.[6] Over half of the federal R&D
funds, or about one-quarter of total national R&D flows through programs directed by DOD. Those federal R&D programs are an important
part of a broader national technology policy that has, until recently, im-
plicitly focused on compartmentalized programs targeted on decentralized
agency missions.

The information technology revolution, however, has increased the
dual-use components of those programs and heightened the importance of
network organizational integration across government agencies and between government, industry, and other research organizations. The
FCCSET coordination process has been useful in at least making each
agency aware of programs in other agencies and in encouraging marginal
adjustments within agency budgets toward dual-use projects, but it has

thus far been less effective in forcing coordination of efforts across agencies. Of the central themes recently proposed for closer interagency coordination, the national information infrastructure, advanced manufacturing, education and training, and government operation initiatives seem most closely targeted on expanding network integration, offsetting market failures, and adjusting organizational structures to exploit information technologies.

Because global R&D and input-output organizational networks move generic information on new products and processes so quickly, technology competition focuses on creating advanced and specific factors that can capture tacit forms of information. International technology regimes must account for both the advantages of global organizational networks and the problems of competitive subsidies to attract those high-value activities in national network nodes. Trade policies are particularly blunt instruments for dealing with those issues for two central reasons. First, their influence on the location of factor creation is indirect, and the side effects can be damaging and difficult to predict. Second, the use of the sector-specific, bilateral, outcome-oriented steps that have the most promise of success also violate the general, multilateral, process-oriented procedures of the GATT framework. As a result, bilateral managed-trade approaches threaten to undermine the very system they are attempting to buttress.[7] Instead, the GATT framework should be expanded to embrace an international technology regime that promotes collaborative efforts in basic science, defines acceptable levels of subsidies at the pre-competitive R&D level, opens government procurement practices, defines acceptable limitations on international investment, and protects international property rights. These are all difficult issues, but they should be addressed directly rather than through bilateral trade pressures that are counterproductive in the long run.[8]

The scale of collaborative dual-use programs between government and industry is still quite small. Further experimentation in techniques for cooperation is warranted, particularly in the period of defense transition, but such programs must still prove their worth in actual commercial applications and in realized spillover benefits, so an effective evaluation scheme should be an integral part of those programs. Recent steps to tie government support to private initiatives supported with at least 50 percent private funding provide a particularly useful framework for capturing essential market feedback. Similarly, screening criteria should emphasize proposals involving several firms or linking private firms to universities, government laboratories, or nonprofit research organizations in order to promote the local network connections that are so important in capturing externalities and in attracting high-value activities. Manufacturing extension services can similarly work to develop network connections at the local level, but such programs should be subject to clear market performance tests with public funds phased out over a fixed time schedule and replaced by private funding if the benefits warrant it.

Improvements in the physical high-speed communications networks that support the information technology revolution are critical, but the private sector has the incentive, capacity, and demonstrated ability to forge those networks. Government can assist in the development of the emerging national information infrastructure by ensuring appropriate linkages among the organizations that make up the national innovation network, particularly in supporting connections to research universities, nonprofit research organizations, and government laboratories, and in promoting more efficient dissemination of the vast store of federal information. Those efforts should include both physical, software, and organization connections in support of evolving private sector architectures. Matching grants to local government and other organizations for network integration provide a particularly useful way of decentralizing the structure of network connections while using federal funds to offset market failures outside the private sector.

Broader arguments for the government to play a role in "information highways" comparable to its role in developing rail and highway networks, however, are off the mark. The appropriate role for government is limited by the relative ease of linking local information networks into larger systems, the absence of eminent-domain problems comparable to obtaining land for rail and highway systems, the rapid pace of changing technology that gives the private sector enormous advantages in finding efficient network connections, and the powerful externalities that serve to lock in network standards through normal market relationships. Indeed, government is far more likely to protect current organizational relationships, such as the boundaries between telephone and cable companies, than to permit the emergence of more efficient future networking relationships that are not yet even envisioned.

In short, U.S. technology policy designed to strengthen the commercial base should emphasize the central importance of market forces and network organizational relationships. Market pressures provide the impetus for the continuous innovation required to meet global standards in a period of rapid technological change. The government's role in this process should expand, but only to resolve clear market failures and to capture externalities that might receive too little attention from private firms. When the government does intervene, it should use market incentives wherever possible. In particular, public agencies should set fixed deadlines for transitions to larger commercial shares of funding for joint projects, insist on clear measures by which the effectiveness of programs will be judged before the fact, and focus on those dual-use technologies in which prior government experience provides insights into effective program design.

MILITARY STRATEGY

National technology policy, in turn, has important implications for the broader military industrial base; for the interaction of military systems, forces, and doctrine; and for the military strategy for using those capabilities in the international arena. The revolution in military affairs and the global R&D and input-output organizational networks driving the information technologies behind that revolution suggest important new ways of thinking about military strategy. The United States now has a large lead in applying those technologies to weapon systems, in force structures designed to integrate those capabilities, and in doctrine required to apply them on the battlefield. But convergence in technological capabilities across the developed regions and global integration of dual-use industries mean that the United States cannot sustain that lead by simply blocking foreign access to current technologies. In fact, the current lead in military technologies can only be sustained by continued access to global technological bases.

Cooperation will be essential to avoid the proliferation and diffusion of increasingly lethal and accurate conventional munitions and delivery systems, to ensure that integrated defense markets serve common goals, and to adjust force structures to new budget realities. The costs of sustaining the current range of U.S. defense capabilities will be prohibitive given the requirement to lower defense outlays as part of the broader objective of lowering annual budget deficits. With reduced forward deployments, arrangements for effective forward presence will increasingly rely on cooperative security arrangements. In addition, as security challenges shift from direct threats to U.S. national existence to less vital, but perhaps even more complex, issues of regional stability, the political legitimacy for the use of force will increasingly lie in multinational arrangements at the regional or global level. Underlying technological, economic, and political trends all point toward the requirement for a cooperative approach to developing, integrating, and applying military forces. That does not imply a loss of U.S. sovereignty in protecting its vital national interests, but it does suggest that the U.S. will need the leverage of cooperative arrangements in pursuing less vital regional interests.

As discussed in Chapter 3, corporations pursuing strategic alliances have learned to identify and protect their core competencies and to concentrate network arrangements on complementary capabilities. C. K. Prahalad and Gary Hamel argue that the corporation itself is a portfolio of competencies rather than a combination of businesses. In their view, the most important core competencies in the global market are those that permit the corporation to develop unanticipated products. They argue that core competence should provide potential access to a variety of markets, make a significant contribution to the customer's evaluation of end products, and be difficult for competitors to imitate. The core competence is often reflected in a core product that can be applied to a number of end products. For example, Honda has a core competence in design and development skills that is reflected in its core product, the Honda engine, and applied to a variety of products designed around that engine. Prahalad and Hamel argue that corporate strategy should focus on developing, sustaining, and applying core competencies, and the people with skills critical to those competencies should be managed as corporate, rather than divisional, assets.[9]

Similarly, military strategy must begin with a clear understanding of the core military capabilities that the U.S. must sustain on future battlefields and the complementary capabilities that can be maintained through organizational network relationships with allies. Complementarity in capabilities should be designed not only to improve the potential to meet anticipated contingencies, but just as importantly to demonstrate political commitment to use military force in concert. In this sense, military cooperation flows not from alliance commitments to respond in particular ways to designated common threats, but from an organizational network understanding that common broad national goals can best be achieved from trust built through the demonstrated benefits of continuing collaboration. Military strategy therefore requires an identification of core competencies, a framework for cooperation on complementary capabilities, and a supporting military technology strategy.

Core Competencies

In World War II, the vital U.S. core competence in mobilization and logistics ultimately overcame large gaps in military technology, doctrine, and training. In the postwar period, nuclear deterrence and forward deployments of substantial forces in collective security arrangements emphasized the importance of forces-in-being in a strategy of flexible response. The U.S. core competence arguably lay in the development and management of strategic nuclear systems and in the integration of heavy maneuver elements in combined arms operations. In the post- coldwar period, strategic nuclear systems are less central and forward basing of heavy forces is more difficult to sustain on economic and strategic grounds. The new U.S. advantages in C^3I, precision delivery, combined arms integration, logistics, and strategic mobility capabilities give it a vital core competency that has now become increasingly important: organizational network formation and maintenance. The key network relationships are being refined at all levels, from R&D to coordination across services to forging an overarching alliance framework.

The information technology revolution provides enormous possibilities for exploiting that core competence in new ways, but unfortunately innovators are rarely in a position to capture the commercial or strategic benefits of their innovation. Leading firms face enormous difficulties in capturing the next technological breakthrough. Technologies tend to follow a trajectory with enormous uncertainty at the outset about how the technology will be used and a proliferation of competing product designs. Over time, one of the designs tends to dominate and products become standardized. Firms develop organizations to produce the standardized product efficiently, but they then encounter problems in adjusting to the possibilities of the next technological breakthrough. New firms seize the promise of the new technology and press on with innovative applications, and the cycle continues.[10]

In many ways, early success locks in patterns of behavior that can block subsequent adaptation to new circumstances. Few dominant military powers have sustained that position through a transition to new technologies. Again, the innovator has difficulty making the organizational adjustments needed to exploit the potential of the innovation. The British provided the initial innovations in the use of "tanks" in World War I, but the Germans were in a better position in the interwar years to make the organizational changes needed to exploit the potential for the use of armor on the battlefield. In the commercial sphere, the key step is the transition from the innovation itself to commercially successful production of the new products that embody the innovation. In a world in which the major economic powers all have access to the same global technology pool, there will be a premium on rapidly adapting military systems, force structures, and doctrine to the new technological possibilities. The commercial idea of "turning inside the competition" is appropriate here. With new technologies and short product cycles, competitive firms must constantly hone their organizations to get quality products to market quickly before the competition is able to react. Similarly, in the military sphere, the key is to develop the organization and doctrine needed to use the innovation effectively in battle.

Those organizational challenges in adapting to a new environment will be just as important at the strategic level. The United States produced the information technology revolution that has created the necessity for adaptation to new international network structures, but the transition from a highly successful cold war strategy of confrontation to a new strategy of cooperative competition based on the new environment will require organizational flexibility and vision. Fortunately, the United States faces an interval of at least a decade in which its military systems and doctrine will exceed the conventional capacities of any foreseeable opponent. In the longer term, however, more rapid adaptation to new technologies will be more important.

In that adjustment process, U.S. military strategy should remain clearly focused on the central role of integration and coordination in sustaining the core competency of organizational network formation and maintenance. That core competency will be reinforced by underlying technological trends, the requirement to use a reduced force structure with greater flexibility, and the need to achieve mass through the integration of fires from dispersed sources. C^3I, coordination of the delivery of precision munitions, logistics, and mobility all build from that central core competency. Complementary security arrangements with other countries should exploit but not sacrifice those core competencies. For example, the extent of forward presence of U.S. forces in other regions and the degree of integration with other national forces in sharing access to those supporting C^3I, fire control, logistics, and force projection organizational networks can be used to lever core competencies into specific patterns of regional influence and cooperation. Military strategy must sustain and improve the core competencies, identify and exploit the potential for cooperative arrangements to expand regional capabilities, and assist in guiding national and regional relationships in directions suggested by broader national strategy.

Cooperative, Independent, and Adversarial Competitors

The United States is involved in an intense competition with other nations and combinations of nations for future economic well-being and national security. That competition for new technologies, commercialization of new products, refinements in production to improve efficiency, and for new military systems, effective force structures, and successful doctrine need not be confrontational. Indeed, most competition for economic markets and for efficient defense systems strengthens the United States by forcing it to meet world standards through continuous innovation. Useful competition proceeds within a framework of cooperation on rules of the game defining forms of competition that are acceptable and those that are harmful, such as the use of force, protectionism, or even competitive currency devaluation, and develops appropriate sanctions for those who violate the rules. In short, the concept of competition is not pejorative. It can have positive or negative consequences depending on the context in which it occurs. That distinction may seem obvious, but it continues to elude many who see competition as an anachronistic cold war concept.

For analytical simplicity, it is useful to consider a range of competitive relationships, including cooperative, independent, and hostile competition. *Cooperative* competitors work to establish cooperative approaches to common goals that define mutually advantageous rules of the game. In military terms, they agree to coordinate complementary capabilities, develop common standards for interoperability, intervene in concert in different crisis situations where they have common interests, and avoid actions that might lead to military confrontation with others in the cooperative network framework. The cooperation permits, indeed even encourages, competition in producing more efficient military systems within defined rules for technology transfer. For example, NATO allies, Japan, and Korea would clearly fall into this category of cooperative competitors.

Independent competitors operate outside the cooperative defense network, but they do not seek to undermine the goals or the operation of the network. China and Russia would arguably fall into this category. *Adversarial* competitors such as Libya, Iran, and Iraq, on the other hand, operate outside the network, flaunt the network's rules of the game, and actively seek to undermine the goals and operations of the cooperative competitors. Military strategy in these terms seeks to deter hostile competitors, defeat them when the hostile behavior spills into combat, and seeks longer-term incentives for shifting hostile competitors into the independent or cooperative categories. More generally, military strategy must deal with behavior as it exists and seek to encourage shifts toward more cooperative network integration.

In addition to differences in competitive relationships, nations and groups of nations have different levels of military capability. Those at the top level might be defined as "peer competitors" of the United States, with global power projection capabilities and the sophisticated capabilities required for the integration and coordination of long-range attacks with precision munitions. At a second level, nations might have capabilities only for regional power projection or have some of the deep-strike technologies but not the capacity for full integration. Such countries may be participating in niches of the revolution in military technology, systems, and doctrine, but they would not be competitive across the whole spectrum of systems. At a lower level, nations might possess limited force projection capabilities and limited access to long-range delivery systems, although they might have asymmetrical capabilities in lower-level technologies or advantages of terrain or organization that would still make them formidable opponents in unconventional combat. Those at this lower-level capability would not be participating in the military technical revolution. The level of capability depends not only on the technology reflected in military systems, but perhaps even more importantly on the force structure, training, and doctrine required to use those systems.

The combination of the nature of the competition and the level of military capability provides a useful format for considering how military strategy might, for example, be used to ensure that potential peer competitors are also cooperative competitors, or how hostile competitors might be prevented from gaining higher-level capabilities. The revolution in military technology, systems, and doctrine provides valuable insights into defining key patterns of integration at each level that might serve as leading indicators of changes in capabilities that deserve particular strategic emphasis.

Although military strategy must deal with the near and present danger from hostile competitors with lower-level military capabilities, in the longer term the most important challenge is to ensure that potential peer competitors remain cooperative competitors. Those are not relationships that can be bound in contract, particularly because threats to mutual interests remain indistinct in these early years of the post-cold war period. The continuing evolution of cooperative relationships will depend on nurturing patterns of mutual trust through intermittent cooperation in crisis management and through patterns of developing complementary, integrated defense capabilities. Military technology strategy can play a central role in that process by linking access to defense networks to patterns of cooperative behavior. Rather than focusing military strategy on any particular anticipated future opponent, the best insurance against the emergence of an opposing peer coalition is to sustain core competence in organizational network formation and maintenance and provide clear incentives for cooperative competition.

Unlike the cold war period, it is highly unlikely that countries or groups of countries will be able to sustain global military power on an isolated economic base. The impact of the information technology revolution in reducing the relative effectiveness of Soviet conventional forces is instructive. Access to the global organizational networks driving the information technology revolution will be required to avoid technological obsolescence. The central strategic challenge will be to ensure a link between access to those global organizational networks and cooperative patterns of competition.

Military Technology Strategy

DOD military technology strategy is being reformulated to deal with the implications of the revolution in military technology, systems, and doctrine, the increased requirement for organizational network relationships across services and R&D and procurement activities, the growing importance of simulation and prototypes, and the requirement to consider both the commercial and military implications of dual-use technologies. Vertical organizations designed to compartmentalize and protect information are fading. Horizontal organizations are taking their place because of the need to absorb and integrate technological changes emerging from dual-use and defense industrial sectors that have increasingly global dimensions.

In Europe, the movement toward a single commercial market has been mirrored in consolidation of the defense sector. That process resulted first in the emergence of national champions in most defense technologies. In the latest phase, those champions have joined in the development of extensive European network organizational relationships to compete for national defense procurement contracts. Because defense contracts constitute a small share of total sales of many of the largest European defense firms, commercial network relationships spill over into defense networks. Firms allied in commercial ventures tend to develop similar relationships in the defense sector. Similarly, Japanese defense firms remain highly diversified, and strong network relationships across firms and between firms and the government dominate the R&D and procurement process.

The defense network integration apparent in other regions has been slower to develop in the United States. The U.S. technological lead in most defense areas, its large base of domestic procurement, the concentration of the leading defense firms on military production, and strict rules on technology transfer have limited the extent of network integration. That trend may be shifting as dual-use technologies become more important, U.S. firms fight to preserve market share in declining global defense markets, and technological convergence continues. U.S. firms have consistently played a large role in both the European and Japanese markets through export sales and coproduction. More recently, there has been evidence of increased interregional teaming for procurement contracts and for some codevelopment arrangements like the FSX.

As total levels of defense expenditure decline and dual-use technologies play an even larger role in military systems, it will be difficult for the United States to sustain the traditional isolation of its defense sector. Thus far, CFIUS reviews of direct foreign investment have served as a deterrent to integration through acquisitions in the narrowly defined defense sector, but there has been no similar restriction in dual-use technologies. Interregional defense collaboration is unlikely to take the form of true multinational consolidation, but the trend toward cooperative joint ventures and interregional teaming should continue, particularly in dual-use sectors.

Such network relationships provide an excellent instrument for promoting cooperative competition, because U.S. firms have strong incentives to lever their technological advantages into agreements that can provide access to foreign markets, and foreign firms need access to U.S. technology. Moreover, all of the developed regions have common interests in avoiding the proliferation of arms sales that could enhance the capabilities of hostile competitors. Because U.S. MOUs for the transfer of defense technology carry restrictions on the export of military systems or the technology itself, defense network integration helps to tighten controls over arms transfers.

The essence of a military technology strategy of cooperative competition centers on opening access to defense markets, encouraging competitive bids for defense contracts, permitting more open technology transfer with Japan and Europe in areas outside core U.S. competencies, and placing tighter restrictions on arms sales or technology transfers outside the three developed regions. In the areas of core U.S. competencies in intelligence, precision strike, logistics, strategic mobility, and combined arms integration, the U.S. should seek to exploit its capabilities through network organizational relationships rather than through technology transfer. By demonstrating willingness to share those competencies with allies in international operations, U.S. strategy can help to eliminate redundancy in allied capabilities and gain force multipliers through a logical division of effort.

Such a policy of pressing for integration in capabilities can help to prevent costly investment in redundant systems and encourage allies to pursue common network standards. The objective is not to attempt to block technological collaboration with allies, but to control the process in a way that promotes further network integration and prevents resolving problems of excess defense capacity through destabilizing arms sales. Cooperative competitors do not need excessively redundant national capabilities, but they do need confidence that they will have access to essential capabilities in a crisis and that their cooperation will not constrain eventual access to advanced systems.

Military technology transfers to independent and particularly hostile competitors should be far more restrictive. One goal of cooperative competition should be to link technological access to cooperative behavior and more complete network integration. In that sense, export control policy can serve as a useful lever in promoting cooperative competition.

CONSISTENCY OF NATIONAL STRATEGY AND SECURITY STRATEGY

Continuing access to global organizational networks will be essential in reaching the economic and security goals of U.S. national strategy, but access alone will not be enough. The strategy must pursue a national environment that will encourage successful competition within those networks. It should also seek to shape the broader rules for the competition in ways that prevent confrontation that might undermine the entire system and inadvertently promote the emergence of independent or hostile peer competitors.

U.S. strategy, then, should promote two mutually reinforcing components of cooperative competition. First, security strategy should build on a framework of cooperative competition in the development, integration, and coordination of defense capabilities to counter hostile competitors and ensure that potential peer competitors remain cooperative competitors. Second, economic strategy should reinforce cooperative competition through multinational institutions and regimes that emphasize the central role of market forces. In particular, it should pursue a framework of cooperative competition to establish the rules that will apply to the intensifying regional competition for the location of high-value, high-technology activities within global organizational networks.

The consistency of security and economic strategy will make each more effective. The first requirement in both areas will be to sustain the U.S. economic base. The second will be to ensure that the regions with current access to the information and military technology revolutions—Europe, the United States, and Japan—remain tied together in cooperative economic and defense organizational networks. The third will be to draw other emerging peer competitors or peer coalitions into the cooperative competition framework, or, in the absence of cooperative behavior, to limit their access to the systems that are driving the military revolution.

The central purpose of the cooperation should be to strengthen democratic institutions and promote equal access to economic markets. The idea of global organizational networks suggests that the institutions developed to those ends need not have a fixed hierarchical relationship. Considerable flexibility will be required and organizational boundaries should be permeable. For example, the United Nations may legitimize common action in various cases, but regional organizations may well be better equipped to mobilize resources and tailor responses to meet local requirements. Indeed, the Conference for Security and Cooperation in Europe (CSCE) or similar organizations in other regions may serve a regional legitimizing role either under the United Nations or independently. Standing collective or bilateral security arrangements, or ad hoc coalitions, might then implement the broader political mandate. Overlapping economic and security institutions would reinforce and expand the network structure. From this perspective, efforts to frame neat organizational hierarchies are less important than an understanding of the implications of overlapping network relationships.

The forward presence of U.S. forces in these terms is required not so much to counter threats that are external to each region as to enhance defense network relationships and provide stability among peer competitors. U.S. forces in Northeast Asia help to stabilize regional relationships involving Japan and Korea, and U.S. forces in Europe work to stabilize regional relationships involving the United Kingdom, France, and Germany, while simultaneously building stronger defense network integration for crisis management.

The strategic role envisioned here for the United States in a strategy of cooperative competition is very similar to the role Michael Lind identifies with the "catalytic state." In his words, "A catalytic state is one that seeks its goals less by relying on its own resources than by acting as a dominant element in coalitions of other states, transnational institutions, and private sector groups, while retaining its distinct identity and its own goals."[11] In the information age, the catalytic state must focus on the operation of global organizational networks, work to develop broad rules for cooperation and competition within those networks, and compete effectively for high-value economic activities and military capabilities within that framework of cooperative competition.

A STRATEGY OF COOPERATIVE COMPETITION

Cooperation

In the post-cold war era, legitimacy for international action will increasingly derive less from narrowly defined security interests and more from international consensus on common approaches to key global problems, such as the environment, the AIDS epidemic, drugs, the proliferation of weapons of mass destruction, the destabilizing consequences of internal wars, and humanitarian relief efforts. The complex problems of economic restructuring and defense conversion in the states of the former Soviet Union, "ethnic cleansing" in Yugoslavia, and starvation in Somalia suggest the scope of problems that will clearly be beyond the resources or the range of legitimate responses available to any great power, including the United States. Cooperative international defense organizational networks that can develop consensus and coordinate responses will be essential in dealing with those challenges.

Local and regional political factors will inevitably change the coalition of potential actors in any given instance, so the international organizational network framework must be flexible enough to accommodate a changing cast of players in each instance. International burden sharing will then be measured in national contributions not to any one effort, but to the longer-term record of cooperation and commitment of resources in those instances permitted by unique national conditions.

The strategy of the United States would be to play the role of strategic broker, forming, sustaining, and modifying international networks to meet a sophisticated array of challenges. U.S. leadership should be focused on creating defense organizational networks that will allow coalitions to act in concert, because in the new global environment unilateral actions will be increasingly ineffective. Although the relative U.S. economic position has declined, it remains the only superpower and it still brings a unique array of advantages to the task of strategic broker, including economic influence, strategic military mobility, advanced communications, ethnic diversity, political stability, a strong democratic tradition, diplomatic alliances, and an established record of assuming an impressive share of the burdens of international responsibility. In short, U.S. strategy would be to help forge an array of international organizational networks that would permit the international community to act in concert without the United States itself being forced to commit a disproportionate share of resources.

Ironically, from this perspective, organizations such as NATO that now appear to some analysts as cold war relics are actually invaluable international networks for coordinating common responses in a host of situations. NATO provides precisely the kind of command, control, communications, intelligence, and logistics networks required for cooperative security or humanitarian efforts. Whether that particular organization will be the instrument for intervention is less important than the organizational network relationships that will make cooperative efforts more feasible and efficient. Although NATO played a relatively minor direct role in Desert Shield and Desert Storm as an organization, the political and military networks it helped create were invaluable. Cooperative regimes for nonproliferation, the United Nations, GATT, the World Bank, the International Monetary Fund, and other similar organizations provide established organizational networks in which the United States has enormous influence and through which it can pursue cooperative competition. This does not suggest a surrender of U.S. sovereignty to international organizations: regional competition will remain intense and the United States has important regional interests. It does, however, imply that U.S. strategy should seek to extend leverage through cooperation in international organizations to shape and restrain the form of regional competition.

Competition

Cooperative competition underscores the importance of economic strength as the foundation of national strategy, and economic strength depends on sustaining high and growing levels of productivity among U.S. workers in the face of intense international competition. Despite the short-term dislocations of international integration, the United States should welcome the competition, because efforts to meet global standards will continue to induce the creation of the specialized and advanced factors of production needed for comparative advantage in strategic sectors. Indeed, global organizational networks channel information, technology, and resources to those economies that provide the best home bases for each industrial sector. The key issue, then, is how each region is positioned for success in the home base competition and what ground rules will be followed in competitive trade, industrial, and technology policies.

The first step will be to get the fiscal house in order and lower the real after-tax cost of capital through increased national savings, deficit reduction, and tax incentives for productive investment. The next tier of potential reforms deals with coordination of strategic-trade, industrial, and technology policies that are more controversial, particularly when they involve replacing market forces in picking the winners of the future. Policies toward particular industries can easily be distorted by special interests, and the record of industrial policies in other countries has been mixed at best. The global network framework also makes it difficult to define national firms or to anticipate the full ramifications of any purely domestic policy. The approaches with the most promise deal with the processes of innovation and factor creation at a level above individual industries, focusing on compensation for market failures and emphasizing the need for competition within global organizational networks. Instead of attempting to block the operation of global networks, effective strategy should center on steps to enhance efficiency within the new global structures.

The center of the strategy lies in revising technology policy to focus on dual-use industries that provide spillover benefits to other commercial sectors and contribute to the military industrial base as well. The first objective must be to ensure that government policies provide as little distortion as possible to underlying market forces. The second objective should be to supplement those forces where there are market failures caused by externalities, particularly externalities that grow from enhanced organizational network connections. That emphasis will help to build the supporting structure for home bases that can compete effectively in new global organizational networks.

The shift in focus in U.S. technology policy requires fundamental adjustments in R&D and procurement practices within the military sector. With limited defense funds and increased emphasis on dual-use technologies, the R&D and procurement system will have to shift to more horizontal structures that are alert to spin-in possibilities from the commercial sector, that exploit integration across traditional service boundaries, and that make effective use of simulation techniques.

The U.S. can no longer rely on technological advantages to sustain economic and military leadership. Economic convergence and global organizational networks will ensure that other advanced regions have access to the same generic technologies after very short intervals. The competition in both areas will focus on adaptations of new technologies in organizational structures that are flexible enough to continuously reinvent themselves and that can exploit the connections made possible by the information technology revolution. To some extent, that integration will depend on new physical networks, and infrastructure investment in those areas will be important to broader organizational adaptation. The real constraints will increasingly shift, however, from access to advanced technology or physical networks to the ability to develop new organizations capable of exploiting precision, flexibility, and integration. The incentives to absorb the inevitable transition costs will come from dynamic, adaptive global organizational networks. The key will not be to protect U.S. institutions from today's competitors, but to nurture patterns of innovation that will exploit new opportunities.

Cooperative Competition

Cooperative competition is a framework for examining strategic options that increasingly cut across economic and military sectors. It does not propose a new world order in the sense of a desired set of outcomes or a fixed set of institutional relationships. Instead, it recognizes that global organizational networks are an integral part of the new economic, military, and political environment and that they will be modified by the strategic brokers of the future. The network perspective provides a flexible format for viewing emerging global regions that have less to do with geographic distinctions than with shifting patterns of interconnection.

Convergence and global organizational networks have changed the economic landscape just as the end of the Cold War has changed the political and military environment. Regional competition for the home bases of global networks poses a challenge for U.S. strategy, and there is a real risk that the competition may erode the international institutions needed to deal with pressing global problems. Without those institutions, the U.S. will be severely constrained in pursuing its national interests, but the nation is also in an excellent position to influence events through those organizational networks. Cooperative competition recognizes that cooperation in building international organizational networks and in the coordinated development of military capabilities and competition in the marketplace and in the evolution of new military systems are not alternatives; they are two sides of the same strategy.

NOTES

1. An earlier version of portions of Chapter 8 appeared in "Economics and National Strategy: Convergence, Global Networks, and Cooperative Competition," *Washington Quarterly* (Summer 1993): 91–114, copyright MIT Press, 1993. The edited material is reproduced here by permission of the *Washington Quarterly* and MIT Press.

2. See Samuel P. Huntington, "Why International Primacy Matters," *International Security* 17 (Spring 1993): 68–83, for a persuasive articulation of this position.

3. The Office of Technology Assessment defines the DTIB as "the combination of people, institutions, technological know-how, and facilities used to design, develop, manufacture, and maintain the weapons and supporting defense equipment needed to meet U.S. security objectives." U.S. Congress, Office of Technology Assessment, *Building for the Future: Strategies for Restructuring the Defense Technology and Industrial Base* (Washington, D.C.: U.S. Government Printing Office, June 1992), 4.

4. Ibid.

5. In the 1960s, a similar shift occurred in the management revolution under Defense Secretary Robert McNamara. At that time, civilian systems analysts in the Office of Program Analysis and Evaluation gained a prominent role in evaluating programs across services, particularly in the area of strategic weapon systems where military experience did not provide an overwhelming advantage in technology debates.

6. Tables 4-1 and 4-2.

7. For a similar conclusion, see Luc Soete, "National Support Policies for Stra-

tegic Industries: The Strategic Implications," in *Strategic Industries in a Global Economy: Policy Issues for the 1990s,* Organization for Economic Cooperation and Development (Paris, 1991), 62–64.

8. For an argument for fundamental reform of GATT and greater emphasis on sector-by-sector approaches to codes of conduct, see Peter F. Cowhey and Jonathan D. Aronson, "A New Trade Order," *Foreign Affairs* 72 (America and the World 1992/93), 193–195.

9. C. K. Prahalad and Gary Hamel, "The Core Competence of the Corporation," *Harvard Business Review* 68 (May-June 1990): 81–85, 90.

10. For an interesting study of why leading firms pursue incremental R&D while new rivals invest in new approaches, see Jennifer F. Reinganum, "Practical Implications of Game Theoretic Models of R&D," *American Economic Review* 74, *Papers and Proceedings* (May 1984): 61–66.

11. Michael Lind, "The Catalytic State," *The National Interest,* No. 26 (Spring 1992): 3.

Selected Bibliography

Abramowitz, Moses. "Catching Up, Forging Ahead, and Falling Behind." *Journal of Economic History* 46 (June 1986): 385–406.

Air Force Institute of Technology. *Critical Technologies for National Defense.* Washington, D.C.: American Institute of Aeronautics and Astronautics, 1991.

Allen, Beth. "Choosing R&D Projects: An Informational Approach." *American Economic Review* 81, *Papers and Proceedings* (May 1991): 257–261.

Ames, Edward, and Nathan Rosenberg. "Changing Technological Leadership and Industrial Growth." *Economic Journal* 73 (March 1963): 13–31.

Aoki, Masahiko. "Horizontal vs. Vertical Information Structure of the Firm." *American Economic Review* 76 (December 1986): 971–983.

———. "Toward an Economic Model of the Japanese Firm." *Journal of Economic Literature* 28 (March 1990): 1–27.

Aoki, Reiko. "R&D Competition for Product Innovation: An Endless Race." *American Economic Review* 81, *Papers and Proceedings* (May 1991): 253–256.

Arrow, Kenneth. "The Economic Implications of Learning by Doing." *Review of Economic Studies* 29 (June 1962): 155–173.

Atlantic Council of the United States, *Transfers of Technology to Industry from the U.S. Department of Energy Defense Programs Laboratories.* Washington, D.C., July 1992.

Baily, Martin Neil, and Alok K. Chakrabarti. *Innovation and the Productivity Crisis.* Washington, D.C.: The Brookings Institution, 1988.

Baldwin, Richard, and Paul R. Krugman. "Market Access and International Competition: A Simulation Study of 16K Random Access Memories." In *Empirical Methods for International Trade,* edited by Robert Feenstra, 171–197. Cambridge, Mass: MIT Press, 1988.

Baldwin, Robert E. "Are Economists' Traditional Trade Policy Views Still Valid?" *Journal of Economic Literature* 30 (June 1992): 804–829.

Baldwin, William L., and John T. Scott. *Market Structure and Technological Change.* New York: Harvard Academic Press, 1987.

Bartlett, Christopher, and Sumantra Ghoshal. *Managing Across Borders: The Transnational Solution.* Boston, Mass.: Harvard Business School Press, 1989.

Baumol, William J. "Productivity Growth, Convergence, and Welfare: What the Long-Run Data Show." *American Economic Review* 75 (September 1985): 806–817.

Baumol, William J., Sue Anne Batey Blackman, and Edward N. Wolff. *Productivity and American Leadership.* Cambridge, Mass.: MIT Press, 1989.

Bernheim, Douglas R. *The Vanishing Nest Egg: Reflections on Saving in America.* New York: Twentieth Century Fund, 1991.

Bernstein, Jeffrey I. "Costs of Production, Intra- and Inter-Industry R&D Spillovers: Canadian Evidence." *Canadian Journal of Economics* (May 1988): 324–347.

Bernstein, Jeffrey I., and M. I. Nadiri. "Interindustry R&D Spillovers, Rate of Return, and Production in High Technology Industries." *American Economic Review* 78, *Papers and Proceedings* (May 1988): 429–434.

Berry, F. Clifton. *Inventing the Future: How Science and Technology Transform Our World.* New York: Brassey's, Inc., 1993.

Bhagwati, Jadish. *Protectionism.* Cambridge, Mass.: MIT Press, 1988.

Bianchi, Patrizio, and Nicola Bellini. "Public Policies for Local Networks of Innovators." *Research Policy* 20 (October 1991): 487–497.

Bleeke, Joel, and David Ernst, eds. *Collaborating to Compete: Using Strategic Alliances and Acquisitions in the Global Marketplace.* New York: John Wiley & Sons, Inc., 1993.

Brander, James A., and Barbara J. Spencer. "International R&D Rivalry and Industrial Strategy." *Review of Economic Studies* 163 (October 1983): 707–722.

Branscomb, Lewis M. "Does America Need a Technology Policy?" *Harvard Business Review* 70 (March-April 1992): 24–31.

Bressand, Albert. "European Integration: From the System Paradigm to Network Analysis." *The International Spectator* 24 (January-March 1989): 21–29.

Brown, Frederick J., Lt. Gen. *The U.S. Army in Transition II: Landpower in the Information Age.* Washington, D.C.: Brassey's (US), Inc., 1993.

Cainarca, Gian Carlo, Massimo G. Colombo, and Sergio Mariotti. "Agreements Between Firms and the Technological Life Cycle Model: Evidence from Information Technologies." *Research Policy* 21 (February 1992): 45–62.

Carlton, Dennis W., and Jeffrey M. Perloff *Modern Industrial Organization.* Glenview, Ill.: Scott, Foresman/Little Brown, 1990.

Carnegie Commission on Science, Technology, and Government. *Science and Technology in US International Affairs.* New York: Carnegie Commission, January 1992.

Carnevale, Anthony Patrick. *America and the New Economy: How Competitive Standards Are Radically Changing American Workplaces.* San Francisco, Calif.: Jossey-Bass Publishers, 1991.

Chandler, Alfred D., Jr. *The Visible Hand: the Managerial Revolution in American Business.* Cambridge, Mass.: Harvard University Press, 1977.

———. "The Evolution of Modern Global Competition." In *Competition in Global Industries,* edited by Michael E. Porter, 405–448. Boston, Mass.: Harvard Business School Press, 1986.

———. *Scale and Scope: The Dynamics of Western Managerial Capitalism.* Cambridge, Mass.: Harvard University Press, 1990.

Chesnais, Francois. "Multinational Enterprises and the International Diffusion of Technology." In *Technical Change and Economic Theory,* edited by Giovanni Dosi, 496–527. London: Pinter Publishers, 1988.

Chinworth, Michael W. *Inside Japan's Defense: Technology, Economics & Strategy.* Washington, D.C.: Brassey's (US), Inc., 1992.

Clinton, President William J., and Vice President Albert Gore, Jr. *Technology for America's Economic Growth, A New Direction to Build Economic Strength.* Washington, D.C.: U.S. Government Printing Office, February 22, 1993.

Cole, Robert E. "Some Cultural and Social Bases of Japanese Innovation: Small-Group Activities in Comparative Perspective." In *The Political Economy of Japan, Volume 3: Cultural and Social Dynamics,* edited by Shumpei Kumon and Henry Rosovsky, 292–318. Stanford, Calif.: Stanford University Press, 1992.

Contractor, Farok J. *Licensing in International Strategy: A Guide for Planning and Negotiations.* Westport, Conn.: Quorum Books, 1985.

Contractor, Farok J., and P. Lorange, eds. *Cooperative Strategies in International Business.* Lexington, Mass.: Lexington Books, 1988.

Cooper, Richard N. *The Economics of Interdependence.* New York: McGraw-Hill, 1968.

———. *Economic Policy in an Interdependent World.* Cambridge, Mass.: MIT Press, 1986.

Crawford, Vincent P., and Hans Haller. "Learning How to Cooperate: Optimal Play in Repeated Coordination Games." *Econometrica* 58 (May 1990): 571–595.

Creveld, Martin van. *Technology and War: From 2000 B.C. to the Present.* New York: Free Press, 1989.

Dasgupta, Partha, and Joseph Stiglitz. "Uncertainty, Industrial Structure, and the Speed of R&D." *Bell Journal* 11 (Spring 1980): 1–28.

David, Paul A. *Technical Choice, Innovation and Economic Growth.* Cambridge: Cambridge University Press, 1975.

———. "Clio and the Economics of QWERTY." *American Economic Review* 75, *Papers and Proceedings* (May 1985): 332–337.

———. "General Purpose Engines, Investment and Productivity Growth: From the Dynamo Revolution to the Computer Revolution." In *Technology and Investment: Crucial Issues for the 1990s,* edited by Enrico Deiaco, Erik Hornell, and Graham Vickery, 141–154. London: Pinter Publishers, 1990.

DeBresson, Chris and Fernand Amesse. "Networks of Innovators: A Review and Introduction to the Issue." *Research Policy* 20 (August 1991): 363–379.

Deiaco, Enrico, Erik Hornell, and Graham Vickery, eds. *Technology and Investment: Crucial Issues for the 1990s.* London: Pinter Publishers, 1990.

Denison, Edward F. *The Sources of Economic Growth.* Washington, D.C.: Committee for Economic Development, 1962.

———. *Accounting for Slower Economic Growth: The United States in the 1970's.* Washington, D.C.: The Brookings Institution, 1979.

———. *Estimates of Productivity Change by Industry.* Washington, D.C.: The Brookings Institution, 1989.

Derian, Jean-Claude. *America's Struggle for Leadership in Technology.* Cambridge, Mass.: MIT Press, 1990.

Dertouzos, Michael L., Richard K. Lester, Robert N. Solow, and the MIT Commission on Productivity Growth. *Made in America: Regaining the Productivity Edge.* Cambridge, Mass.: MIT Press, 1989.

Diwan, Romesh K., and Chandana Chakraborty. *High Technology and International Competitiveness.* New York: Praeger, 1991.

Dosi, Giovanni. "Sources, Procedures, and Microeconomic Effects of Innovation." *Journal of Economic Literature* 26 (September 1988): 1120–1171.

———. "The Nature of the Innovative Process." In *Technical Change and Economic Theory,* edited by Giovanni Dosi et al., 221–238. London: Pinter Publishers, 1988.

Dosi, Giovanni, et al., eds. *Technical Change and Economic Theory.* London: Pinter Publishers, 1988.

Dowrick, Steve, and Duc-Tho Nguyen. "OECD Comparative Economic Growth 1950–1985: Catch-Up and Convergence." *The American Economic Review* 79 (December 1989): 1010–1030.

Drezner, Jeffrey A. *The Nature and Role of Prototyping in Weapon System Development.* Santa Monica, Calif.: RAND, National Defense Research Institute, 1992.

Encarnation, Dennis J. *Rivals Beyond Trade: America Versus Japan in Global Competition.* Ithaca, N.Y.: Cornell University Press, 1992.

Ernst, Dieter, and David O'Connor. *Technology and Global Competition.* Paris: Organization for Economic Cooperation and Development, 1989.

Faulhaber, Gerald R., and Gaultiero Tamburini, eds. *European Economic Integration: The Role of Technology.* Boston: Kluwer Academic Publishers, 1991.

Fecher, Fabienne, and Sergio Perelman. "Productivity Growth and Technical Efficiency in OECD Industrial Activities." In *Industrial Efficiency in Six Nations,* edited by Richard E. Caves et al., 460–488. Cambridge, Mass.: MIT Press, 1992.

Federal Reserve Bank of Kansas City. *Policies for Long-Run Economic Growth.* Kansas City, Kans.: Federal Reserve Bank of Kansas City, 1992.

Feenstra, Robert C., James R. Markusen, and William Zeile. "Accounting for Growth with New Inputs: Theory and Evidence." *American Economic Review* 82, *Papers and Proceedings* (May 1992): 415–421.

Ferguson, Charles H. "Computers and the Coming of the U.S. Keiretsu." *Harvard Business Review* 68 (July-August 1990): 55–70.

Ferguson, Charles H., and Charles R. Morris. *Computer Wars: How the West Can Win in a Post-IBM World.* New York: Times Books, 1993.

Franz, Roger S. *X-Efficiency: Theory, Evidence and Applications.* Boston: Kluwer Academic Publishers, 1988.

———. "X-Efficiency and Allocative Efficiency: What Have We Learned?" *American Economic Review* 82, *Papers and Proceedings* (May 1992): 434–438.

Freeman, Christopher. *The Economics of Industrial Innovation.* 2nd ed. London: Francis Pinter, 1982.

———. *Technology Policy and Economic Performance: Lessons from Japan.* London: Francis Pinter, 1987.

———. "Japan: A New National System of Innovation?" In *Technical Change and Economic Theory,* edited by G. Dosi et al., 330–348. London: Francis Pinter, 1988.

Freeman, Christopher, and L. Soete, eds. *New Explorations in the Economics of Technical Change.* London: Francis Pinter, 1990.

Gansler, Jacques. *The Defense Industry.* Cambridge, Mass.: MIT Press, 1980.

———. *Affording Defense.* Cambridge, Mass.: MIT Press, 1989.

Gentsch, Eric L., and John W. McInnis. *A Profile of Defense Manufacturing Costs and Enabling Technologies.* Bethesda, Md.: Logistics Management Institute, January 1992.

Gerschenkron, Alexander. *Economic Backwardness in Historical Perspective.* Cambridge, Mass.: Harvard University Press, 1962.

Gilpin, Robert. *The Political Economy of International Relations.* Princeton, N.J.: Princeton University Press, 1987.

Golden, James R. *The Dynamics of Change in NATO: A Burden-Sharing Perspective.* New York: Praeger, 1983.

———. *NATO Burden-Sharing: Risks and Opportunities,* The Washington Papers 96. New York: Praeger, 1983.

Golden, James R., Daniel J. Kaufman, Asa A. Clark, and David H. Petraeus, eds. *NATO at Forty: Change, Continuity, and Prospects.* Boulder, Colo.: Westview Press, 1989.

Graham, Edward M. and Paul R. Krugman. *Foreign Direct Investment in the United States.* 2nd ed. Washington, D.C.: Institute for International Economics, 1991.

Graham, Otis L. *Losing Time: The Industrial Policy Debate.* Cambridge, Mass.: Harvard University Press, 1992.

Griliches, Zvi, ed. *R&D, Patents, and Productivity.* Chicago: University of Chicago Press, 1984.

———. "Productivity, R&D and Basic Research at the Firm Level in the 1970's." *American Economic Review* 76 (March 1986): 141–154.

———. "Productivity Puzzles and R&D: Another Nonexplanation." *Journal of Economic Perspectives* 2 (Fall 1988): 9–21.

Grossman, Gene M. "Promoting New Industrial Activities: A Survey of Recent Arguments and Evidence." *OECD Economic Studies* 14 (Spring 1990): 87–125.

Grossman, Gene M., and Elhanan Helpman. *Innovation and Growth in the Global Economy.* Cambridge, Mass.: MIT Press, 1991.

Gugler, Philippe. "Building Transnational Alliances to Create Competitive Advantage." *Long Range Planning* 25 (February 1992): 90–99.

Hagedoorn, John, and Jos Schakenraad. "Leading Companies and Networks of Strategic Alliances in Information Technologies." *Research Policy* 21 (April 1992): 163–190.

Hart, Jeffrey A. *Rival Capitalists: International Competitiveness in the United States, Japan, and Western Europe.* Ithaca, New York: Cornell University Press, 1992.

Helpman, Elhanan, and Paul R. Krugman. *Market Structure and Foreign Trade: Increasing Returns, Imperfect Competition, and the International Economy.* Cambridge, Mass.: MIT Press, 1985.

Helpman, Elhanan, and Paul R. Krugman. *Trade Policy and Market Structure.* Cambridge, Mass.: MIT Press, 1989.

Helpman, Elhanan, and Assaf Razin. *International Trade and Trade Policy.* Cambridge, Mass.: MIT Press, 1991.

Hickman, Bert G. *International Productivity and Competitiveness.* New York: Oxford University Press, 1992.

Hippel, Eric von. *Sources of Innovation.* New York: Oxford University Press, 1988.

Holland, Harrison M. *Managing Defense: Japan's Dilemma.* New York: University Press of America, 1989.

Huntington, Samuel P. *American Military Strategy.* Berkeley, Calif.: Institute of International Studies, University of California, 1986.

———. "The U.S.—Decline or Renewal?" *Foreign Affairs* 67 (Winter 1988/1989): 76–96.

———. "Advice for a Democratic President: The Economic Renewal of America." *The National Interest,* No. 26 (Spring 1992): 14–19.

Imai, Ken-ichi. "Japan's Corporate Networks." In *The Political Economy of Japan, Volume 3: Cultural and Social Dynamics,* edited by Shumpei Kumon and Henry Rosovsky, 198–230. Stanford, Calif.: Stanford University Press, 1992.

Irwin, Douglas A. "Strategic Trade Policy and Mercantilist Trade Rivalries." *American Economic Review* 82, *Papers and Proceedings* (May 1992): 134–139.

Jacobs, Michael T. *Short-Term America: The Causes and Cures of Our Business Myopia.* Boston, Mass.: Harvard Business School Press, 1991.

Jaffe, Adam B. "Technological Opportunity and Spillovers of R&D: Evidence from Firms' Patents, Profits, and Market Value." *American Economic Review* 76 (December 1986): 985–1001.

Jorde, Thomas M., and David J. Teece. *Antitrust, Innovation, and Competitiveness.* New York: Oxford University Press, 1992.

Jorgenson, Dale W. "Productivity and Postwar U.S. Economic Growth." *Journal of Economic Perspectives* 2 (Fall 1988): 23–41.

Jorgenson, Dale W., Frank M. Gollop, and Barbara M. Fraumeni. *Productivity and U.S. Economic Growth.* Cambridge, Mass.: Harvard University Press, 1987.

Jorgenson, Dale W., and Ralph Landau, eds. *Technology and Capital Formation.* Cambridge, Mass.: MIT Press, 1989.

Kamien, Morton I., Eitan Muller, and Israel Zang. "Research Joint Ventures and R&D Cartels." *American Economic Review* 82 (December 1982): 1293–1306.

Katz, Michael L., and Carl Shapiro. "Network Externalities, Competition, and Compatibility." *American Economic Review* 75 (June 1985): 424–440.

Kaufman, Daniel J., David S. Clark, and Kevin P. Sheehan, eds. *U.S. National Security Strategy for the 1990s.* Baltimore, Md.: The Johns Hopkins University Press, 1991.

Kaufman, William W., and John D. Steinbruner. *Decisions for Defense: Prospects for a New Order.* Washington, D.C.: The Brookings Institution, 1991.

Kendrick, John W. "Policy Implications of the Slowdown in U.S. Productivity

Growth." In *Productivity Growth and Competitiveness of the American Economy,* edited by Stanley W. Black, 75–109. Boston: Kluwer Academic Publishers, 1989.

Kennedy, Paul. *The Rise and Fall of the Great Powers.* New York: Random House, 1987.

———. *Preparing for the Twenty-First Century.* New York: Random House, 1993.

Keohane, Robert O. *After Hegemony: Cooperation and Discord in the World Political Economy.* Princeton, N.J.: Princeton University Press, 1984.

Keohane, Robert O., and Joseph S. Nye. *Power and Interdependence.* 2nd ed. Harper Collins Publishers, 1989.

Kim, Duk-Choong. "Open Regionalism in the Pacific: A World of Trading Blocs?" *American Economic Review* 82, *Papers and Proceedings* (May 1992): 79–83.

Kindleberger, Charles P. "International Public Goods Without International Government." *The American Economic Review* 76 (March 1986): 1–13.

———. *The International Economic Order: Essays on Financial Crisis and International Public Goods.* Cambridge, Mass.: MIT Press, 1988.

Kitschelt, Herbert. "Industrial Governance Structures, Innovation Strategies, and the Case of Japan: Sectoral or Cross National Comparative Analysis." *International Organization* 45 (Autumn 1991): 453–493.

Kleinknecht, Alfred, and Jeroen O. N. Reijnen. "Why Do Firms Cooperate on R&D? An Empirical Study." *Research Policy* 21 (August 1992): 347–360.

Krasner, Stephen D., ed. *International Regimes.* Ithaca, NY: Cornell University Press, 1983.

Krueger, Anne O. "Government, Trade, and Economic Integration." *American Economic Review* 82, *Papers and Proceedings* (May 1992): 109–114.

Krugman, Paul. *Rethinking International Trade.* Cambridge, Mass.: MIT Press, 1990.

———. *The Age of Diminished Expectations: U.S. Economic Policy in the 1990s.* Cambridge, Mass.: MIT Press, 1990.

———. *Geography and Trade.* Cambridge, Mass.: MIT Press, 1991.

———, ed. *Strategic Trade Policy and the New International Economics.* Cambridge: MIT Press, 1986.

Kumon, Shumpei. "Japan as a Network Society." In *The Political Economy of Japan, Volume 3: Cultural and Social Dynamics,* edited by Shumpei Kumon and Henry Rosovsky, 109–141. Stanford, Calif.: Stanford University Press, 1992.

Kumon, Shumpei, and Henry Rosovsky, eds. *The Political Economy of Japan, Volume 3: Cultural and Social Dynamics.* Stanford, Calif.: Stanford University Press, 1992.

Lane, Sarah J. "The Determinants of Investment in New Technology." *American Economic Review* 81, *Papers and Proceedings* (May 1991): 262–270.

Langlois, Richard N., and Paul L. Robertson. "Networks and Innovation in a Modular System: Lessons from the Microcomputer and Stereo Component Industries." *Research Policy* 21 (August 1992): 297–314.

Laussel, Didier. "Strategic Commercial Policy Revisited: A Supply-Function Equilibrium Model." *American Economic Review* 82 (March 1992): 84–99.

Leamer, Edward E. *Sources of International Comparative Advantage: Theory and Evidence.* Cambridge, Mass.: MIT Press, 1984.

Lee, Thomas H., and Proctor P. Reid. *National Interests in an Age of Global Technology.* Washington, D.C.: National Academy Press, 1991.

Leibenstein, Harvey. "Allocative Efficiency vs. X-Efficiency." *American Economic Review* 56 (June 1966): 392–415.

———. *Inside the Firm: The Inefficiencies of Hierarchy.* Cambridge, Mass.: Harvard University Press, 1987.

Levin, Richard C., Wesley M. Cohen, and David C. Mowery. "R&D Appropriability, Opportunity, and Market Structure: New Evidence on Some Schumpeterian Hypotheses." *American Economic Review* 75, *Papers and Proceedings* (May 1985): 20–30.

Libicki, Martin C. *What Makes Industries Strategic.* Washington, D.C.: The Institute for National Strategic Studies, National Defense University, November 1989.

Lind, Michael. "The Catalytic State." *The National Interest,* No. 26 (Spring 1992): 3–12.

Maddison, Angus. "Growth and Slowdown in Advanced Capitalist Economies: Techniques of Quantitative Assessment." *Journal of Economic Literature* 25 (June 1987): 649–98.

———. *Dynamic Forces in Capitalist Development.* New York: Oxford, 1991.

Mankiw, N. G., D. Romer, and D. N. Weil. "A Contribution to the Empirics of Economic Growth." *Quarterly Journal of Economics* 107 (May 1992): 407–437.

Mansfield, Edwin., et al. "Social and Private Returns From Industrial Innovations." *Quarterly Journal of Economics* 91 (May 1977): 221–240.

McKinsey Global Institute et al. *Service Sector Productivity.* Washington, D.C.: McKinsey Global Institute, October 1992.

Moran, Theodore H. "The Globalization of America's Defense Industries." *International Security* 15 (Summer 1990): 57–99.

———. "International Economics and National Security." *Foreign Affairs* 69 (Winter 1990/1991): 74–90.

———. *American Economic Policy and National Security.* New York: Council on Foreign Relations Press, 1993.

Mowery, David C. "The U.S. National Innovation System: Origins and Prospects for Change." *Research Policy* 21 (February 1992): 125–144.

———, ed. *International Collaborative Ventures in U.S. Manufacturing.* Cambridge, Mass.: Ballinger Publishing Company, 1988.

Mowery, David C., and Nathan Rosenberg. *Technology and the Pursuit of Economic Growth.* Cambridge: Cambridge University Press, 1989.

Muroyama, J. H., and H. G. Stever, eds. *Globalization of Technology: International Perspectives.* Washington, D.C.: National Academy Press, 1988.

National Science Board, *Science and Engineering Indicators—1991.* 10th ed. Washington, D.C.: U.S. Government Printing Office, 1991.

National Science Foundation. *Researching Priorities in Networking and Communications.* Washington, D.C.: April 1992.

———. *Promoting the Progress of Science and Engineering, Budget and Program Strategy Fiscal Year 1994.* Washington, D.C.: March 1993.

Nelson, Richard R. "Research on Productivity Growth and Differences: Dead Ends and New Departures." *Journal of Economic Literature* 19 (September 1981): 1029–1064.

———. *High Technology Policies: A Five-Nation Comparison.* Washington, D.C.: American Enterprise Institute, 1984.

———. "Institutions Supporting Technical Change in the United States." In *Technical Change and Economic Theory,* edited by G. Dosi et al., 312–329. London: Francis Pinter, 1988.

———. "U.S. Industrial Competitiveness: Where Did It Come From and Where Did It Go?" *Research Policy* 19 (February 1990): 117–132.

———, ed. *National Innovation Systems.* New York: Oxford University Press, 1993.

Nelson, Richard R., and Sidney G. Winter. *An Evolutionary Theory of Economic Change.* Cambridge, Mass.: Belknap Press of Harvard University Press, 1982.

Nelson, Richard R., and Gavin Wright. "The Rise and Fall of American Technological Leadership: The Post-War Era in Historical Perspective." *Journal of Economic Literature* 30 (December 1992): 1931–1964.

Nguyen, Sang V., and Edward C. Kokkelenberg. "Measuring Total Factor Productivity, Technical Change, and the Rate of Returns to Research and Development." *Journal of Productivity Analysis* 2 (February 1992): 269–282.

Nye, Henry R. *The Myth of America's Decline: Leading the World Economy Into the 1990s.* New York: Oxford University Press, 1990.

Ohmae, Kenichi. *The Borderless World.* New York: Harper Business, 1990.

———. "Rise of the Region State." *Foreign Affairs* 72 (Spring 1993): 78–87.

Olson, Mancur. *The Logic of Collective Action.* Cambridge, Mass.: Harvard University Press, 1965.

———. *The Rise and Decline of Nations: Economic Growth, Stagflation, and Social Rigidities.* New Haven, Conn.: Yale University Press, 1982.

———. "The Productivity Slowdown, the Oil Shocks, and the Real Cycle." *Journal of Economic Perspectives* 2 (Fall 1988): 43–69.

Olvey, Lee D., James R. Golden, and Robert C. Kelly. *The Economics of National Security.* Wayne, N.J.: Avery Publishing Group, 1984.

Organization for Economic Cooperation and Development. *Innovation Policy: Trends and Perspectives.* Paris, 1982.

———. *Technical Cooperation Agreements Between Firms: Some Initial Data and Analysis.* Paris, 1986.

———. *Choosing Priorities in Science and Technology.* Paris, 1991.

———. *Technology in a Changing World,* The Technology/Economy Programme. Paris, 1991.

———. *Strategic Industries in a Global Economy: Policy Issues for the 1990s.* Paris, 1991.

———. *Globalisation of Industrial Activities: Four Case Studies: Auto Parts, Chemicals, Construction, and Semi Conductors.* Paris, 1992.

———. *Main Science and Technology Indicators, 1991/2.* Paris, 1992.

———. *Structural Change and Industrial Performance: A Seven Country Growth Decomposition Study.* Paris, 1992.

————. *Information Networks and New Technologies: Opportunities and Policy Implications for the 1990s.* Paris, 1992.

Ouchi, William G., and Michele K. Bolton. "The Logic of Joint Research and Development." *California Management Review* 30 (Spring 1988): 9–33.

Peck, Morton J. "Joint R&D: the Case of Microelectronics and Computer Technology Cooperation." *Research Policy* 15 (October 1986): 219–231.

Pfaff, William. "Redefining World Power." *Foreign Affairs* 70 *America and the World* (1990/1991): 34–48.

Pierre, Andrew J., ed. *A High Technology Gap?: Europe, America and Japan.* New York: Council on Foreign Relations, 1987.

Porter, Michael E. *Competitive Advantage: Creating and Sustaining Superior Performance.* New York: Free Press, 1985.

————. *The Competitive Advantage of Nations.* New York: Free Press, 1990.

————, ed. *Competition in Global Industries.* Boston, Mass.: Harvard Business School Press, 1986.

Powell, Colin L. "U.S. Forces: Challenges Ahead." *Foreign Affairs* 71 (Winter 1992/1993): 32–45.

Prahalad, C. K., and Gary Hamel. "The Core Competence of the Corporation." *Harvard Business Review* 68 (May-June 1990): 79–91.

Prestowitz, Clyde V. *Trading Places: How We Allowed Japan to Take the Lead.* New York: Basic Books, 1988.

Reich, Robert B. *The Work of Nations: Preparing Ourselves for 21st Century Capitalism.* New York: Alfred A. Knopf, 1991.

Romer, Paul. "Increasing Returns and Long Run Growth." *Journal of Political Economy* 94 (October 1986): 1002–1037.

Rosecrance, Richard. *America's Economic Resurgence: A Bold New Strategy.* New York: Harper & Row, 1990.

Rosenau, James N. *Turbulence in World Politics.* Princeton, N.J.: Princeton University Press, 1990.

Rosenberg, Nathan. *Perspectives on Technology.* Cambridge: Cambridge University Press, 1976.

Rosenberg, Nathan, Ralph Landau, and David C. Mowery, eds. *Technology and the Wealth of Nations.* Stanford, Calif.: Stanford University Press, 1992.

Sandholtz, Wayne. "ESPIRIT and the Politics of International Collective Action." *Journal of Common Market Studies* 30 (March 1992): 1–21.

Sandholtz, Wayne, Michael Borrus, John Zysman, Ken Conca, Jay Stowsky, Steven Vogel, and Steve Weber. *The Highest Stakes: The Economic Foundations of the Next Security System.* New York: Oxford University Press, 1992.

Saxenian, AnnaLee. "The Origins and Dynamics of Production Networks in Silicon Valley." *Research Policy* 20 (October 1991): 423–437.

Scherer, Frederick M. "Research and Development Resource Allocation Under Rivalry." *Quarterly Journal of Economics* 81 (August 1967): 359–394.

————. *Industrial Market Structure and Economic Performance.* Chicago, Ill.: Rand McNally College Publishing Company, 1980.

————. *Innovation and Growth: Schumpeterian Perspectives.* Cambridge, Mass.: MIT Press, 1984.

————. *International High Tech Competition.* Cambridge, Mass.: Harvard University Press, 1992.

Schmookler, Jacob. *Invention and Economic Growth.* Cambridge, Mass.: Harvard University Press, 1966.

Schumpeter, Joseph A. *The Theory of Economic Development.* Cambridge: Harvard University Press, 1934.

———. *Capitalism, Socialism and Democracy.* New York: Harper & Row, 1942.

Sharp, Margaret. "Tides of Change: the World Economy and Europe in the 1990s." *International Affairs* 68 (January 1992): 17–35.

Shetty, Y. K., and Vernon M. Buehler, eds. *The Quest for Competitiveness: Lessons From America's Productivity and Quality Leaders.* New York: Quorum Books, 1991.

Sköns, Elisabeth. "Western Europe: Internationalization of the Arms Industry." In *Arms Industry Limited,* edited by Herbert Wolf, 160–190. Solna, Sweden: Stockholm International Peace Research Institute (SIPRI), 1993.

Smith, Helen Lawton, Keith Dickson, and Stephen Lloyd Smith. "'There are Two Sides to Every Story': Innovation and Collaboration Within Networks of Large and Small Firms." *Research Policy* 20 (October 1991): 457–468.

Snidal, Duncan. "The Limits of Hegemonic Stability Theory." *International Organization* 39 (Autumn 1985): 579–614.

Solow, Robert. "Technological Change and the Aggregate Production Function." *The Review of Economics and Statistics* 39 (August 1957): 312–320.

———. "Growth Theory and After." *The American Economic Review* 78 (June 1988): 307–317.

Spencer, Barbara J., and James S. Brander. "International R&D Rivalry and Industrial Strategy." *Review of Economic Studies* 50 (October 1983): 707–22.

Steinberg, James B. *The Transformation of the European Defense Industry: Emerging Trends and Prospects for Future U.S.-European Competition and Collaboration.* Santa Monica, Calif.: RAND, National Defense Research Institute, 1992.

Steindel, Charles. "Manufacturing Productivity and High Tech Investment." *Federal Reserve Bank of New York Quarterly Review* (Summer 1992): 39–47.

Storper, Michael, and Bennett Harrison. "Flexibility, Hierarchy, and Regional Development: The Changing Structure of Industrial Production Systems and Their Forms of Governance in the 1990s." *Research Policy* 20 (October 1991): 407–422.

Strange, Susan. "States, Firms, and Diplomacy." *International Affairs* 68 (January 1992): 1–15.

Sullivan, Gordon R., and James M. Dubik. *Land Warfare in the 21st Century.* Carlisle, Penn.: U.S. Army War College, Strategic Studies Institute, February 1993.

Suzumura, Kotaro. "Cooperative and Noncooperative R&D in an Oligopoly With Spillovers." *American Economic Review* 82 (December 1982): 1307–1320.

Teece, David J. "Profiting from Technological Innovation: Implications for Integration, Collaboration, Licensing and Public Policy." *Research Policy* 15 (December 1986): 285–305.

———. "Technological Change and the Nature of the Firm." In *Technical Change and Economic Theory,* edited by G. Dosi et al., 256–281. London: Francis Pinter, 1988.

———. "The Dynamics of Industrial Capitalism: Perspectives on Alfred Chandler's

Scale and Scope." *Journal of Economic Perspectives* 31 (March 1993): 199–225.

Thurow, Lester. *Head to Head: The Coming Economic Battle Among Japan, Europe, and America.* New York: William Morrow and Co., Inc., 1992.

Tyson, Laura D'Andrea. *Who's Bashing Whom?: Trade Conflict in High-Technology Industries.* Washington, D.C.: Institute for International Economics, 1992.

U.S. Congress, Office of Technology Assessment. *Arming Our Allies: Cooperation and Competition in Defense Technology.* Washington, D.C.: Office of Technology Assessment, 1990.

———. *Federally Funded Research: Decisions for a Decade.* Washington, D.C.: U.S. Government Printing Office, May 1991.

———. *Global Arms Trade: Commerce in Advanced Military Technology.* Washington, D.C.: Office of Technology Assessment, June 1991.

———. *Miniaturization Technologies.* Washington, D.C.: U.S. Government Printing Office, November 1991.

———. *Global Standards: Building Blocks for the Future.* Washington, D.C.: U.S. Government Printing Office, March 1992.

———. *Building Future Security: Strategies for Restructuring the Defense Technology and Industrial Base.* Washington, D.C.: U.S. Government Printing Office, June 1992.

———. *Defense Conversion: Redirecting R&D.* Washington, D.C.: U.S. Government Printing Office, May 1993.

U.S. Department of Defense. *Defense Science and Technology Strategy.* Washington, D.C.: Director of Defense Research and Engineering, June 1992.

U.S. Department of the Army. *Army Science and Technology Master Plan,* Vols. I and II. Washington, D.C., November 1992.

U.S. Federal Coordinating Council for Science, Engineering, and Technology, Office of Science and Technology Policy. *Grand Challenges 1993: High Performance Computing and Communications, The FY 1993 U.S. Research and Development Program,* A Report by the Committee on Physical, Mathematical, and Engineering Sciences. Washington, D.C.: Office of Science and Technology Policy, 1992.

———. *FCCSET Initiatives in the FY 1994 Budget.* Washington, D.C.: Office of Science and Technology Policy, April 8, 1993.

U.S. House of Representatives, Committee on Science, Space, and Technology, *Science, Technology and American Diplomacy, 1992.* Washington, D.C.: U.S. Government Printing Office, 1992.

U.S. Joint Chiefs of Staff. *National Military Strategy of the United States.* Washington, D.C.: Department of Defense, January 1992.

U.S. National Security Council Staff. *National Security Strategy of the United States.* Washington, D.C.: U.S. Government Printing Office, January, 1993.

Van Huyck, John B., Raymond C. Battalio, and Richard O. Beil. "Tacit Coordination Games, Strategic Uncertainty, and Coordination Failure." *American Economic Review* 80 (March 1990): 234–248.

Vernon, Raymond. "International Investment and International Trade in the Product Cycle." *Quarterly Journal of Economics* 80 (May 1966): 190–207.

———. "The Product Cycle Hypothesis in a New International Environment."

Oxford Bulletin of Economics and Statistics 41 (November 1979): 255–267.

Williamson, Jeffrey G. "Productivity and American Leadership: A Review Article." *Journal of Economic Literature* 29 (March 1991): 51–68.

Wright, Gavin. "The Origins of America's Industrial Success, 1879–1940." *American Economic Review* 80 (September 1990): 651–668.

Wriston, Walter B. "Technology and Sovereignty." *Foreign Affairs* 67 (Winter 1988/1989): 64–75.

Yarbrough, Beth V., and Robert M. Yarbrough. *Cooperation and Governance in International Trade*. Princeton, N.J.: Princeton University Press, 1992.

Yoffie, David B., ed. *International Trade and Competition: Cases and Notes in Strategy and Management*. New York: McGraw-Hill, 1990.

Zysman, John, with Laura Tyson, Giovanni Dosi, and Stephen Cohen. "Trade, Technology, and National Competition." In *Technology and Investment: Crucial Issues for the 1990s*, edited by Enrico Deiaco, Erik Hornell, and Graham Vickery, 185–211. London: Pinter Publishers, 1990.

Index

About the Author

JAMES R. GOLDEN, Colonel U.S. Army, served as a senior staff economist on the President's Council of Economic Advisers and presently is Professor and Head of the Department of Social Sciences at the U.S. Military Academy at West Point. His previous works include *Economics of National Security* (co-authored, 1983), *NATO Burden Sharing* (1983), and *The Dynamics of Change in NATO* (1984).